CHANGING PARKS

A camping scene at Crown Lake, Algonquin Provincial Park, Ontario, 1912.

(*National Archives of Canada* C56127)

Changing PARKS

THE HISTORY, FUTURE AND CULTURAL CONTEXT
OF PARKS AND HERITAGE LANDSCAPES

JOHN S. MARSH *&* BRUCE W. HODGINS, *Editors*

NATURAL HERITAGE / NATURAL HISTORY INC.

Acknowledgements

This complex project has called upon the hands and hearts of many. It would be impossible to mention everyone, but to Robin Brass, Kerry Cannon, Barry Penhale and Erik Hanson must be extended our heartfelt gratitude. Their professionalism and generosity of spirit thread through, and bind this work together.

Taken from *Coming to Canada,* Carol Shields' "Pioneers: Southeast Ontario" is published with permission of the publisher, Carleton University Press.

Changing Parks

Published by Natural Heritage / Natural History Inc., P.O. Box 95, Station "O," Toronto, Ontario M4A 2M8

Design: Robin Brass Studio
Printed and bound in Canada by Hignell Printing Limited, Winnipeg

Canadian Cataloguing in Publication Data

Main entry under title :

Changing parks : the history, future and cultural context of parks and heritage landscapes

Includes index.
ISBN 1-896219-06-3

1. National parks and reserves – Canada. I. Marsh, John S., 1942– .
II. Hodgins, Bruce W., 1931– .

FC215,C43 1997   367.6'8'0971   C96-930475-7
FIOII.C43 1997

THE CANADA COUNCIL | LE CONSEIL DES ARTS
FOR THE ARTS | DU CANADA
SINCE 1957 | DEPUIS 1957

Natural Heritage /Natural History Inc. acknowledges the support of The Canada Council for the Arts for our publishing program and the assistance of The Association for the Export of Canadian Books, Ottawa.

Contents

Author Biographies vii

Introduction xiii
JOHN S. MARSH

Great Rivers, Small Boats: Landscape and Canadian Historical Culture 1
JOHN H. WADLAND

Ontario's Provincial Parks and Changing Conceptions
of "Protected Places" 34
GERALD KILLAN

The Aboriginal Presence in Ontario Parks and Other Protected Places 50
BRUCE W. HODGINS & KERRY A. CANNON

The Ontario Experiments in Forest Reserves 77
BRUCE W. HODGINS, R. PETER GILLIS & JAMIE BENIDICKSON

The History of National Parks in Ontario 94
DENNIS CARTER-EDWARDS

Landscapes, Waterscapes, Inscapes: Putting The People Back
into Pukaskwa 107
BRIAN S. OSBORNE

Where He Didn't Spend His Summer Vacation: Martin Luther King,
Racism, and Fundy National Park 135
ALAN MACEACHERN

Conservation, culture et identité : La création du Parc des Laurentides
et du Parc de la Montagne Tremblante, 1894-1938 140
YVES HÉBERT

At the Foot of the Mountain: Preliminary Thoughts on the
Alpine Club of Canada, 1906-1950 160
PEARLANN REICHWEIN

The Evolution of World Heritage in Canada 177
NANCY ELLIOT

The Creation of National Parks and Equivalent Reserves in Ontario
and the Antipodes: A Comparative History and its Contemporary
Expression 189
JOHN SHULTIS

The Elusive Scottish Park System 209
LOUISE LIVINGSTONE

Canadian Parks Legislation: Past, Present and Prospects 221
IAN ATTRIDGE

Parks – A British Columbia Perspective 238
BRUCE K. DOWNIE

Parks Past, Present, Future: A Northern Perspective 250
RONALD G. SEALE

Greenways: The Second Park Movement 256
GEORGE B. PRIDDLE

Ecotourism and Parks: Do or Die 261
PAUL F.J. EAGLES

Parks and Protected Areas and Sustainable Development 279
J.G. NELSON

Index 295

Author Biographies

Ian Attridge

Ian Attridge is an environmental lawyer with training in resource management, ecology, environmental politics and law. Attridge provides policy advice and legal research on protected areas legislation, natural heritage stewardship techniques and land trust organizations as a Legal Analyst with the Ontario Ministries of Natural Resources, and Environment and Energy.

Before establishing his current legal practice, Ian Attridge was employed in legal services branches of both Ministries. In addition he is a Research Associate of the Canadian Institute for Environmental Law and Policy in Toronto, the author of a number of publications on private land stewardship and biodiversity law and policy, a lecturer at Toronto's York University and a speaker at conferences across North America.

Dennis Carter-Edwards

Dennis Carter-Edwards is currently Head of the History-Archaeology section of Parks Canada, Ontario. A graduate of Trent University, Carter-Edwards has served for the past 20 years as a Project Historian for Parks Canada, specializing in military and canal history. Carter-Edwards is a past president of the Ontario Historical Society and is actively involved in the preservation and presentation of Ontario's heritage.

Kerry Cannon

Kerry Cannon is the Managing Editor of the *Journal of Canadian Studies*. Cannon holds a Master's degree from Trent University's Frost Centre for Canadian Heritage and Development Studies. She has written and co-authored several articles on Aboriginal issues and Canadian studies. Cannon is co-editor with Bruce W. Hodgins of *On The Land: Confronting the Challenges to Aboriginal Self-Determination in Northern Quebec and Labrador* (Toronto, 1995).

Bruce Downie

Bruce Downie is a Protected Areas Planning Consultant based in Victoria, BC. Over the past 15 years he has conducted projects throughout western and northern Canada, as well as internationally. Prior to the creation of his consulting practice, Downie worked as a planner for BC Parks, Parks Canada and the Ontario Ministry of Natural Resources.

Paul Eagles

Paul Eagles is a Biologist and a Planner with a professional interest in environmental planning. Eagles has experience in parks management in a dozen countries. Currently he is a member of the IUCN's Commission on National Parks and Protected Areas. In that capacity Eagles chairs the Global Task Force on Parks and Tourism.

Peter Gillis

Peter Gillis is the Principal Consultant with RPG Information Services. Gillis is working on a variety of information policy issues, including assisting the governments of Alberta and British Columbia in the implementation of freedom of information and privacy legislation. He is also writing a "Privacy Handbook for Public Sector Managers" with Government Technology Conferences of Sacramento, California.

Yves Hébert

Yves Hébert est diplômé de l'université Laval (maîtrise en historie). Il a travaillé pour l'Institut québécois de recherche sur la culture et publié Bibliographie de la Côte-du-Sud. Il est co-auteur de Archives paroissiales de la Côte-du-Sud, Inventaire sommaire et de Histoire de la Côte-du-Sud. Il a été chercheur au Dictionnaire biographique du Canada et à la faculté d'Education de l'université Laval. Agissant comme historien consultant, il a travaillé pour plusieurs organismes gouvernementaux et il a réalisé l'iconographie historique de trois livres. En juin 1996, il a publié un ouvrage de vulgarisation sur l'histoire de la ville de Montmagny. Dans le domaine de l'histoire environnementale, il a publié un article sur la genése de la pensée écologique au Québec dans Thêmes canadiens, périodique édité par l'Association d'études canadiennes. Il s'intéresse à l'étude des relations entre les représentations, les savoirs scientifiques et la protection de la nature dans l'histoire du Québec. Yves Hébert vit à Lévis, près de la ville de Québec.

Bruce W. Hodgins

Bruce W. Hodgins has been teaching at Trent University since 1965. From 1980 to 1983 he was Chair of History and, from 1986 to 1992, was the Director of Trent University's Frost Centre for Canadian Heritage and Development Studies. He is published widely in the fields of Aboriginal affairs, resource management, parks, wilderness and recreation, federalism and the North.

Recently he has been the co-author with Jamie Benidickson of *The Temagami Experience: Recreation, Resources, and Aboriginal Rights in the Northern Ontario Wilderness* (1989) and with Gwyneth Hoyle, *Canoeing North into the Unknown* (1994). Hodgins has also co-edited with Margaret Hobbs, *Nastawgan* (1986), with John Milloy and Shawn Heard *Co-existence? Studies in Ontario-First Nations Relations* (1991), and with Kerry Cannon, *On the Land* (1995).

Since 1956 he has been involved with Camp Wanapetei in Temagami. As well as being an experienced northern canoe trip leader, Hodgins is also very active with the Canadian Canoe Museum.

Gerald Killan

Gerald Killan is a Professor of History and the Academic Dean at King's College, the University of Western Ontario. He is the author of *Protected Places: A History of Ontario's Provincial Parks System* (1993), the award winning *David Boyle: From Artisan to Archaeologist* (1983) and *Preserving Ontario's Heritage: A History of the Ontario Historical Society* (1976). Killan is a past president of both the Champlain Society and the Ontario Historical Society and is currently a trustee of the Quetico Foundation and a member of the Ontario Conservation Review Board.

Alan MacEachern

Alan MacEachern is a PH.D. student in history at Queen's University, Kingston, Ontario. He has co-developed and taught North American Environmental History at Queen's, both as a lecturer and with their correspondence course. Alan's dissertation is on the changing philosophy of the Canadian National Parks Branch from the 1930s to the 1970s, as seen in the creation and development of the first four parks in Atlantic Canada. Recent work has included "Rationality and Rationalization in Canadian National Parks Predator Policy," published in *Consuming Canada: Readings in Environmental History*.

J.G. Nelson

J.G Nelson's field of interest is human ecology. Most of his research has been done at the interface between scholarship and public policy and practice. His research largely has been built on an historical approach, notably through studies of land use history and landscape change and their relevance for planning, management and decision-making. This work has ranged from studies in the history of ideas – for example, the history of the concept of wilderness – through to detailed analyses and mapping of land use and landscape change in Canada, Europe and Southeast Asia, principally Indonesia. While his work has been wide-ranging, he has focused considerable concentration on national parks, protected areas and assessments of shores or coastal zones.

Brian Osborne

Brian Osborne is Professor of Geography at Queen's University, Kingston. A historical geographer, his research over the past thirty years has focused on several themes concerned with the "construction" of places and peoples' identification with them: the industrialization of Welsh rural society and the emergency of the "Valleys"; the settlement, development and "construction" of the Ontario countryside; the development of the national postal system in Canada; colonization, settlement, and promotion of the West by the Canadian National Railway; the role of art, literature and mass-communications in identification with place and the development of social memory.

George B. Priddle

George Priddle's research has moved from being primarily concerned with people management in parks to an interest in Greenways. He served as Chairman for the Ontario

Parks Council for the first seven years of its existence. Currently Priddle is actively involved in a number of trail organizations with a particular interest in the development of "rails trails."

In recent years he has also developed an interest and has been teaching and advising students in the area of waste management.

PearlAnn Reichwein

PearlAnn Reichwein holds an M.A. and a PH.D. in Canadian history from Carleton University and has won numerous academic awards. Her specialized interests include environmental history, heritage conservation, national parks, public policy and the history of the Canadian Rockies. Reichwein's work has been published in periodicals such as *The Beaver* and *The Canadian Alpine Journal*. Her recent doctoral thesis, "Beyond the Visionary Mountains: The Alpine Club of Canada and the Canadian National Park Idea, 1906 to 1969," examines the history of climbers as a key user group in the mountain national parks. Reichwein has worked for Carleton University in Ottawa and Parks Canada in Banff National Park.

Ronald G. Seale

After teaching at the University of Windsor, Ontario for five years, Ron Seale joined Parks Canada in 1974. He held various positions in that agency, in the fields of interpretation, visitor services, finance, system planning and public liaison, as well as serving as Park Superintendent. He has worked in field locations at Banff and Fundy National Parks, South Moresby/Gwaii Haanas National Park Reserve, as well as at Headquarters and the Prairie and Northern Regional Office.

From 1990-1996, Seale was seconded to the Government of the Northwest Territories, working in park planning and policy development, and in the establishment of new national parks, territorial parks and Canadian Heritage Rivers in the Northwest Territories. He left Parks Canada in 1996 to join IUCN and work as a Park Planning Advisor with the National Parks Agency in Uganda.

John Shultis

John Shultis is an Assistant Professor in the Resource Recreation and Tourism Programme at the University of Northern British Columbia. After graduation from Trent University with a joint major in Geography and Environmental and Resource Science (Honours B.SC.), time was spent working as a paleontologist and travelling around the world. Shultis's doctoral dissertation, prepared for the Department of Geography at the University of Otago, Dunedin, New Zealand, examined the historical and contemporary attitudes to unmodified environments (wilderness), the natural environment and protected areas in New Zealand. A nation-wide survey of adult residents of New Zealand (N=847) was compared with a representative sample of backcountry users in New Zealand's protected areas system (N=233) with regards to their attitudes to and perceptions, images, and utilization of wilderness, natural environments and protected areas. Prior to arriving at UNBC in 1995, he taught for two years in the School of Outdoor Recreation, Parks and Tourism at Lakehead University, Thunder Bay, Teaching and research include the comparative history of protected areas, parks planning and management, environmental interpretation, special event tourism, areas and facilities planning, and social and behavioral dimensions of resource recreation and tourism.

John H. Wadland

John H. Wadland is a graduate in History of McMaster (B.A., 1965), Waterloo (M.A., 1968) and York (PH.D., 1976) universities. He has taught in the interdisciplinary Canadian Studies Program at Trent University since 1972. He was Chair of the Program from 1984 to 1993 and Editor of the *Journal of Canadian Studies* from 1980 to 1984. He concentrates his teaching in the fields of environmental history, art history, land policy, bioregionalism, and interdisciplinary methods. He has published a book-length academic biography of the Canadian artist and naturalist Ernest Thompson Seton (New York, 1979) and numerous articles and book reviews. Most recently he completed, with Margaret Hobbs, two folio plates for Volume II of the *Historical Atlas of Canada* (Toronto, 1993). In 1993 Professor Wadland received both the Ontario Council of University Faculty Associations and the Lieutenant Governor of Ontario Awards for Excellence in Teaching. He is currently Director of the Frost Centre for Canadian Heritage and Development Studies at Trent University in Peterborough, Ontario.

INTRODUCTION

John S. Marsh

Canada has had national and provincial parks now for over 100 years. In 1993, we celebrated the Centennial of Algonquin Park, and the Ontario Provincial Park system, the oldest provincial park system in the country. Trent University, with the support of the Ontario Ministry of Natural Resources, contributed to this celebration by hosting a conference in Peterborough, Ontario entitled "Changing Parks: A Conference on the History, Future and Cultural Context of Parks and Heritage Landscapes." The title was chosen to suggest that parks had changed over the last 100 years, were being forced to change now by new economic and political circumstances, and would have to change substantially in the years to come. Accordingly, a conference programme was developed to consider the history of non-urban parks, cultural and comparative perspectives on parks, current issues facing parks, as well as likely and desirable future directions for parks and other protected areas, especially in Ontario. Conference participants were urged to consider, in particular, the following questions:

1. What is the changing cultural context of parks and conservation?

2. How have parks and conservation evolved, and what have we learned?

3. What is happening to parks and conservation outside Ontario?

4. What environmental, social, cultural, economic, administrative, management and political issues are now facing parks and conservation?

5. What conceptual and practical solutions exist or are required to address park and conservation issues?

6. What future directions should we take with parks and conservation?

This book includes most of the papers presented at this conference and addresses, in various ways, the topics as well as most, if not all, the questions above. The conclusions I offered at the conference and the specific contributions of the authors are summarised below.

Humankind has had increasing impacts on the environment and there has been growing concern since the mid-nineteenth century, but especially in recent decades about these impacts. The environment and ideas about our place in it have evolved. Parks have emerged in response to these environmental and ideological changes. In current parlance, parks are both landscapes and ideas. The first article by John Wadland, dealing with the relationship between landscape and ideas, and the significance of rivers and wilderness in Canadian culture, provides a context for considering the historical evolution of parks.

Parks have been a great idea, and practical response to environmental concerns, and have flourished since Banff National Park was established in 1885, and Algonquin Provincial Park in 1893. Parks have persisted despite recessions, wars, technical change, political interests and various threats to their integrity. National parks have spread throughout Canada, so there are now 39 national parks, located in every province and territory. Furthermore, every province and territory now has provincial or territorial parks. The number of parks in Ontario has increased to 265. Gerald Killan reviews the changing conceptions of protected places in Ontario, from places for profit to places for ecological protection. Dennis Carter-Edwards discusses the history of national parks in Ontario, while Ian Attridge traces the development of protected area legislation in Canada.

Other protected areas have been designated, especially by government, to support nature conservation and provide recreation. We have, for example: forest reserves, wildlife areas, and greenways. Bruce Hodgins, Peter Gillis and Jamie Benidickson discuss Ontario's historical experiments in Forest Reserves, such as Temagami, and how some became parks. George Priddle reviews the benefits of, and potential for greenways. Increasingly, protected areas are being given additional recognition and protection by also designating them as world heritage sites, heritage rivers and biosphere reserves. Nancy Elliot summarises the evolution of World Heritage Sites in Canada. In recent decades private landowners have been assuming more responsibility for stewardship of the land, and co-operating with government agencies to protect cultural landscapes.

There has been sustained public interest in parks, and groups have been advocating their establishment and protection since the turn of the century. The Alpine Club of Canada and the National Parks Association of Canada were early supporters of national parks, and in the last 30 years many more groups, notably The Canadian Parks and Wilderness Society, World Wildlife Fund, the

Canadian Nature Federation, the Wildlands League and the Federation of Ontario Naturalists have encouraged the creation and protection of parks. Recently, Friends groups have played an important role in supporting individual parks, such as Algonquin or the Trent Severn Waterway. PearlAnn Reichwein considers the historical relationship of the Alpine Club of Canada to national parks.

In recent years there has been growing recognition that most park environments, while relatively natural compared with urban areas, have been modified by human activity. Many areas now designated parks were used for hundreds, even thousands, of years by Native peoples. Furthermore, prior to designation, and even afterwards, many park environments, such as Algonquin and Banff, were modified by resource extraction, transport development and tourism. Gradually we are appreciating the place of people in parks and coming to regard them more as cultural landscapes. Thus, Brian Osborne makes the case for "putting the people back into Pukaskwa" National Park.

Parks and Native peoples have long been related often, unfortunately, to the detriment of the Aboriginals. Many have been displaced to establish parks, and their traditional uses of park areas have been curtailed. Recently, however, Native peoples have often been allies in establishing parks, and other protected areas, for example while reaching land claim agreements. Bruce Hodgins and Kerry Cannon discuss the Aboriginal presence in Ontario's parks and protected areas.

Parks have sometimes been regarded as elitist institutions, serving only the needs of the more established and privileged in society. In relation to this, Alan MacEachern uncovers historical evidence of a racist response to a particularly distinguished park visitor. It has been argued, therefore, that more attention must be paid by park agencies to minority groups and recent immigrants, if parks are to serve and be suppported by a wider public.

Comparisons of the evolution of parks in Canada and other countries, and of Ontario and other provinces and territories, reveal both similarities and differences. As John Shultis explains, national park ideas diffused from the United States to Canada, Australia and New Zealand, so all began park creation for similar reasons before 1900. In contrast, Scotland has still not established national parks, for reasons discussed by Louise Livingstone. Yves Hébert reveals the distinct approach of Quebec to the creation and development of Laurentides and Mont Tremblant provincial parks. Current perspectives on parks in British Columbia and the Northwest Territories are offered by Bruce Downie and Ron Seale, respectively.

Expressions of concern were voiced generally at the conference, and are evident in some of the articles, about the challenges facing parks, such as budget and staff reductions, the demoralisation of staff and park supporters, and the lower priority apparently being accorded the environment. At least some participants, however, believed these challenges could be met by administrative renewal, the development of revenue generating ecotourism, new planning legislation, and the future support of young people, such as those attending the conference. Paul Eagles discusses the need for more business-like park organisations, and the potential benefits of ecotourism in parks.

Gradually we are adopting a more comprehensive view of parks. We are recognising that they have a regional even global context. Their integrity depends on what goes on around them, and how they are perceived by adjacent populations. The final article, by Gordon Nelson, again stresses the context of parks, and urges greater appreciation and communication of the benefits of linking parks and sustainable development.

Since the conference, there have been some major and rapid changes in Canada that have had a substantial impact on parks. In particular, governments, both federal and provincial, have been reducing their responsibilities, budgets and staffing. Accordingly, the Canadian Parks Service and most provincial park agencies, notably the Ontario Provincial Parks, have also had to reduce their budgets, staff and programmes. They have been forced to find ways to operate more efficiently, generate revenue, and encourage the private sector and non-governmental organisations to take on, often through partnership arrangements, some of their former responsibilities. Opinion remains divided on whether these changes and responses will in the long run lead to the improvement or deterioration of parks.

In summary, this book explores the historical evolution of parks, as well as their current characteristics and challenges, especially in Ontario. As such, it also provides a rich basis for discussing, planning and actually creating the park system of the next century.

JOHN S. MARSH

GREAT RIVERS, SMALL BOATS:

LANDSCAPE AND CANADIAN

HISTORICAL CULTURE

John H. Wadland

The sayd men did moreover certify, unto us, that there was the way and beginning of the great river of Hochelaga and ready way to Canada, which river the further it went, the narrower it came, even into Canada, and that there was fresh water, which went so farre upwards, that they had never heard of any man who had gone to the head of it, and that there is no other passage but with small boates.

JACQUES CARTIER, "A SHORT AND BRIEFE NARRATION" (1535), IN RICHARD HAKLUYT, *THE PRINCIPAL NAVIGATIONS, VOYAGES, TRAFFIQUES, AND DISCOVERIES OF THE ENGLISH NATION* (1589)

Landscape

This essay is really about *oikos* or home place. It assumes that described landscapes constitute the essential benchmarks of an evolving human affinity with terrain, occupied or unoccupied. Landscape is a social construction. It is a text that explains "a way of seeing the world, and imagining our relationship to nature. It is something we think, do and make as a social collective" (Wilson: 1990). The year 1993 witnessed the centennials of two significant monuments to the cultural measurement of landscape. One was the Frontier Thesis of

Frederick Jackson Turner; the other was the establishment of Algonquin Park.[1] I take these as points of departure for situating, and differentiating, modern American and Canadian landscapes of the imagination.

There is no international taxonomy of landscapes. Although non-Native Canadians and Americans may share a common language of landscapes, they ascribe to this language meanings that reveal fundamentally different apprehensions of *oikos*. At the risk of oversimplifying what is ultimately an extraordinarily complex project, I propose to address four macro landscapes: the wilderness, the frontier, the agrarian and the urban.

For my purposes here, the Turner thesis is important for its articulation of relationships between the four macro landscapes underlying environmental historical discourse on this continent for the past century. Not even the brilliant work of revisionist scholars – notably Donald Worster, William Cronon, Annette Kolodny, Max Oelschlaeger and Alfred W. Crosby – has been able to dislodge these spaces from the collective consciousness.[2] Turner's frontier landscape was a westward advancing margin of settlement depending for its existence upon the wilderness into which it marched and out of which it carved an apparently nobler pastoral or agrarian space. The wilderness was reclaimed from waste and brought to the service of civilization, the highest expression of which was the city. Turner's thesis was animated by the most recent census that had demonstrated to him, regardless of the amount of empty land yet remaining to be filled by eager yeomen, that the frontier had reached the Pacific and that wilderness, as an organic element in the shaping of American democracy, had vanished. In Turner's analysis, the wilderness is in the west. Except for its protected presence in the form of parks, artifacts of legislation like the Wilderness Act of 1964, wilderness remains a voiceless, vanquished landscape, only to be sentimentally remembered and mythologized. The frontier, too, is gone, deprived of its host, though in its name all manner of technological achievement continues an unrelenting march along pathways of material progress. The agrarian and urban landscapes predominate. The former abandons its population to the latter as mechanism overtakes the farm, by increments rendering human habitation of the land almost an anachronism, except during holidays. Turner read his paper to the American Historical Association in Chicago, the White City, host to the 1893 World's Columbian Exposition. The Battle of Wounded Knee had occurred in December 1890, concluding 30 years of Indian wars in the west and symbolically silencing the true voices of the land. The Sierra Club was established by John Muir in 1892 to fight for the preservation of remnant pockets of wilderness, to champion the cause of parks.

In the year Turner read his paper, Algonquin Park was opened approximately 140 km north of Toronto. By 1850 all the good agricultural land of southern Ontario was under cultivation. Colonization roads, such as the Opeongo Road that reached Bark Lake, just outside the present park boundary, in 1855, were intended to lure aspiring farmers north onto the Canadian Shield. In 1878 Alexander Kirkwood and J.J. Murphy published *The Undeveloped Lands in Northern and Western Ontario* in which they maintained that the area was suitable for agriculture and could support a population "of at least half a million of souls." Farming was attempted in several pockets with predictable results. By 1886 it was the same Alexander Kirkwood who was championing the establishment of Algonquin Park. He argued poignantly, in a letter to the Commissioner of Crown Lands, that "In adopting the word [Algonquin], we perpetuate the name of one of the greatest Indian nations that has inhabited the North American continent" (Kirkwood 1886: 8). While like its Banff predecessor, the park was intended to support recreation, its primary purpose were to prohibit agriculture and to protect the watershed feeding the Muskoka, Petawawa, Bonnechère and Madawaska rivers from farming and a rapacious forest industry. Regulated logging was still permitted, but the prior claim of water governed the terms of use. The relative success of this policy is measured visually in the paintings of Tom Thomson, who made Algonquin a spiritual home from his first visit in 1913 until his mysterious death there, at Canoe Lake, in 1917.[3] In Thomson's work we find rivers, lakes, creeks, swamps and small reservoirs in rich profusion, centrepieces to a landscape form emulated and enlarged by his friends, Varley, MacDonald, Carmichael, Johnston, Lismer, Jackson and Harris. The ubiquitous Group of Seven, Canada's national school of landscape painters, symbolically launched its first canoe in Algonquin Park.[4] Several members of the Group lived in Toronto and had worked with Thomson at Grip, a commercial advertising firm servicing urban materialism. Its primary patron, one of its own number, had inherited the wealth of a successful manufacturer of farm implements. It is puzzling, as Jonathan Bordo has remarked, that the wilderness images of these men are characterized by the erasure of the Algonkian presence. This is especially noteworthy when we consider that British Columbia artist Emily Carr, the one woman seriously linked to the Group, actually privileged the Native presence in a large segment of her work – a factor suggesting a sensibility more akin to that of nineteenth-century painters like Paul

Kane, Peter Rindisbacher and William Armstrong.[5] My point is that far from being the primal innocence of a Tom Thomson painting, the northern wilderness of Algonquin is a landfill site for various kinds of cultural baggage. That baggage anticipates the attempts by Canadian historians over time to locate the place of wilderness in the social vision of Canada.

The progenitor of these acts of writing wilderness into the account of Canada as a society is Harold Adams Innis. His staples approach essentially followed Canada's evolution through the development of the country's natural resources; however, the approach is grounded in an understanding and love of the land; it aspires to grasp the country as more than a complex political economy in search of absolute definition. Each Innis text – whether examining the cod fishery, the fur trade, forestry, agriculture, mining, hydroelectricity – is couched in cultural insights marrying biology, geography, economy, history, even the arts, in connecting patterns reflecting eclectic reading and an intensely felt sense of place. *The Fur Trade in Canada* (1930) begins with an examination of the ecology and ethology of the beaver, as then understood in the science of his sources (who included Ernest Thompson Seton) at the time of writing. His work on forestry explored the contribution of lumbering and pulp and paper production, examined conservation practices and the social contexts of logging. But it also understood that Canada's forest industry, still our leading export sector, would only have been marginally successful by modern standards had it not been for the discovery, in the mid-nineteenth century, that wood fibre could be manufactured into paper. The transition from rag paper to newsprint transformed the entire communications industry within and without the country. Innis understood that the canoe and paper were symbiotic partners in the enlightenment of people. Just as important as the wealth they helped to generate were the ideas they carried and to which they themselves gave rise. Marshall McLuhan repeatedly deferred to the Innis of *Empire and Communications* (1950) and *Media and Communications* (1951), an Innis who was not only wrestling with the tensions between oral and written traditions, between time- and space-binding media, but who was working through the ultimate extension of his staples approach.[6] There is a fundamental unity in all his work; each of its component parts is linked by elements animal, vegetable, mineral and hydrological. Towards the end of his life, poised also on the edge of the birth of Canadian television, Innis was most deeply fascinated by the oral tradition. One cannot help but think of his enchantment with the oral in the context of his early work, which reveals respect and admiration for Native peoples and a particular understanding of the diverse, indigenous cultures encountered by successive waves of alien Europeans. He understood that myths and stories, voices of the land, constituted the collective memory and governed the ethical behaviour of whole linguistic groups. While partial to the time-binding qualities of the oral tradition, which emphasized community, the local and the spiritual, his analysis also grasped the implications of the canoe as an instrument for extending empires across space when appropriated by non-Native colonists and traders.

Donald Creighton absorbed Innis's central premises, retooled them in his own magnificent prose and articulated most eloquently what we have come to style historiographically the Laurentian thesis. In *The Commercial Empire of the St. Lawrence* (1937) we encounter

> the one great river which led from the eastern shore into the heart of the continent.... The river meant mobility and distance; it invited journeyings; it promised immense expanses, unfolding, flowing away into remote and changing horizons.... The river meant movement, transport, a ceaseless passage west and east, the long procession of river-craft – canoes, bateaux, timber rafts and steamboats – which followed each other into history.... The river was not only a great actuality: it was the central truth of a religion. Men lived by it, at once consoled by its promises; its whispered suggestions and its shouted commands; and it was a force in history, not merely because of its accomplishments but because of its shining, ever-receding possibilities (Creighton 1956: 6-7).

The river is the pathway to possibilities. Although agriculture is one of those possibilities, and certainly a governing one in the context of this particular book (which covers the period 1760-1850), it does not stand alone. Even here, "The St. Lawrence and the lakes gradually superseded the Ottawa as the main channel of western commerce; and the new staples timber, wheat and potash replaced the old staple, fur" (1956: 89). The commercial age of the canoe ends symbolically at Montreal in 1821 with the death of the North West Company and the ground breaking ceremonies announcing construction of the Lachine Canal. Carl Berger translated Creighton's insights to modern readers from a broader perspective:

> In Creighton's book the river was a colossal presence, men were Lilliputians in comparison. Living on its shores and responding to its dic-

tates they were but frail instruments of its purposes. Ultimately their hopes were dashed on its rocks. The feeling that pervaded Creighton's narrative had much in common with that evoked by the paintings of the Group of Seven. The landscapes of a northern terrain, for the most part without human figures, moulded the national character. What the painters had only implied, Creighton (and Innis) documented historically. The landscape of rivers, lakes and shield was the matrix of Canadian institutions, economics and national hopes (Berger 1986: 214).

The river and the wilderness landscape to which it provided access, both imposed and underlined limitation. Nature dictated the terms.

Innis was a decentralist who resisted bureaucracy, ideology and the forces of homogenization. Creighton, on the other hand, was a traditional conservative with a strong centralist bias. Historiographically, the factor most distinguishing them is one of emphasis. In recognizing the east-west axis and the economic forces shaping its development, Innis stressed the individual staples popping up along the way, like beads on a chain. These staples existed for the most part outside the agrarian landscape as they still do. They helped to feed regionalisms associated with themselves and with their markets; they formed relationships, marrying the interests of regions. Creighton, for his part, carried the implications of his earlier insights into the twentieth century in *Dominion of the North* (1944). He drew the attention of the next generation of readers to John A. Macdonald's National Policy as the synthetic definition of national purpose for three of the macro landscapes. The railroad was an extension of the river and the canoe; the tariff protected urban manufacturing; immigration brought settlement to the agrarian west. All were locked in a cycle of mutual dependency at the centre of which lay the wilderness. Though its location was imprecise, its ingredients elusive, it was the through-which and out-of-which everything else emerged. Thus, in spite of the different inflections they give it, in both Innis and Creighton the frontier is not a landscape; it is simply an ambiguous, confusing word, not even really a concept. It evokes a sense of "out there." Spaces witnessed, but never held. Borderless.

The third partner in shaping the macro landscapes with which we must wrestle is J.M.S. Careless. In his famous essay, "Frontierism, Metropolitanism, and Canadian History" (1954), and its reincarnation, *Frontier and Metropolis: Regions, Cities and Identities in Canada before 1914* (1989), we first find a clear definition of a Canadian frontier landscape distinct from its Turnerian parallel.

Unlike his mentors Innis and Creighton, both of whom he admired and deferred to, Careless felt compelled to tackle the Frontier Thesis head on, and to
theorize the result. The American frontier, Careless argued, was basically "a
socio-economic and socio-cultural marginal zone between 'civilization' and
'savagery' – an area grasped at by transforming settlement, expansively and not
defensively, to open up more lands and resources" (1989: 38). The Canadian
frontier, on the other hand, was

> a dependent, not a determinant, and directed by metropolitan out-thrust,
> not itself a director.... It is a marginal area extended into natural wilds by
> a society engaged in acquiring and developing the soils or other resources
> of this rudimentary hinterland, through which process the margin gains
> its own newly emergent community (1989: 40).

Careless emphasizes especially the fact that the agrarian landscape is far less
important to the Canadian imagination than it is to the American:

> ...Canadian territories abundantly featured northern forests, rock masses,
> muskeg, or tundra barrens. And the fertile areas that could support
> substantial rural populations were much restricted in central Canada, still
> more so in Atlantic and Far Western regions. The unrelenting granite of
> the Precambrian Shield straddled the midst of the country, not the richly
> fruitful Mississippi Basin, agrarian heartland of the United States. There
> were no cotton or subtropical kingdoms to develop here, or millions of
> acres of mid-western cornfields. Agricultural frontiers that loomed so
> large in Turnerian perspectives were in no way as predominant in the
> vistas of the north (Careless 1989: 41).

In Canada, the wilderness, and the frontiers reaching outward from metropolitan centres, are located in the north. A post-frontier agrarian landscape exists in the south and in the west, but the north is distinguished by the absence
of the agricultural possibility, despite the teasing Peace River country and Great
Clay Belt. And this north, this wilderness, is the dominant landscape.

Careless carries forward the pride of place accorded economics in the work
of Innis and Creighton. The east-west Laurentian axis is intact, metropolitan
nodes strung out at intervals along its length. But in Careless's writing each of
these nodes has taken on a life of its own. Relationships with other nodes con-

tinue on the axis, but the local or regional expression of dominance describes ever-expanding concentric circles of development, in a south-north direction, into the hinterland.

> The term "metropolis" ... denotes a dominant large city, whose commanding status essentially expresses the commercial, transport, industrial and financial functions of control or influence which it exerts over extensive and productive hinterland territories. These four economic attributes ... work in concert with political, social and attitudinal factors that contribute to the city's role of headship, but the economic aspects of the metropolis are most fundamental (1989: 61).

Arthur Lower, though unreasonably neglected, is close to all the historians whose work we have examined. He alone among them had actually been at Harvard during the tenure of Norman S. B. Gras, the Canadian economic historian whose *Introduction to Economic History* (1922) first explored the metropolis/hinterland concept. He had actually studied under Frederick Merck, in turn a student and disciple of Frederick Jackson Turner. The influence of these scholars is evident in *Settlement and the Forest Frontier in Eastern Canada* (1936), *The North American Assault on the Canadian Forest* (1938) and more recently in *Great Britain's Woodyard* (1973). Perhaps his personal experience of the wilderness landscape, gleaned from work as a fire ranger in northern Ontario and as an employee of the Department of Fisheries on James Bay, as well as his skills as a canoeist and his wide reading of natural history, brought to his analysis of staple extraction a uniquely sceptical eye.[7] Whatever the cause, to use Careless's words, Lower "espoused the pejorative view of metropolitanism as inherently subjugating and exploitative, sucking a territory dry because 'business had to go on'" (1989: 54). Careless characterizes this perspective as rather myopic, but does argue that dominance should be seen neither as "naturally benign" nor as "innately baneful":

> ... to display metropolitan workings as essentially oppressive and parasitical, pushing dominated areas deeper and deeper into backwardness is [not] historically convincing. There is altogether too much counter-evidence. It thus looks sensible to consider chief-city dominance as a widely evident historical fact that can have either positive or negative consequences according to circumstances (1989: 52).

As Rosemary Ommer demonstrates in her most recent work on the New-foundland fishery, negative consequences may very closely approximate Lower's estimation.[8]

Certainly Careless's frontier/hinterland landscape is a dependency; its shape and health are mutable, determined by the nature of the staples for which capital develops it. Capital is located in the metropolis and it is in the service of those who occupy and shape the urban landscape that the frontier exists as an idea and as a place. Frontier landscapes, seen from the vantage point of urban valuation, have no intrinsic value; they find redemption in the ways by which they contribute to the creation of capital. Very much as our use of the word "environment" accords second place to nature, privileging the "us" environed, the metropolis/hinterland dialectic effectively diminishes non-urban space, making it merely a supplier to a reality in which it, itself, is not equally a participant. When hinterland ceases to be useful to the metropolis it does not move on to become a Turnerian agrarian landscape. It stops dead in its tracks, awaiting its recovery by the wilderness.

Finally, Careless leaves us with a conception of region in which a metropolis and its hinterland combine around the forces of extraction and production to constitute a community with a discernible identity, part of which will be derived from the set of cultural, social, economic and political sub-communities of which it is composed. "A natural region can be defined by its physical aspects; a historical region displays the interaction of human and geographic elements over time" (1989: 21-22). The material contents of regions "appeared in rural landscapes, resource workplaces and urban locales" while "the immaterial aspects ... were revealed in the collective sense of common qualities of life and interests that developed within each broad territory, though powerfully influenced in all by physical conditions" (1989: 23-24). Careless's model thus subsumes all four macro landscapes within an organic region governed, in its most dignified incarnation, by "reciprocity and mutual reinforcement" (1989: 75). This, he posited, was the relationship to be hoped for as between regions and nation. But the troubling question of dependency remains unresolved. There are unequal places in the relationship.

The concept of regionalism leads us to our final architect of the early Canadian landscape tradition, W.L. Morton. Morton is best remembered as the leading voice of his own home, the prairie west. In its particulars his outstanding contribution to western historiography supports and reinforces for his agrarian landscape the staples, Laurentian and metropolitan approaches of his

colleagues. What he resented in Innis and Creighton, and expressed in his famous essay, "Clio in Canada" (1946), was the implication that the west was
merely a colony of the imperial centre, that "a uniformity of the metropolitan
culture throughout the hinterlands" was a necessary corollary of their perspectives. The prairie landscape and its inhabitants, he said, were distinct:

> The West is plains country, with few, though great resources, a harsh and
> hazardous climate, and an inflexible economy. So domineering is this
> environment that it must change people and institutions greatly from
> those of the humid forest regions of the East (Morton 1967: 47).

Morton liked the metropolitan thesis for its flexibility, and one must imagine that Careless, in turn, was shaped in his redefinition of the ideas of Norman
Gras by Morton's conception of cultural diversity, particularly ethnic diversity,
and its relationship with land.

I want to conclude this section by examining a Morton essay that is seldom
discussed but which bears directly upon the landscape question. In "The
'North' in Canadian Historiography" (1970) he gives us a compelling definition
of the north as "all that territory beyond the line of minimal growth of the
known cereal grains" (Morton 1970: 32) – one assumed hinterland deriving its
explanation from another:

> As the agricultural frontier moved westward it left an open flank to the
> north. This became a permanent frontier, an enduring demarcation line
> between wilderness and farmland, between north and south. Ragged,
> flexible, moving far north in the far northwest, it is nevertheless an im-
> penetrable as well as a permanent frontier. It may be vaulted; it cannot be
> removed (Morton 1970: 35).

The hallmark of this final frontier, then, is that it stands still. It is absolutely
limiting. On its nether side is a wilderness distinctive for its absolute denial of
the agricultural possibility. If cities were not already dependent on the trading
of staples, either raw or finished, drawn from their hinterlands, the north itself,
in the form of long winters and cold temperatures, moves symbolically from its
home on a predictable, seasonal round to limit urban landscapes, to demand
behaviours, "furnishing that contrast of civilization and wilderness" (1970: 37).
The north forced the European to live among Native peoples, to respect and

learn from them. The Métis "make this country significantly unlike the United States" (1970: 38). As he wrote this paper Morton was witnessing national debates surrounding the discovery of oil at Prudhoe Bay, the voyage of the *Manhattan*, Arctic Waters Pollution Prevention legislation, Richard Rohmer's Mid-Canada Corridor project. It struck him as odd that the north had never figured prominently in the generalizations of his colleagues, though he noted that Morris Zaslow[9] was ready in the wings. The north had been absent, he implied, because it was a force of limitation, not of progress, the "ultimate and comprehensive meaning" of a Canadian history awaiting articulation:

Not only in the North, but in nearly all Canada, life and wealth are possible only on the North's conditions. The North makes necessary an absolute dependence on one's fellows, on cooperative skills, on communal capital. So, in ever lessening degrees southward, does southern Canada. In the North the average does not govern, the extremes do. So, in degrees ever dwindling southward, do they in the South (1970: 40).

A general statement of the macro landscapes of Canada, derived from historical tradition, is a complex project whose surfaces we have only tentatively rubbed. Let us conclude simply by observing that the received landscapes of the Canadian historical imagination are dramatically distanced from their American equivalents. They live in different places, are subjected to different forces, and in their marriage with the people who inhabit them and leave marks, they make texts telling different stories. Economics and rivers have been central protagonists in the Canadian story. But as W. L. Morton suggested at the end of the period we have just examined, limitation had also been written into the plot.[10]

Rivers
The epigraph to this paper was written by Jacques Cartier in 1535.[11] It is beautiful in its simplicity, recognizing at first hand the majesty and power of the Ottawa and St. Lawrence rivers and foretelling in some measure their roles in a national history which has been recorded around the work of scholars like Innis, Creighton and Careless. Each of these men is bound to the others through a sequence of ideas that follows the grand river to the interior on what Northrop Frye once characterized as a "journey without arrival." The indispensable partners on the journey were the Native inhabitants of the place. Their small boat, the canoe, became the *sine qua non* of travel, of communication and

of trade. In an ironic twist of fate it also became the vital tool of imperialism. The Native portage, too, was essential to the journey, joining lake to river, river to river, space to space, culture to culture through a seamless web of networks thousands of years old.[12] Approaching from the sea, Cartier understands that the remaining journey will be "farre upwards," towards the north and against the current.

The Canadian tradition of imagining a wilderness north, is obviously, much older than Tom Thomson or W. L. Morton. It also cuts across all of the disciplines. Politicians often return to John Diefenbaker's celebrated speech of 1958 in which he articulated his "northern vision." " Sir John A. Macdonald opened the west. He saw Canada from east to west. I see a new Canada," thundered the Prime Minister from Prince Albert, Saskatchewan, "a Canada of the North!" (Colombo 1974: 152). *The Idea of North* was the title chosen by musician Glenn Gould for his famous "contrapuntal radio" documentary in five voices which first aired on CBC *Ideas* in 1967 and which resurfaced most recently as the centrepiece for François Girard's *Thirty-Two Short Films About Glenn Gould* (1993). The baggage of practical, mythical and symbolic purposes loaded onto the idea of north by southerners is ably explored in the fine work of historians like Carl Berger, Ian MacLaren, Stuart Houston and Shelagh Grant.[13] Since the early 1960s Quebec geographer Louis-Edmond Hamelin has been refining a "nordicity index" with which to measure nuanced gradations of northness.[14] To southerners the north has always been a landscape of mystery. So few of us have gone there, wherever it is, that it becomes a place of easy imaginings. Correctives exist for us to read, whether in the lyrical postmodern text, *Enduring Dreams: An Exploration of Arctic Landscape* (1994) by John Moss, or in James Raffan's moving collaborative account of the ways in which three cultures – Dene, Inuit and Euro-Canadian – have apprehended a single, sacred, northern place.[15] In the Clarendon Lectures delivered at Oxford University in 1991 Margaret Atwood rehearsed the entire literary construction of north in the English Canadian canon, beginning with John Franklin's *Narrative*. Reflecting on the ill winds infecting the north with urban pollution, she concluded poignantly:

> Canadians have long taken the North for granted, and we've invested a large percentage of our feelings about identity and belonging in it.... The edifice of Northern imagery ... was erected on a reality; if that reality ceases to exist the imagery, too, will cease to have any resonance or mean-

ing, except as a sort of indecipherable hieroglyphic.... The earth, like trees, dies from the top down. The things that are killing the North will kill, if left unchecked, everything else (Atwood 1995: 115-16).

In the 25 years separating Morton's paper from the publication of Atwood's lectures, Canadian sensitivity to the north has been stirred up by dramatic events that affirm the symbiotic relationship uniting all four macro landscapes, augmenting their mutual dependency. Each event marks a step towards grasping the informing role of Native peoples and their understanding of place.

In the late 1960s and early 1970s, the oil and gas industry, pipelines, highways, hydroelectric power projects, sovereignty – practical things – glued our attention to the north. But the economic issues motivating concern were paralleled by Native peoples' return, after a prolonged absence, to the national political culture. Southerners had brought their vision to a north peopled by Dene, Cree, Inuit and Métis who had learned the lessons of treaties. After the Trudeau government's ill-advised 1969 White Paper they made clear their opposition to any decisions altering the northern landscape to which they themselves were not privy. The Inuit Tapirisat was established in 1971. The Dene Declaration followed in 1975, the same year in which the James Bay and Northern Quebec Agreement was signed. The Calder Case of 1973 established in law the principle of aboriginal rights, and the British Columbia lawyer, Thomas Berger, who had represented the Nishga position, was one year later charged with the responsibility of conducting Canada's first serious environmental and social impact assessment, the Mackenzie Valley Pipeline Inquiry. The Berger Report, *Northern Frontier, Northern Homeland* (1977), still stands as the single finest non-Native examination of the northern condition – testimony to the fact that Berger travelled to and heard evidence from all the indigenous communities along the routes of two proposed gas pipelines. The moratorium on development recommended by the Report demonstrated that traditional ecological knowledge carried just as much (in this case more) weight than all the science that urban industrial money could buy.

Not coincidentally, other manifestations of environmental concern were appearing simultaneously. The Canadian Arctic Resources Committee began publication of *Northern Perspectives* in 1972. Trent University, which had launched the country's first Native Studies Program in 1969, introduced the radical environmental magazine, *Alternatives*, in 1971. Donald Chant's Pollution Probe arrived on the scene in 1969. Environment Canada became part of the federal bureaucracy in 1970, coinciding exactly with the establishment of Greenpeace and the Committee for an Independent Canada.

The journey "farre upwards" is at the centre of some of the most challenging non-Native Canadian essays, fiction and poetry of the period following 1970. The work is often, though not always, historical. If not historical, it is heavily laden with metaphorical allusions to ancestry. It is marked as well by deeply introspective questions about contact with indigenous peoples and about the meaning of inhabitation – as distinguished from merely living in or travelling through place. In this work, journeying sometimes takes place on foot, but most often, on a river, by canoe. An early expression of the genre was Al Purdy's *North of Summer: Poems from Baffin Island* (1967). More recently the voice of Quebec speaks, from a different perspective, through Gilles Vigneault's lyrical *Portages* (1993). Certainly Margaret Atwood's *Surfacing* (1972), Harold Horwood's *White Eskimo* (1972), Wayland Drew's *The Wabeno Feast* (1973) and *Halfway Man* (1989), Peter Such's *Riverrun* (1973), Brian Moore's *Black Robe* (1985) and M.T. Kelly's *A Dream Like Mine* (1987) and *Out of the Whirlwind* (1995) articulate sensibilities craving engagement with the true voices of the land. Wayland Drew, a fine Canadian author about whose work far too little is written, has even carried the wilderness journey into science fiction with his Erthing Cycle – *The Memoirs of Alcheringia* (1984), *The Gaian Expedient* (1985) and *The Master of Norriya* (1986) – a complex trilogy, building upon Scandinavian mythology, which imagines a victorious wilderness, reclaiming the city as its own.

Out on the agrarian prairie a number of authors have followed the lead of W. L. Morton, their spiritual mentor, in journeying north. Robert Kroetsch in *Gone Indian* (1973), Aritha van Herk in *Places Far From Ellesmere* (1990) and Rudy Wiebe in *A Discovery of Strangers* (1994) come immediately to mind. In *Playing Dead: A Contemplation Concerning the Arctic* (1989), his prelude to the latter book, Wiebe reveals some of the insights which first inspired this paper. He begins by reflecting on the rivers in his life, and those he has read about, marvelling at the stories they might tell of their ceaseless journeys to whichever of three oceans is their ultimate destination. For example, this reflection on Franklin's expedition of 1819-22:

... in the summer of 1821, when nothing more was known about Canada's western Arctic coast than the two deltas Hearne and Mackenzie had seen as it were for a moment, in 1821, 764.5 miles of Arctic Coast was mapped by five English sailors who got there by following river systems across the tundra from the present site of Yellowknife ... north via Winter Lake and down the Coppermine River to the sea. French Canadian voyageurs paddled them there and then through the ice in birchbark canoes (Wiebe 1989: 14).

English sailors, French voyageurs, Indian canoes, combined in a river to the sea, to make a map, true landscape painting, of the place. The stories of Franklin, Back and King are the stories of water, of rivers:

> [They] made their entry into the Arctic landscape by means of water and ... for most of the last four hundred years of Arctic encounter the whites have not wanted land there ... because they do not want to stop in the Arctic at all: they merely want it to be a convenient passage to another place altogether.
> And the Arctic has never cooperated.... The image of water ... affirms the idea that movement within a landscape, whether on water or occasionally land, can be seen in the linear image of water moving down to the sea, or ... of the rivers being the tentacles of the protean sea reaching over the land. In other words, the movement (life) of human beings is always analogous to the line water draws upon land (77-78).

Wiebe is unromantic throughout his narrative about the warring and violence historically in evidence between Native groups, Dogrib against Yellowknife, Yellowknife against Inuit. But it is the beauty of their language and of their stories that enthrals him, the voice of the land itself. Having heard this voice, he ends by echoing Morton: "I desire true NORTH, not PASSAGE to anywhere."

> I need wisdom ... to understand why Canadians have so little comprehension of our own *nordicity*, that we are a northern nation and that, until we grasp imaginatively ... in word, song, image and consciousness that North is both the true nature of our world and also our graspable destiny we will always ... be wishing ourselves something we aren't, always stand staring south across that mockingly invisible border... (111, 114).

The culture of water is one of the most significant variables distancing Canadian environmental history from its American equivalent, an observation reinforced by any good hydrological atlas. Canada ranks third only to Russia and

Brazil in terms of total river flow. The Ottawa River alone drains more water than all the rivers in England and Wales combined.[16] Yet despite their role in our history, and somewhat paradoxically, rivers have largely been taken for granted. Their neglect and abuse have, at length, stirred the institutional mind to action. One notable product is the Canadian Heritage Rivers System, established in 1984 by a joint initiative of the federal, provincial and territorial governments, with the goal of establishing "a system of Canadian Heritage Rivers that reflects the diversity of Canada's river environments and celebrates the role of rivers in Canada's history and society. The dream is to ensure that rivers in Canada flow into the future, pure and unfettered as they have since the meeting of the vast Pleistocene ice sheets" (Canadian Heritage Rivers Board Pamphlet: 1994). Twenty-five rivers have already been designated to fulfil the objectives of this lofty prose.

But rivers outside a Heritage Rivers system, like the wilderness landscapes outside parks, do not receive equal treatment. Most rivers, even some Heritage Rivers, are locked into human purposes supporting the sustenance and enlargement of agrarian and urban landscapes. Without rivers these landscapes would diminish, be lost. They are dependent on the rivers, not the rivers on them. Or is it really too late to say this? As Atwood implied earlier, in another context, history has made of them mutual dependencies.

In Canada, agriculture has been, historically, a minor player in the water withdrawal enterprise, as recently as 1986 accounting for only 8.4 per cent of national intake.[17] But the amount of land under irrigation has been growing exponentially in the modern period, more than quadrupling to almost 900,000 hectares between 1950 and 1988. Over 90 per cent of irrigated land exists in Saskatchewan, British Columbia and Alberta, the last province alone accounting for 60 per cent. These figures can be deceiving if not placed in another context. In the three prairie provinces 2.4 per cent of improved farmland is irrigated. Yet this irrigation accounts for 46 per cent of water withdrawal and a staggering 69 per cent of total consumption on the prairies. By contrast, municipal use accounts for 7 per cent of withdrawal and 3 per cent of consumption. Fully 23 per cent of total water consumption on the prairies is explained by evaporation from reservoirs. Over time irrigation technology has evolved from surface ditching and lined canals to reservoir, pipeline and sprinkler systems. Each improvement brings more water to the land, in consequence increasing agricultural productivity. But as recent controversies surrounding the Oldman and Rafferty-Alameda projects have demonstrated, each improvement sets in motion a huge chain reaction of ecological implications involving flooded forests, fish and wildlife habitat, sediment deposition and streambed erosion.[18] The increased demand for chemical fertilizers and pesticides on irrigated lands can lead to nutrient loading and pollution in adjacent streams and groundwater. Salinization has been a measurable consequence of irrigation worldwide since the collapse of Mesopotamia. On the prairies, riparians downstream from irrigation works receive dissolved salts and (especially in drought conditions) reduced water volume, thereby often suffering from benefits accruing to others. Rather than continuing our adaptation to the land, as in dryland farming, we have chosen to adapt the land to ourselves.

To date Canada has engineered a larger volume of interbasin water transfers than the United States and Russia combined – most of it for hydroelectric power production. In 1906 Ontario Hydro became the first crown-owned electrical utility in Canada, setting the stage for development in the rest of the nation. By 1988 Canada serviced 62 per cent of its electrical needs with falling water at 400 generating stations, making this country, with a capacity exceeding 60,000 MW, the world's major producer of hydroelectricity. Production has increased dramatically since the 1960s. Forward from the First World War federal politicians had forcefully opposed long-term power exports to the United States, with its proven capacity for developing a dependency. Not until W.A.C. Bennett confronted Ottawa over his "Two Rivers Policy" did the climate really change. The resulting Columbia River Treaty of 1964, debated and by many Canadians lamented to this day, spawned a big dam mentality the first efflorescence of which appeared on the Peace River in 1967, bearing the name of British Columbia's premier.[19] The Mica Dam followed on the Columbia in 1972; the Churchill Falls development generated its first power in Labrador in 1971; in Manitoba, the Churchill River diversion into the Nelson River was completed in 1976. Phase One of the James Bay Power Project, commenced in 1971 but not completed until 1984, brought the number of large dams in Quebec to 189, representing a gross storage capacity almost half of Canada's total. Like its parent on the Peace, the La Grande complex (and its still threatened offspring on Grande Baleine and on the Nottaway-Broadback-Rupert river systems) stands as a monument to the vision of a premier, this time Robert Bourassa.

Dam building has generated, besides electricity, flood control and irrigation, enough controversy to keep historians busy for years. Whether or not dams are intended to sustain the cultures of agrarian or urban landscapes their impacts are felt most emphatically on the land whose voices they manipulate, reinvest with new meaning or simply silence. Often wherever a new dam is located a Native group is affected. This is true of the Oldman River, of the Peace and the La Grande. As the reservoir at Williston Lake began to fill behind the Bennett Dam, the Métis at Fort Chipewyan, hundreds of miles downstream on the Peace-Athabasca Delta, watched their muskrat-based trapping economy disintegrate while a wetland dependent on annual spring floods was transformed into a terrestrial ecosystem. Increased levels of methyl-mercury, first discovered in the Churchill-Nelson diversion, have also appeared in the James Bay region, leached in the flooding of organic matter. A traditional dietary staple of the Cree at Chisasibi, local fish species are now so badly contaminated as to be inedible. The James Bay and Northern Quebec Agreement, negotiated in 1975 to legitimize the project and its consequences and to calm political fears of an invasive federal presence in Quebec affairs, provided for Inuit and Cree involvement in subsequent environmental and social impact assessments in the region. But this was of little moment for a *fait accompli* engineered to fortify the urban landscape. The transmission lines running from James Bay effectively reversed a current running to the sea. And dams have made water just another staple commodity; *Power from the North* (1985) as Robert Bourassa called it in his book, to the powers of the south. Democracy.[20]

The language of dams is not the language of rivers described by Rudy Wiebe. The language of dams is the language of methyl-mercury, zebra mussels, purple loosestrife and acid rain. It is the language of urban landscapes that have forgotten their dependence on rivers and the north. The histories of the automobiles we drive, of the fuel that powers them, of the roads they follow, of the parks which constitute their holiday destinations, all of these are the history of the wilderness landscape consumed by human purpose. The urban landscape is made out of wilderness. Wilderness invests with power those who do not know it. Or care.

Relationships

Ecology. The word was first used in the organic sense we now understand by Ernst Haeckel, a German zoologist and science popularizer, in his *Generelle Morphologie* in 1866. Ecology is derived from the Greek word *oikos*, signifying "dwelling" or "home" and means, literally, "The knowledge of home." Haeckel defined ecology as "the science of relations between organisms and their environment." *Economy* is formed from the same Greek root.

As used by Aristotle [*oekonomie*] originally meant the proper functioning of a household unit.... A soundly organised working household was the basis of a viable state. It was as self-sufficient as possible. It husbanded its resources, and avoided waste and disorder. It was not a methodologically individualist concept, but implied a self-contained group; the nation, the tribe, the organism (Bramwell 1989: 41).

Traditionally, ecology has been treated as a branch or subdiscipline of biology. Biology, like all other sciences shaped by the European Enlightenment, is reductionist. The emphasis is on the individual, "on fragmentary parts of larger home-systems or ecosystems. But home is more than the creatures in it.... And the study of home involves more than the study of its inhabitants." Therefore, to quote University of Saskatchewan plant ecologist Stan Rowe, "biology, rightly understood, is a subdiscipline of ecology." In other words, "organisms do not stand on their own; they evolve and exist in the context of ecological systems that confer those properties called life.... Biology without its ecological context is dead" (Rowe 1989: 229). The same may be said of every discipline. History outside its ecological context should also be considered dead.

Here, *context* means the setting or "home" of human civilizations in nature, and the uses and abuses to which those civilizations subject the natural environments within which they are niches, even while the civilizations are themselves shaped by the constraints of their natural setting. The term *context* therefore introduces into history a circular, non-linear account of change and causality – an emphasis on relations rather than upon particulars. In *In Defense of the Land Ethic* (1989) J. Baird Callicott writes that

relations are "prior to" the things related, and the systematic wholes woven from these relations are prior to their component parts. Ecosystemic wholes are logically prior to their component species because the nature of the part is determined by its relationship to the whole That is, ... a species has the particular characteristics that it has because those characteristics result from its adaptation to a niche in the ecosystem (110-11).

In this perspective, the particular alienated for the sake of observation and control from its context in an ecosystemic whole is dead. This is as true for the organisms isolated by biology as for the particulars of history placed under a magnifying glass by the orthodox historian.

Ecology then is not merely a science; it constitutes a way of looking at the world. In addition to context and relationship, ecology implies a diversity of life-forms that they describe and contain and without which they cease to exist. The term always points to systems of interacting and interdependent constituents, the alteration or elimination of one of which may set in motion a sequence of unimagined change to which civilizations, like all other organisms, must adapt or die.

As environmental historians, our main objective, according to Donald Worster, must be "to discover how a whole culture, rather than exceptional individuals in it, perceived and valued nature," understanding that, at least to this point in time, "no culture has ever really wanted to live in total harmony with its surroundings" (Worster 1988: 303). A growing body of literature in both the United States and Canada suggests that the best place to begin this exercise is in the microregion or bioregion we know best – our own immediate *oikos*, or home, the ecosystem in which we as individuals are practising participants. If earth is to be understood as our environment, those who are its stewards have a responsibility to articulate a sense of place that gives voice to the other than human entities of that locale. This task requires that we understand science as part of lived culture:

> The kinds of soils and rocks under our feet; the source of the waters we drink; the meaning of the different kinds of winds; the common insects, birds, mammals, plants, and trees; the particular cycles of the seasons; the times to plant and harvest and forage – these are things that are necessary to know. The limits of resources; the carrying capacities of its lands and waters; the places where it must not be stressed; the places where its bounties can best be developed; the treasures it holds and ... withholds – these are the things that must be understood. And the cultures of the people, of the populations native to the land and of those who have grown up with it, the human social and economic arrangements shaped by and adapted to the geomorphic ones, in both urban and rural settings – these are the things that must be appreciated (Sale 1985: 42).[21]

This bioregional perspective, far from being parochial and inward, is essential to an understanding of national history apprehended as the relationship between its parts. It becomes quite literally a grassroots study, seen from the ground up. It is a history meant to be guided by a felt sense of place, attuned to the subtleties and nuances of the particular in its various circuits of relatedness, a history which accepts limitation. On the ground, and at the root, is the landscape of the place. No cultural activity occurs exclusive of the environment required to sustain it. On the face of the landscape is written the record of success and failure.

The concept of regionalism has been with English-Canadian historiography at least since 1937 when Walter Sage argued that the Maritimes, Quebec, Ontario, the Prairies and British Columbia (he left out the north) were more closely related to adjacent areas of the United States than to each other. Ramsay Cook introduced the idea of "limited identities" in 1967 and J.M.S. Careless began to run with it in 1969. Thus the period following the Centennial can again be regarded as a watershed, fragmenting to those of a centralist predisposition, but empowering to those outside the dominant culture. Regional academic journals such as *BC Studies* (1968), *Prairie Forum* (1976) and *Acadiensis* (1971) voiced the priorities of place often marginalized in established periodicals. Small regional book publishers (with names such as Coach House, Anansi, James Lorimer, Harvest House, Western Producer, Hurtig, Breakwater, Talonbooks, Ragweed, Douglas and McIntyre) were born during this period, frequently with writers themselves in the front office. The voice of region was joined by the voices of women. The Royal Commission on the Status of Women, convened in 1967, reported in 1970. The National Action Committee, formed in 1971, was followed by the *Canadian Newsletter of Research on Women* (now *Resources for Feminist Research*) in 1972. *Québécoises deboutte!* appeared in 1971, *Kinesis* in 1974. Labour was represented by *Labour/Le Travail* (1976). With *Canadian Ethnic Studies* (1969), the University of Calgary took on multiculturalism, a new concept emerging with sufficient force, in volume four of the Laurendeau-Dunton report (1969), to warrant the creation of its own federal ministry (1972). The Canadian Consultative Council on Multiculturalism commenced its work in 1973. The postcolonial discourse was launched on all fronts simultaneously with environmentalism, the recognition of aboriginal rights and the revisioning of the north.

The vitality of what has been called "The New Regional History" (Gaffield 1991) is best measured in the extraordinary work of the *Institut québécois de recherche sur la culture*. Since 1979, the *Institut* has been embarked on a systematic exploration of Quebec's micro regions – Saguenay-Lac St. Jean, Gaspésie, Laurentides, Outaouais, Mauricie, Abitibi, etc. – which engages professional historians with local citizens in the joint creation of detailed and gritty texts examining the physical and cultural landscapes of local place. As the first phase of the project begins to wind down, Fernand Harvey, the Director of Research, has set in motion his own synthesis. One of the objects is to determine whether this collage bears any resemblance to the big picture of the dominant tradition.[22] In English Canada, macro regionalism has been with us for a long time. On the prairies, for example, we have already identified the leadership of W.L. Morton. To his work we may add that of scholars like John Warkentin, Ronald Rees, Douglas Francis, Sharon Butala, Bill Waiser, Don Gayton, Doug Owram, David Jones, David Breen, John Herd Thompson, Gerald Friesen – a ceaselessly renewing procession of authors for whom the landscape centres the discourse.[23]

Bioregionalism emerges from this background but narrows its spatial range, emphasizing instead the complex ecological relationships at work within the home place, or micro region. In some ways bioregionalism addresses questions posed by George Woodcock's thesis on the anti-nation in the early 1970s,[24] but it fastens on natural (as distinct from political) boundaries. Bioregions are most often defined by watersheds. In its modern incarnation, bioregionalism finds its empirical measures in systems theory. Donald McTaggart asks us to consider "three dimensions of differentiation," what he calls the "biophysical system," the "inhabiting system" and the "network system," all in the context of place or community.

> Society and community are not envisaged as social systems which happen to be located in an ecosystem. They are part of the place system, and place is the focus of attention. Human society does not only have to respond to ecology in general; perhaps more significantly, particular communities – rural, urban, tribal, industrial – have to learn to be part of their own particular place systems, through a slow process of historic continuity (McTaggart 1993: 314, 317).[25]

Considerations of this kind guided the analysis of David Crombie in two pathbreaking reports, *Watershed* (1990) and *Regeneration* (1992), answering the terms of reference of the Royal Commission on the Toronto Waterfront. As Commissioner, Crombie adopted an ecosystem approach[26] that understood the relationship between history and ecology, built and natural heritage. He realized very early in his deliberations that in our culture of rivers lay the explanation of many of the problems on the Lake Ontario waterfront. Accordingly he defined and mapped a "Greater Toronto Bioregion" centred not on the urban landscape but on the Oak Ridges Moraine to the north, a huge deposit of sand and gravel formed by retreating glaciers, "the headwater to most north and south flowing rivers in the area. " Crombie's reports regard the city "as a natural ecosystem," concluding that "Economic development ... cannot be sustained in an ecologically deteriorating environment" (Crombie 1992: 455). They also demonstrate the importance of recognizing the north, rivers, urban, agricultural, frontier and wilderness landscapes in the context of the place where one apprehends them. These quantities live everywhere among us.

The final, perhaps the most important, point to make in the context of bioregionalism is its openness to what the literature calls traditional ecological knowledge (or TEK). Traditional ecological knowledge is described as

> a cumulative body of knowledge and beliefs, handed down through generations by cultural transmission, about the relationship of living things (including humans) with one another and their environment. Further, TEK is an attribute of societies with historical continuity in resource use practices; by and large, these are non-industrial or less technologically advanced societies, many of them indigenous or tribal (Berkes 1993: 3).

The incorporation of traditional ecological knowledge into environmental impact assessment, assumed by many to be the sole preserve of professional scientists, has become increasingly common since the Berger Inquiry. It is now generally agreed that because it "avoids scientific reductionism" and "encompasses the biophysical, economic, social, cultural, and spiritual aspects of the environment," traditional ecological knowledge is "in many instances better suited to answer scientists' many questions" (Sallenave 1994: 19). Seen from a bioregional perspective, traditional ecological knowledge must be understood as history emerging from place, the closest we shall ever come to the true voice of the land. Perhaps the creation of Nunavut may be considered evidence that the penny has finally dropped.

> If knowledge truly *is* power, then appropriate decision making power must be transferred to those at the source of the knowledge to be used. They may then use their power to protect the environment, culture and way of life of northern aboriginal communities (Sallenave 1994: 19).[27]

* * *

This essay is about *oikos* and the interpretation of home place in Canadian history. It argues that the *eco* of economy governed historical writing about land in the period leading up to the watershed of the Centennial. After 1967, however, an emerging shift in approach to the *eco* of ecology was discernible, emphasizing limitation by the land rather than material progress measured by resources extracted from it. This is not to suggest that economic issues were abandoned by historical discourse. Far from it. An analysis of changes in attitude toward the wilderness, frontier, agrarian and urban landscapes has attempted to demonstrate the growth of a dynamic tension between economy and ecology since 1967. Canadian literary culture has kept alive the imaginary properties of the journey "farre upwards" on which W.L. Morton embarked in 1970. Employing one of its dominant metaphors, the river winding its way through all four landscapes and carrying its cargo of economic and ecological priorities, I have concluded by urging consideration of a new bioregional approach to history. This approach marries the models of community economic development (CED)[28] and traditional ecological knowledge (TEK) in a paradigm that recognizes the nation as a system of mutually dependent, localized relationships. This interpretation recognizes the complex diversity of local place ecosystems and the historical dependence of people on them. It also challenges historians to rethink the anthropocentric agenda by better familiarizing themselves with the science of ecology and with the language and traditions of Native and rural peoples. Bioregional history is a hinterland/metropolis history. It reverses the dependency relationship and asks us to investigate new patterns. Our dominant landscape, the wilderness, a metaphor for ecology, lies in the north of our imagination. It is and always has been peopled.

* * *

Ramsay Cook has become one of Canada's most eloquent voices in the wilderness.[29] But years ago, back on the watershed, he argued

> that the concept of the "frontier" has never really touched the Canadian imagination so deeply as it has the imagination of the United States. Far more influential ... has been the concept of the North, which provided many imaginative and nationalistic Canadian writers a nature symbol to develop. If the cowboy was the hero of the frontier in the United States, the Royal Canadian Mounted Policeman was the Canadian symbol – a symbol not only of law and order, but of metropolitan penetration of the frontier (Cook 1971: 172-73).

By recognizing the shared hundredth anniversary of the Turner thesis and Algonquin Park, I opt for another metaphor. As I see it, the central informing symbol of America is the horse, an imported domestic animal charged with the job of carrying cowboys, pulling wagons full of settlers, dispatching the cavalry against the Indians. The equivalent symbol for interior Canada must surely be the canoe. This apparently simple technology was indigenous to the place, the product of thousands of years of evolution, expressing in different forms, from Micmac to Haida, the variety of Native cultures spanning the continent. When the descendants of Cartier moved inland they travelled riverine highways in these craft, guided by their makers on whose skills and knowledge they depended for survival. The birch canoe engaged the French, and later the British, with the land, drawing them on Frye's journey without arrival. These voyageurs, like this country, were in a constant condition of becoming. Learning the language of the place from its own voices. The paddler and the river were joined by the paper thin bark of a tree. The paddler had to know what strokes were appropriate to the conditions, where the V in the current lay, often in hiding between treacherous boulders. The paddler went where the river led, learning by stages to become it. And when an impasse was reached the paddler found the portage and carried the canoe to the next body of water. Eric Morse researched, recorded and mapped many of the intricate routes that took paddlers from one end of Canada to the other. He published the result, *Fur Trade Routes of Canada/Then and Now* (1969) on the watershed. The introduction is signed by Pierre Trudeau. In this book Morse discussed the extraordinary hardship but also the drama of the journey. He examined the variants of canoe used in specific conditions – the 600-pound, 36-foot *canot de maître* to Lake Superior, the 300-pound, 25-foot *canot du nord* to points west. But he emphasized the partnership between Native and non-Native in the experience:

> The Indian showed the trader how: the fur canoe was the ordinary Indian birchbark canoe but developed to its maximum strength and capacity; the provisions for the voyageurs while en route were almost entirely Indian in origin.... The Indian, moreover, showed the trader where, for the fur trade canoe routes were not discovered and engineered by white explorers: some had been in use since the passing of the last ice age (21).

The canoe: a domesticated tree.
Great rivers, small boats.

Note

I wish to acknowledge with gratitude, the generous assistance of the Social Sciences and Humanities Research Council of Canada towards the research for this paper. Warm thanks are extended also to the many readers of prior versions: James Struthers, Bruce Hodgins, James Raffan, Ramsay Cook, Wayland Drew, Jean Manore, Jack Matthews, Michèle Lacombe, Christl Verduyn, Sandy Lockhart, Fernand Harvey, Ivan Ashbury, Jonathan Bordo, Shelagh Grant, Kerry Cannon and Sean Kane. While their help has been essential, I alone take full responsibility for all errors and omissions.

Works Cited

Atwood, Margaret. *Strange Things: The Malevolent North in Canadian Literature*. Oxford: Clarendon Press, 1995.

—. *Surfacing*. Toronto: McClelland & Stewart, 1972.

Berger, Carl. *The Writing of Canadian History: Aspects of English-Canadian Historical Writing Since 1900*. 2nd ed. Toronto: University of Toronto Press, 1986.

Berger, Thomas. *Northern Frontier, Northern Homeland: The Report of the Mackenzie Valley Pipeline Inquiry*. Ottawa: Government of Canada, 1977.

Berkes, Fikret. "Traditional Ecological Knowledge in Perspective." *Traditional Ecological Knowledge: Concepts and Cases*. ed. J.T. Inglis. Ottawa: International Program on Traditional Ecological Knowledge and International Development Research Centre, 1993.

Bourassa, Robert. *Power From the North*. Scarborough: Prentice-Hall, 1985.

Bramwell, Anna. *Ecology in the Twentieth Century: A History*. New Haven: Yale University Press, 1989.

Callicott, J. Baird. *In Defense of the Land Ethic: Essays in Environmental Philosophy*. Albany: State University of New York Press, 1989.

Careless, J.M.S. *Frontier and Metropolis: Regions, Cities and Identities in Canada Before 1914*. Toronto: University of Toronto Press, 1989.

—. "Frontierism, Metropolitanism and Canadian History." *Canadian Historical Review* 35.1 (March, 1954): 1-21.

—. "'Limited Identities' in Canada," *Canadian Historical Review* 50 (1969): 1-10.

Colombo, John Robert ed. *Colombo's Canadian Quotations*. Edmonton: Hurtig, 1974.

Cook, Ramsay. "Canadian Centennial Celebrations." *International Journal* 22 (1967).

—. "Frontier and Metropolis." *The Maple Leaf Forever: Essays on Nationalism and Politics in Canada*. Toronto: Macmillan, 1971. 166-175.

Creighton, Donald. *Dominion of the North: A History of Canada*. Toronto: Macmillan, 1944.

—. *The Empire of the St. Lawrence*. Toronto: Macmillan, 1956.

Crombie, David. *Regeneration: Toronto's Waterfront and the Sustainable City. Final Report of the Royal Commission on the Future of the Toronto Waterfront*. Ottawa: Ministry of Supply and Services, 1991.

—. *Watershed. Interim Report of the Royal Commission on the Waterfront*. Ottawa: Ministry of Supply and Services, 1990.

Drew, Wayland. *The Gaian Expedient*. New York: Ballantine, 1985

—. *Halfway Man*. Ottawa: Oberon Press, 1989.

—. *The Master of Norriya*. New York: Ballantine, 1986.

—. *The Memoirs of Alcheringia*. New York: Ballantine, 1984.

—. *The Wabeno Feast*. Toronto: Anansi, 1973.

Gaffield, Chad. "The New Regional History: Rethinking the History of the Outaouais." *Journal of Canadian History* 26.1 (Spring, 1991): 64-81.

Girard, François. *Thirty-Two Short Films About Glenn Gould*. Montreal: Rhombus Films, 1993.

Gould, Glenn. *The Idea of North: Sound Documentary*. Toronto: CBC Learning Systems, 1971 . Vinyl Disk.

Gras, N.S.B. *An Introduction to Economic History*. New York: Harper, 1922.

Horwood, Harold. *White Eskimo: A Novel of Labrador*. Toronto: Doubleday, 1972.

Innis, Harold Adams. *The Bias of Communication*. Toronto: University of Toronto Press, 1951.

—. *Empire and Communications*. Oxford: Clarendon Press, 1950.

—. *Essays in Canadian Economic History*. Toronto: University of Toronto Press, 1956.

—. *The Fur Trade in Canada: An Introduction to Canadian Economic History*. New Haven: Yale University Press, 1930.

—. *The Strategy of Culture*. Toronto: University of Toronto Press, 1952.

Kelly, M.T. *A Dream Like Mine*. Don Mills: Stoddart, 1987.

—. *Out of the Whirlwind*. Don Mills: Stoddart, 1995.

Kirkwood, Alexander. *Algonkin, Forest and Park, Ontario letter to the Honourable T.B. Pardee, M.P.P., Commissioner of Crown Lands for Ontario*. Toronto: Warwick, 1886.

Kirkwood, Alexander and J.J. Murphy. *The Undeveloped Lands in Northern and Western Ontario: Information Regarding Resources, Products and Suitability for Settlement – Collected and Compiled from Reports of Surveyors, Crown Land Agents and Others, with the Sanction of the Honourable the Commissioner of Crown Lands*. Toronto: Hunter, Rose, 1878.

Kroetsch, Robert. *Gone Indian*. Toronto: New Press, 1973.

Lower, A.R.M. *Settlement and the Forest Frontier in Eastern Canada*. Toronto: Macmillan, 1936.

—. *The North American Assault on the Canadian Forest: A History of the Lumber Trade Between Canada and the United States*. Toronto: Ryerson, 1938.

—. *Great Britain's Woodyard: British America and the Timber Trade, 1763-1867*. Montreal: McGill-Queen's University Press, 1973.

McTaggart, W. Donald. "Bioregionalism and Regional Geography: Place, People and Networks." *Canadian Geographer* 37.4 (1993): 307-319.

Moore, Brian. *Black Robe*. Toronto: McClelland & Stewart, 1985.

Morse, Eric W. *Fur Trade Canoe Routes of Canada: Then and Now*. Toronto: University of Toronto Press, 1969.

Morton, W. L. "Clio in Canada: The Interpretation of Canadian History." *Approaches to Canadian History* ed. Ramsay Cook et al. Toronto: University of Toronto Press, 1967. 42-49.

—. "The 'North' in Canadian Historiography." *Transactions of the Royal Society of Canada*. Series 4.8 (1970): 31-40.

Moss, John. *Enduring Dreams: An Exploration of Arctic Landscape*. Concord, ON: Anansi, 1994.

Purdy, Al. *North of Summer: Poems from Baffin Island*. Toronto: McClelland & Stewart, 1967.

Rowe, J. Stan. *Home Place: Essays on Ecology*. Edmonton: NeWest, 1990.

—. "The Importance of Conserving Systems" in *Endangered Spaces: the Future for Canada's Wilderness*. ed. Monte Hummel. Toronto: Key Porter, 1989.

Sale, Kirkpatrick. *Dwellers in the Land: The Bioregional Vision*. San Francisco: Sierra Club Books, 1985.

Sallenave, John. "Giving Traditional Ecological Knowledge its Rightful Place in Environmental Impact Assessment." *Northern Perspectives* 22.1 (Spring 1994): 16-19.

Such, Peter. *Riverrun*. Toronto: Clarke, Irwin, 1973.

Van Herk, Aritha. *Places far from Ellesmere*. Red Deer: Red Deer College Press, 1990.

Vigneault, Gilles. *Portages*. Montreal: Nouvelles éditions de l'arc, 1993. These poems first appeared as songs in a recording titled *Le Chant du Portageur*. Editions Le Vent qui vire et Polymuse, 1992 (SOCAN).

Wiebe, Rudy. *A Discovery of Strangers*. Toronto: Knopf, 1994.

—. *Playing Dead: A Contemplation Concerning the Arctic*. Edmonton: NeWest, 1989.

Wilson, Alexander. *The Culture of Nature: North American Landscape from Disney to the Exxon Valdez*. Toronto: Between the Lines, 1991.

Worster, Donald. "Doing Environmental History" in *The Ends of the Earth: Perspectives on Modern Environmental History*. ed. Donald Worster. Cambridge: Cambridge University Press, 1988. 289-307.

Endnotes

1. For textual celebrations of these centennials, see Richard White and Patricia Nelson Limerick, *The Frontier in American Culture*, ed. James R. Grossman (Berkeley: University of California Press 1994); Gerald Killan, *Protected Places: A History of Ontario's Provincial Park System* (Toronto: Dundurn, 1993). For a particularly lucid analysis of the legacy of Frederick Jackson Turner, see Patricia Nelson Limerick, "Turnerians All: The Dream of a Helpful History in an Intelligible World," *American Historical Re-*

view 100.3 (June, 1995): 697-716. The pivotal paper, on which my point turns, is Frederick Jackson Turner, "The Significance of the Frontier in American History," American Historical Association, *Annual Report for 1893* (Washington, 1894), 199-227.

2. See especially, Donald Worster, *An Unsettled Country: Changing Landscapes of the American West* (Albuquerque: University of New Mexico Press, 1994); William Cronon, *Changes in the Land: Indians, Colonists and the Ecology of New England* (New York: Hill and Wang, 1983); Alfred W. Crosby, *Ecological Imperialism: The Biological Expansion of Europe, 900-1900* (New York: Cambridge University Press, 1986); Annette Kolodny, *The Land Before Her: Fantasy and Experience of the American Frontiers, 1630-1860* (Chapel Hill: University of North Carolina Press, 1984); Max Oelschlaeger, *The Idea of Wilderness: From Prehistory to the Age of Ecology* (New Haven: Yale University Press, 1991).

3. For the definitive study of Thomson, see Joan Murray, *Tom Thomson: The Last Spring* (Toronto: Dundurn, 1994).

4. The most recent study of the Group is Charles C. Hill, *The Group of Seven: Art for a Nation* (Ottawa: National Gallery of Canada; Toronto: McClelland & Stewart, 1995). Of particular importance, in the context of this paper, is Roald Nasgaard, *The Mystic North: Symbolist Landscape Painting in Northern Europe and North America 1890-1940* (Toronto: University of Toronto Press, 1984).

5. I have no interest in joining the debate on cultural appropriation in this paper. What fascinates me is Carr's link with the romantic representation of Native peoples in the work of Canada's nineteenth-century artists. Whatever its failings, and however easily it may be dismissed as evidence of the colonizing vision, much of this work, seen as a product of its time, was animated by a spirit not of exploitation, but of respect. Sentimentality is a measurable quantity in most Canadian paintings of the Victorian period, but the acknowledgement of the Native presence, and specifically outside a warring context, sets the work in opposition to parallel American images of the same period. That Carr maintained this link while Thomson and the Group abandoned it is worthy of reflection. As I have suggested elsewhere, the issue is far more involved than much of the postcolonial discourse on the subject allows. See John H. Wadland and Margaret Hobbs, "Images of Canada," *Historical Atlas of Canada*, Vol. II ed. R. Louis Gentilcore (Toronto: University of Toronto Press, 1993), Plate 1, and 154-55. I am deeply indebted to Jonathan Bordo for redirecting my eye in these matters. See his "Jack-Pine – Wilderness Sublime or the Erasure of the Aboriginal Presence from the Landscape," *Journal of Canadian Studies* 27.4 (Winter 1992-93): 98-128. This I mean neither to dismiss nor to demean the very real and legitimate concerns of contemporary Native scholarship in Canada and elsewhere. See, especially, Deborah Doxtator, *Fluffs and Feathers: An Exhibit on the Symbols of Indianness. A Resource Guide* (Brantford: Woodland Cultural Centre, 1988); Deborah Doxtator et al. *Revisions* (Banff: Walter Phillips Gallery, 1992); Richard Hill, "One Part Per Million: White Appropriation and Native Voices," *Fuse* 15.3 (Winter 1992): 12-22. For the rea-

son I have explicitly made these points, see Robert Fulford, "The Trouble With Emily," *Canadian Art* 10.4 (Winter, 1993): 32-39. I am trying to understand what exactly it was that moved non-Native artists to paint what they painted, to omit what they did not. What was the intent? What are the assumptions shaping this intent? For those who will want to point out that Tom Thomson and the Group of Seven left out *all* reference to the human presence, aboriginal or not, it is first of all necessary to say that they are wrong. Next, I would direct them to Eli Mandel, "The Inward, Northward Journey of Lawren Harris," *artscanada* 222-23 (October-November, 1978) 7-24 for a good read by a prairie poet which speaks directly to the thesis of this paper.

Several Canadian historians have embarked on journeys of self-scrutiny in treating Native history. No one has been at this longer than University of Calgary Professor, Donald Smith. His studies in life writing stand out for never having compromised on the vital, often uncomfortable, questions that must be addressed by readers of this paper who, without being indigenous to place, legitimately aspire to become autochtonous. See Donald B. Smith, *The Native People in Quebec Historical Writing on the Heroic Periods (1543-1663) of New France* (Ottawa: National Museums of Canada, 1974); *Long Lance: The True Story of an Imposter* (Toronto: Macmillan, 1982); *Sacred Feathers: The Reverend Peter Jones (Kahkewa-quonaby) and the Mississauga Indians* (Toronto: University of Toronto Press, 1987); "The Life of George Copway or Kah-ge-ga-gah-bowh (1818-1869) – and a Review of His Writings," *Journal of Canadian Studies* 23.3 (Fall 1988): 5-38; *From the Land of Shadows: The Making of Grey Owl* (Saskatoon: Western Producer Prairie Books, 1990). For a fuller statement of my sense of this important work see John H. Wadland, "The River That Flows Both Ways," *American Review of Canadian Studies* 22.3 (Autumn 1992): 407-413.

6. See James W. Carey, "Harold Adams Innis and Marshall McLuhan," in *McLuhan: Pro and Con* ed. Raymond Rosenthal. (Baltimore: Penguin, 1968), 270-308.

7. Lower was an ardent naturalist and loved to be on the water. See A.R.M. Lower, *My First Seventy-Five Years* (Toronto: Macmillan, 1967); *Unconventional Voyages* (Toronto: Ryerson Press, 1953).

8. Rosemary E. Ommer, "One Hundred Years of Fishery Crisis in Newfoundland," *Acadiensis* 23.2 (Spring 1994): 5-20.

9. Morris Zaslow published two books in the Canadian Centenary Series of which Morton was the General Editor. *The Opening of the Canadian West, 1870-1914* (Toronto: McClelland & Stewart, 1971); *The Northward Expansion of Canada, 1914-1967* (Toronto: McClelland & Stewart, 1988).

10. The theme of limitation was seized upon by several Canadian intellectuals in the 1970s. None was more eloquent than Wayland Drew, "Wilderness and Limitation," *Canadian Forum* 52 (February 1973): 16-19.

11. It is believed that this source constitutes the first mention of the word "Canada."

12. There are many good sources on the subject of the canoe. See especially, Kenneth G. Roberts and Philip Shackleton, *The Canoe: A History of the Craft from Panama to the*

Arctic (Toronto: Macmillan, 1983); C.E.S. Franks, *The Canoe and White Water* (Toronto: University of Toronto Press, 1977); Bruce W. Hodgins and Margaret Hobbs, eds. *Nastawagan: The Canadian North by Canoe and Snowshoe* (Toronto: Betelgeuse, 1985); James Raffan and Bert Horwood, eds. *Canexus: The Canoe in Canadian Culture* (Toronto: Betelgeuse, 1988); David Gidmark, *Birchbark Canoe: The Story of an Apprenticeship with the Indians* (Burnstown, ON: General Store Publishing, 1989). For a chronicle of virtually every major non-Native canoe journey in the Canadian north, see Bruce W. Hodgins and Gwyneth Hoyle, *Canoeing North into the Unknown: A Record of River Travel 1874-1974* (Toronto: Natural Heritage, 1994).

13. Carl Berger, *The Sense of Power* (Toronto: University of Toronto Press, 1970); S. D. Grant, "Myths of the North in the Canadian Ethos," *Northern Review* 3-4 (Summer, 1989): 15-41; I.S. MacLaren, " The Aesthetic Mapping of Nature in the Second Franklin Expedition," *Journal of Canadian Studies* 20.1 (Spring, 1985): 39-57; "From Exploration to Publication: The Evolution of a 19th Century Arctic Narrative," *Arctic* 47.1 (March 1994): 43-53; "The Pastoral and the Wilderness in Early Canada," *Landscape Research* 14:1 (1989), 15-19; "The Poetry of the New Georgia Gazette or Winter Chronicle, 1819-1820," *Canadian Poetry* 30 (Spring-Summer 1992): 41-73; "Samuel Hearne and the Landscapes of Discovery," *Canadian Literature* 103 (Winter 1984): 27-40; "Touring at High Speed: Fur Trade Landscape in the Writings of Frances and George Simpson," *Musk-Ox* 34 (Spring 1986): 78-87; C. Stuart Houston, ed. *Arctic Artist: the Journal and Paintings of George Back, Midshipman with Franklin, 1819-1922* (Kingston: McGill-Queen's University Press, 1994); *Arctic Ordeal: The Journal of John Richardson, Surgeon-Naturalist with Franklin, 1820-22* (Kingston: McGill-Queen's University Press, 1984); *To the Arctic By Canoe, 1819-21: The Journal and Paintings of Robert Hood, Midshipman with Franklin* (Montreal: Arctic Institute of North America, 1974). This list makes no attempt to be definitive. Each of the authors represented skips across the disciplines to render historical verdicts. MacLaren is actually a Professor of literature. He and Stuart Houston, both westerners, have contributed much to the northern imaginary through their work. Both have also had a profound influence on Rudy Wiebe, about whom more later.

14. Louis-Edmond Hamelin, *About Canada: The Canadian North and its Conceptual Referants* (Ottawa: Department of the Secretary of State, 1988).

15. James Raffan "Frontier, Homeland and Sacred Space: A Collaborative Investigation into Cross-Cultural Perceptions of Place in the Thelon Game Sanctuary, Northwest Territories." Unpublished PhD Dissertation, Queen's University, 1992. See also his *Summer North of Sixty: By Paddle and Portage Across the Barrens Lands* (Toronto: Key Porter, 1990).

16. Robert Legget, *Ottawa Waterway: Gateway to a Continent* (Toronto: University of Toronto Press, 1975) 6.

17. Unless otherwise noted, all of the statistical data reported below is taken from Canada, *The State of Canada's Environment* (Ottawa: Minister of Supply and Services,

1991) Chapters 3, 12 and 26; P.H. Pearse et al., *Currents of Change: Final Report Inquiry on Federal Water Policy* (Ottawa: Environment Canada, 1985); M.C. Healey and R.R. Wallace, eds. *Canadian Aquatic Resources* (Ottawa: Department of Fisheries and Oceans, 1987). For those who want to take the route of the imagination, the classic book remains Hugh MacLennan, *Seven Rivers of Canada: The Mackenzie, the St. Lawrence, the Ottawa, the Red, the Saskatchewan, the Fraser, the St. John* (Toronto: Macmillan, 1961). This book was revised and enlarged to include photographs by John de Visser in 1974. See Hugh MacLennan, with the camera of John de Visser, *Rivers of Canada* (Toronto: Macmillan, 1974).

18. Andy Russell, *The Life of a River* (Toronto: McClelland & Stewart, 1989); George N. Hood, *Against the Flow: Rafferty-Alameda and the Politics of the Environment* (Saskatoon: Fifth House, 1994).

19. John Elliott, "The Columbia River Treaty: Growth Versus Development and the Implications." *The Sociology of Natural Resources* (Toronto: Butterworths, 1981) 160-214.

20. Michael Posluns, *Voices from the Odeyak* (Toronto: NC Press, 1993) supports my view. Sean McCutcheon, *Electric Rivers: The James Bay Project* (Montreal: Black Rose, 1991) would question it. See also William Hamley, "Economic Development and Environmental Preservation: The Case of the James Bay Hydro-Electric Power Projects, Quebec," *International Journal of Canadian Studies* 4 (Fall 1991): 29-48. By far the best reflections on the political implications of such issues are contained in Bruce W. Hodgins and Kerry A. Cannon, eds. *On the Land: Confronting the Challenges to Aboriginal Self-Determination in Northern Quebec and Labrador* (Toronto: Betelgeuse, 1995).

21. For a more lyrical statement of the same point, see Sean Kane, *Wisdom of the Mythtellers* (Peterborough: Broadview Press, 1994).

22. See Fernand Harvey, "L'histoire régionale, rural et urbaine," Jacques Rouillard, dir, *Guide d'histoire du Québec* 2nd éd. (Montréal: Editions du Meridien, 1993) 229-52; Fernand Harvey, dir., *La région culturelle. Problématique interdisciplinaire* (Québec: Institut québécois de recherche sur la culture, 1994). Recently the *Institut* has become affiliated with *l'Université du Québec*. It has changes its name to *l'Institut national de la recherche scientifique – culture et société*.

23. John Warkentin, ed., *The Western Interior of Canada: A Record of Geographical Discovery, 1612-1917* (Toronto: McClelland & Stewart, 1964); Ronald Rees, *New and Naked Land: Making the Prairies Home* (Saskatoon: Western Producer Prairie Books, 1988); R. Douglas Francis, *Images of the West: Changing Perceptions of the Prairies, 1690-1960* (Saskatoon: Western Producer Prairie Books, 1989); Sharon Butala, *The Perfection of the Morning: An Apprenticeship in Nature* (Toronto: Harper Collins, 1994); Bill Waiser, *The Field Naturalist: John Macoun, the Geological Survey and Natural Science* (Toronto: University of Toronto Press, 1989); Don Gayton, *The Wheatgrass Mechanism: Science and Imagination in the Western Canadian Landscape* (Saskatoon: Fifth

House, 1990); Doug Owram, *Promise of Eden: The Canadian Expansionist Movement and the Idea of the West, 1856-1900* (Toronto: University of Toronto Press, 1980); David C. Jones, *Empire of Dust: Settling and Abandoning the Prairie Dry Belt* (Edmonton: University of Alberta Press, 1987); David H. Breen, *The Canadian Prairie West and the Ranching Frontier, 1874-1924* (Toronto: University of Toronto Press, 1983); John Herd Thompson, *The Harvests of War: The Prairie West, 1914-1918* (Toronto: McClelland & Stewart, 1978); Gerald Friesen, *The Canadian Prairies: A History* (Toronto: University of Toronto Press, 1984).

24. George Woodcock, "A Plea for the Anti-Nation," *Canadian Forum* 52 (April, 1972): 16-19. See also, George Woodcock, "There are No Universal Landscapes," *artscanada* 222-23 (October-November, 1978): 37-42.

25. On bioregionalism see also, Christopher Plant and Judith Plant eds., *Turtle Talk: Voices for a Sustainable Future* (Gabriola Island, BC: New Society Publishers, 1993); Doug Aberley, ed., *Boundaries of Home: Mapping for Local Empowerment* (Gabriola Island, BC: New Society Publishers, 1993).

26. For the development of the ecosystem approach, see Stephen Bocking, "Visions of Nature and Society: A History of the Ecosystem Concept," *Alternatives* 20.3 (July-August 1994): 12-18.

27. The leading non-Native authority on traditional ecological knowledge is Milton M.R. Freeman. For a concise statement see his "The Nature and Utility of Traditional Ecological Knowledge," *Northern Perspectives* 20.1 (Summer 1992): 9-12. For a Native perspective, see Martha Johnson, ed., *Lore: Capturing Traditional Environmental Knowledge* (Ottawa: Dene Cultural Institute and International Development Research Centre, 1992).

28. Burt Galaway and Joe Hudson, eds., *Community Economic Development: Perspectives on Research and Policy* (Toronto: Thompson Educational Publishing, 1994); David J. A. Douglas, ed., *Community Economic Development in Canada* (Toronto: McGraw-Hill, Ryerson, 1994) 2 vols.

29. I intend the comment as laudatory. See, e.g. Ramsay Cook, "Cabbages not Kings: Towards an Ecological Interpretation of Early Canadian History," *Journal of Canadian Studies* 25.4 (Winter 1990-91): 5-16; *1492 and All that: Making a Garden Out of A Wilderness* (North York: Robarts Centre for Canadian Studies, York University, 1992).

Ontario's Provincial Parks
and Changing Conceptions of
"Protected Places"

Gerald Killan

O ver the course of the past century, popular understanding of provincial
parks as "protected places" has undergone considerable change. When
Alexander Kirkwood first proposed the creation of Algonquin Park over a century ago, he conceived of protection as efficient commodity management, that
is, the conservation of forest, fish, wildlife, waterway and scenic resources for
perpetual use and profit. According to this line of utilitarian thinking, a park
could be managed so as to "protect" natural resources from destruction and
depletion while at the same time permitting such things as supervised commercial logging and tourism activities. Today, however, when park advocates speak
of protection they mean preservation of biotic diversity, communities and processes, including the representation in parks of all the province's major earth and
life science features. In contrast to conservationists of Kirkwood's ilk, modern
preservationists argue that timber and mineral extraction and other forms of
commercial exploitation are incompatible with the protectionist objectives of
provincial parks. As a case in point, in early 1993, the leaders of the Wildlands
League were so angered by the impact of logging, hunting, roadbuilding and
recreational development in Ontario's first park that they called for "the re-
moval of Algonquin from the provincial parks system by the end of 1993 unless
substantive progress is made" in reducing the threat posed by these influences.

"It's time we call [Algonquin] what it is," declared Kevin Kavanagh, the league's president, "and not let the government lead the public along by classifying this area as protected. It's not – plain and simple!"[1]

Since the beginning of the Ontario provincial parks system, both utilitarian conservationists and preservationists have been players in the parks story, although the latter's influence was undeniably limited until the founding of the Federation of Ontario Naturalists (FON) in 1931. The FON's first major impact on parks policy came in 1938 when a campaign against logging in Algonquin prompted Frank MacDougall, superintendent of the park (1931-41), and later deputy minister of lands and forests (1941-66), to introduce the policy of multiple-use which struck a new balance between utility and preservation in park management policy. Later, following the Second World War, as ecological science became popularized and as the environmental movement waxed in the late 1960s across North America, the preservationist movement came to the fore and successfully jostled aside the utilitarian conservationists for a more prominent place in the park sun.

The Primacy of Utility and Profit

Ontario's original pre-1954 provincial parks – Algonquin, Lake Superior, Quetico and Sibley to the north, Ipperwash, Long Point, Presqui'ile and Rondeau to the south along the southern Great Lakes shoreline – were all set aside for utilitarian conservationist reasons. In Algonquin's case, the primary motive for creating the park was to maintain the water supply in the rivers originating in the Nipissing highlands by sustaining the forest cover in the headwaters area. Notwithstanding the importance of watershed protection, Alexander Kirkwood, one of the chief proponents of the park idea, did not see this objective involving a choice between water and wood. Logging, too, would have its place in the park. "The timber need not be permitted to rot down," he argued, "the mature trees can be cut in due season to allow the next in size a chance for growth." In this way, "utility and profit will be combined: the forest will be of great benefit as a producer of timber, and will add to the provincial revenue" (Kirkwood 1886: 4). Game protection ran a close second to watershed protection in importance and utility as a reason for creating Algonquin Park. As a wildlife sanctuary, Algonquin was to serve as a breeding ground to restock large portions of the province to the everlasting delight of sport hunters and tourist interests.

In Rondeau's case, recreation and conservation formed the basis of the argument presented by residents of southwestern Ontario when they petitioned for a park in 1894. The beaches and forested areas of Pointe aux Pins had long made the area "a popular and favourite resort for picnic and pleasure parties" numbering in the thousands.[2] Besides recreation, the petitioners argued that a park would protect the timber stand so necessary for maintaining Rondeau Bay as a harbour of refuge and commerce. Fifty years later, in 1944, tourism considerations lay back of the decision to create both Sibley and Lake Superior Provincial Parks along the proposed route of the Trans-Canada Highway.[3] Preservation had nothing to do with the creation of these parks. No one realized that Lake Superior Provincial Park possessed natural significance until four years after it had been established. In 1948, after undertaking field work in the area, C.H.D. Clarke, a biologist with the division of fish and wildlife in the DLF, discovered to his surprise that "this park more nearly approached the scenic and biological standards generally associated with [major nature preserves] in various parts of the world" and recommended that it should in time be managed according to international protectionist standards.[4] That proved to be a vain hope; a major provincial highway was constructed through the length of the park while the timber companies subjected it to decades of highgrade logging practices.

Prior to the 1930s, only the occasional voice could be heard demanding that natural areas be set aside to preserve scenery, flora and fauna, or wilderness for its own sake. In the 1880s and early 1890s, as various interests lobbied for a park in the Nipissing highlands, members of the Canadian Institute in Toronto occasionally expressed such sentiments.[5] In the provincial legislature in 1893, during the debates over the Algonquin Park Act, the Conservative MLA for West Kent, James Clancy, stood alone in calling for a logging ban in the park. "It would be a great pity," he argued, "if the forests were not maintained in their natural state in the park."[6] The existence of logging would mean that "the park would exist wholly on paper." No one else spoke in support of this position. Indeed, according to Thomas W. Gibson, "If the establishment of the Park had depended upon the preservation of the pine, the scheme would have had to be abandoned" (Gibson 1896: 123). Not only did the province want the revenues, but the survival of many communities contiguous to Algonquin depended upon ongoing logging opportunities in the park. It was no coincidence that the government auctioned off all the available timber berths in the proposed park area a few months before passing the Algonquin Park Act. To his credit, the plucky Clancy reiterated his no-logging proposal during the debate on the Rondeau Park Act in 1894.[7]

Clearly, preservationists possessed minimal political influence at the beginning of the Ontario parks story. It was mainly their wise-use counterparts who shaped policy. Not that it mattered at the outset, or for several decades thereafter, since both conservationists and preservationists were of one mind in their desire to set aside the first parklands as a protective measure against settlers and encroaching urban and industrial development.

Not surprisingly, given the reasons for establishing the first parks, utilitarian conservationist attitudes conditioned most aspects of management policy in the first half century of park development. Administrators and politicians accepted the proposition that parks should be managed for "use and profit" as Alexander Kirkwood put it. Commercial timber operations continued in the forests of Algonquin and Quetico often with detrimental effects on scenic, recreational and natural resources. For instance, without regard for scenic values, the timber operators regularly logged the shorelines of canoe routes and left unsightly slash for all to see. They dammed outlets to lakes to facilitate log driving and sometimes maintained the high water levels into summer thereby creating an ugly fringe of dead and fallen trees along miles of waterways (Killan 1993: 38-44).

Wildlife management also came to be viewed in utilitarian terms by park officials. As early as 1896, the superintendent of Rondeau constructed an aviary and commenced a program of raising native and exotic game birds, a program that included selling, purchasing and bartering eggs and the sale of adult birds. The priority given to the aviary operation effected other aspects of wildlife management. With DLF blessing, an effort was made to eliminate game bird predators – hawks, owls, weasels, skunks and foxes – by poisoning and trapping.[8] From 1910 to 1920, rangers in Algonquin and Quetico trapped so-called surplus fur-bearing animals and sold the pelts on the fur market.[9]

Similarly, the "use and profit" philosophy extended beyond timber and wildlife management to encompass recreational and tourism development. Beginning in 1905, lands and forest officials promoted the growth of leasehold cottage resorts in Algonquin and Rondeau, and later, during the 1920s, in Long Point and Presqu'ile. Once entrenched, leaseholders pressured officials (park commissions in Presqui'ile and Long Point) to develop and manage the parks to suit the interests of the cottage communities. The impact of these communities was invariably detrimental to natural values. At Long Point, for the worst case example, some 550 cottages had been constructed by 1949 leaving a trifling six of the original 76 hectares of the park for public use. "Generally speaking," reported a Department of Municipal Affairs official in 1950, "the development which has taken place has tended away from the conception that the Park was to be an area for general use of the public ... towards the creation of a colony of summer cottage occupants, whose desires and interests clash with the avowed purposes for which the Park was set aside."[10] The original Long Point Provincial Park had to be abandoned in 1956 and a new park relocated on adjacent property.

The Advent of Multiple Use

"Use and profit" management policies eventually occasioned a backlash from recreational and preservationist forces within the conservation movement, people alarmed about the negative effects these policies were having on scenic and natural values. The first organized reaction came in 1928 with the formation of the Minnesota-based Quetico-Superior Council (QSC) – its Canadian allies eventually evolved into the Quetico Foundation. The QSC came into existence to thwart the plan of timber baron Edward Backus to construct a series of dams along the boundary waters area between Quetico Provincial Park and the Superior National Forest in Minnesota. It took decades of sustained effort, but the QSC did ultimately succeed in convincing authorities on both sides of the international border to protect the shorelines from the effects of logging, flooding and other forms of industrial exploitation (Killan and Warecki 1988: 328-55).

It was not until 1931, however, with the formation of the Federation of Ontario Naturalists, that an organization emerged to champion an ecological or preservationist perspective in park policy. In 1934, the FON published *Sanctuaries and the Preservation of Wild Life in Ontario* that made the case that utilitarian conservation considerations alone should not solely determine what was protected in parks. The federation insisted that there were sufficient scientific and educational reasons to justify creating a system of nature sanctuaries or reserves in provincial parks and elsewhere on Crown land for "the preservation of representative samples of the natural conditions" of Ontario. "The need for nature preservation," the naturalists argued, "does not depend only on the economic value of the natural life usually considered worthy of consideration."

The establishment of the FON marked the beginning of an ongoing tension between the "wise use" conservationists and the preservationists. For almost four decades, a harmony of interest about creating parks had existed between the two currents in the conservationist stream: now, because of park management issues, their parallel courses were about to bend in on one another to create turbulent crosscurrents. This occurred in 1938 when waves of recreationists flowed into Algonquin following the completion of Highway 60. As these people explored the interior of the park, complaints rose about the destructive practices of the timber operators. Accordingly, the FON initiated the campaign to ban logging in the park, and to challenge the primacy of the gospel of "use and profit."[11]

The superintendent of Algonquin, Frank MacDougall, quickly responded to the problem by introducing the policy of multiple-use, a policy already in favour to the south on federal lands administered by the U.S. Forest Service. Multiple-use endeavoured to embrace both the utilitarian conservationist and the preservationist positions and to strike a new balance in park management policy. Multiple use doctrine held that "where two or more ... main uses can be served at the same time on the same area they are carried forward side by side....Whenever two of these uses come into conflict, some authority determines which is likely to render the greater public service.... On principle [sic] areas of the national forests recreation is an incidental use; on some it is a paramount use; on a few it becomes the exclusive use" (Allin 1982: 68). For MacDougall, multiple use in parks like Algonquin and Quetico meant that wherever a clash occurred between recreationist and logger, then scenic protection and recreational values were to be given primacy in management policy.[12] As applied by MacDougall, multiple use led to a number of innovations in park policy including: the introduction of standardized shoreline and scenic reserves in Algonquin and Quetico; the designation of a nature reserve zone in Algonquin to protect small stands of old-growth pine; and the creation in 1941 of the Wildlife Research Area.

All in all, Frank MacDougall's efforts succeeded in striking a *modus vivendi* between logger and recreationist, and between conservationist and preservationist. Not until the 1960s when wilderness enthusiasts, environmentalists and recreationists confronted what had become a year-round, heavily mechanized logging industry dependent on diesel trucks and elaborate road systems, skidders and chain saws, did MacDougall's conflict resolution formula break down and the search for a new balance between conservationist and preservationist begin again in earnest.

Recreation-Preservation Imbalance

After the Second World War, the provincial parks picture was dramatically altered by a remarkable boom in outdoor recreation, a phenomenon which lasted nearly 30 years. This great rush to get outdoors was fuelled by rapid population growth, by sustained urban and industrial growth, by a rising standard of living, by increased levels of leisure time (the 40-hour, five-day work week became the norm for working-class Ontarians), by more personal mobility, and by an increasingly better educated and younger population.

Although they resisted these pressures at first, the foresters in the Department of Lands and Forests (DLF) eventually responded to the public's demand for more parkland with beaches, picnic and camping facilities, and natural areas, all within a few hours motoring distance of the province's major urban places. After Frank MacDougall despatched his regional foresters to study the practices of state park systems to the south, the Frost government created the Division of Parks within the DLF in 1954 and gave it the task of developing as rapidly as possible a network of provincial parks around the shorelines of the southern Great Lakes and at regular intervals along the major northern tourism highways. The park system quickly expanded from eight in 1954 to 108 operating parks in 1970 (Killan chapter 3).

Despite this extraordinary parkland expansion, the demand for campsites, beaches and recreational space still outstripped supply. Alas, the massive user pressure (the number of park visitors jumped from two million in 1957 to 12 million in 1970), combined with the rapid expansion in the number of parks, proved to be fraught with difficulties. By the early 1960s, the provincial park system was in a state of management adrift. "Here in Ontario," Chief of Parks A. B. Wheatley candidly admitted in 1961, "our parks are planned and decisions made on a day to day basis.... Literally speaking, we have no long range plans and ... no qualified staff available to prepare research programs."[13] Three years late, Alan R.K. MacDonald, a parks planner, confessed that the "Parks Branch is slowly but surely stagnating. This has been brought about because of the tremendous growth in the system and a lack of parallel growth in professional and technical staff, both in the field and head office."[14] Under these circumstances, parks officials were scarcely able to cope with an almost overwhelming set of management problems including: environmental degradation caused by recreational overuse; a shortage of campsites in southern regions; rowdyism; crowded and littered canoe routes; and heightened tensions between hunters and naturalists, motorboat fishermen and wilderness trippers, loggers and environmentalists.

Lacking an official parks policy, management decisions were often made at the whim of bureaucrats and politicians. The decision to locate a radio observatory in Algonquin Park in 1959 is a case in point. Without a hint of public consultation, on the recommendation of Deputy Minister Frank MacDougall, the Frost government provided a 2,200 hectare area near Lake Traverse for radio astronomy purposes by the National Research Council of Canada. This project required an access road, laboratory buildings and residences, several large antennae, and a series of dishes (some 30 metres in diameter) spread out in a line over several kilometres. Patrick Hardy, managing director of the Canadian Audubon Society, reflected the thinking of the province's conservation groups when he wrote: "It is inconceivable to me that there is not another spot in the whole of Ontario which is sufficiently isolated and interference-free for the location of the radio telescope." What the province required, he added, was "legislation which would prevent incursions of any kind on our provincial parks without first having the matter thoroughly aired in debate."[15]

Aware of the implications of the lack of an official policy statement, the Federation of Ontario Naturalists submitted in 1958 an "Outline of a Basis for a Parks Policy for Ontario," the first attempt to define "the principles which should govern the establishment and management of public parks" and nature reserves from an ecological perspective. The document would not have been possible without the many advances made by professional ecologists in Britain and North America during the previous quarter century, the period when ecology – the branch of biology concerned with the normal but extremely complex interrelationships among all forms of plant and animal life in time and space – came of age. At the heart of the ecologists' creed, popularized in North America by Aldo Leopold's *A Sand County Almanac* (1949), lay a genuine respect for all forms of life, based on an understanding that every living thing was part of an intricate, interdependent, dynamic biotic community, that every living thing filled a special niche, and played a unique role in maintaining the character and stability of the shared environment. To remove or damage one element in the system inevitably undermined the healthy operation of the whole, sometimes imperceptibly, but sometimes drastically. In this view of the natural order, humankind was merely one dependent species of the biotic community to which it belonged but could make no claim to possess.

In the FON's view, parks served five purposes – recreational, aesthetic, educational, historical and scientific. It was the government's responsibility to establish parks to fulfill those needs, and to manage parkland in such a way as to harmonize recreation and ecology, give primary consideration to the protection of natural areas, and minimize influences such as commercial logging, trapping and sport hunting. The FON also returned to a theme it had first raised in 1934, that the province should set aside "for purely scientific purposes" a system of nature reserves representative of Ontario's life science features.

The FON's "Outline of a Basis for a Parks Policy for Ontario" was arguably the most sophisticated statement on the subject yet produced, and Premier Leslie Frost recognized this immediately. He responded in part by passing the Wilderness Areas Act (1959) – the first legislative recognition in Ontario for the nature reserve concept (albeit under the misnomer wilderness area). The act also provided for the protection of historical sites on Crown land such as the petroglyphs site near Stoney Lake (today Petroglyphs Provincial Park). Alas, the Wilderness Areas Act contained a serious deficiency from a preservationist perspective. In deference to the mining interests who feared that vast tracts of Crown land would be "sterilized," the government restricted full protection to those areas under 640 acres in size and made larger ones subject to "development and utilization" (Killan 1993: 134).

While the Wilderness Areas Act represented a small step forward for natural areas protection, it did nothing to address the problems besetting provincial parks arising out of the recreation-commercial utilization-preservation imbalance. By the mid-1960s, a consensus emerged among park administrators, conservationist groups of all stripes, and politicians that the only way to resolve the management problems, conflicts and confusion in the parks was to introduce a parks classification and zoning scheme as the central framework of parks policy. No one park, it was now clear, could be all things to all people. Different types of parks had to be established for different user groups, and managed to achieve specific objectives. In a more complex and effective way than the multiple use approach, parks classification and zoning provided a conflict resolution mechanism to meet the needs of preservationist, utilitarian conservationist and recreationist alike.

James Keenan, then the land use supervisor in the Parks Branch, drafted the first parks classification framework that received approval in 1967. The scheme classified provincial parks into five categories – natural environment, nature reserve, primitive, recreation and wild river (Killan 1993: 165-7).

For a brief time all was roses in the provincial parks garden as one park initiative followed another in the wake of the classification breakthrough. During 1967-8, Polar Bear Primitive Park was created, the first seven nature reserves established, a nature reserve advisory committee appointed, and wild river inventories undertaken (sections of the Mattawa and Winisk rivers were slated as the first such parks). The Robarts government also appointed Leonard Gertler to conduct a study of the Niagara Escarpment to identify areas worthy of protection for their recreational and environmental values. His report subsequently led to special funding for parkland along the escarpment during the seventies.

The euphoria over the classification policy and these noteworthy initiatives proved to be short-lived, a lull before the preservationist storm. As it turned out, the implementation of the 1967 classification policy came to a grinding halt over the issue of primitive parks. With the exception of Polar Bear (above the tree line and in an area of low mineral potential), timber and mining interests opposed all proposals for new primitive parks, as well as proposals to reclassify and/or rezone the large natural environment parks – Algonquin and Quetico, Killarney and Lake Superior.

And so it was in 1968 that the wilderness question emerged as a major political issue in Ontario politics. Two new organizations appeared to join the FON to champion the wilderness cause: the National and Provincial Parks Association of Canada (NPPAC, today the Canadian Parks and Wilderness Society), established in 1963, became a force to be reckoned with once Gavin Henderson assumed the executive director's position in November 1964; and the Algonquin Wildlands League, created in 1968, under the inspired leadership of such worthies as Douglas Pimlott, Abbott Conway, Walter Gray and Patrick Hardy.

The quickening preservationist impulse was part of a larger, strengthening phenomenon – the North American environmental movement. Modern environmentalism, according to Samuel P. Hays in *Beauty, Health, and Permanence* (1987), emerged out of the social and economic transformations following the Second World War and the concomitant general rise in living standards. Many North Americans reached a level of affluence that enabled them to look beyond the acquisition of necessities and conveniences to give priority to quality of life considerations. For instance, the newly affluent came to value outdoor recreation space, undefiled natural areas, and clean air and water as essential aspects of a better standard of living.

During the 1950s, the post-war outdoor recreation boom helped shape, and in turn was sustained by, new environmental attitudes. The participants in the great rush to get outdoors began to view natural areas differently than their utilitarian forbears. Public conceptions of forests and rivers changed in this period. In contrast to earlier conservationists who viewed forests as tree farms to be managed on a sustained yield basis, or who valued rivers primarily for navigation, irrigation and hydroelectric purposes, the environmentally inclined population conceived of forested areas and waterways both as environments with biological merits and as "aesthetic resources that provided amenities and enhanced daily life." Accordingly, the first phase of environmental politics in the United States largely involved "the amenity values of wild lands" (Hays 1987: chapter 1). Under pressure from preservationist organizations like the Sierra Club, the Wilderness Society and the National Wildlife Federation, the administrations of presidents John F. Kennedy and Lyndon B. Johnson responded with a long list of legislation dedicated to the protection of "the aesthetic qualities of nature and wildlands" – the Wilderness Act (1964), the Land and Water Conservation Fund (1965), the National and Scenic Rivers Act (1968) and the National Trails Act (1968).

Concern over air and water pollution became the hallmark of the second phase of environmental activism that came to the fore in the mid-1960s. Public anxiety over the enormous deleterious impact that pollution was having on natural environments and the threat this posed to general health and well-being built up during the radioactive fallout scares of the late 1950s and early 1960s, and peaked over the pesticide scare stimulated by the publication of Rachel Carson's *Silent Spring* (1962). Carson wrote about ecology – "the web of life-or death" she called it – in terms average people could understand, and explained to her shocked readers how humankind was poisoning itself by introducing DDT into the food chain. *Silent Spring* opened the floodgates of discussion on environmental issues of all kinds. It became apparent that no one could avoid the effects of air, land and water pollution. This realization did not sit well with the generation of North Americans who had grown affluent during the post-war economic expansion, and who now placed increasing importance on matters of life style and family, home and leisure. With pollution and economic and urban expansion threatening the areas in which they lived and played, more and more people began to heed the environmentalist message.

During the 1960s, Ontarians imbibed a steady stream of information and commentary on environmental questions and realized that their province was not immune to the problems plaguing many parts of the world. When they read of killer smog in London or Los Angeles, their thoughts went to the 1962 Grey Cup game rudely interrupted when a thick blanket of fog, partly caused by dirt and sulphur fumes, settled over the Canadian National Exhibition Stadium in Toronto. Five years later, they were shocked by a CBC television documentary – "Air of Death" – that claimed that toxic air threatened the lives of the residents of Port Maitland. Ontarians also faced the fact that a water pollution crisis of immense proportions threatened the Great Lakes. In the mid-

1960s, scientists declared Lake Erie "near death" due to eutrophication (Ashworth 1986: chapter 12). Revelations about other new environmental threats appeared regularly in newspaper articles and popular magazines.

For those interested in natural areas protection these were worrisome times. "Our generation is witnessing a world-wide disaster to overtake the thin film of life that paints our planet green," commented R. Yorke Edwards. In previously remote areas, "exploitation of the landscape by man has already destroyed much of their wilderness, and from all of them come warnings of wildlife about to be literally pushed off the earth" (Edwards 1967: 1). In such a world, concluded the environmentalists, the preservation of natural areas was urgently required. In view of their own steadily deteriorating environment, many informed southern Ontarians came to believe that the quality of their lives, and perhaps even their survival, depended on their shrinking natural inheritance. Gavin Henderson put it bluntly: "In all nature, environment is the key to success of every organism. If the habitat is favourable a species will thrive. If it is unfavourable it will die out."[16]

This powerful context of environmental awareness explains the intensity of the emotions behind the fight in Ontario for more wilderness, nature reserve and national parks that erupted in 1968. Over the next six years, the Algonquin Wildlands League, the FON, the NPPAC, and their allies succeeded in generating widespread public support for wilderness preservation; indeed, they made the issue a litmus test of the government's commitment to environmental reform (Killan and Warecki 1992). By 1974, the preservationist lobby had achieved impressive results. Logging had been banned in Killarney and Quetico, and both parks had been designated primitive in 1971 and 1973 respectively. The Davis government had agreed to the establishment of Pukaskwa National Park. Public consultation had been entrenched as part of the provincial park master planning process, and the Provincial Parks Advisory Council appointed to serve as a watchdog over the system and to seek public input on significant policy matters. And while commercial logging remained in the forests of Algonquin (under the auspices of the Algonquin Forest Authority) and Lake Superior, in all other parks, a new timber policy excluded timber licences, and henceforth parks were to be operated as Crown Management Units. If logging was deemed necessary, the cutting would be carried out by private companies as a ministry project, and each operation would have as its main purpose the management of the forest for environmental values.

The Gospel Relating to Parks

During the years when wilderness preservation commanded the public's attention, the Parks Division and the regional offices of the Ministry of Natural Resources underwent profound changes in both the quality and quantity of their personnel. Of particular significance, parks planning and management became professionalized with the addition of specialists from a wide spectrum of disciplines. By the late 1970s division personnel had introduced park master and system planning programs second to none in North America. Their work climaxed in 1978 with the approval by the Davis cabinet of an official parks policy and the release of the so-called "Blue Book," the *Ontario Provincial Parks Planning and Management Policies* manual.

The "blue book" was an accomplishment of historic importance; it has been aptly called "the gospel relating to parks." Based on a decade of scientific, recreation and leisure research, it provided answers to a host of complex questions: What were the goals and objectives of the provincial parks system? How many parks of each class did Ontario require and why? Where should these parks be located and why? What activities should be permitted/prohibited in each class of park and zone and why? The new policy also added historical parks to the system. Primitive parks became wilderness parks and the wild river designation metamorphosed into waterway parks.

Once possessed of a clear idea of what the optimum Ontario parks system should look like, regional and district personnel accelerated the earth and life science inventories and field surveys required to determine how many new parks were required to meet the targets prescribed for each class of park in the "blue book." This work came to fruition in 1981 with the completion of regional parks system plans for each of the MNR's administrative regions. These plans identified 245 candidate provincial parks which the planners deemed necessary to achieve policy objectives. The significance of these documents and the policy frameworks upon which they rested (the "Blue Book" in particular) can scarcely be exaggerated. They provided administrators and politicians with a clear direction, but more importantly, they provided an agenda and a mission for park advocacy groups in the decade ahead, and inspired them to extraordinary action.

In 1981-2, the MNR began the process of dovetailing the park system into the larger, ongoing Strategic Land Use Planning (SLUP) process; in other words, the 245 candidate provincial parks were tossed into the land use planning hopper to compete against the land and water requirements of other ministry programs and users of Crown land. To the surprise of most everyone, the parks issue immediately dominated the remainder of the SLUP process. The seven candidate wilderness parks and 151 nature reserves evoked a negative reaction from timber and mineral interests and sport hunters among others. In effect, SLUP turned into an unprecedented, epic struggle between environmentalists and utilitarians, that is, between advocates of the two clashing perceptions of parks as protected places (Killan 1993: chapter 9).

The struggle over SLUP climaxed on 2 June 1983 when Minister of Natural Resources Alan Pope announced his decision on the implementation of the provincial parks system plan. He declared in the legislature that five new wilderness parks had just been placed into regulations, that 149 new provincial parks of various classes would be created in the immediate future, and that the province was prepared to enter into negotiations with the federal government to establish a national park on the Bruce Peninsula. Regrettably, these spectacular advances for the parks system were soured by two other features of Pope's announcement. Ninety of the candidate parks under review during the SLUP process had been rejected (76 would have been nature reserves), while drastic cutbacks had been made in the size of many of the remaining candidate parks. Worse still, Pope revealed that the Davis government intended to discard the "Blue Book" as the management tool for all the post-1983 parks. Henceforth, new parks, including wilderness and many nature reserve parks, were to be opened to what the "blue book" had defined as non-conforming uses in these places – mineral exploration, sport hunting, trapping and commercial tourism. This was a retrograde step that took the park system back to the old pre-1954 period of "use and profit" management policy. In the see-saw balance between the preservation and utilitarian conservation concepts of parks, the latter was once again in the ascendancy.

As it happened, dramatic changes in provincial politics provided an opportunity to review Pope's ill-conceived parks policy. In June 1985, Ontario's remarkable 42-year Tory dynasty came to an end when the Liberals under Premier David Peterson ascended to power. It required three years of intensive lobbying by preservationist groups and a great deal of internal cabinet wrangling and hand-wringing, but on 17 May 1988, the Liberals reinstated the "blue book" policies for the post-1983 parks.

Predictably, those utilitarian conservationists who subscribed to multiple-use ideas were outraged at the policy reversal and complained bitterly about the "total protectionism" which now prevailed in park management.[17] In point of fact, nothing could have been further from the truth. Rather than total protectionism, the hallmarks of the 1988 Liberal parks policy were balance, trade-offs and flexibility. For instance, hunting and commercial tourism – activities deemed exploitive by preservationists – remained in selected historical, natural environment, recreation and waterway class parks. The Peterson government also substantially modified "blue book" policy to permit existing commercial tourism operations to remain in wilderness parks, and to allow some fly-in operations and the use of motorboats outside access areas. Sport hunting was already being accommodated in 66 parks. And status Indians were allowed to continue their traditional activities including hunting, trapping and wild rice harvesting in all classes of parks located within their treaty areas, and to retain their hunt camps in wilderness parks. All in all, these were scarcely the policy prescriptions one would associate with total protectionism.

Clearly, then, in resurrecting the "Blue Book" for the post-1983 parks, the Peterson Liberals did not entirely forsake the traditional doctrine of utility and profit. Further proof of this can be seen in the "use and profit" mentality at work in the tourism and marketing strategies pursued with enthusiasm by many park managers, and the oft-repeated description of provincial parks as "products" to be "packaged" and "promoted" through paid advertising campaigns and customized park-specific marketing plans.[18]

In point of fact, Ontario's park policies embrace both the traditional conservationist notion of "protected places" based on the gospel of "utility and profit," and the new ecological conception of protection. Despite the influence of environmentalism, "ecology" did not displace "utility" in Ontario's parks. Both ecology and utility became variables in the decision making equation. Most debates over our "Changing Parks" have involved, and will continue to involve, differences of opinion over which of the two variables should be given priority. If the history of Ontario's provincial parks system teaches us anything, it is that the balance between utility and protection is always at risk of being shifted by the winds of political, economic and social change.

References

Allin, C.W. (1982). *The Politics of Wilderness Preservation*. Contributions in Political Science No. 64. Westport, Conn.: Greenwood Press.

Ashworth, W. (1986). *The Late Great Lakes: An Environmental History*. New York: Alfred A. Knopf.

Edwards, R.Y. (1967). "The Preservation of Wilderness: Is man a part of nature – or a thing apart?" *Canadian Audubon*, January-February, 1-7.

Gibson, T.W. (1896). "The Algonquin National Park of Ontario." Ontario Clerk of Forestry, *Report*, 119-132.

Hays, S.P. (1987). *Beauty, Health and Permanence: Environmental Politics in the United States, 1955-1985.* Cambridge, Mass.: Cambridge University Press.

Killan, G. (1993). *Protected Places: A History of Ontario's Provincial Parks System.* Toronto, Oxford and Lewiston: Dundurn Press in association with the Ontario Ministry of Natural Resources.

Killan G. and Warecki, G. (1988). "Saving Quetico-Superior, 1927 to 1960" in R. Hall, W. Westfall, and L. S. MacDowell (eds), *Patterns of the Past: Interpreting Ontario's History*: Toronto and Oxford: Dundurn Press with the Ontario Historical Society.

Kirkwood, A. (1886). *Algonkin Forest and Park, Ontario. Letter to the Honorable T. B. Pardee, M.P.P., Commissioner of Crown Lands for Ontario.* Toronto: Warwick and Sons.

Endnotes

1. "1993: Action Before Celebration," *Wildland News*, Vol. 25/No. 1 (Spring 1993), 2.

2. Kent County Council Minutes, 26 January 1894, Petitions, 439. "Petition to the Hon. Sir Oliver Mowat, Premier of Ontario, and the Members of the Executive Council to the Members of the Executive Council to the Province of Ontario, 26 January 1984. Provincial Archives of Ontario (PAO), RG-8, 1-7-F-2, petitions 1894, no. 23, "Petition of the Town Council of Chatham, Praying that Pointe Aux Pins may be set apart as a Public Park, February 8, 1894."

3. For the origins of Sibley Provincial Park see Land Records (LR), Queen's Park, Whitney Block, file 110765, *passim.* For Lake Superior see LR-125864, *passim.*

4. LR-125864 C. H. D. Clarke to W. J. K. Harkness, 27 January 1948.

5. *Ontario Sessional Papers* (OSP), No. 7, 1888. *Report of the Canadian Institute 1886-7*, 1; *Transactions of the Canadian Institute* 3 (1891-92), 60.

6. Newspaper Hansard, 9 May 1893.

7. *Ibid.*, 23 March 1894.

8. OSP, No. 5, 1896, Superintendent's Report, 281.

9. OSP, No. 34, 1909-10, Superintendent's Report, 98; *ibid.*, No. 3, 1910-11, 99; *ibid.*, No. 3, 1912-13, 93; *ibid.*, No. 3, 1920-1, 117.

10. LR-30477 Vol. 50 H. L. Cummings to W. W. Orr, 29 April 1950 and *passim.*

11. LR-79218 *passim* 1938. See Toronto *Globe and Mail*, 3 November 1938.

12. LR-119915 Algonquin Park *Newsletter*, Vol. 8, No. 3, 20 April 1939.

13. PAO, RG-1, 1A-3, box 4, file 2-3-4, A. B. Wheatley to G. H. U. Bayly, 7 December 1961.

14. PB, file 10-1, Parks Planning General, A. R. K. MacDonald to A. B. Wheatley, 16 June 1964.

15. LR-164940, Patrick A. Hardy to J. W. Spooner, 25 November and 17 December 1959.

16. Quoted in *Quetico Newsletter* 10, no. 3 (Winter 1964).

17. John Power, "Trapping, Hunting Ban a Blow to Democracy," *Toronto Star*, 21 May 1988. John Kerr, "Crisis in Our Parks," *Ibid.*, 25 May 1988.

18. "Marketing Strategies for Provincial Parks," Policy PM6.5, 1 September 1986.

THE ABORIGINAL PRESENCE

IN ONTARIO PARKS AND OTHER

PROTECTED PLACES

Bruce W. Hodgins & Kerry A. Cannon

In Ontario, Aboriginal First Nations historically had a sustainable, and self-governing presence on nearly all the lands and waterways of what later became parks (provincial and federal) and other protected places. Since 1784 most treaties between the Crown and First Nations, either implicitly or explicitly, confirmed their right to continued presence on those portions of their former hunting and living territories which remained "crown land" – land not patented or ceded to individuals or corporations. In other words, aspects of their aboriginal rights were incorporated as treaty rights in and over crown land.

All parks and most other protected areas are on crown land. Aboriginal rights on these lands, though limited, are now increasingly entrenched in the Constitution and further guaranteed by recent Supreme Court decisions. Often, the specific, on-site details have yet to be settled. Furthermore, there are First Nations and some Métis groups who claim often that they hold land unceded and therefore protected under provisions of the Royal Proclamation of 1763, or that lands once retained by them as reserve Indian lands were wrongly appropriated or sold out from under them, or that land belonging to one First Nation was ceded to the Crown by a different First Nation. All of this will have to be sorted out, hopefully in the next ten or so years.

Controversy, misunderstanding, misrepresentation, and confusion still exist. Draft temporary agreements have been or are presently being negotiated. Some deep wilderness ecologists and many non-Native consumptive anglers and hunters remain embittered and unreconciled. We, on the other hand, like many other moderate environmentalists and park supporters, are enthusiastic about these recent positive developments.

The Government of Ontario and the present Government of Canada both recognize the "inherent right" of Aboriginal First Nations to self-government – still not clearly defined – even if that inherent right failed to be entrenched when the Charlottetown Accord was defeated in October 1992. Indeed, former Premier Bob Rae has entered into a binding agreement with most of the Chiefs of Ontario that all collective relations between Ontario and First Nations will be on a "government-to-government" basis.[1] The clock cannot be turned back on inherent rights. It is still to be determined in most cases how the inherent right to self-government will relate to collective First Nations co-management, or at least concrete involvement in the management of parks and other protected areas. The direction that the provincial government is leaning towards, however, is becoming clearer. An environmental assessment panel recently recommended that the Ministry of Natural Resources give "natives an opportunity to share in the social and economic benefits of the forest, and to involve their input in timber management planning."[2]

For our purposes, the 1850 Robinson Treaties, involving most of the large Canadian portions of the watersheds of Georgian Bay, the North Channel and Lake Superior, were the most important agreements between Aboriginal peoples and the Crown in Ontario. Negotiated in Sault Ste. Marie by the Torontorian W.B. Robinson for the imperial Crown, the Indians ceded most of their ancestral lands, received special grants, reserves and a treaty annuity, as well as the now very significant "full and free privilege" to hunt and fish on the unpatented portions of their traditional lands – then close to 100 percent and now still over 80 percent of their territories. In other words, all of their aboriginal rights were not given up in exchange for new and different treaty rights. Much of this continuum was implied or stated in the earlier treaties and certainly made manifest in the latter ones.

In 1860 the united Province of Canada was given control over Indian Affairs by the imperial government. It negotiated in 1862 the Manitoulin Island Treaty. After Confederation, the Canadian Crown negotiated in 1873, Treaty 3, involving the Ojibwa and OjiCree communities of what became the Kenora-Rainy

River-Lake of the Woods districts of northwestern Ontario. In 1905-06, Canada, with the help from and presence of Ontario representatives, negotiated with the Crees and others, the James Bay Treaty 9 covering, with the adhesions of 1929, the entire huge far north of the province. The pattern held. In 1923, the Roberts Treaty, covering a large area south of the Mattawa – Ottawa River line vainly attempted to clarify cessions, terms, and territories with several First Nations of central Ontario.

Meanwhile, Confederation had vastly confused the situation with regard to relations between federal and provincial governments and the First Nations. Though "Founding Peoples," the First Nations were not active participants in the creation of the Canadian federation. The British North America Act, by section 91, item 24, gave the Government of Canada the responsibility to make laws for "Indians and Lands reserved for the Indians." Section 92, item 5, gave Ontario and the other original provinces power over "The Management and Sale of the Public Lands belonging to the Province, and of the Timber and Wood thereon," and section 109 gave the provinces control over "All Lands, Mines, Minerals, and Royalties...."[3] So Indians and Indian Reserves were a federal responsibility, while crown lands and natural resources were provincial responsibilities. It was and has remained ever complicated. The trinity of the single Crown – imperial, federal, and provincial was to be expressed in three "rights," with the imperial right being a rapidly declining one, with little power but much intrusive history and legality.

Then came the federal Indian Act of 1876, with its several precursors and later amendments down to 1951 and beyond. Now severely constitutionally and ethically challenged, the Indian Act soon came to be recognized as superior to the solemn treaties between the imperial or the Canadian Crown and the self-governing First Nations. The Indian Act dramatically curtailed aboriginal self-government, explicitly until at least the mid-1970s and in some measure even today. In the shield country and in the James Bay lowlands, where most of the large provincial parks and other protected areas are located, the Aboriginal presence on much of the so-called crown land long continued, and 95 percent of the land in northern Ontario is today still unpatented, that is not under private ownership. Aboriginal treaty rights to a presence on and to a use to these lands therefore endure. If one excludes the metropolitan limits of the five major urban centres of northern Ontario, well over two-thirds, perhaps three-quarters of the land mass of northern Ontario has an Aboriginal majority on it. Trapping and the use of the land for country food, often as part of the informal economy, has remained important.

By various devices, legislative, administrative, juridical, and simple *force majeure*, Ontario proceeded after Confederation, working basically from the southern shield northward, to restrict the Aboriginal presence and the rights of First Nations to fish, gather, hunt and even trap in parts of the crown domain. Some of this action was site specific. Some was broad, by using laws of "general application" to involve Indians as well as others. Some such action has been successfully challenged in the courts, and other actions are now being challenged. Much have simply been withdrawn or not enforced. Most of the action was probably always illegal.

When the first great parks were established, that is Algonquin in 1893 and Quetico in 1913, the rights of Aboriginal peoples were largely ignored or severely curtailed. Though lumbering long remained and was extremely widespread in the Parks, many Ontarian "first visitors" and their great artistic representatives (Tom Thomson and the Group of Seven) tended to see "their" wilderness as pristine.

In the past, First Nations consistently challenged Ontario's legislative authority over Native issues in order to protect both their traditional relationship with the federal government and to assert their aboriginal rights to self-government. More recently, this approach has changed profoundly because of Ontario's growing support for First Nations, including their claims to self-government in a broad sense and in the most recent rounds of the constitutional reform process. First Nations had been reluctant to have any relations with Ontario, partly because of decisions such as the *St. Catherine's Milling* case of 1888.[4] This case involved the Ontario government and the federal government (supported by the St. Catherine's Milling and Lumber Company) competing for resources, specifically timber allotments, in the disputed area of present-day northwestern Ontario. Eventually, the court ruled that although the Indians had ceded the lands to the Canadian Crown, Ontario then immediately secured rights to the underlying or radical title to all former Indian lands. It was not surprising, therefore, that First Nations were cautious in dealing with Ontario because it appeared that the province had secured the ability to undermine all their traditional rights.

Following the Second World War, Ontario became slowly, but increasingly, involved in the provision of services to First Nations, because Canada wanted to reduce its costly responsibilities, and Ontario wanted to expand its jurisdiction and power over Native lands and resources. In 1948, the Special Joint Committee of the Senate and the House of Commons proposed the devolution of powers such as social services, and fish and game laws from the federal to the provincial governments. Heretofore provinces were apprehensive about the legislative position of First Nations as a collective group with special status and rights. Consequently, in 1951, when the Indian Act was mildly revised, a new section was added which stated that provincial laws were extended to include Indians except when the laws conflicted with the Indian Act or violated their treaty rights. This clause provided the impetus for Ontario to become more involved in Native affairs; even though, Aboriginal peoples feared that any "... move to the provinces will jeopardize or even nullify their, aboriginal, treaty, and corporate land and resource rights under the Constitution Act, 1867."[5]

In March 1976 the Office of Land Claims was established under the Ministry of Natural Resources. In 1978 the name was changed to the Office of Indian Resource Policy. The office had the prime responsibility of dealing with Indian land claims and other Indian land matters.[6] In that same year, the federal government, the provincial government, and the First Nations of Ontario entered into formal tripartite discussions on First Nations self-government. This process was originally facilitated by a tripartite council which included among its members the federal minister of Indian Affairs, the minister responsible for the then provincial Native Affairs portfolio, and the Chiefs of Ontario.[7] A number of working groups were established including one that focused on land claims. The new process was seen as a departure from unilateral decision-making in the exercise of government responsibility and as a meaningful change to the existing notion of First Nations-Government relations. It was significant because it allowed for the participation of Aboriginal peoples in the development and implementation of initiatives affecting their lives, and secondly, "With the commitment to achieving change through mutual agreement, the government(s) acknowledged Indian self-determination."[8] Despite these advantages, the successful resolution of Native issues and claims was impeded by the long debate over the concept of specific self-governing aboriginal rights which Native peoples cannot compromise and which the Ontario government refused, until recently, to recognize.[9] Without accepting that Aboriginal peoples were entitled to these rights, the utility of the discussions seemed limited.

In 1985 a new Liberal government, led by David Peterson, was elected in Ontario. Almost immediately, this government demonstrated a much more pro-active stance regarding Native issues than that taken previously. A Cabinet Committee on Aboriginal Affairs was struck with membership from among the more prominent members of cabinet (Ian Scott, the Attorney General and a high-profile senior minister, was given the additional responsibilities of Minister Responsible for Native Affairs). The Minister Responsible for Native Affairs was supported by what was now to be called the Ontario Native Affairs Directorate (ONAD). The Directorate played a lead role in moving toward the development of a provincial aboriginal affairs policy and acted as a central agency in seeing that individual ministries lived up to the spirit of such an evolving policy. The Peterson Government was committed to beginning the settlement of land claims and, in the latter months of its mandate, to the establishment of an Aboriginal share in the management of what heretofore had been regarded as crown land totally under the control of the Ministry of Natural Resources. This commitment was best demonstrated with the signing of a Memorandum of Understanding with the Teme-Augama Anishnabai in April 1990.

With the election of Bob Rae and the New Democratic Party, in September of 1990, the relationship between Ontario and its Aboriginal peoples was further altered. The new government pledged to deal with First Nations on a government-to-government basis, in an atmosphere of co-operative co-existence. This commitment was recognized by the First Nations of Ontario and the province when they signed a Statement of Political Relationship on 6 August 1991 which stated in part that the Ontario government would

> facilitate the further articulation, the exercise and the implementation of the inherent right to self-government within the Canadian constitutional framework, by respecting existing treaty relationships, and by using such means as the treaty making process, constitutional and legislative reform and agreements acceptable to the First Nations and Ontario.[10]

By implementing this policy, the provincial government had, in effect, changed the philosophy and the structures formed by past governments to deal with Aboriginal peoples. This development demonstrated that Ontario was no longer fearful that the recognition of Native peoples' right to self-government would jeopardize its monopoly over revenues derived from public lands and resources as guaranteed under the BNA Act. Because Ontario recognized the First Nations' right to self-government and the federal government had only done so recently and with many restrictions – except the declaratory ones connected with the aborted Charlottetown Accord of 1992[11] – First Nations are strengthening their relationship with the province. This has far-ranging implications not only for constitutional affairs, but for the social and economic sectors of the province as well.[12] Representative of the new approach, the province was adapting to addressing aboriginal issues was its willingness to enter into negotiations concerning land claims, self-government and the joint management of resources with First Nations, such as the Saugeen Ojibwa, the communities on Manitoulin Island, the Algonquins of Golden Lake, and the Northern Nishnawbe-Aski Nation.

The policies of the NDP Government, to broaden the acknowledgement of aboriginal and treaty rights on the unpatented lands, including parks and other protected places, of their former living and hunting territories, has been supported by a series of Supreme Court of Canada decisions.[13] In 1967, for instance, the Nisga'a of British Columbia brought a suit before the Supreme Court asking the Court for a declaration that their aboriginal title had never been extinguished. Even though, in 1973 the Nisga' lost in a split decision, the result was, nevertheless quite significant because it was the first time that the Supreme Court recognized that aboriginal title existed at the time of colonization as a legal right derived from the aboriginal peoples historical occupation and possession of the land, independent of any proclamation or treaty. More recently, in 1990 the Supreme Court ruled on a case (Regina vs. Sioui) which involved a community of Huron people in Quebec who broke some of the regulations for the Jacques-Cartier Park by cutting down some trees and building fires. The Court ruled that the provincial parks rules were not entirely valid because the Huron's rights had not been extinguished by treaty. The Huron people had been treated as a nation by the French and then the British therefore, the Hurons were recognized as having considerable autonomy in their internal affairs and a continual role in their former hunting territory (even though they had moved there from Huronia in the 1650s). The judgement implied that unless First Nation resource rights were specifically extinguished by legislation or treaty these rights still existed.

The case which has the greatest influence to ensuring that Aboriginal peoples are included in the cooperative management of natural resources is Regina vs. Sparrow (1990). A member of the Musqueam First Nation in the Vancouver area, Reginald Sparrow was charged in 1984 under Federal Fisheries Act with using a drift net that was longer than what was permitted by the term of his band's food-fishing license. In his defence, Sparrow argued that he was exercising his existing aboriginal right to fish, a right which according to the 1982 Constitution Act could not be extinguished by the Crown. The Court ruled that the Federal Fisheries Act had not distinguished an inherent aboriginal right to fish and that members of the band could continue to exercise their fishing activities. Furthermore, it dictated that aboriginal rights could only be infringed or extinguished with justification that is "consistent with the honour of the Crown and fiduciary or trust relation."[14]

The Rae Government was committed to expanding the land base of self-governing Aboriginal peoples and to their role in resource management. Furthermore, more than their federal counterpart, Ontario showed a higher commitment to negotiate rather than litigate, Aboriginal land claims. Perhaps rivalled only by the Temagami question inherited from the Peterson years, the highest profiled aboriginal issue belonged to what has been described by critics as "the fight" for Algonquin Park.

Nine years after the signing of the Royal Proclamation, the Algonquins, in July of 1772, made their first formal assertion of aboriginal title.[15] They identified the area of the Ottawa River Valley between the Long Sault Rapids and Lake Nipissing on the south side and Lake Timiskaming on the northeast side as their aboriginal lands. This 8.5 million-acre area includes most of the watershed of the Ottawa River Valley, north to the Mattawa River. Historical records show that the Algonquins warned that they were prepared to take direct action to clear these identified lands of European trespassers. Hector Cramahe, the Acting Governor of Quebec, promised the Algonquins that he would deal with the problem, thus apparently acknowledging that the Algonquins had an interest in these lands.[16] Since 1791 the band has filed 20 petitions with the Governor General that support its claim, reminding the Crown of the guarantees they were promised in the Royal Proclamation and requesting protection and compensation as outlined in that document. On several occasions, the government acknowledged the existence of this claim but failed to act to resolve it. Some of the outer reaches of the original overly broad assertion or claim – in the south and west – were ceded to the Crown by other First Nations in 1783 (involving some Oka Algonquin signatures), in 1819, and 1850. The Mississaugas and Chippewas (Ojibwa) ceded most of their own and Algonquin territory to the Crown by the Williams Treaty in 1922-23. The Crown accepted the surrenders even though the Mississaugas told the treaty commissioners that they had no authority to surrender another First Nation's territory. Therefore, the Algonquins never ceded title to the northern part of their ancestral homeland in Ontario. In 1873, Ontario had sold 632 hectares (1,561 acres) to Canada to be set apart as a reserve for the Algonquins living at Golden Lake. It is here where 300 of the 990 members of the Golden Lake Algonquin First Nation currently reside; the majority of Algonquins, of course, reside in nine communities in Quebec.

In the 1970s the Algonquins of Golden Lake began to reassert their land rights. Much of their efforts were focused on Algonquin Park, which is partly located inside their ancestral territory. They filed their principal petition in 1983, requesting that the land claim issue be accepted for negotiation by the federal and provincial governments. In 1987, Ontario did reply that "its land claim policy would continue as before: disposition of Crown land would proceed without any requirement for notice to or consent, from the Algonquins."[17] Ontario announced that the Whitney area, which lies at the centre of the band's land claim area, was to be designated as a Primary Development Area, meaning land was to be made available to developers at subsidized rates.[18] Road construction within the land claim area has also been increased. As the claim bogged down in the federal bureaucracy, the band asserted its right to the land through injunctions against proposed developments, information pickets on the highway through the Park and attempts to work out land management agreements with the province.

In August of 1988 the band proposed an offer of settlement to the federal and provincial governments that it take over the administration and control of Algonquin Park. Since the Park's inception, the Golden Lake First Nation had been denied any real influence in the use and management of the park. Away back in March 1893 the Ontario government announced in the provincial legislature that it was examining the idea of creating a park in the shield country north of Toronto. Subsequently, the Royal Commission on Forest Reservation and National Park, led by Alexander Kirkwood, was appointed to determine the character of the area and to calculate "the mode system and cost of maintaining such reservations as the Adirondack and the Yellowstone Parks."[19] The Kirkwood Commission cited the maintenance of the water supply and game protection as the two most important reasons for having a park.

Aboriginal peoples and their stake in these lands were not considered by the commissioners. This was evident by the fact that the act that was passed to create the Park and Forest Reservation outlawed the traditional activities of the Algonquins; they were not allowed to hunt or trap, and all fishing activities were controlled by a permit system. It was not until after the Park was created that Crown Lands Commissioner Hardy acknowledged the omission:

> It will be a ticklish business to prevent Indians killing wild animals in the Park where they have been in the habit of hunting, and their ancestors before them. I am free to say this Indian hunting did not occur to me at

the time the whole matter was under discussion. Now I see nothing for it but to exclude the Indians as well as the white men. But great care and tact will be required to handle these people so as not to embitter them or leave them feeling they have a substantial grievance.[20]

By contrast, logging companies were well accounted for in the commission's report. Most of the land that now made up Algonquin Park was already under licence for timber extraction. The park act permitted the harvesting of pine to continue with restrictions. In 1900 the pine was being eliminated in commercial quantities in some places, the act was revised to permit the cutting of other species including spruce hemlock cedar and black ash. As the president of the Federation of Ontario Naturalists stated in a 1991 editorial, "The precedent for non-conforming uses was thus well established by the turn of the century."[21]

Throughout the Park's evolution, few changes were made to accommodate the needs of the Algonquin of Golden Lake. Algonquins assert, however, that as an aboriginal right they continued to "poach" and trap illegally in some eastern parts of the Park; the province has "allowed" them limited trapping rights there since 1958. In that year, commercial trapping was approved in several provincial parks, the rationale being that it did not "conflict with recreation and did not have a significant effect upon the number of animals seen by summer visitors."[22] The Golden Lake band immediately began working 19 registered traplines on the eastern side of the park. Moreover, in 1961, after the addition of Clyde and Bruton townships to the southwestern limit of Algonquin Park, the Departments of Lands and Forests also allowed the hunting of moose and deer in these townships on a controlled basis. The activity was, of course, not restricted to status Indians, but was an open policy that resulted in the creation of a significant number of hunting lodges (there are presently 70) in the southern part of the park. Interestingly, the flexible hunting policy proved to be workable, and few user conflicts were reported.

In October of 1988, after the band had staged a protest over the Labour Day weekend at the east entrance to Algonquin Park, senior representatives of the Ontario government came to Golden Lake to discuss the claim. They advised the band that before a decision could be made, more detailed information demonstrating aboriginal use of the land was necessary. At this time the Peterson government agreed to work with the band to establish an "interim agreement" which would resolve some of the issues of mutual concern. In May of 1989 the band met with representatives of ONAD and were advised that the provincial government would not likely agree to negotiate the Golden Lake claim until after the federal government formally accepted it for the purposes of settlement. The province did, however, agree to enter into discussions with the band, parallel yet separate from the land claim process, one which would attempt to address some of the immediate needs of the Algonquins of Golden Lake.

In 1991, the Algonquins notified Ontario and Canada that they were beginning legal action, and in the same year they served Ontario with a Notice of Claim under the Proceedings Against the Crown Act. The Algonquins asserted that they: 1) did not sign any treaties that may have removed their Aboriginal title; 2) are distinct from any Aboriginal groups that did sign treaties; 3) have not taken any treaty benefits; and 4) have used lands and resources in the Ottawa Valley since before the arrival of European settlers. Their claim involved 36, 260 square km on the Ontario side of the Ottawa Valley watershed, including 7700 square km of Algonquin Park.

Meanwhile, the new Ontario administration was eager to show that it was now willing to bargain in good faith. For this reason it expanded upon a strategy employed the previous year by the Liberal regime. For over a year, band members had hunted openly in the Park pending the settlement of the land claim, testing their constitutional rights to hunt for food in their traditional lands. In 1989, 42 charges had been laid against seven members of the Golden Lake First Nation who had openly violated the law by driving illegal pick up trucks into protected areas. In response, the minister, Ian Scott argued, that had the question of aboriginal and hunting rights gone to the courts, the outcome might have been total unrestricted access to the Park. In June 1990, the first 40 of the charges had been dropped by Ontario. In January 1991, the two remaining charges of trespassing and illegal hunting in the Park were dropped against Clifford Meness, the Chief of the Algonquins of Golden Lake. Shortly thereafter, the Ministry of Natural Resources (MNR) issued a directive to park rangers instructing them not to enforce most hunting and fishing regulations against band members. In a speech to the Ontario Federation of Anglers and Hunters on 22 February 1991, MNR Minister Bud Wildman said that the Ministry was modifying its enforcement policy "so that we recognize the rights Native people have to hunt and fish for food for personal and community use."[23] The policy will "also seek to minimize the number of instances where Native people might be charged under such acts as the Game and Fish Act." This meant that the Algonquins were no longer to be charged with violations of hunting and fishing laws in Algonquin Park. Known as the Interim Enforcement Policy, the policy

was designed to minimize legal conflicts. In accordance with the Sparrow ruling, it ensures that the exercise of Aboriginal rights was to be consistent with
responsible fish and wildlife management. The policy stated that status Indians
who are able to identify themselves as such, and who were harvesting or
transporting wildlife or fish as food for personal consumption and for social or
ceremonial purposes, should not be subject to enforcement procedures except
in specific circumstances.

After six months of negotiation, including public consultation meetings in
the communities of Golden Lake, Mattawa, Barry's Bay, Pembroke, Huntsville,
Bancroft and Ottawa, the province of Ontario in October 1991 entered into a
one-year renewable agreement with the Algonquins of Golden Lake. From
Ontario's perspective, this Agreement recognized the band's rights but imposed
restrictions necessary to protect the Park.

From the First Nation's perspective, they were simply asserting their rights
to their ancestral homelands. They were five major points that the Agreement
focused on: a delineated hunting season (October 15 to January 15); hunting was
restricted to the northeast half of the park, away from main routes used by wilderness canoeists; restrictions on off-road vehicle use (the Algonquins agreed
not to use all terrain vehicles or snowmobiles for hunting in the park); and there
were annual harvest limits. In total, the band could harvest up to 100 moose and
175 deer, which was considered enough to meet the community's food needs and
what biologists believe to be fully sustainable for the herds. This Agreement is up
for renewal each year that the land claim negotiations continue.

Despite some attempts at public consultation, the Agreement was very controversial. Two of the most critical opponents to the plan were the Ontario Federation of Angler and Hunters led by Rick Morgan and the newly formed Ad
Hoc Committee to Save Algonquin Park, led by Peter Ward and Scott Hayden
whose 650 members feared that the government might turn over the "administration and control of Algonquin Park" to the Indians. The Ad Hoc Committee undertook research to challenge the validity of the Golden Lake claim, organized demonstrations and news conferences and issued regular information
bulletins. A publicity and media campaign was initiated which attempted to
appeal to those who were not familiar with the issues and convince them that
the government was not protecting their interests.[24] Consider the words of one
poster: "The Ontario NDP has stated its intention of turning over *your* land and
natural resources to natives to finance their demands for native self-government." These attacks existed despite the fact that hunting and fishing rights

were Supreme Court-upheld Aboriginal Rights. Meetings were held throughout the eastern part of the province and attendance was high. An editorial in the *Eganville Leader* called one well-known, and particularly spirited meeting held in Pembroke, "an evening of Indian bashing." In another episode, a man from Marathon protested the Court's interpretation of Aboriginal hunting rights by throwing a dead moose fetus at a judge's feet – he was subsequently fined $1,000.[25]

In many ways these responses are lacking in sound judgement and are more than tainted with racism. Consider the facts: Save Algonquin Park Committee and OFAH have used the argument that the First Nations' harvesting principles violate conservation principles. The fact is that the Park is home to 4,000 deer and none of the species hunted by Aboriginals is near extinction. Native people harvest only about one per cent of the moose and about five per cent of the fish taken every year in Ontario. Golden Lake negotiator Greg Sarazin estimated that the community would actually take no more than half the allotted moose and less than a third of the deer quota: "We are not sportsmen – WE do not play with our food, we eat it."[26] In its courageous support of the Agreement the Federation of Ontario Naturalists argued that there were much bigger threats to the Park's moose than the Aboriginal hunters. They are attacked by a disease carried by deer that feed in areas cleared by loggers. Many are hit by cars or shot by hunters when they cross the park boundary and non-Natives are able to hunt moose from about 70 licensed camps from the southwest of the park. The rhetoric of the opponents of the Algonquins of Golden Lake negotiations seems not to be based on evidence.

In the first year after the Agreement was signed there were several developments. The Negotiating Committee released a Ministry of Natural Resources biologist's finding that the moose population in the park has remained stable or increased since the signing of the 1991-92 interim hunting Agreement. The Algonquins took 47 per cent of their maximum agreed-upon harvest of 100 moose, and about 20 per cent of their maximum agreed-upon harvest of 175 deer.[27] In the second year the Algonquin harvest of 34 deer represented about one quarter of one per cent of the deer taken by all hunters in the entire land claim area. The Algonquin harvest of 47 moose was 11.5 per cent of the total number taken by all hunters in the land claim area.[28] Eighty-nine moose were harvested by the Algonquins in their land claim area. All 89 were harvested within a northeastern portion of Algonquin Provincial Park designated for this use by the Agreement. By comparison Non-Algonquin hunters harvested 331 moose within the Algonquins' land claim area; of these, 57 were in Clyde and Bruton Townships in the southern tier of the Park, and 274 outside of the Park.

Ontario and the Algonquins of Golden Lake First Nation completed and signed a second Interim Hunting Agreement on October 13, 1992. There were several major changes from the original Agreement. In an improvement from the earlier Agreement, one that was suggested by the Algonquins' negotiators, the hunting season for mature female moose was shortened to avoid harvesting female moose that were in the late stages of pregnancy. The Algonquins agreed that all-terrain vehicles or snowmobiles should not be used to engage in the actual hunt inside the park, and that cars and trucks should not be used off-road except to retrieve game. To address the question of who was participating in the hunt, a change was made which meant that the terms of the Interim Hunting Agreement do not apply when members of the Algonquins of Golden Lake First Nation hunt with non-Algonquin people. In cases where Algonquins hunt in a party with non-Algonquins, they are all subject to the provincial regulations governing sport hunting.

In 1993, the harvest was set at the same quota – 100 moose and 175 deer within the Park. The Algonquins developed some innovative conservation methods. They have implemented an age and sex specific hunting harvesting system (or tag system), which will further protect the biological sustainability of the moose population. The system was found to be effective in protecting moose in age and gender sets that are important for breeding purposes. By harvesting after the main breeding season and over a larger area, the Algonquins were able to distribute more evenly pressure on the moose population. They have also agreed to restrict hunting in Algonquin Park's nature reserves, wilderness zones, and historic zones, prohibit the hunting of wolves, loons, and species that are rare, threatened or endangered and establish a tribunal to administer conservation methods.[29]

In many ways, parallels may be drawn between what has, and what is presently occurring in Algonquin Park and Quetico Wilderness Park. In both cases, the role of Aboriginal people in the use and management of the parks has proven to be a very contentious issue. The primary difference between these two site-specific examples is that while the Algonquins of Golden Lake maintain that they are not a party to any treaty agreement, the people of the Lac La Croix First Nation argue that they are only attempting to assert its rights as guaranteed under Treaty Three.

In 1913, the same year that the Provincial Parks Act was passed, Quetico Provincial Park was also created. The desirability for a Park in this region of north-western Ontario that is bordered by the state of Minnesota was identified by the Evans Commission report of 1911. The report outlined the devastating impact that large-scale poaching was having on the moose and other big game in the area. It found that the moose population was being threatened by two groups: sportsmen who prized the animal's antlers and professional hunters who were employed by lumbering camps to provide food for their workers. The United States, the Government of Minnesota, and the American lobbies also pressured Ontario to provide conservation measures similar to those which they had implemented in the Superior National Forest and the Boundaries Water Canoe Area.

Like their counterparts whose ancestral lands encompassed Algonquin Park, the Lac La Croix First Nation and the Ojibwa of Sturgeon Lake found themselves isolated and unable to participate in their traditional activities once the Park was founded. This was not the original intention of Aubrey White, the deputy minister of lands, forests, and mines as was demonstrated when he wrote in 1909: "the Indians would not be interfered with."[30] The Sturgeon Lake Ojibwa had been a signatory to Treaty 3 in 1873. Under the terms of this treaty, this band had surrendered their territory, and in return, it received reserve lands known as 24C and a guarantee that it could continue to exercise its Aboriginal rights to hunt, trap and fish in the region.

In 1910, a search for a sufficient supply of food gradually forced most of the people of Sturgeon Lake to relocate their community to Hunter's Island, which, unbeknownst to them, was now part of the Quetico Forest Reserve and was subject to provincial government regulations.[31] Because this type of settlement violated the conditions under which the Forest Reserve operated, Ontario officials forced the breakup of the camp. The implications for the Sturgeon Lake people were devastating. Unable to survive the winter without food, members of the community sought the support of other Ojibwa First Nations, in particular those of the Lac La Croix, located beside what had become the southwestern corner of Quetico Park. Many moved there. In 1915 without discussion with members of the Sturgeon Lake community, the federal and Ontario governments declared their Reserve 24C extinct.

This was not the only difficulty that posed a challenge to the survival of the Lac La Croix First Nation. Once Quetico Park had been created, community members were arrested for participating in hunting, trapping, and fishing – activities which were affirmed under Treaty 3 – and they were prevented from visiting sacred ceremonial grounds. As a former Chief of the First Nation Steve

Jourdain stated: "These activities of Ontario had a devastating effect upon the people of the Lac La Croix First Nation, and grievously hurt the people of Lac La Croix, both collectively and individually."[32]

Over the last 80 years, the First Nation has been able to assert some of its inherent rights that the Ontario government had attempted to extinguish effectively. In 1948, the Indian Affairs Branch of the Department of Mines and Resources in Ottawa, recognizing the issue of chronic unemployment, appealed to the province to allow Indians to trap in Quetico, thus providing a source of employment. The Lac La Croix band were soon working twenty-one registered traplines in the northwest sector of Quetico Park.[33] The use of outdoor motors on a limited basis for the purpose of guiding was also agreed upon by the Ontario government. In 1971, the province also adopted a flexible position when M.N.R. Minister Bernier promised outdoor motor would also be prohibited, but the policy would be phased in, to reduce the impact it would have on the livelihoods of the La Croix Indian band who served as Park guides. At the time, Bernier thought these policies would do much to reduce user conflicts, but as history has shown the problems have instead escalated.

In early 1991 members of the Lac La Croix First Nation (including descendants of the Sturgeon Lake group) filed a land claim against the federal and the provincial governments. This treaty entitlement claim is for land identified as Sturgeon Lake Indian Reserve #24C in Quetico Provincial Park. They argue that this land has not been surrendered and that is still Indian Reserve land. As well, they claim, quite correctly, that their treaty rights have been violated as a result of action connected with the creation of Quetico Park, through their inability to practice unrestricted their aboriginal rights to hunt, fish, and trap.

On 3 June 1991, the Ontario government proffered an historic apology for its actions. Bud Wildman promised to redress the treatment of the Lac La Croix First Nation, by improving the economic and social conditions of the band. To this end, Mr. Wildman promised immediately to expand the opportunities to guide tourists and to make further expansions after public consultation, on balancing more access with preservation of the park as a natural region. He also accused the federal government of not "acting in a manner fitting of the crown." Subsequently, he invited the federal government to participate in land claims; although, he noted the federal governments' slow performance on this issue. He affirmed that the province would "move quickly and negotiate matters that are within provincial jurisdiction."[34]

When Quetico was declared a Wilderness Park in 1977 the Lac La Croix First

Nation was granted a "temporary" exemption to use outdoor motorboats on six lakes and part of a river inside the park adjacent to the reserve. At the same time, all forms of mechanized travel including outdoor motors, aircraft, all terrain vehicles and snow mobiles within the 4500 square km were banned. Hunting and logging also were forbidden. In order to expand the employment opportunities through guiding, additional motorboat access in Quetico Park is seen as fundamental by the First Nation. There are two requests that the provincial government must consider. The Quetico Guides Association, which is a group of Aboriginal trappers and guides who work in the Atikokan area primarily for a Non-Native outfitter, have requested permission to use motorboats on French, Pickerel, and Batchewaung lakes along the northern edge of the park. The lakes are accessible by road and provide many visitors to Quetico with their only opportunity to experience the wilderness quality of the park. Secondly, the Lac La Croix First Nation with motorboat access to six lakes within the park, has requested further access to interior lakes together with accompanying docks and boat caches.

There are essentially two competing interests: on the one hand, the Ontario government's has made a commitment to deal fairly with Aboriginal issues; and on the other hand, it is trying to maintain and extend the system of protected areas and for all wildlife of the province. Predictably these actions on behalf of Aboriginal people create controversy. Wilderness and environmental groups protested the opening of Quetico to motorboats and float planes, preferring instead other arrangements that would provide a sound economic base for the Lac La Croix people. For instance, Kevin Proescholdt of Friends of the Boundary Waters argued – "Motorboat use and airplane landings destroy the essential character of places like Quetico and the Boundary Waters on our side of the border....The thrust of the policies for Quetico since 1971 has been to eliminate non-conforming uses such as logging and motorized uses and to enhance Quetico's priceless wilderness character. This character should not be degraded for any reason particularly for the commercial gain of private businesses."[35]

Also of concern is the secretive way in which these proposals are being handled. There has been minimal open discussion or public consultation. That consultation took the form of two public meetings by the Ontario Provincial Parks Council at Atikokan and Thunder Bay. The MNR also received 600 briefs, half of them from Americans represented by the Friends of the Boundary Waters Canoe Area (BWCA), as well as from the Federation of Ontario Naturalists, the Wildlands League, and the Friends of Quetico Park, a 400

member organization composed largely of area residents. Quetico Superintendent Jay Leather summarized the majority of opinions held by these groups: "If
the economic and social needs of the Lac La Croix band lead to expanded use
of the park, most people want those rights sunsetted (expiration dates fixed) so
that the wilderness character of the park can be preserved."[36]

Although MNR remains reluctant to discuss the state of the negotiations, on
28 September 1993 Chief Leon Jourdain released details of the draft Agreement
which awaits confirmation by the province. It consists of three main items:The
Lac La Croix First nation will obtain mechanized access by motorboat or float
plane to lakes lying southwest of Sturgeon Lake, in an area about a third the
size of the park, beginning in the Spring of 1994; a co-management area is
established west of the Reserve where Aboriginal people will have a say in
development; and a parks administration building and cultural healing centre
will be established on the reserve to diversify the band's economy. The extent to
which this plan will be fulfilled is still unclear. In many ways, parallels may be
drawn between what has, and is presently occurring in Algonquin Park and
Quetico Wilderness Park. In both cases the role of Aboriginal people in the use
and management of the parks has proven to be a very contentious issue. The
primary difference between these two site-specific examples is that while the
Algonquins of Golden Lake maintain that they are not a party to any treaty
agreement, the Lac La Croix First Nation argues that it is attempting to assert
its rights as guaranteed under Treaty Three.

In contrast to the way in which Aboriginal people were, until recently, virtually ignored in the establishment of parks in this province, the creation of Polar
Bear Provincial Park in 1967 was different. The process involved the recognition and participation of the people, all Cree who lived in the area. Lands and
Forests Minister Rene Brunelle insisted, when the park plan was being formulated, that the "traditional hunting and trapping rights of the indigenous Indian population be guaranteed."[37] What separated this statement from others
historically was that it was not simply political rhetoric; it was matched with
action. Consultation with the Attawapiskat Band did occur – steps were taken
to ensure that the information and materials available were in Cree and thus the
information was accessible to the community.

Because Attawapiskat was somewhat isolated and is located a great distance
from the nearest urban centre, many members of the community continued to
live off the land. Hunting and fishing also remained the primary source of employment for community members. Consequently, Lands and Forests imple-

mented a policy which favoured the local Aboriginal community. Only members of the coastal communities along Hudson and James Bay (now linked together in the Mushkegowuk Tribal Council) could guide in the Park. Non-native tourist operators were prohibited from practising these activities in the region. Documented in the park's Master Plan was the guarantee that the annual goose hunting camps would continue within the Park. A similar strategy was employed when the Winisk Wild River, now Waterway, Park was created in 1969.

Today, an equitable balance persists between the conservational interests of Aboriginal people and those of the province. In 1992 a discussion paper for the review of the Polar Bear Provincial Park Management Plan was released. It contains the following resolution by the Mushkegowuk Tribal Council:

> Whereas it is the intention of the Weenusk First Nation to maintain in perpetuity the wilderness state of the Hudson Bay Lowland while at the same time guaranteeing that First Nations people continue to earn a living from the land by having the right to pursue economic opportunities that do not conflict with the perpetual wilderness concept; Whereas outside interests are pursuing mineral development in lands adjacent to Polar Bear Park; Therefore be it resolved that Mushkegowuk Council support the Weenusk First Nation in seeking to have the Polar Bear Park extended to include the lands bounded by the 54th parallel and 87th longitude with necessary conditions to allow First Nations to pursue appropriate economic opportunities.[38]

The Attawpiskat, Fort Severn and Peawanuck First Nations assert that the growth of the park is a positive development, not the threat that is often perceived by other Aboriginal groups in the more southern portions of the province. Their resolution recognized that only park protection has the muscle to safeguard their homeland from the inroads of resource extraction. The support for an increase in the size of the park has won the support of those groups not always in support of Aboriginal assertions, such as the Federation of Ontario Naturalists. In keeping with the resolution, the Council has also drafted a co-management proposal for consideration that would give the bands significant input into matters involving wildlife, tourism, education and economic development.

In contrast, Aboriginal issues remain unclear with regards to Killarney Provincial Park. Aboriginal people were ignored when the Park was created in 1967. They were, however, allowed to continue trapping. In 1974, the United Chiefs and Councils of Manitoulin initiated their claim against the Canadian and Ontario governments relating to lands on Manitoulin Island not yet sold for their benefit. In 1992 in what was probably ONAS's greatest achievement to date, the Manitoulin issues were basically settled to broad general satisfaction. But an unresolved corollary of the Manitoulin question was the matter of the extent of the Point Grondine Reserve on the mainland, established following the Robinson Treaty of 1850. Point Grondine is situated between the mouth of the French River and Collins Inlet, adjacent to Killarney Park. Being an isolated spot, the people on Point Grondine had gradually moved to Wikwemikong on the Island – a move completed in the late 1940s. In 1968, the community merged totally with Wikwemikong.

At issue now is a large tract of land surrounding this uninhabited Point Grondine. First Nation negotiators convincingly insist that their ancestors in 1850 believed that the Reserve was to be surveyed according to the French league measurement (one league being about five kilometres long). Government surveyors, however, measured the Reserve so that a league was equal to approximately one English mile. Furthermore, the First Nation believes that the Reserve should have been set out along the coast not in a north-south block. All of this might mean that the Reserve could be enlarged from the current 24 to 176 square kilometres, perhaps stretching into the Park's southern boundaries.

Directly related to this discussion is the affect that the claim could have on Killarney (48000 square hectare), located northwest of Point Grondine. Chief Henry Peltier and his negotiators say all of the Park is subject to negotiation. "When the government established Killarney Park it didn't consider the history behind what the Indian lands were or what possible claims would be in future years. They just went ahead and established the Park. The Ontario government already admits there was a grave error made back in 1850."[39] Some MNR officials have expressed hope that the impact on the Park will be minimal, but that they are concerned that a settlement might award Indians exclusive hunting and fishing rights in the park. Paul Wyatt, the Sudbury District Manager of MNR has said "If it became part of a reserve property, public use of it would change... if they (First Nations) wish to retain it for their own band use."[40] In contrast, other officials of the Ontario government believe that the claim will have absolutely no effect on Killarney Park.[41] Of course, as in Algonquin, the Sparrow decision affects residual Aboriginal Rights within Killarney.

Approximately 3,300 Saugeen Ojibwa from the Bruce Peninsula are also in-volved in a long-standing dispute with the provincial government over unsold-surrendered land.[42] Under the Treaty No. 72 signed in 1854, the Saugeen ceded the rest of the Bruce Peninsula (50,000 acres), except for specific reserves, to the Crown (The Saugeen were also signatories to a treaty signed with Sir Francis Bond Head in 1836). Much of the land was to be held in trust and sold for their benefit. The Saugeen Ojibwa have documented evidence dating from the 1870s showing that the Crown did not obtain fair market value in sales of surrendered land and thus violated the terms of the treaty.

From 1985-86 the Saugeen Ojibwa were involved in tripartite discussion to establish ownership of approximately 50,000 acres of unsold land. In spite of the negotiations regarding the status of the unsold lands, Ontario continued to deal in the lands. Most recently, in 1989, the Ontario government began to transfer land to the federal government for the establishment of a the new Bruce Peninsula National Park. The province ignored the First Nation's request to stop the proceedings until the land claim was settled, because the transfers might pre-determined the value and utility of the land. In the spring of 1992, the Saugeen First Nation won a favourable court decision on commercial fishing rights in and around the Bruce Peninsula.

Nevertheless, negotiations with Ontario over the Ojibwa fishing rights that the Court upheld seem to be going nowhere. In January 1994 Lester Anaquot, a spokesman for the First Nation told the Royal Commission on Aboriginal Peoples: "Even though the Saugeen Ojibway have won a significant court victory that confirmed their right to fish commercially, it is not being translated in any meaningful way to a recognition of jurisdiction, co-management or what their stake really is in the fisheries around the Bruce Peninsula."[43] Instead of talks, the province seems to have resorted to unilateral action, such as reimposing a fish quota without consultation, and instituting a pattern of having conservation officers laying charges.

Apart from the Lady Evelyn-Smoothwater Wilderness Park (established in 1983), the three new and adjacent Waterways Parks, and the old but small Finlayson Point Park, nearly all of the remaining portions of the Temagami country are outside park boundaries. But by tradition much of it, including skyline and shoreline reserves, prohibitions against mainland developments on the main lakes, limited access, etc. all point to the vague but vital heading of "protected places." The story of the place and role of the Teme-Augama Anishnabai [T-AA] (who had not signed the Robinson treaties) is long, complicated and stormy.[44] They have, of course, trapped, fished, hunted and gathered in their N'Daki Menan, although Ontario has at times attempted to restrict these activities. Confrontations peaked in 1988-89, with road blockades and arrests. After that, under the Memorandum of Understanding of April 1990, signed by Lynn MacLeod and Chief Gary Potts and implemented with an Appendum by Bud Wildman and Chief Potts, in May of 1991. The following were agreed upon: 1) the Wendaban Stewardship Authority, with six T-AA appointed members and six Ontario appointed members was established[45] to manage or steward the lands and resources in the four townships at the core of the previous Old Growth Forest and road access controversies. 2) The T-AA secured a major, structured, consultative role in the management of the entire Temagami Forest and have since secured four guaranteed seats on the overall Comprehensive Planning Council. 3) Processes were put in place whereby an Agreement-in-Principle [AIP] would be negotiated dealing with the division of Temagami lands among the T-AA jurisdiction, joint jurisdiction, and Ontario and municipal jurisdiction, regardless of the then forthcoming decision of the Supreme Court of Canada on the land claim.

In August 1991, the T-AA did not win in the Court, but most of their history was upheld, and the Crown was found to have failed in its fiduciary responsibility to the T-AA and effectively was told to proceed to rectification. The AIP was to lead to federal involvement and the constitutional entrenchment of a Treaty of Co-existence. Perhaps no where else in Ontario is the self-governing, aboriginal presence role, use, and influence in and over protected lands and waters projected to be so thorough and significant.

Alas, the draft AIP agreed upon by Ontario and the T-AA in December 1993 has not secured acceptance (as demanded by Ontario) by the federally recognized, status-only Temagami First Nation (formerly styled the Temagami Indian band). The AIP secured the trifold division of land, financial compensation, and a joint stewardship body, with one-third Aboriginal membership, over a very wide area around Lake Temagami and north westward to the Wilderness Park. It secured continued T-AA involvement in all resource and development decisions, outside the municipalities, provided by their own timber lease for an area beyond their own lands, and a projected significant role in the management of the Lady Evelyn-Smoothwater Park.

Only a few but most of the largest parks and other protected places have been examined in this study. In most, the situation is still influx or deep in protracted negotiations. With respect to Petroglyphs Provincial Park (near Peterborough), a site which remains a special aboriginal spiritual place, there is growing controversy over local aboriginal requests for unrestricted access and for formal co-management or perhaps full aboriginal control. Ironically, in the Petroglyphs area, First Nations demand a total no hunting policy while MNR has allowed a very short term, bow and arrow deer hunt and even a one-day rifle hunt, to prevent over population. Previously, there were concerns regarding open aboriginal graves at nearby Serpent Mounds Provincial Park; MNR has carefully addressed those concerns.

Another example of where co-management to a certain extent is being implemented is Rondeau Park in southwestern Ontario and involves the Caldwell First Nation. In November 1993 a deer cull began in the Park in an effort to control the overpopulation of these animals. Under the supervision of the MNR , representatives of nine First Nations, and in particular the Caldwell First Nation, harvested 320 deer over a four week period. Opposition to the cull was widespread. Cottagers wanted the deer spared and hunting associations acknowledged that there were too many deer in the park but worried that the cull could devastate the entire deer population of Kent County. Others suggested that the cull should be open to all hunters and not just to First Nations. In many ways, this experiment was a success. The MNR met its goal of conservation and the Carolinian forest has been preserved for the time being. Native elders and members of the First Nation who were in need were the primary recipients of the venison. It has not been established as to whether the experiment will proceed in the future, but it has established precedence for that area in terms of co-management practices.[46]

The pattern is clear. The special Aboriginal presence in and use of these places, while still short on detail, is constitutionally entrenched and undoubtedly will increase.[47] The highest principles of conservation and stewardship are not endangered. Such principles are all threatened more by other long-standing "conforming" and "non-conforming" uses in the parks. Protected wilderness and natural environments in Ontario will have an Aboriginal presence, as well they should. Some Aboriginal Canadians, like many Euro-Canadians, will be polluters and bad stewards. Such people will have to be restrained and if necessary prosecuted. Yet during the great heroic age of the fur trade and the canoe, the wilderness had an autonomous Aboriginal presence. That presence was expected, wanted, and revered. Human beings were an integral part of the ecosystem. Aboriginal people, at that time, affected and over modestly modified while conserving that ecosystem. If the Aboriginal presence violates a basically American definition of wilderness, the Ontario definition will simply have to be quite different.

In January 1992, Bud Wildman who had been the Minister of Natural Resources and was still the Minister Responsible for Native Affairs, summed up the situation when praising the protection of "endangered spaces" and describing the process for the establishment of new parks. "No decision respecting the acceptability of candidate sites, he noted, will be made without involvement and participation by Aboriginal peoples."[48] Regarding park matters in Ontario, First Nations will increasingly play a significant role and their aboriginal and treaty rights can hardly be compromised.

Endnotes

1. For a discussion of the relationship between First Nations and the province of Ontario please see various essays in Boyce Richardson, ed., *Drumbeat: Anger and Renewal in Indian Country* (Toronto: Summerhill Press for the Assembly of First Nations, 1989), and Bruce W. Hodgins, Shawn Heard, and John S. Milloy, *Co-existence? Studies in Ontario – First Nations Relations* (Peterborough: Frost Centre for Canadian Heritage and Development Studies, 1992). See also: Fiona Sampson, "Ontario Aboriginal Policy With an Emphasis on the Teme-Augama Anishnabai," unpublished Master of Arts thesis, (Peterborough: Frost Centre for Canadian Heritage and Development Studies, Trent University, 1990).

2. Darcy Henton, "Ontario Forests Now Officially For All," *Toronto Star*, 23 April 1994, B6.

3. All Lands, Mines, Minerals, and Royalties belonging to the several Provinces of Canada, Nova Scotia, and New Brunswick at the Union, and all Sums then due or payable for such Lands, Mines, Minerals, and Royalties shall belong to the several Provinces of Ontario, Quebec, Nova Scotia, and New Brunswick..." Canada, Constitution Act 1867, Section 109.

4. See: Barry S. Cottam, "The Twentieth Century Legacy of the *St. Catherine's* Case: Thoughts on Aboriginal Title in the Common Law," *Co-existence? Studies in Ontario – First Nations Relations* eds. Bruce W. Hodgins, Shawn Heard, and John S. Milloy (Peterborough: Frost Centre for Canadian Heritage and Development Studies, 1992) 118-127; and Ian G. Scott and J.T.S. McCabe, "The Role of the Provinces in the Elucidation of Aboriginal Rights in Canada," *Governments in Conflict? Provinces and Indian Nations in Canada*, eds. J. Anthony Long and Menno Boldt (Toronto: University of Toronto Press, 1988) 59-71.

5. Long and Boldt 5.

6. In February 1988 the Office was incorporated into the Ontario Native Affairs Directorate.

7. In the second year of the tripartite process, First Nation representation was expanded to include the Union of Ontario Indians, the Association of Iroquois and Allied Indians, Nishnawbe-Aski Nation and Grand Council Treaty No. 3. The reason for this change

was that the associations had argued that the diversity of regional/treaty interests and local conditions could not be adequately represented by the Chiefs of Ontario alone.

8. Glenn Brennan, Policy Analyst, Operational Policy – Ontario Region, Indian and Northern Affairs Canada, Personal Letter, 8 February, 1993.

9. Fiona A. Sampson, "An Historical Consideration of Ontario Aboriginal Policy," *Co-existence? Studies in Ontario-First Nations Relations*, eds. Bruce W. Hodgins, Shawn Heard, and John S. Milloy (Peterborough: Frost Centre for Canadian Heritage and Development Studies, 1992) 22.

10. "Statement of Political Relationship," 6 August, 1991.

11. In the Charlottetown Accord, Section 35.1 stated: "The Aboriginal peoples of Canada have the inherent right of self-government within Canada. The right referred to in subsection (1) shall be interpreted in a manner consistent with the recognition of the governments of the Aboriginal peoples of Canada as constituting one of three orders of government in Canada...." Canada, Draft Legal Text, based on the Consensus Report on the Constitution of 28 August 1992, 9 October 1992. The Charlottetown Accord was defeated in a national referendum on 26 October 1992; thus, no revisions were made to the Constitution Act of 1982.

12. John S. Milloy, Shawn Heard, and Bruce W. Hodgins, "Introduction," *Co-existence? Studies in Ontario-First Nations Relations* 2.

13. See: Peter Kulchyski, *Unjust Relations: Aboriginal Rights in Canadian Courts* (Toronto: Oxford University Press, 1994).

14. Richard Bartlett, "Indian Summer in the Supreme Court: The Sparrow Quartet," *Resources: Newsletter of the Canadian Institute of Resources Law* 32: 6-7.

15. For a broad discussion of the Golden Lake First Nation's claim note Greg Sarazin, "Algonquins South of the Ottawa – 200 Years of Broken Promises" *Drumbeat* ed. Boyce Richardson (Toronto: Summerhill Press, 1989) 167-201.

16. Ontario, Ontario Native Affairs Secretariat "The Algonquins of Golden Lake Negotiations," Issue No. 1, May 1992. Note also Peter Heisel, *The Algonkin Tribe* (Arnprior: Kichesippi, 1987); Peter N. Ward, "Major Flaws in the Golden Lake Land Claim to Algonquin Park," Ad Hoc Committee to Save Algonquin Park, *Information Bulletin* No. 1 (15 June 1991). Ward and to a degree Heisel ultimately reject the legitimacy of all the Golden Lake Claims.

17. Sarazin 194.

18. Sarazin 194.

19. Gerald Killan, *Protected Places: A History of Ontario's Provincial Parks System* (Toronto: Dundurn Press, 1993) 14.

20. Audrey Saunders, *Algonquin Story* (Toronto: Ontario Department of Lands and Resources, 1963) 98.

21. "Groundswell: Algonquin Park and the Golden Lake Band," *Seasons* (Summer 1991): 46.

22. Killan 137.

23. Peter Gorrie, "Hunting the Middle Ground," *Toronto Star*, 9 October 1991, A8.

24. A survey of recent titles of articles published about the aboriginal presence in provincial parks gives a clear picture of the bias involved: "A Clash of Values," "Hunting-Ground Havoc," "A Tradition Torn – Aboriginal Hunting and Fishing Rights," "Betraying the Wilderness," "Bargaining Away Algonquin," and "Indians Might Get Killarney Park."

25. Darcy Henton, "Native rights spark battle over Ontario's great outdoors," *Toronto Star*, 2 March 1991, A1.

26. Peter Gorrie, "Hunting the Middle Ground," *Toronto Star*, 9 October 1991, A8.

27. Ontario Native Affairs Secretariat, "Algonquin Negotiating Bulletin," No.2, July 1992.

28. Ontario Native Affairs Secretariat, "Algonquin Negotiating Bulletin," No.4, July 1993.

29. Ontario Native Affairs Secretariat, "Algonquin Negotiating Bulletin," No.5, December 1993.

30. Killan 25.

31. See David T. McNab, "'Principally Rocks and Burnt Lands': Crown Reserves and the Tragedy of the Sturgeon Lake First Nation in Northwestern Ontario," *Aboriginal Resource Use in Canada* Kerry Abel and Jean Friesen eds. (Winnipeg: University of Manitoba Press, 1991) 157-173.

32. As reported in "Ontario Apologizes to Indians," *Globe and Mail*, 4 June 1991, A2.

33. Killan 137.

34. As reported in "Ontario Apologizes to Indians," *Globe and Mail*, 4 June 1991, A2.

35. Robert Reguly, "Rallying to Keep the Wilderness Wild," *Globe and Mail* (Metro Edition), 18 May 1992, A11.

36. Ibid.

37. Ontario Archives, RG-1, 1C, temporary box 4, accession no. 14195, OPIB Polar Bear file, Report to OPIB, 8 March 1971, as quoted in Killan 334.

38. As quoted in "Cree to Co-Manage Polar Bear Provincial Park," *Ontario Out of Doors* 23.9 (March 1992): 3.

39. "Indians Might Get Killarney Provincial Park," *Ontario Out of Doors* 24.6 (July 1992):22.

40. Ibid.

41. ONAS, *Point Grondine Report*, July 1992.

42. See Peter S. Schmalz, *The Ojibwa of Southern Ontario* (Toronto: University of Toronto Press, 1991) and Peter S. Schmalz, *The History of the Saugeen Indians* (Toronto: Ontario Historical Society, 1977).

43. "Royal Commission Told Aboriginal Rights Are Not Respected," *Globe and Mail* (Metro Edition) 4 November 1993, A7.

44. Bruce W. Hodgins, "The Temagami Dispute: A Northern Ontario Struggle Toward Co-Management," *White Pine Symposium Proceedings* (Duluth, UMD, 1992); Bruce W.

Hodgins and Jamie Benidickson, *The Temagami Experience: Recreation, Resources, and Aboriginal Rights in the Northern Ontario Wilderness* (Toronto: University of Toronto Press, 1989); ONAS/T-AA, *Memorandum of Agreement*, April 1990, *Addendum*, May 1991, *Agreement-in-Principle* (draft), December 1993; Paper and Reports of the Wendaban Stewardship Authority, Temagami, 1991-94; and Reports and Minutes of the Comprehensive Planning Council (and its TAC predecessor), 1989-94, and ONAS *Bulletins*, 1990-94.

45. One of whom (Hodgins) is an author of this paper.
46. Debora Van Brenk, "Deer Cull Suspended," *Chatham Daily News*, 27 November 1993, C12.
47. For comparable issues and breakthroughs in the Yukon, see Sarah Locke, "Vuntut National Park: a New Kind of National Park," *Borealis* 5.1 (Spring 1994) 26-32.
48. Ontario Ministry of Natural Resources, *News release*, "Minister Announces Commitment to Protect Endangered Spaces," 23 January 1992, also cited in Killan *Protected Places* 383.

THE ONTARIO EXPERIMENTS

IN FOREST RESERVES

Bruce W. Hodgins, R. Peter Gillis & Jamie Benidickson

During the late-nineteenth century, significant groups and individuals in central Canada, especially Ontario, became aware that the natural abundance of the forests was not unlimited.[1] In particular, the valuable and extensive pine stands of the Canadian Shield were threatened. Conservationist ideas then popular elsewhere in the British Empire, in Europe and in the United States readily appealed to those in the region concerned with the future of their woodlands and with the stability of the forest industries dependent on them. To forestall the imminent depletion of this critical resource, proposals based on conservationist proposals were advanced, concerning land classification, timber regeneration and improved harvesting practices. Efforts were also made to train professional foresters.

Implementation of such measures required the active participation of government: nearly all extensive forest lands in Canada, especially in Ontario, remained part of the Crown or public domain and were licensed rather than sold to lumbermen. Bernhard E. Fernow underscored the need for government responsibility in his forestry lectures at Queen's University, Kingston, Ontario, in 1903:

> The interest in the future lies with the state, the state must interfere, wherever the interests of the future clearly demand it…. Special stress is to be laid upon the necessity of including the interest of the future com-

munity in this consideration, calling for the exercise of providential functions on the part of the state.[2]

Algonquin Park (1893) was an important creation and was also called, at first, a
Forest Reservation, but the most dramatic way in which governments could
begin to meet this obligation toward forest conservation was to set up forest
reserves. The Province of Ontario responded by establishing a network of reserves, beginning with Temagami in 1901. These actions were mirrored by other
provinces, especially Quebec, which at times was ahead of Ontario in this
policy domain.

The new forestry initiative proved attractive to both government officials
and the major lumber interests. It was also politically popular with the elector-
ate. The reserves made possible the achievement of objectives common to government and private interest, including improved forest fire surveillance and
protection of large watersheds from the threat of soil erosion. But above all, the
system was intended to conserve existing stand of timber, thus promising the
forest industries a more dependable supply of raw materials and the provincial
government a steady source of revenue. By the turn of the century, mills in parts
of central Canada were already beginning to suffer from a decline in both quality and quantity of logs. To businessmen seeking stability for their industries,
the reserves appeared to guarantee continuing access to merchantable timer.
The provincial government was willing to aid these operators because in the
late-nineteenth century it derived 20 per cent of its revenue from the forests.[3]
Finally, land classification was viewed by bureaucrats and lumbermen alike as a
way of excluding agricultural settlers from marginal farming areas and reclaiming areas laid waste by decades of overcutting and accompanying forest fires.

In the long run, however, the forest reserves failed to meet these diverse ex-
pectations. They certainly did not become the cornerstone of new provincial
forestry policies, as their more ambitious promoters had hoped. The reasons for
this failure, complex though they were, stemmed from one basic problem. The
early conservationists were practical persons. They had hoped that the Reserves
would be used to introduce the principles of scientific forestry into the management of public woodlands. They did not fully comprehend, however, either
the scientific principles underlying modern forestry or the tremendous political commitment required to establish and maintain an effective forest management system on public lands. When these complexities became apparent in the
period after 1914, the various provincial governments showed neither the incli-

nation to finance effective systems nor the political determination to confront the resource-use controversies.

Only with the Forestry Act of 1927 did some dynamism reappear, by giving a mandate for research forests and establishment of a few new small Crown reserves. This was complemented in 1929 by the Provincial Forest Act, which redesignated the five principal Ontario forest reserves as provincial forests, added modestly to the size of several, and created three new provincial forests. The Depression of the 1930s halted progress, however, and this plus the larger lack of commitment obstructed effective forestry measures in the province until well beyond World War II.

After 1947, as these more modern forestry measures began to form part of provincial policy, the provincial forests lacked much significance. They were eventually abolished around 1964. By this time, several of the more significant one, but not that of Temagami, had been converted, or were being converted into provincial parks. Then, in very recent years, the concept of special "protected places" outside the parks, where forestry might be practised in very careful or very restricted ways and new settlement was prohibited or highly restricted, has been reintroduced. This concept finds or is about to find implementation in regimes such as community forests (both with federal and with provincial initiatives), co-management schemes such as the Wendaban Stewardship Authority, and the now recommended special areas of protected old growth forests.

Beginnings

Well before Canadian Confederation in 1867, agrarian settlers in Ontario and Quebec had entered the coniferous forests of the "broken country" beyond the southern edge of the rough Canadian Shield. Here, except in a few fertile valleys (and, later, in the northern Clay Belts), agriculture has always been marginal and precarious. The choices facing the prospective Canadian settler during the late-nineteenth century were, therefore, threefold: turn to the prairie over 1,000 miles to the west; emigrate to the United States; or try one's luck with a clearing on the Shield. Some chose the third alternative and, as a result, many of the great pine forests were either cut down quickly to clear land or wastefully burned over. Thus, settlers and lumbermen clashed over the use of forestlands, especially in the Ottawa-Huron Tract of Ontario and a smaller area of central Quebec.

In Quebec and a few adjacent areas of eastern Ontario, collective settlement was promoted by a French-speaking, Roman Catholic "colonization movement."[4] In Ontario, settlement was usually individual, though sometimes ethnically clustered. The long-term wisdom of such settlement was questioned even by the provincial authorities who encouraged it through generous homesteading conditions. Yet even if agricultural prospects were questionable, both Ontario and Quebec maintained a naively optimistic faith in their northern frontiers. For Ontario, at least, such optimism had been confirmed in the mid-1880s when construction of the Canadian Pacific Railway, pushing west from Mattawa on the Ottawa River, led to the discovery of rich copper-nickel deposits near Sudbury. These discoveries were soon followed by large-scale industrial prospects at Sault Ste. Marie that continued to attract interest northward toward "New Ontario."[5]

At the same time, some lumbermen and a few civil servants began to realize that the forest resources of central Canada, especially the pine, were not inexhaustible, as the popular myth proclaimed.[6] Southern areas were already showing signs of depletion, while in northeastern Ontario and adjacent Quebec lumbermen were approaching the northern extremities of growth for the pine species. Prospective shortages of raw materials encouraged leaders of the central Canadian lumber industry to advocate forest conservation programs. They wanted both land classification aimed at keeping settlers out of prime pine areas and more efficient utilization of existing resources; lumbermen also sought longer-range cutting plans for limits or leasing areas that would include fire protection and thus the possibility of woodland regeneration.[7] All such programs would help stabilize the lumber industry and protect industry leaders' investments.

These major operators wielded a great deal of political influence with the provincial governments of both Ontario and Quebec – influence derived from their leadership in the largest non-agricultural industry in Canada, an industry that provided rich revenues to the provincial governments.[8] Since a decline in the lumber industry would be disastrous in the private and the public sectors, the operators' support of the conservationist cause lent the movement respectability and a sense of urgency as far as provincial authorities were concerned.

Conservation itself came of age in Canada with the meeting of the second Congress of the American Forestry Association in Montreal in 1882. The Congress attracted a variety of eminent Canadians – including scientists, politicians, interested laymen and lumbermen.[9] All were in agreement with the general resolutions of the Congress, which declared that forest fires, wasteful cutting practices, poor wood utilization, and improper land clearing were depleting the forests of North America. Led by representatives of the lumber industry, conferees called for more extensive co-operation between governments and timber operators to maintain parts of the public domain as perpetual forestlands.

The immense success of the Montreal Congress was followed by a spate of provincial and federal legislative activity, especially regarding suppression of forest fires. Fire was a principal menace to the forest. Not only did it destroy much standing timber, it also made more difficult the natural reproduction of valued white pine. Quebec took the first steps toward fire protection in 1883 by locating rangers on its timber limits under the authority of a fire superintendent. The system was fully paid for by the limit-holders.[10] Ontario followed suit in 1885 but provided for a shared-cost arrangement between the provincial government and the licensees.[11] The larger, more progressive lumbermen firmly supported these fire-protection systems. The groundwork laid through the co-operative systems in Ontario and Quebec had, by the early 1920s, slowly expanded into province-wide fire-protection organizations.

The second major initiative taken immediately after the Montreal Congress was the appointment of federal and provincial officials to gather and disseminate forestry information. In 1883 the federal Conservative administration of Sir John A. Macdonald appointed J.H. Morgan commissioner of forestry, responsible to the Department of the Interior.[12] He was charged with investigating the forestlands of most of western Canada and examining the need for tree planting. Morgan compiled a number of reports before being released from his position in 1890. In Ontario a more permanent arrangement was made in 1883 when Robert W. Phipps was appointed clerk of forestry within the provincial Department of Agriculture. He reported on problems arising from the settlement of lands unfit for agriculture, on reforestation, and on the value of forest reserves, but was interested primarily in tree planting and forestry in settled areas of southern Ontario.[13] Not until Thomas Southworth, a former journalist, took over the clerkship in 1896 was there a change in emphasis from farm forestry to timberlands.[14] The office was moved to the Department of Crown Lands, a move Southworth interpreted as an attempt to bring forestry closer to the forest. He began to stress the need for forest reserves, the observance of a 12-inch diameter minimum limit for timber cutting, and improved forest protection. He also began a casual study of white pine regeneration.[15]

Southworth's work pushed the Ontario conservation program in the direction of establishing timber reserves, the third and last legislative response to the challenges presented by the Montreal Congress. From his office, now renamed the Bureau of Forestry, Southworth actively promoted an awareness of the ultimate limits of Ontario's forest resources. He emphasized the distinctive forest characteristics of the Ontario northland and the possibilities for the natural regeneration of pine. Large parts of the northern region were unsuited for agriculture, he pointed out, but "excellently suited for the production of successive growth of timber if growing conditions were closely controlled."[16] Like the lumbermen, he regarded fire as the major threat to pine reproduction. But Southworth went further, blaming careless lumber operators for causing such blazes.

Southworth's campaign for protecting Ontario's pine forests soon led to legislative action. In June 1897 a provincial Royal Commission – which included two prominent Ontario lumbermen, E.W. Rathbun of Deseronto and John Bertram of Toronto – was appointed to examine the subject of "restoring and preserving the growth of white pine and other timber trees upon lands in the province which are not adapted for agricultural purposes or settlement."[17] The commission's investigations resulted in Ontario's Forest Reserves Act of January 1898, which authorized the lieutenant-governor in council "to set apart from time to time such portions of the public domain as may be deemed advisable for the purposes of future timber supplies."[18] Forestry enthusiasts welcomed the act as "the inauguration of a scientific forestry system in Ontario" and as "the initial step in preparing for a rational system of forestry intended to ensure proper harvesting of existing stands of timber and to provide a perpetual source of income to the province."[19]

Ontario and the Rise of the Forest Reserve Idea

In 1893, even before Southworth's efforts and the establishment of the Royal Commission on Forest Protection, the Ontario government had established Algonquin Park as a "public park and forest reservation, fish and game preserve, for the advantage and enjoyment of the people of the Province."[20] Lumbermen operating in this central watershed area were cautiously optimistic that the park would enable the government to provide additional fire protection for lands in the park without greatly interfering with their cutting rights. As well, leading timber operators had had a major influence on the report of the Forest Protection Commission and viewed the Ontario Forest Reserves Act as a positive step.

Crown lands officials moved quickly to designate other reserve areas, including the small Eastern Forest Reserve in the southeastern counties of Frontenac and Addington, containing about 80,000 acres. Much of this region, including some burned-over sections, was under licence. Licence holders were given five years to remove mature timber and were not eligible for renewals. Another small reserve of 45,000 acres was set aside in the township of Sibley on the north shore of Lake Superior. Both were regarded as regeneration projects for cutover and burned areas that had once been rich pineries.

In 1901 the Ontario Liberal government set up the huge Temagami Forest Reserve. The designated area comprised 2,200 square miles centred on Lake Temagami and was described as "the largest body of pine timber in Ontario still in the hands of the Crown."[21] Situated north of the transcontinental Canadian Pacific Railway in northeastern Ontario, the area was being lumbered only on its peripheries and contained large groves of virgin pine and other species. While French-Canadian colonization was stringing out along the Canadian Pacific Railway and pushing into the fertile valley of the lower Sturgeon River, settlement had not penetrated these woodlands, whose rugged, lake-strewn topography was quite unsuited for farming. Only recreational canoeists and the local fur-trading Indian population travelled Temagami's waterways, and their views were largely ignored in creating the reserve. Two years later, in response to the popularity of the initial designation, the Reserve was enlarged to 5,900 square miles. Expansion permitted closer regulation of recreational activities and secured adequate conditions for fire protection. The reserve's new northwestern boundary lay over the divide into the Arctic watershed, just beyond the limits of pine.[22]

The plans of the provincial government were now obvious; it wished to remove prime forest areas from the pressures of frontier resource exploitation and to control future cutting in the reserves. Recreational canoeists and other sportsmen might use these lands, but the primary aim was to protect the pine. Licences were let in the reserves only if timber was judged to be mature or damaged by wind or fire. The policy had some merit: it would serve to classify substantial lands for forestry purposes, aid in retaining a forest cover on major watersheds in order to prevent erosion and wastage of hydraulic power, and protect future provincial revenues derived from the timber industries. On this basis a belt of forest reserves was established across northern Ontario, including Mississagi, a pine area of 3,000 square miles west of Temagami set up in 1903 and enlarged by 2,000 square miles in 1913; Nipigon, a pulpwood area of 7,300 square miles created in 1905; and the Quetico Boundary Reserve of 1,795 square miles in western Ontario, created in 1909.[23] In 1904 E. J. Davis, commissioner of crown lands in the province's Liberal administration, reaffirmed government Reserve policy:

> ... these are areas that will not be used for settlement, and can be worked as permanent reserves, disposing annually of the timber that is ripe, and allowing that which is not fully developed to remain until it is at the proper stage for cutting to the best advantage.[24]

If the Temagami Forest is any example, however, the Ontario plan, almost from the beginning, fell short of the comprehensive forestry policy that had been touted by the provincial civil service and the press. In the southwest corner of the reserve, large pulpwood concessions were granted, and cutting along the railway right-of-way was authorized even though no rules had yet been devised for harvesting mature timber in the reserve. Furthermore, after 1903 outside forces made the establishment of a policy much more difficult. Construction began on the provincially owned Temiskaming and Northern Ontario Railway northward from the rail junction at North Bay. The line was designed both to tap the known mineral resources of the entire region and to open up a prospective agrarian district known as the Little Clay Belt. It passed through the Temagami Forest and by the northeast corner of Lake Temagami itself. Railway construction led to the discovery of silver near what became Cobalt, northeast of the lake, and the resulting silver rush soon spread westward into the reserve, threatening the priority given lumbering over other resource use. By the time regular service began on the Temiskaming and Northern Ontario Railway, steamboats were in service on Lake Temagami and recreational hotels, fishing resorts and youth camps were already appearing on its islands.[25]

Such problems became provincewide in 1905 when 34 years of Liberal rule in Ontario ended with the victory of James Whitney and his Conservatives over Premier George Ross. Ottawa Valley lumbermen, with their keen interest in northeastern Ontario, clearly no longer could command the influence that they had enjoyed in the old regime.[26] In fact, the allegedly deleterious role of the Ottawa lumber barons and other "monopolists" had been one of the chief issues dividing the two political parties. The Conservatives were champions of progressive, democratic reform and liberal capitalism. Initially, conservation for them had more to do with popular control over resources and their accessibility than it did with long-range planning and sustained-yield forestry measures. The new government pushed ahead aggressively with northern development, focusing on railways, mining, and the increased extraction of resources generally. Northerners, represented by Frank Cochrane, the Sudbury mineral speculator who became minister of the reorganized Department of Lands, Forests and Mines, secured considerable influence in the new government.[27]

The lumbering interests were still awaiting a general cutting policy for the reserves when the government changed. As far as they were concerned, the matter was relatively simple: the reserves existed to provide a secure renewable timber supply that would be harvested by the major private operators under long-term leases. This would benefit the provincial treasury and the provincial economy. But only in regard to fire suppression could the government be persuaded to move with dispatch.

Temagami again provides an excellent example. As early as 1901, a few rangers were appointed, and each year the number was increased. The year 1902 brought regulations controlling access and travel and the lighting of fires. On paper, prospecting and mining were to exist only under strict controls. Activities potentially harmful to young pine, such as roasting sulphurous mineral ores, were prohibited, and regulations on railway smokestacks and furnace screens were issued. Nevertheless, competing pressures increased. The Conservative government immediately took the several hundred islands in Lake Temagami out of the reserve, setting up long-term leases for cottages, resorts and youth camps.[28] The local Indians continued to protest the alienation of their resources. In 1906 silver was discovered within the reserve near Maple Mountain; production commenced and a boom started on the northeastern frontier. In 1907 the silver boom struck both sides of Elk Lake – a widening of the Montreal River that served as the reserve's northeastern boundary. Then in the spring of 1909 prospectors staked claims around Gowganda in the heart of the reserve, setting fires and cutting pine haphazardly. Finally, in 1911 and 1912 the silver rush evolved into a gold rush, centred on the rich Porcupine-Timmins fields just beyond the northwest protrusion of the Temagami Forest. The Conservative government responded by eliminating the northernmost townships from the reserve.[29]

Temagami may have been more susceptible than other areas to pressures from interests wishing to exploit the natural resources of Ontario's northland, but the experience of Temagami was symptomatic of the inability of Ontario officials to formulate and implement an effective forestry policy for the reserves. Opposition from other resource users and a boom psychology in New Ontario contributed a great deal to this failure. Equally important was the view espoused by laymen, like Thomas Southworth, who did not comprehend the public commitment necessary for true sustained-yield forest management. Southworth saw the reserves not as evolving management units but rather as banks of timber for the future, to be licensed slowly under controlled conditions.[30]

If Southworth was blind to the need for scientific forestry, few others in the bureaucracy cared enough to advocate new measures.[31] Thus, while it created the Ontario forest reserve system, the Ontario government was unwilling either to establish adequate reserves (in 1913 the system entailed 12 million acres, while Southworth had envisaged 40 to 50 million acres) or to inaugurate a timber management administration based on forestry principles.[32] This lack of action was to have dire consequences for Ontario's northern woodlands and to bring the system itself under increasing criticism from professional foresters, federal forestry officials and some representatives of the forest industries themselves.

The Decline of the Ontario Forest Reserves
Ontario remained incapable of establishing clear harvesting guidelines based on sustained-yield management for its system. Legislation was passed in 1908 authorizing the sale of cutting rights within reserves for mature and fire-damaged pine, but consistent regulations for enforcement were not forthcoming.[33] This left some lumbermen uneasy, for the absence of an official commitment to long-term leases forced them to deal with the provincial government on an ad hoc basis.

The Temagami Forest again demonstrates the problem. A major clearing program near the line of the Temiskaming and Northern Ontario Railway continued into the 1920s, allegedly for fire prevention. Between 1908 and 1916 a series of limits were let throughout the reserve, ostensibly because there had been fire and wind damage. The licences were repeatedly renewed generally for areas much larger than those originally damaged. Pulp concessions, especially in the Sturgeon River valley and along the Macobe and Montreal rivers, assumed greater importance.[34] Similarly, salvage cutting was authorized in the Mississagi Forest, the major operator being the Spanish River Lumber Company (working in four townships in 1913). Yet in all cases the only dynamic feature of provincial interest in the reserves was an increase in fire ranging staff. No other forestry measures were established.

By 1914 the conservationist ethic within the Ontario government, which had made the provincial reserve system possible, was actually in eclipse. It remained alive among a growing body of professional foresters, at the University of Toronto's Faculty of Forestry, and among some leaders in the forest industries, but during this period all these interests were gradually put on the defensive by the government's woodland policies. Judson Clark, the only professional forester within the Bureau of Forestry, left in 1907 after disagreements over forest-management procedures.[35] Bernhard E. Fernow, dean of the Faculty of Forestry at the University of Toronto from 1907 to 1919, moved from extolling the reserve system to open criticism of provincial policy. A proponent of state-run, German-style forestry, Fernow had enthusiastically promoted the idea of a contiguous belt of northern reservations. He became convinced, however, that since the Conservatives had come to power forest management on the reserves had been limited to concern for timber revenues alone. He predicted that within 25 years, at existing rates of cutting, the supply of pine would be exhausted and other merchantable species badly affected. "The scant supply of forest products with the exception of pulpwood is evident," he wrote. Even the bulk of that, he noted, was north over the divide into the Arctic watershed and thus relatively inaccessible.[36] There were ample reasons for his pessimism. During their departmental reorganization in 1905, the Conservatives had once again transferred the director of forestry to the Department of Agriculture and limited his responsibility to reforestation of southern woodlots and prevention of fires along rail lines. E. J. Zavitz, who became provincial forester in 1912, was a professionally trained forester; but his mandate was not expanded until 1917, when he was placed in charge of all fire-control services for the province. He was not responsible for general reserve policy."

The short-lived United Farmer administration (1919-1923) made some modest attempts to revive the faltering Ontario reserve system. Former Provincial Forester Judson Clark was called back temporarily in 1922 to give advice on a proposed reorganization of the Department of Lands and Forests. Clark pointed out, in effect, that the reserves had only served as land-classification units, enjoying some success in fire suppression but failing miserably as forest-management units.[37] Unfortunately, Clark's analysis was buried in the larger, more controversial issue of corruption and wrongdoing in the administration of forestlands, especially under former Conservative Minister Howard Ferguson. The situation was investigated by the Riddell-Latchford Timber Commission, whose report, although full of conservationist exhortations and suggestions for specific reforms, made little reference to the reserves. The commissioners merely recommended that management practices, associated in the popular mind with these areas, be applied to all crown land.[38] The return of the Conservatives to power in 1923, with Howard Ferguson now as premier, meant that no basic structural changes were made.

Only in 1926, when the dedicated forestry advocate William Finlayson became minister, did some dynamism reappear. His Forestry Act of 1927 aimed at restricting marginal agricultural settlement outside the reserves and establishing a Forestry Board to undertake research. It also provided for the creation of small crown forest reserves for the "preservation or reproduction" of pine and other species.[39] This legislation was followed in 1929 by a Provincial Forest Act, which redesignated the five principal Ontario reserves as provincial forests, added modestly to the extent of Temagami, Eastern and Mississagi, and created three new provincial forests – Georgian Bay, Wanapitei and Kawartha. In addition, the minister was given the power to create other provincial forests. The forests were to be protected from agricultural settlement and administered "according to the best forestry practice." Timber was to be sold only if damaged or deemed mature. Pulpwood as well as pine cutting was to be controlled on a sustained-yield basis.[40] The new Wanapitei Forest, which lacked mature commercial species, was established as a northern scientific research area.[41]

Nevertheless, despite Finlayson's sincerity, the government as a whole lacked the commitment to carry through its legislative good intention. The Depression of the 1930s dried up funds and the Forestry Board disappeared. The only visible sign of a new hand was in the Temagami Forest, where a small existing survey was expanded into a major forest inventory, despite inadequate funding. Thus by 1930 the ambitious forest reserve system of Ontario had largely come to naught.

Retrospect and Innovation

By the early 1930s, the policy of provincial forests in land management, heralded after the turn of the century as the cornerstone of bold new forestry initiatives, had failed to provide the basis of sustained-yield production. Ontario, which had pioneered the reserve system, faltered in the face of a resurgence of liberal democracy and serious conflict over northern land-use priorities. The province set up large reserves, such as Temagami and Mississagi, without devising an adequate policy for their ongoing administration. In areas like Temagami, cutting policies simply developed on an ad hoc basis well into the 1920s. Some licenses were let out after fire or wind damage, but in 1924 a berth was sold without any reference to such conditions.[42] Actual cutting in the forest revealed large quantities of over-mature pine that should have been harvested years before.[43] Obviously, simple banking of timber within reserves was inadequate. In response, the Ontario government opened large accessible areas for lease in 1927, and continued to do so thereafter for both pine and pulp species. This new departure in the Temagami Forest was defended by E.H. Finlayson, the minister responsible, as "rotation of crop and perpetuation of forest wealth."[44] In effect, it was hardly more than long-overdue harvesting. Large-scale exploitation continued until slowed by the Depression of the 1930s. The only tangible evidence of scientific forestry in Temagami took place in an area linked to the Faculty of Forestry of the University of Toronto. Here selective planting resulted in a second crop of pine.[45] The university lands, however, were operated independently of the rest of the reserved lands. Otherwise, Temagami was typical of the other forests. Throughout the province, the forest industries declined in economic status in favour of mining, railway development and recreation. Moreover, lumbering declined in relation to pulp and paper production. In the face of these developments the Ontario reserve system became largely a dead letter during the Depression years.

After 1947, with the Report of the Kennedy Royal Commission on Forestry, overall regulating of timber cutting and silvacultural activities improved modestly throughout the Ontario Crown domain, and the gap between practices inside and outside the provincial parks narrowed. (In parks, of course, lumbering soon ceased or, as in Algonquin, was severely restricted). There was at least a policy commitment to the goals of sustainable yield forest management. Specifically the Crown Timber Act of 1952 allowed alternative uses of land within provincial forests, so long as the proper and careful harvesting of forest products remained paramount.

For Temagami, in a study undertaken in 1958, it became evident that there was virtually no difference between land use practices and regulations within the Forest and many areas outside it.[46] There were, however, important special provisions protecting the skyline preserve for Lake Temagami itself, as well as the accompanying prohibition against mainland development on that Lake (the Islands having been taken out of the Forest in 1905). Elsewhere in the Temagami Forest, all sorts of private land patents had been and were being granted under the Public Lands Act, despite their apparent prohibition under the Forest Reserves and Provincial Forest Acts.[47]

In 1964, the provincial government slipped a short clause into a revision of the Crown Timber Act that simply and very quietly abolished all surviving provincial forests.[48] In the Temagami country, lodges, outfitters and youth camps, before and for sometime after 1964, continued to use the wildlands-sounding forest reserve designation in their promotional material.

The notion of the inexhaustible forest died hard in Ontario. In the early-twentieth century it was perhaps too much to expect a full-fledged effective forestry program to emerge merely from the forest reserve policy and an evolving parks policy. Most early proponents of that policy did not appreciate the full requirements of such a program, and, when they did, provincial governments would not commit the financial resources or muster the political will to bring about an effective forestry system based on the reserves. Under these circumstances, the forests served only to prevent some inappropriate marginal farming and to slow the pace of cutting, thereby helping to preserve some broad lake and river shoreline country and some old growth forest remnants, for the enjoyment of future generations and the overall protection of some of the ecosystems.

So, certainly not all was lost. Indeed parts of several of the great forest reserves reappeared as provincial parks. Quetico was totally converted in 1913 and later enlarged, with logging eliminated from 1946 to 1961 and since 1971. Sibley (now Sleeping Giant) became a park in 1944. In 1971, the (upper) Mississagi Wild River (later Waterway) Park was created and thereafter, to the south, the small Mississagi Park appeared, both within the former Provincial Forest. Also in 1971, Petroglyphs Provincial Park was created in the core area of the Kawartha Provincial Forest. Inside the old Temagami Forest, the Lady Evelyn Wild River Park was established in 1971, and then in 1983 the rather large Lady Evelyn-Smoothwater Wilderness Park was created in a major core section of the old Forest. Adjacent to it, followed the Waterways Parks of the Makobe-Greys, Obabika, Solace, and the (upper) Sturgeon; the co-management lands of the Wendaban Stewardship Authority are another example.[49] In different ways, they are all special, protected places.

Other regimens for protected places, analogous to the old forest reserve system, have also been established. They include the Areas of Natural and Scientific Interest (ANSI), much of the land under the guidance of the Niagara Escarpment Commission, the Provincial Nature Reserves, the specially protected Wetlands, the lands of the Nature Conservancy of Canada and the recent "Keep It Wild" Natural Heritage Areas. Current moves to protect many of the surviving old growth forests would also fit the tradition – although most of the above examples are more preservationist in concept than the old forest reserves.

Stewarded, sustained yield policies are, however, at the centre of the recent establishment of official community forests. This is true whether they arise from provincial and local initiatives (such as that at Geraldton) or from federal and local initiatives (such as that near Elk Lake). They flow directly from the forest reserve philosophy and clearly show the power of its legacy with the added benefit that they must have solid local "stakeholder" support, both politically and philosophically.

Endnotes

1. Most of this paper first appeared in the *Journal of Forest History*, 26. 1 (January 1982), as part of an article entitled, "The Ontario and Quebec Experiments in Forest Reserves, 1883-1930." Note also Bruce W. Hodgins and Jamie Benidickson, *The Temagami Experience: Recreation, Resources, and Aboriginal Rights in the Northern Ontario Wilderness* (Toronto: UTP, 1989); and Peter R. Gillis and Thomas R. Roach, *Lost Initiatives: Canada's Forest Industries Forest Policy and Forest Conservation* (New York: Greenwood, 1986).

2. B. E. Fernow, "Lectures on Forestry," in Ontario, Director of Forestry, *Annual Report, 1903* (Toronto, 1905) 69.

3. In Ontario between 1867 and 1899, about 20 per cent of revenue was obtained from the forests. See *Report of the Commission on Finance* (Toronto, 1900) 6, 24; H. V. Nelles, *The Politics of Development: Forests, Mines and Hydro-Electric Power in Ontario. 1849-1941* (Hamden, Connecticut: Archon Books of Shoe String Books, 1974) 18-19.

4. For a summary of the motivations behind this movement, see J. Little, "La Patrie: Quebec's Repatriation Colony, 1875-1880," in Canadian Historical Association, *Historical Papers, 1977* (Ottawa, 1978) 66-85; Bruce W. Hodgins, *Paradis of Temagami* (Cobalt, 1976); G. C. Brandt, "The Development of French-Canadian Social Institutions in Sudbury, Ontario, 1883-1928," *Laurentian University Review* 11 (February 1979): 5-22.

5. Margaret Van Every, "Francis Hector Clergue and the Rise of Sault Ste. Marie as an Industrial Centre," *Ontario History* 56 (September 1964): 191-202.

6. R.P. Gillis, "The Ottawa Lumber Barons and the Conservation Movement, 1880-1914," *Journal of Canadian Studies* 9 (February 1974): 14-29.

7. *Ibid*. 22.

8. *Ibid*.

9. Richard S. Lambert with Paul Pross, *Renewing Nature's Wealth: A Centennial History of the Public Management of Lands, Forests and Wildlife in Ontario, 1763-1967* (Toronto: Ontario Department of Lands and Forests, 1967) 162-63, 177-82, 525-27.

10. Gillis, "Ottawa Lumber Barons," 20.

11. *Ibid.*; Lambert with Pross, *Renewing Nature's Wealth*, 161-62.

12. File 69113, Vol. 81, Department of the Interior, RG15, Public Archives of Canada (hereinafter cited as PAC), Ottawa.

13. Lambert with Pross, *Renewing Nature's Wealth*, 182-84.

14. *Ibid.*

15. *Ibid.*

16. Ontario, Clerk of Forestry, *Annual Report*, 1896, 22-23.

17. B. E. Fernow, "Forest Resources and Forestry," in Adam Shortt and A. G. Doughty, eds., *Canada and its Provinces: A History of the Canadian People and Their Institutions*, vol. 18, *The Province of Ontario* (Toronto: Glasgow, Brook & Co., 1914-1917) 595.

18. *Toronto Globe*, 29 December 1897, 8.

19. Nelles, *Politics of Development*, 205; Ontario, Director of Forestry, *Annual Report, 1899*, 6-9.

20. Ontario, 56 Victoria (1893), cap. 8.

21. Ontario, Department of Lands and Forests, *Woods and Forest Report, Book IV*, 102; "Memorandum for the Honourable Commissioner of Crown Lands," 7 January 1901; Ontario, Director of Forestry, *Annual Report, 1900-1901*, 6. See Bruce W. Hodgins and Jamie Benidickson, "Resource Management Conflict in the Temagami Forest, 1898-1914," in Canadian Historical Association, *Historical Papers, 1978* (Ottawa, 1979) 148-75. Note also Bruce W. Hodgins and Jamie Benidickson, *The Temagami Experience: Recreation, Resources, and Aboriginal Rights in the Northern Ontario Wilderness*, (Toronto: UTP, 1989).

22. Ontario, Director of Forestry, *Annual Report, 1904*, 12.

23. Lambert with Pross, *Renewing Nature's Wealth*, 285.

24. *Toronto Globe*, 19 February 1904, 8.

25. Jamie Benidickson, "Temagami and the Northern Ontario Tourist Frontier," *Laurentian University Review* 11 (February 1979): 43-69.

26. Gillis, "Ottawa Lumber Barons," 24-29.

27. Lambert with Pross, *Renewing Nature's Wealth*, 258-63.

28. OC 53/156, 12 August 1905, RG3, Public Archives of Ontario (hereinafter cited as PAO), Toronto.

29. Ontario, 2 George V (1912), cap. 6.

30. In 1903 Southworth prophesied, "the people of Ontario need have no fears of direct taxation until the public expenditures of the Province are enormously in excess of the amount now annually expended." He had missed the opportunity to spend some revenue on actual forest management. Ontario, Director of Forestry, *Annual Report, 1903*, 8.

31. Nelles, *Politics of Development*, 207-14; Gillis, "Ottawa Lumber Barons," 24-29.

32. Ontario, Director of Forestry, *Annual Report, 1903*, 8; Fernow, "Forest Resources and Forestry," 596; Clyde Leavitt, "Forest Protection in Canada, 1912," in Canada, Commission of Conservation, *Annual Report, 1913*, 145.

33. 14 August 1905, OC53/243, RG3, PAO: I-7-B-2, PG8, PAO; *Ontario Sessional Papers, 1908*,

65; J. F. Turnbull, A. B. Doran, and A. C. Thrupp, "Logging Operations on Temagami Forest Reserve in Ontario," *Canada Lumberman* 40 (15 November 1921): 42-43.

34. The authors are particularly indebted to Isy St. Martin for original research assistance on the subject of pine and pulp cutting within the Temagami Forest Reserve from 1914 to 1940. For information, note especially Ontario, *Orders-in-Council*, 7 August 1909, and 10 September 1912; Ontario, *Burnt Timber Books*, references for 1914, 1915, and 1916; "Sturgeon Falls Pulp Company Agreement, 6 October 1898," Ontario, *Sessional Papers, 1898-99*, no. 74; "Sturgeon Falls Pulp Company Agreement, 15 December 1901," Ontario, *Sessional Papers, 1902*, no. 67; Ontario, Department of Lands and Forests, *History, of the Swastika Forest District* (Toronto, 1964) 24; T. W. Dwight, *Forest Fires in Canada*, 1914-15-16, Forestry Branch Bulletin 64 (1918) 37; F. J. Kelly, "The Spanish River Lumber Company," *Sylva* 5 (July-August 1949): 25-29.

35. Lambert with Pross, *Renewing Nature's Wealth*, 186-88.

36. Fernow, "Forest Resources," 596-99.

37. Ontario, Department of Lands and Forests, *Annual Report, 1922*, 282

38. Ontario, *Report of the Timber Commission* (Toronto, 1922).

39. Ontario, 17 George V, cap. 12.

40. Ontario, 19 George V, cap. 14.

41. *Ibid.*; "Ontario Forestry Board" file, History Committee Records, 2-16-3, BB, RGI, PAO.

42. Ontario, *Timber Sales Books*, 1924, entries for Riddell and Law townships.

43. "G. A. Mulloy, "A Visit to the Forest in the Sudbury-North Bay Districts," *The Forest Chronicle* I (December 1925): 27-30.

44. Ontario, Department of Lands and Forests, *Annual Report, 1928, 12-13*

45. W.C. Cain, "Forest Management in Ontario," *The Forest Chronicle* 15 (March 1939): 23.

46. Larry E. Hodgins, "Economic Geography of the Lake Temagami District," (BA Dissertation, University of Toronto, 1958).

47. Hodgins and Benidickson, *The Temagami Experience*, 208-09 and 230-39.

48. *An Act to Amend the Crown Timber Act*, 1964, cop. 16, sec. 11: "Section 46 of the Crown Timber Act is repealed." That Section (of the 1952 Act) had heretofore maintained the existence of the provincial forests.

49. Wendaban Stewardship Authority, Papers, Reports and Documents, Temagami, 1991-94.

THE HISTORY OF NATIONAL PARKS

IN ONTARIO

Dennis Carter-Edwards

The conference theme, "Changing Parks: The History, Future and Cultural Context of Parks and Heritage Landscapes," provides a useful frame of reference for examining Ontario's five national parks: St. Lawrence Islands, Point Pelee, Georgian Bay Islands, Pukaskwa and Bruce Peninsula National Park. The establishment and subsequent development of these parks over the past century reflects in a tangible way the change in thinking about conservation principles and practices adopted by the federal government in responding to the twin demands of protection and public use. This paper focuses on the key steps in the development of Ontario's National Parks program over the past century and the underlying values and assumptions which were manifested through the park making and park managing process – in other words, the "cultural context" for the national park program in Ontario.

The first formal steps towards national parks reservations in Canada were initiated by the discovery of the mineral hot springs near Banff, Alberta in November 1883 by crew members working on the CPR line. Conflicting claims by interested parties who tried to secure private ownership of this valuable resource prompted the federal government to withdraw this tract from public sale.[1] In June 1887 the Macdonald government passed the Rocky Mountains Park Act that created Canada's first national park. The purpose of the act was set out in Clause #2:

The said tract of land is hereby reserved and set apart as a public park and pleasure ground for the benefit, advantage and enjoyment of the people of Canada subject to the provisions of this act and of the regulations hereinafter mentioned.... [2]

The "benefits" and "advantages" anticipated by this government initiative were closely identified with the broader goals of Macdonald's National Policy. As R. Craig Brown has pointed out, early park policy was based on the assumption of limitless natural resources capable of exploitation as a shared venture between government and private enterprise.[3] The region's natural beauty and the curative powers of the mineral springs were recognized as "resources" to be exploited for commercial benefit. This could best be accomplished by creating the necessary facilities, such as hotels and trails, in partnership with the private sector. Profit, rather than any intrinsic aesthetic value inherent in the landscape, was the government's primary concern.

While the initial legislative efforts for the establishment of national parks focused on the west, *public* interest in park formation was originally centred in Ontario. It was the scenic Thousand Islands in the St. Lawrence River and the risk that these islands might be reserved for private developers that prompted one of the first substantive public discussions on the issue of conservation, public enjoyment and park designation.

The islands situated in the St. Lawrence River between Brockville and Kingston were originally claimed by the Alnwick Band of Mississauga. They surrendered title to the Crown in 1856 on the understanding that the islands were to be administered by the Government of Canada for their benefit.[4] By the 1870s, however, squatters had taken up residence on the islands, cutting down the timber and farming the cleared lands. To forestall further unremunerative exploitation of the property, the Indian Affairs Branch of the Department of the Interior, decided in 1873 to offer the islands for sale at public auction.[5] This proposal drew a mixed local reaction. D. Jones, MP for South Leeds, remarked at a public meeting that "either the Dominion Government ... should retain them as they were or the County Council should purchase and hold them as a park for the use of the whole Dominion."[6] Perhaps the most striking comment came from an anonymous writer in London, Ontario who argued that the islands should be retained by the Crown for public benefit.

The beauty of these far famed islands is one of our national possessions ... [and] should be carefully preserved as a pleasure ground for our people in perpetuity. Our neighbours, utilitarian as they are, have set aside.... Yellow stone Reservation. Why should not our Government be foreseeing ... and set apart such "reservations," especially in the case of the Thousand Islands where nature seems to indicate such a use for them.

The writer went on to warn of the dangers of uncontrolled private development.

Instead of being the secluded bit of wild nature that it is at present [it] ... would soon teem with villages, as the American islands are already beginning to do.... We should have a sort of Cockney suburb, where we now have the quiet solitude of nature, which once broken, can never be restored.... Any Government which would do this for pecuniary considerations would transmit to posterity a memory of Vandalizing associations.[7]

Fine words indeed, but a philosophy of preserving natural settings in their verdant state for the spiritual renewal they offered the visitor was out of step with the concept of "usefulness" adopted by the government. As a compromise to the opponents of outright sale of the islands, the Crown offered leases on island properties and gave long-term squatters an opportunity to purchase land at market value; however, sales were far from brisk and the issue of a park reservation abated. Over the next few years, rapid growth on the American side of the river sparked renewed interest in land sales. The Canadian Government responded by again advertising islands for sale in 1894, although this time provision was made for reserving a select group of islands for "park purposes."[8] While some applauded the government's action, others opposed the concept of a national park, arguing that only private developers would create the necessary tourist facilities that would stimulate local construction and economic growth. The *Gananoque Reporter*, reflecting the strong boosterism of the period, argued, "We believe the Canadian government has done the right thing in placing the islands on the market ... real estate allowed to be idle or undeveloped never will contribute to a country's greatness."[9] The reserved islands were formally recognized as St. Lawrence Islands National Park by Order in Council in September 1904.[10] This decision to create a national park from a few islands in the St. Lawrence River did not stimulate a wider discussion on the purposes and principles of national parks or spark interest in creating additional parks. Rather, it was a pragmatic response to a particular situation consistent with the doctrine of "usefulness" reflected in earlier park developments.

Such was not the case when Point Pelee National Park was established in 1919. This park initiative was the result of an extensive discussion on the benefits of conserving an important wildlife habitat and honouring Canada's commitment through international treaty to safeguard migratory birds.

Point Pelee is a triangular shaped sand spit formed some 10,000 years ago at the western end of Lake Erie. It is strategically located on the fly route for migratory birds and butterflies and contains a unique collection of resident Carolinian flora and fauna. The British Naval Department originally designated Pelee as a naval reserve because of the extensive stands of timber; however, this did not prevent scatters from taking up residence during the early part of the century, farming the cleared lands, harvesting the fish, muskrats and other wildlife resident on the Point and shooting the many ducks, swans and other birds frequenting the area.[11]

The extensive bird population that visited the Point attracted the attention of numerous naturalist and conservation clubs formed on both sides of the border in the latter part of the nineteenth century. In 1905 for example, The Great Lakes Ornithological Club toured Point Pelee. Other naturalists conducted regular scientific observations and ornithological studies from their "Shack" at the Point.[12] Included in this group was Percy Taverner, staff ornithologist with the Museums of Canada. Taverner was a key figure since he also served on the federal Commission of Conservation that had been set up by the Laurier government in 1909 to act as an advisory body responsible for collecting and disseminating information on the efficient management of Canada's natural resources.[13] In a report to the commission in 1915, Taverner highlighted the unique scientific, aesthetic, recreational and economic benefits associated with Point Pelee and recommended that it be "reserved, not only for our contemporaries, but for posterity as well."[14]

Another key figure in the campaign to protect the Point was Gordon Hewitt, Dominion Entomologist for the Department of Agriculture and Secretary to the Advisory Board on Wildlife Protection, established in 1916 to develop policies for wildlife conservation. Born and educated in England, Hewitt brought an extensive background on conservation issues and an energetic personal commitment to his professional duties.[15] He toured the Point early in 1917 as the guest of the Essex County Wild Life Association. His visit and meetings with area residents convinced him of the need to protect Point Pelee. Hewitt and Taverner consulted with J.B. Harkin, the Dominion Parks commissioner on getting Pelee designated as a national park. Although sensitive to the commercial potential of national parks, Harkin was supportive of the principle of protecting wilderness areas for their intrinsic values. He once remarked, "Will we ever be able to educate the man in the street to realize that it is as much a desecration to mar this natural harmony as to draw a razor across the Mona Lisa."[16] The result of this discussion was a strongly worded report by the Advisory Board on Wildlife Protection recommending Point Pelee be set aside as a national park.[17] The minister approved the report and in May the following year, Point Pelee National Park was established by Order in Council.[18] Unlike earlier park designations, Pelee was recognized primarily for its significance as a wildlife habitat rather than for its potential commercial benefits. This decision reflected a shift, modest though it may have been, from the notion of usefulness to that of protecting wildlife.

Interest in park development for the Georgian Bay area was first expressed by an archaeologist rather than a naturalist. In 1920 Dr. Rowland B. Orr, the director of the Provincial Museum in Toronto and a seasoned excavator who had worked extensively in the Penetanguishene area wrote to J.B. Harkin suggesting that Beausoleil Island be set aside as a national park.[19] The circumstances were similar to those at St. Lawrence Islands with the Department of Indian Affairs acting as the custodian department "managing" the properties on behalf of First Nations. As one of the few island left in the public domain, Orr felt Beausoleil should be retained and protected by the Crown. His recommendation was given valuable political support by Senator W.H. Bennet of Midland who wrote to the Minister of the Interior stressing the important tourism benefits that would accrue to the area by designating the site a national park.[20] After reviewing the costs and suitability of the property, Harkin recommended the purchase of Beausoleil and several adjacent islands for park purposes. Included in the adjacent properties was Flower Pot Island which, apart from its geological interest, was felt to have potential pre-contact archaeological importance.[21] While the necessary funds were allocated as early as 1924, the actual purchase of the land and gazetting of Georgian Bay Islands National Park was not finalized until 1929 when the necessary funds were transferred to the Department of Indian Affairs.[22]

In the case of each of these parks, there were particular circumstances and key individuals who were able to marshall sufficient support to accomplish the desired goal. In these early years of the parks' program, there was no comprehensive process for evaluating potential candidate sites against a set of national criteria to insure the best, most endangered or the most representative regions were protected as national parks. Instead, government action was more a gratuitous response to well-directed political pressure either from the general public or senior bureaucrats. Yet, over the period, there had been a gradual evolution in thinking regarding the purpose and benefits of national parks. From purely public recreational grounds as was the case at St. Lawrence Islands to the need to conserve wildlife habitats or significant natural and archaeological features as was the case with Point Pelee and Georgian Bay Islands, the government was recognizing the importance of protecting these areas.

This growing realization that parks had to be protected in some fashion if they were to be of value to future users was reflected in new legislation. In 1930 Parliament approved a new National Parks Act which set in place streamlined procedures for the designation of national parks. More importantly, the Act made reference to basic conservation principles to be reflected in the parks program. Article #4 of the Act stated:

> The parks are hereby dedicated to the people of Canada for their benefit, education and enjoyment subject to the provision of this Act and the Regulations and such Parks shall be maintained and made use of so as to leave them unimpaired for the enjoyment of future generations.[23]

While emphasis would still be placed on benefits and enjoyment for the next 20 years, the government recognized that parks had to be developed and operated in a way that sustained the resources and associated values that made these places "special."

Although each of the first three national parks in Ontario were created under unique circumstances, their subsequent development followed a common pattern. Having decided that certain areas were worth setting aside for public use and enjoyment, the department moved quickly to provide some basic amenities for the comfort and enjoyment of the visitors. At St. Lawrence Islands, builders under contract with the department, constructed wharfs, picnic tables and pavilions for island visitors. These primitive facilities were later upgraded through the auspices of the Department of Labour as make work projects during the 1930s.

At Point Pelee, similar facilities were provided including picnic tables, improved roads, campgrounds, change houses and washroom facilities to cater to the growing number of visitors coming to the park. Campsites, picnic shelters, change houses and a dock were also built on Beausoleil Island for the convenience of tourists.[24] Thus, through the 1920s and 1930s the parks were operated and maintained primarily for the recreational opportunities they provided although other development options were entertained. While the notion of "exploitive" use of park resources had been eliminated with passage of the National Parks Act in 1930, there was still support by the federal government for private, development-oriented activities within the boundaries of national parks. Point Pelee presented the most extreme case of this policy. In the 1920s a substantial part of the park was acquired by a private American developer who proposed subdividing the land into extensive cottage lots. Several parcels of land were sold off and private cottages built before the scheme was cancelled.[25] A more public spirited but nevertheless development-oriented use of park land occurred at Georgian Bay Islands where private campgrounds for youth groups had been leased to the YMCA prior to the creation of the national park. In 1938 the Lions Club of Toronto obtained permission to erect a camp ground at Turtle Bay where extensive new facilities were constructed on what later turned out to be sensitive archaeological resources.[26] During this period, however, little thought was given to conducting environmental screening for natural or cultural resources prior to initiating development activities.

The management of this growing infrastructure of services, facilities and personnel along with enforcement of park regulations required more accountable administrative procedures. The part-time caretakers who initially had responsibility for the management of the parks and maintenance of their assets gave way to permanent public servants with long-term career interests in supervising park activities. These early efforts at creating a bureaucratic administrative structure were impromptu with each park following a different course. In 1941 J.C. Browne replaced the park warden at Georgian Bay Islands and was subsequently confirmed as the park superintendent. In 1951 he assumed responsibility for Point Pelee and St. Lawrence Islands, although there were still work crews, usually under a warden, to look after the day to day activities at the sites.[27] The gradual evolution of a professional administrative bureaucracy for the national parks is indicative of the increasing importance and responsibility attributed to the proper management of the parks and their assets.

The post-war years brought a dramatic shift in public attitudes and park usage. An increase in leisure time and personal income contributed to a significant rise in visitation levels at national parks. By the 1950s a steady stream of visitors placed heavy demands on park facilities and staff. Nowhere was this trend more apparent than at Point Pelee where pressures from a rapidly expanding clientele – upwards of 600,000 visitors a year on an extremely small land base – prompted the department to reassess the future direction of this and other parks. The approach taken was in keeping with the more interventionist role played by the federal government in directing overall social and economic policy in the post-war period.

In order to carry out these new functions, the department required the necessary professional staff for the development and implementation of policies and programs. In 1958 a Planning Section was added to the National Parks Service. The following year an Interpretation and Education Division was established to develop and co-ordinate interpretive programming at the sites. One of the first tasks for the new Planning Division was the preparation of a long-range development concept for Point Pelee. After considerable discussion with park staff they completed the Point Pelee National Park Development Plan in 1961. The plan contained a number of key recommendations including:

1. Preservation of the Park's "natural environment" by identifying specific areas where recreational activities could occur.

2. Setting a maximum limit for number of visitors permitted within the park and then designing facilities to match that target.

3. Developing the park for day use through the gradual elimination of campgrounds and buying up private property within the park boundaries.

4. Reducing vehicular traffic by introducing a transit system.

The plan introduced several innovative concepts, including for the first time, the use of a *zoning system* based on reliable scientific data to insure the identification and protection of significant natural features from uncontrolled disturbances.[28] These principles represented a significant departure from past practice where every effort had been made to accommodate the needs of the visitors.

The increasing emphasis on protection and presentation rather than recreation and public use was indicative of the new approach by the department. This new direction reflected the growing environmental awareness of the 1960s, improved scientific knowledge on resource management issues and employment of specialists both within the department and at the field units. This new thinking regarding national parks was codified in a comprehensive policy statement issued by the Minister, the Honourable Arthur Laing in September 1964. The basic purpose of the national parks system, he stated, was to preserve:

... for all time areas which contain significant geographical, geological, biological or historic features as a national heritage for the benefit, education and enjoyment of the people of Canada. The provision of urban type recreational facilities is not part of the basic purpose of National Parks. Such recreation facilities in harmony with the purpose and reservation of a park may be introduced as required to meet recreational needs; but always so as to minimize impairment and not at all if substantial impairment is inevitable.[29]

The redefinition of national parks policy and the development of new planning and management tools were only a few of the innovations in the national parks program during this period. The designation of the three national parks in Ontario early in the century had clearly demonstrated the difficulty inherent in the approach to creating new parks. Point Pelee, St. Lawrence Islands and Georgian Bay Islands resulted from political whim and circumstance rather than a rational, systematic approach to protecting the diverse natural regions in the country. These initiatives had also been conditional on the availability of land already owned or managed by the Crown. After the National Parks Act of 1930 the context for park establishment changed. Unalienated Crown lands were transferred to the province. Thus, new parks would require the co-operation of the provinces – something that was difficult to achieve. For example, attempts during the 1930s to create a national park out of the provincially owned Sibley Forest Reserve near Thunder Bay foundered on the rocky shoals of federal-provincial relations that were already strained by the sparring between Mitch Hepburn and Mackenzie King.[30] Although there was a requirement for a more effective mechanism for creating parks, the government did not address this issue until quite late. In 1970 the department outlined the need for a comprehensive, systematic approach to the establishment of new national parks:

There has long been a need to formulate a plan which would insure a system of National Parks in Canada that would present in true proportion, a representative, outstanding and unique sampling of Canadian landscape and natural phenomena. Such a plan would have to be objectively laid out, using criteria which would be both acceptable to and understandable by all agencies and individuals concerned. Of necessity, the methodology for such a plan would have to be based on the natural sciences and would have to be relatively free of political and social influences.[31]

Drawing heavily on models developed in the United States, the department divided the country up into 39 distinct natural regions based primarily on geophysical characteristics [32] and launched an aggressive program of creating new parks to fill the gaps in the system, especially in Ontario and Quebec. [33]

During the late 1960s, the Minister responsible for National Parks, the Honourable Jean Chrétien actively pursued negotiations with the Ontario Government to determine interest in getting new national parks established in the province. After some initial reluctance, the province agreed and signed a formal Memorandum of Intention with Respect to the Proposed Pukaskwa National Park, in July 1971, which committed the two governments to the establishment of a national park in Region 18, The Central Boreal Uplands. [34] A working committee with staff from both departments and a representative of the First Nations to present the concerns of area band councils began a series of meetings to finalize the details of the land transfer from the province to the federal government for park purposes. The final agreement signed February 1978 formally established Pukaskwa National Park. The approved Management Plan, completed in 1982 established the park's purpose which was "to protect for all time, a representative area of Canadian significance of the Central Boreal Uplands natural region and the Great Lakes shoreline and to encourage public understanding, appreciation and enjoyment of this natural heritage to as to leave it unimpaired for this and future generations." [35] Pukaskwa was to be developed in a low key manner to protect the unique wilderness experience offered by the site. Hiking trails rather than paved roads, backpacking stations rather than formal campgrounds and low level interpretive signage reflected the department's new approach to the twin mandates of preservation and public use by placing greater emphasis on resource protection and sustainable recreational activities in keeping with the values of the surrounding landscape.

Bruce Peninsula National Park, the most recent addition to the system of national parks in Ontario resulted from a similar identification and consultation process. Park planners were concerned with the low level of park representation in Region 29, the St. Lawrence Lowlands. In December 1981 the Minister of the Environment announced that public consultations would begin to determine the feasibility of establishing a new national park on the Bruce Peninsula. After extensive public consultation and a detailed Socio-economic Impact Assessment of the proposed park, the two governments ratified a formal agreement in 1987 establishing the Bruce National Park and Fathom Five Marine Park. [36]

In looking ahead to the future of park making and park managing in Ontario, there are no shortage of guides and directions for this process. The new Parks Canada Policy statement, "Guiding Principles and Operational Policies," released by the minister of Canadian Heritage in 1993, the federal Green Plan adopted in 1990, the Ontario Region's Strategic Plan – "Focus on the Future" adopted in 1992 and the regional Business Plan will all contribute to future national park direction in Ontario. Increasing attention will be given to an ecosystem based management approach that will focus on broader ecosystems rather than specific natural regions. This will also involve greater partnerships and interagency co-operation, particularly in an era of continuing fiscal restraint and development pressures. These issues have influenced the national parks program for the past century, however, and will continue to challenge park planners and park promoters as we head into the twenty-first century.

Endnotes

1. By Order in Council dated 25 November 1885, some 26 square kilometres on the northern slopes of Sulphur Mountain were "reserved from public sale or settlement ... in order that proper control of the lands [including] these springs may be vested in the Crown." See W.F. Lothian, *A Brief History of Canada's National Parks* (Ottawa: Department of the Environment, 1987) 17.

2. *Ibid.* 23.

3. R. C. Brown, "The Doctrine of Usefulness: Natural Resource and National Parks Policy in Canada, 1887-1914," J.G. Nelson (ed.) *Canadian Parks in Perspective*, (Canada: Harvest House Ltd., 1969) 59.

4. T. Bates, "A Community Vanished A History of Grenadier Island in the St. Lawrence River," Parks Canada, Ontario Region, Manuscript on File, Chapter 2: Native Claims and Surrenders.

5. S. W. Smith, *The First Summer People The Thousand Islands 1650-1910*, (Toronto: Stoddart Publishing Co. Ltd, 1993) 86.

6. *The Gananoque Reporter*, 20 June 1874.

7. *Ibid.* 30 May 1874.

8. St. Lawrence Islands National Park files, quote from the Supplementary Estimates for 1894-1895 that Gordon Island shall be reserved from sale for park purposes. How this decision was arrived at is not clear from the material consulted. While there had been much public discussion on the benefits of establishing a park, the surviving paper trail on the actual decision to include a park in the Order in Council has eluded this researcher.

9. *The Gananoque Reporter*, 2 November 1901, quoting from the Alexandria Bay *Sun*.

10. St. Lawrence Islands National Park files, copy of Order in Council, #108122 20 September 1904.

11. R. Tiessen, *The DeLaurier House and Family Study*, Microfiche Report Series, #8 (1979).

12. J. Foster, *Working for Wildlife: The Beginning of Preservation in Canada* (Toronto: University of Toronto Press, 1971) 194-95.

13. *Ibid.* 40.

14. Commission of Conservation *Annual Report*, (1915), Appendix III, 303.

15. Foster, op.cit., 137.

16. *Ibid.* 125.

17. J.G. Batten, "Land use history and landscape change, Point Pelee National Park," MA Thesis, University of Western Ontario, 1975, Chapter VI; The Commission of Conservation in their Ninth Annual Report (1918) reiterated their position that Pelee be set aside as a park because of "its scenic value, the southern nature of its birds and plant life, its importance as a main route for migratory birds and the exceptional opportunities it affords ... for a national reservation."

18. *Ibid.*

19. F. Lothian, *A History of Canada's National Parks,* Vol. I (Ottawa: Parks Canada, 1976) 87.

20. *Ibid.*

21. *Ibid.*

22. *Ibid.* 88.

23. Statues of Canada, 20-21 George V, Chap. 33; W. Lothian, op.cit. Vol. II, 30-31.

24. Lothian, op.cit., Vol. I, 77-88.

25. *Ibid.* 82.

26. *Ibid.* 88-89; personal communication with staff archaeologist, Brian Ross.

27. *Ibid.* 83.

28. M.J. Cox, "Point Pelee National Park – A Case Study of Policy Evolution," manuscript on file, Parks Canada, Ontario Region (1976) 5.

29. National Parks Policy, National Parks Branch, Department of Northern Affairs and National Resources, Ottawa (1964), manuscript on file, Parks Canada, Ontario Region 4.

30. G. Killan, *Protected Places: A History of Ontario's Provincial Parks System,* (Toronto: Dundurn Press, 1993) 33.

31. *National Parks System Planning Manual,* Indian Affairs and Northern Development, Parks Canada (1071) 3.

32. *National Parks System Plan,* (Ottawa:Environment Canada Parks Service, 1990).

33. The Honourable Jean Chrétien, in his opening remarks to the Canadian National Parks: Today and Tomorrow Conference held in October 1968 stated, "I put a very high priority on the need to establish more such parks in the two central provinces Quebec and Ontario. Such additional parks would meet a great need, and their role

in helping to forge a richer Canadian union is of fundamental importance." J. Chretien, "Our Evolving National Parks System," in J. Nelson et al (eds.) *The Canadian National Parks: today and tomorrow* Conference (Calgary: University of Calgary, 1968) 10.

34. G. Killan, op. cit., pp. 194-195; for the wording of the memorandum, see, Memorandum of Intention.... Ontario Region, Parks Canada, manuscript on file.
35. Pukaskwa National Park Management Plan, Ontario Region, Parks Canada (1982) 3.
36. The Environmental Applications Group Ltd., *Investigations of NACS and NSCS in the Georgian Bay Shoreline Area of Region 19* (1978) 1.

Landscapes, Waterscapes, Inscapes:

Putting the People

Back into Pukaskwa

Brian S. Osborne

An oral history of a wilderness park appears to be a contradiction in terms. By definition, wilderness implies the absence of humans and the dominance of the natural environment. But the reality of many of our present wilderness areas is that they have witnessed the retreat of humans and the reassertion of the natural: that is, to the extent that they can ever be "natural" again after human intervention. While natural ecosystems apparently dominate the scene, an underlying surface of material relics and remembered landscapes survives.

Perhaps this is where Carol Shields's poem fits in: it is called "Pioneers":

> They existed. Butter bowls
> and hayrakes testify,
> and ruined cabins
> their grievous roofs
> caved in.
>
> But they're melting to myth,
> every year harder to believe in,
> and the further we travel away
> the more we require
> in the form of proofs.

Of course
you still meet those who
are old enough to
claim kinship, but eye
witnesses are scarce
now and unreliable.
We want sealers, cutlery, clods
of earth, flames from their fires,
footsteps, echoes, the breath
they breathed,
a sign, something to
keep faith by
before they go the way
of the older gods.
    (Carol Shields 1992: 45)

This is very much the case with Pukaskwa National Park. Through those "scarce and unreliable eye witnesses" that Shields talks about, the now invisible landscapes and waterscapes of human activities are restored "before they go the way of the older gods."

Landscapes, Inscapes, "Real" Geography

For geographers, the visual expression of the imprint of culture on the land is manifest in the "landscape." In its original application (Sauer, [1925], 1963), the landscape was seen to be a material expression of a super-organic culture that imprinted its values on the land producing a sort of palimpsest of human impressions. This approach has been challenged by interpretations of the culturally fabricated world that privilege human agency: the cultural landscape produced by societies is a social construct that demonstrates human needs, priorities and even idiosyncracies. To understand the processes producing these "lived in worlds" we need to seek out the symbolic meaning of "ordinary landscapes" (Meinig, 1979; Tuan, 1974, 1977, 1982; Stilgoe, 1982; Jackson, 1984; Lowenthal, 1985). Current literature in the social sciences has taken this approach further with the "reading" of the "text" of landscape for hidden meanings, figurative images and the imaginary geography of places and spaces. Landscapes are now being interpreted via the concepts of discourse, text and metaphor in order to expose controlling social and cultural mechanisms (Zelinsky, 1988; Cosgrove and Daniels, 1988: Osborne, 1988, 1992, 1992a; Porteous, 1990; Shields, 1991; Short, 1991; Barnes and Duncan, 1992).

The point is that a fuller appreciation of landscapes requires an understanding of the symbolic significance of the physical world, material artifacts, and place-specific events. We have to come to appreciate how it is that places become imbued with symbolic meanings that bond people to their identity in time and space (Werlen 1993). People function in a material world that they have fashioned according to what Gerard Manley Hopkins called "inscapes," mental constructs that serve as templates for human actions and decisions. The degree to which material landscapes represent these cognitive inscapes becomes a critical point of inquiry. Sometimes there are clues. For example, vestigial place-names often evoke original meanings now lost to us, though we mouth their sounds and locate ourselves by them as we move through our own worlds. They are like fragments of an undeciphered text waiting to be decoded.

But this is where the real power of interpretation is: the emotive records of people's experience of place and lives in place. Barry Lopez has referred to this as the "real geography." It refers to the "local expertise" that "resides with men and women more or less sworn to a place, who abide there, who have a feel for the soil and history" (1989). Essentially populist in philosophy and methodology, this approach requires the student of place to engage the people in the context of the material and psychic landscapes they have created. As Lopez explains it:

> If I were now to visit another country, I would ask my local companion, before I saw any museum or library, any factory or fabled town, to walk me in the country of his or her youth, to tell me the name of things and how, traditionally, they have been fitted together in a community. I would ask for the stories, the voice of memory over the land.... I would want first the sense of a real place, to know that I was not inhabiting an idea. I would want to know the lay of the land first, the real geography, and take some measure of the love of it in my companion before I stood before the paintings or read works of scholarship (Lopez 1989: 19-21).

In this way, the recollections of the living population personalize, validate and re-appropriate past histories and geographies in terms of the lived experiences of the people involved, in their own voices.

Certainly, the tried and true methodology of oral history, and its more recent manifestation as "interactive-research" and "story-telling," has the potential for making several contributions in our engagement with the "remembered past."[1]

Initially, the principal objective for oral history was evidentiary: the "discovery" and recording of facts and information. Associated with this was the need for "interpreting" the past: that is, a concern for the more qualitative and impressionistic recollections of actions, events, practices and norms. And all of this was motivated by the principle of "conservation" and "preservation": that is, capturing the fleeting resource of human memory before it was eroded by the actuarial verities of human mortality.

But there have always been critics of this enterprise. Oral history has been charged with being unreliable: it is subjective and too romantic; it lacks authenticity, veracity, and credibility; it is "soft" evidence. For those preferring the equally suspect paper trail, the counter-argument is that oral evidence must always be scrutinized for the expertise, authority, reliability and competence of the source and that, indeed, no more or less is expected of it than is expected of the written record.

But reconstructing accurate renderings of the past is more than facts and evidence. It must be given a human context. This is what moved Raymond Williams in his novel, *The Volunteers*, to complain that, even in the best intentioned assemblages of people's "material history" in folk-museums and parks, the human experience of the past is missing:

> It is pleasant, of course, to walk through the farmhouses and the stables and the dairies and the kitchens: to see the beds, chair, cradles, knives, churns, presses, flails, coppers, stoves, casks, lying all so naturally and so clean to hand. But there are no people here, except as spectators and guides. There are no marks of use – the crumpled sheets, the stained knives. There are a few sheep in the pens, a few flowers and herbs in the gardens, but not much in the drains, no ashes on the hearths. For this is a cleaned-up history, of only part of the material. The people are implied by the shapes of their tools and their furniture, but are essentially absent, not only physically but in the version that is given of them: polished shells of their lives (Williams 1978: 28-29).

The point is that such collections lose touch with the "lived in world" of the human subjects and as such, therefore, lose their essential meaning.

This is the particular value of oral history. Apart from contributing "facts" – dates, locations, techniques – it also allows impressionistic details of emotions, attitudes and perceptions, those crucially important aspects of the lived experience that are so often inaccessible through other sources. Moreover, its very strength is the "humanizing" of history. The verbal colouring vitalizes the lived-experience through the seductive allure of the well told story.

How can the diligent researcher not be charmed by the wit and directness of these responses: "I wish my legs had lasted as well as my tongue has"; "I'm getting to be a real old blatherer"; "Oh, these dates kill me!"; and "but I'm not a story-teller. Anything I tell has got to be the truth, or I don't tell it to you." But another of my sources-cum-fellow-researcher says it all for me:

> Yea, them were experiences, you know, that I remember so well! Every move we made and the likes of that, you know... And it's a good thing that an old person's memory don't fail him, that he forgets all these things because it keeps him alive. To turn back the pages of time and know exactly what was done and why and everything like that, you know. And that's why I say, "Give the truth and nothing but the truth the way it happened to you, or when you witnessed it. Not what the other fellow told you." No, I say, "Throw that in the garbage, what the other people told you," Although you know it could be.[2]

But the whole matter of what is credible or not becomes an interesting question. As Fentress and Wickham put it in their recent study, *Social Memory: New Perspectives on the Past:*

> The social meaning of memory, like its internal structure and its mode of transmission, is little affected by its truth; all that matters is that it be believed, at least at some level.... Social memory is, in fact, often selective, distorted, and inaccurate. None the less, it is not necessarily any of these; it can be extremely exact, when people have found it socially relevant from that day to this to remember and recount an event in the way it was originally experienced. The debate about whether it is inherently accurate or not is thus sterile; and it will remain so as long as memory is treated as a "mental faculty" whose workings can be described in isolation from the social context (1992: xi-xii).

And finally, it is more than a mere academic exercise: there is a powerful ideological agenda. By allowing insights into how people constitute their daily life, oral history establishes the identity of the principal actors in history, the "ordinary" people. This is important as so often the subtleties of historiographic constructs and scholarly interpretations have alienated people from their own history. The inclusion of real people in the construction of their own history is an ideologically charged initiative that "reifies" history. People are returned to their important place in space and time. It's not writing history from the bottom-up, but rather from the inside out – and doing so in a sensitive, insightful and socially responsible way.

Perhaps this is why oral history has come to be so important for research and interpretive programs in monuments, museums and parks. The protected and displayed landscapes, both natural and cultural, need to be understood. The didactic voice of authorative science and history can only go so far. The voices of those who have lived in these environments and who have produced the landscapes speak with a different authority: the insights of having being involved in the "real" geography and "real" history of places. And the thousands of "ordinary" people who are busily making their own histories identify with this.

Pukaskwa Remembered

Pukaskwa is a distinctive piece of Canadian geography. The contact of the Central Boreal Uplands with the pristine shoreline of Lake Superior makes it so. It also constitutes a distinctive piece of Canadian history. Isolated from so many of the developments on the landward side for so long, it was relatively protected from economic development. It looked to the lake. Rivers such as the Pic, White and Pukaskwa afforded corridors of access, but much of human contact was restricted to the Lake Superior littoral. For the people who constructed the ancient Pukaskwa Pits as well as for fur-traders, fishermen, lumbermen and prospectors, access to the region was by lake in the summer, and by the river valley routes at other times.

But little material evidence of these human presences now remains, except for the memories and stories that still lie on the land.[3] Indeed, the park may be said to have a "ghost" population. In the past, hundreds of characters were once involved in economic systems whose presence, however ephemeral, are nevertheless part of the natural history of this part of Canada. The lake fishery, logging on the White River, trapping, prospecting and outfitting are all recaptured as living elements of the "remembered worlds" of Pukaskwa National Park. They contribute to what may be called a "psychic" landscape that must not be forgotten.

a) The Fishermen

There have been a succession of fisheries throughout the Great Lakes, from the fishery integrated into the fur-trade activities, through the pioneer subsistence-fishery, into the modern commercial fishery. Indeed, it is becoming apparent that the Great Lakes experienced a mobile resource frontier akin to that on the land, with the fishery and fishermen moving from the lower lakes into the upper lakes in search of fresh fish stocks (Adams and Kolinosky 1974; Baldwin and Saalfield 1962; Osborne 1990; McCullough 1989). As such, the waters off Pukaskwa have seen the transitions from fur-trade fishery (1830-70), through the era of the independent commercial fisherman (1870-1939), into the contemporary fishery. Much of the technical, economic and social history of these activities can only be recaptured from fragmentary historical records, but the recollections of some of the old-timers have fleshed out the picture through their "living memories." Much of their experienced history validates the written record: the commercial organization of the fishery by external metropolitan forces; the different techniques of seine-net, gill-net and pound-net fishing; the fundamental shifts in technology with the application of steam-power and gasoline motors to boats and "lifters," and the replacement of linen nets by nylon; and the general decline of the fishery, but whether it was cause by the lamprey or by overfishing was a topic in itself.

What was novel with the oral-history project, however, was the opportunity to tease out the way in which the fishermen viewed the lake fishery in terms of patterns of time and place that fitted their knowledge of the habitats and regimens of fish-species with the dictates of the fishing operation. They viewed the waters off Pukaskwa as a "waterscape" that they had been taught to interpret by generations of lore and experience.

They knew the shore-line too. They had to. The extended field of operations, together with the uncertainty of Lake Superior required it. Whether they were operating from the northern set of bases at Rossport, Jackfish and Port Coldwell, or the southern bases of Michipicoten Harbour, Gargantua, Batchawana Bay and Montreal River, they were often more than 100 kilometres away from home. One strategy was to establish a seasonal fishing station such as the one maintained by the Purvis Company at Quebec Harbour on Michipicoten Island. Each year, the establishment there consisted of a fishing crew of 35 to 40 men, a cook and two helpers, and a book-keeper, with the community sometimes swelling to over 60 people when some families relocated there. One of the regulars recalls the facilities consisting of docks, tugs, twine

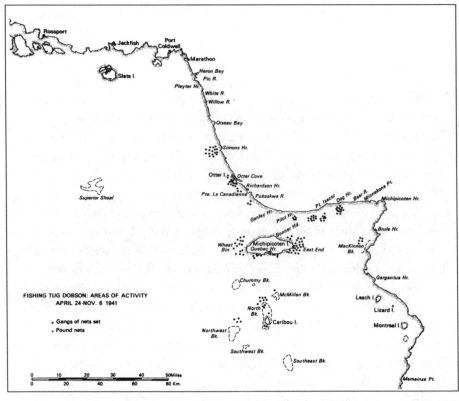

FISHING TUG DOBSON: AREAS OF ACTIVITY
APRIL 24–NOV. 6 1941

• Gangs of nets set
○ Pound nets

Rossport
Jackfish
Port Coldwell
Marathon
Heron Bay
Pic R.
Slate I.
Playter Hr.
White R.
Willow R.
Oiseau Bay
Simons Hr.
Otter I. Otter Cove
Richardson Hr.
Pte. La Canadienne Pukaskwa R.
Superior Shoal
Ganley Hr.
Pilot Hr.
Pt. Isacor Dog Hr. Bear R.
Minnekone Pt.
Michipicoten Hr.
Brule Hr.
Bonner Hd.
Wheat Bin
Michipicoten I.
Quebec Hr.
East End
MacKinnon Bk.
Gargantua Hr.
Chummy Bk.
McMillan Bk.
Leach I.
North Bk.
Lizard I.
Caribou I.
Montreal I.
Northwest Bk.
Southwest Bk.
Southeast Bk.
Mamainse Pt.

0   10   20   30   40   50 Miles
0   20   40   60   80 Km.

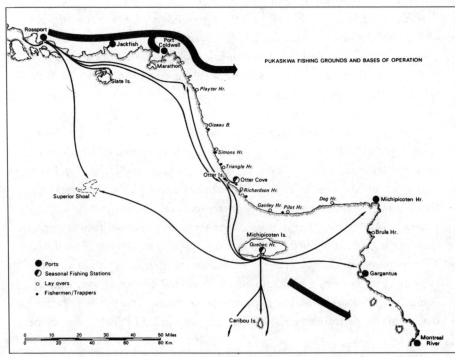

PUKASKWA FISHING GROUNDS AND BASES OF OPERATION

● Ports
◑ Seasonal Fishing Stations
○ Lay overs
• Fishermen/Trappers

Rossport
Jackfish
Port Coldwell
Marathon
Slate Is.
Playter Hr.
Oiseau B.
Simons Hr.
Triangle Hr.
Otter Is. Otter Cove
Richardson Hr.
Superior Shoal
Ganley Hr. Pilot Hr.
Dog Hr.
Michipicoten Hr.
Michipicoten Is.
Quebec Hr.
Brule Hr.
Gargantua
Caribou Is.
Montreal River

0   10   20   30   40   50 Miles
0   20   40   60   80 Km.

sheds, coal-dump, fish-shed, freezing-plant, bunkhouses, blacksmith's shop, some houses for families and a house for Mr. Purvis. This community continued at Michipicoten from May until October, when most returned to the mainland, leaving behind a skeleton crew of four men to mend the nets and put up ice. One who stayed behind remembers that, "We hibernated like a bear." Similar, if less well established, satellite fishing stations were located for a while at such locations as Otter Cove, Old Dave's Cove, Simon's Harbour and Morrison Harbour.

But apart from these bases, there were also "lay-over" harbours. When tugs were operating too far from their home base to get back before night-fall, or when they were driven off the lake by bad weather, crews would have recourse to several sheltered harbours: Playter Harbour, Morrison Harbour, Oiseau Bay, Simon's Harbour, Triangle Harbour, Old Dave's Cove, Otter Cove, Richardson Harbour, Ganley Harbour, Pilot Harbour, Dog Harbour and many others. One fisherman remembers "double headers" when they would decide to stay at Simon's Harbour rather than "run home" and "we'd meet with the boys from Port Coldwell and those places and we'd have a real evening. It was a real party getting together you know." Others remember "double headers" at Otter Cove and Richardson Harbour:

> We laid alongside of one another there in different harbours because we were from the north and they were from the south.... We used to have a lot of good evenings there talking about the different fishing and the different sets ... and the different boats. There, we were mingling all the time with the different crews of them old time boats, you know, and their children aboard some of the boats, you know, same as us.

On another occasion, the refuge was Spruce Harbour:

> And Lake Superior was throwing up an "Old Damnerer" as they called it. And, oh, there was nothing showing its face out on the lake that day and a half that we were there.... We laid there with the Purvis tugs when they came up that far. They always went into that harbour because it was a good safe harbour.

Locations such as these must have often took on the appearance of transient, water-hamlets, as fishermen cooked, told yarns and socialized. But they are empty now.

Apart from locales along the shore, the lake itself was known to the fishermen in term of fishing grounds, shoals and regions of customary use. Each group's location at any time depended on the season, the run of the fish, proximity to home base facilities, and, to some extent, recognition of traditionally used territories.

The fishing grounds off Pukaskwa constitute a divide in the area of operations between two main groups of fishermen. To the northwest, fishermen from Rossport, Jackfish and Port Coldwell usually fished around islands of Nipigon Bay in the spring, and moved out onto the lake shoals in the summer months. They never went much beyond the Pic River to the east until after August when they fished as far south as Otter Head and the mouth of the Pukaskwa River for the fall run of lake trout. Those from the southeast, from Gargantua, Batchawana Bay and Michipicoten, fished south to Caribou Island, as far north as Simon's Harbour, and occasionally to the mouth of the Pic River. For example, the season would open along the Pukaskwa coast with the arrival of the Purvis tugs from their base at Quebec Harbour and they would set their nets from Old Woman Bay and Michipicoten Bay up to the shoals near the Pic River, and the shoals around Caribou Island and Otter Island. By mid-June, they set their nets for whitefish in the shallower waters off Richardson Harbour, Triangle Harbour and Simon's Harbour, but never went further north than the Gravel River because that was the beginning of the Port Coldwell sphere of operation. Apart from the overlap in their activities between Oiseau Harbour and Otter Cove, both groups also pushed out into Lake Superior to fish at the Superior Shoal. These were the "blue water" fishermen as opposed to the "red water" fishermen who clung to the shore.

But that's only the macro-geography. Each fishermen carried with him a detailed knowledge of specific grounds and their yields. Consider the following micro-geography of the waters off Pukaskwa:

...there's a ridge of banks just off the Pukaskwa that we used to fish pretty hard. These banks are very funny banks. And we couldn't fish close to Pukaskwa River anyway because we would get loaded up with sticks. But we used to have some wonderful lifts out and around this area. Fifty or sixty hundred a lift ... two and a half ton and that would be in October, eh. Anywhere's from the first to the end of October and then the fish would seem to move in a little bit. But then we didn't bother because it was too dangerous for us. We'd lose too much twine. And, like I say, in the spring of the year, we fished in the deep water, out to sixty, seventy, and eighty fathom all down this area past Pukaskwa. There's two sets off Canadian Point that we used to do pretty well at, and we fished the shallower water. Why we weaved in where the whitefish and trout were together, like, eh. They would run about a third whitefish and two-thirds trout, eh. And then we would move in and pick that up for, oh, approximately three weeks. And then after that, when the leaves started to turn colour ... as soon as they started to fall, well then we started to work in those banks where they spawned, and shallower places along the shoreline where we could get in.

And if the spatial characteristics of the fishery were known so also were the temporal. As one fisherman put it, "You see, the lake's harvest is the same as your grains and everything on land, eh. There's certain times for harvest on the lake, the same as on the land." But it also helped to know other factors: "They [trout] move according to the moon, and in the dark of the moon you get real good fishing up in shallow water, eh. And in the light of the moon you won't. You wouldn't get a third in the light of the moon that would in the dark of the moon there." But such niceties aside, the seasonal sequence was generally accepted by all: first coastal, then deep water, then the shoals at Superior Shoal and around Caribou Island, and then back to coastal. As one put it:

Well, in the spring of the year here, as soon as we could get out, we'd try to work our way up towards what we called Nipigon Bay ... what we called "The Flats" up in there; shallow water; three or four fathoms. Trout and whitefish went in there early in the spring. Really good fishing. And that's where we would fish until that run of fish was gone. And then we would have to take all our nets out of there. Then we'd work all around the islands and work at different depths.... You've got to find the fish, eh. The fish don't come to you. You gotta go to the fish. Then mostly during July and August we'd be out in the deep water for these ciscoette. And then in the fall we'd come back ashore for the run of big trout when they come into spawn.

With details such as this, the empty waters off Pukaskwa come to be seen as a rich resource with as much of a human involvement as agriculture, lumbering, or mining on land. The fishermen too had their techniques and expertise. The daily regimen was quite routine: "Get out. Find you buoy. Lift your seven miles of nets. Clear them all out. Set them back and come home." Others were less laconic and fleshed out the details of the operation. "Setting the nets," for example, was a technique that required "spinning," "tailing," "cleaning" and "liming" by the crew of three deck-hands. The reverse process of "lifting" the nets consisted of "tailing in," "clearing" and "boxing." As for navigating, what differentiated the "blue water" sailor from the "red water" sailor was knowing how to get to the best grounds, out of sight of land, with only a compass and a watch – and always, "watching for the bad three sisters that's coming on us there and is going to submerge us, probably dive right into us."

For the hundreds of fishermen that have tracked across the waters off Pukaskwa, the environment was a rich, if challenging one. They survive by their detailed knowledge of the lake-fishery, the shelter afforded by the shoreline, and ingenuity. The comment, "it was a good life ... kind of rough at times," seems to be an understatement.

b) The Lumbermen

The forest have not always been so silent either. At one time, the sights and sounds of an active lumbering economy were concentrated on three locations: the White River watershed, the Pukaskwa River watershed and Oiseau Bay. Each of these locations was associated with an intense, if transient, human settlement, and still contain the debris and relics of perhaps the most concentrated and intense human activity within the park. Lumbering introduced large numbers of people into the region, constructed depots, produced a network of trails and lines of movement, and was generally the dominant modifier of the landscape. Of the three, the White River lumbering operation was the most established. Commencing as a salvage operation following a fire in 1936 in the Herrick and Hayward Lake area, lumbering intensified in the 1942-43 season, and a new headquarters was established on the railway at Regan which became the main supply depot for men, horses, supplies and equipment. In all, the Abitibi Power and Paper Company controlled some 2,000 square miles of timber rights with the White River operation yielding an average of 100,000 to 150,000 cords per annum.

There were three discrete elements in the White River logging operation: the White Lake area was the centre of the logging activity; after being rafted across the lake, the logs entered the river proper for the run down to Lake Superior; at the rafting camp at the mouth of the river, the logs were assembled into rafts ready for the last leg, the "Big Tow" to Sault Ste. Marie.

The last White River drive, and the last "Big Tow" of White River logs took place in the summer of 1965. Those who were part of the operation remember the routine and challenges of their life in the woods: the "cruising" and tallying of the area to be lumbered out; the hard work of cutting, hauling, piling, and scaling the logs; the river drive; rafting and the "Big Tow"; and the distinctive life in the camps.[4] Of these, the spring river drive and the subsequent lake-tow bulk large in the remembered history of Pukaskwa.

After a winter of cutting, hauling, piling, and scaling the logs, the river drive commenced in May and lasted well into July, and was divided into the main drive and the "rear drive." Having been towed across White Lake in small rafts, the main drive commenced with logs being driven downstream by eighteen men operating in three crews of six based at four "drive camps": the Dam camp, Angle Falls, Swamp Creek and the rafting camp at the mouth of the river. The flow of logs was regulated by oar-driven pointers, steam powered "alligators," and winch-operated booms at critical points. Various types of booms were used: "glance" booms were positioned across bays and inlets; "trip" booms were located above rapids and controlled manually to control the flow of logs; "holding booms" were sited at various locations along the river for flow control; "bow" booms were large holding booms located at the outflow of White Lake and the mouth of the White River. The "rear drive" started in early July with some 50 men operating in crews of six to a "pointer," a 36-foot-long boat of shallow draught. Using dynamite, hooks called "jam dogs," and winches, these crews cleared up log-jams and dislodged logs stranded along the shore. The "rearing" crews moved along the river, camping out under canvas at tenting grounds on grassy flats along the river.

The recollections of the river drive were vivid for those who participated in it as it was obviously an exciting time marking the culmination of a winter's work. It was also strenuous:

> Keep the wood running. See that it didn't stop...."We only had one jam on the White River. It was a dilly. I don't know, the man in charge let too much wood go, and it got down to the boom at the mouth of the river, and he kept letting it run from above. It backed up to the Falls, and got in there, and piled in there. There were over two rafts of wood in that jam. A raft of wood was 10,000 or 9,000 cords. Boy we had some digging.... I just kept picking away. Dynamite and "pickroons" and pike-poles till we got it out. It took pretty near a month to get that out of there.

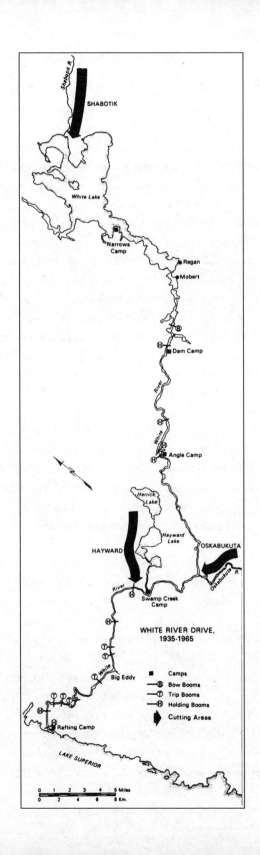

WHITE RIVER DRIVE,
1935-1965

Camps
Bow Booms
Trip Booms
Holding Booms
Cutting Areas

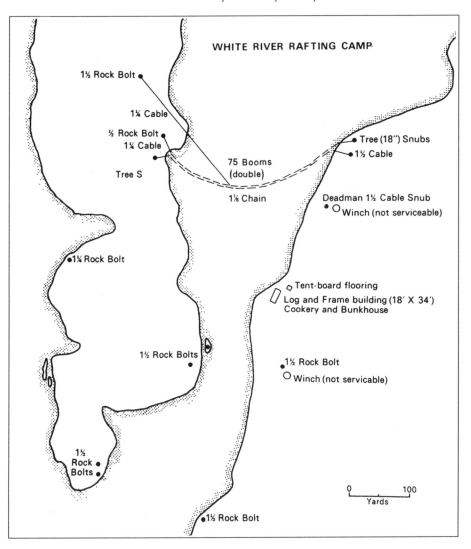

WHITE RIVER RAFTING CAMP.

1½ Rock Bolt

1¼ Cable

½ Rock Bolt
1¼ Cable

Tree S

75 Booms
(double)

Tree (18") Snubs
1½ Cable

1⅛ Chain

Deadman 1½ Cable Snub
Winch (not serviceable)

•1¼ Rock Bolt

Tent-board flooring
Log and Frame building (18' X 34')
Cookery and Bunkhouse

1½ Rock Bolts

1½ Rock Bolt
Winch (not servicable)

1½
Rock
Bolts

0 _____ 100
Yards

•1½ Rock Bolt

Another recalls, "They used a lot of dynamite anyway.... Well, you would just holler and let her go. God, the way, they used dynamite, it didn't seem to frighten anybody." But it could get exciting:

> He said, "Now boys, there's only two logs to be taken out and away she's going to go." They were the key-logs they called them. So he says to the boys, "Make for shore." So they all headed for shore and I stood beside him. "You'd better go, sonny," he said. I didn't know him. He didn't know me either. "Well," I said, "Can I help you?" And he said, "It's pretty dangerous." "Well," I said, "If it's dangerous for you, maybe it's dangerous for me too, but if I can help you I'll stay with you." So he said, "For heaven's sake, when she breaks, follow right in my footsteps or you'll be crushed by the logs coming down." So anyway we took this log out and, of course, away she went with a roar like thunder and Amable said, "Run!" So he offed for the shore and I followed right in his footsteps, I'll tell you, and we landed safely.

No wonder the river drivers took pride in their work and skills; as one put it, "I really had the best fun in my life on that drive":

> You see, you could really get on the loose, as they called it, from the logs. A big timber like that and you take a nice drive down a few hundred yards and jump off on the shore and come back just to make sure the logs are flowing and no signs of jams forming, you see. The proudest moment in my life is when I got my Fraser driving boots.

With the arrival of the last logs at the river mouth, the river drive was complete and the preparations for making up the rafts for the "Big Tow" commenced. Each year, about 10 rafts, each containing about 10,000 cords, would leave the White River for Sault Ste. Marie, towed by tugs with cables of 1,400 to 1,800 feet in length. The rafts were contained by two inner strings of 100 boom logs (2,500 feet), and two outer "wrapper" booms of 125 boom logs (3,125 feet), the whole having a perimeter of approximately one mile in extent. With the wrapper-booms anchored to the shore, the "bow" beams were opened to allow the logs to flow into the raft until the limit of 10,000 cords was reached. The bow-boom was then closed and the wrapper-booms chained around the rear of the raft. One account summarizes the whole process efficiently:

Well the wood is held at the mouth of the river in a boom, a big boom, a double boom with logs from eighteen to twenty-four inches in diameter, one inch chain snubbed at each end with an inch cable.... First they attached the tug's boom to each side of the river and then they opened the bow boom and then the wood went in by itself. There was quite a current there into the lake. They filled the boom with wood, eight, ten, 12,000 cords. I think they did take a 13,000 cord one down one time because they couldn't get the boom closed. The current was too high. And then the raftsmen would tie the wood in and then they would be gone.

The tow tug with its crew of eight men moved along at a speed of about one knot, only stopping after the first eight hours of towing to take up the slack in the boom and double it around the rear of the raft. One of the raftsmen recalls his duties:

...every morning I'd get up and walk around on the booms. It takes maybe three-quarters of a mile all the way round. They were double booms of great big British Columbia pine and with big chain links the size of my fists. And I'd check every one of them as I'd go around to see that they weren't wore out or broke off or something. And then look at the back to see how the wood was.... You see, you could only go a mile an hour with the tug because the pulp wood would all drift to the back of the boom. And then if you'd go any faster than that it would either go under the boom or over the boom. So we just go a mile an hour. It would take a long time to take a raft from Pukaskwa to Sault Ste. Marie.

Before entering the channel on the approach to the mills at the Sault, the rafts were "banded," or reduced to five "bags," each about 500-feet wide and held together by banding wires thrown across them. The tug then returned up lake for the next load of logs that had been accumulating at the booming ground, the round trip taking about 10 days to the Sault and back to the mouth of the White (MacDonald, 1974).

And there's so much more. The seasonal and daily regimen in the camps and the specialized activities of the walking boss, clerk, doctor, warehouse man, scaler, harness maker, blacksmith, cook, packers and itinerant missionaries ("shantymen") are also all part of the story of Pukaskwa.

c) The Itinerants

Trappers, prospectors, tourist guides and tourists are characterised by their seasonal use of the region, their limited number and their consequent limited impact upon the environment. And while the tourists and prospectors were often external to the area, only visiting it seasonally, some of the trappers and guides were permanent residents and important depositories of local lore. Moreover, all of them travelled through the park extensively and possessed a detailed knowledge of bush lore, past activities and ways of life.

Perhaps the most detailed knowledge of Pukaskwa fauna, flora and the general lay of the land was held by those who had trapped there for many generations. Traditionally, Indian trappers moved out from their base at Mobert into the headwaters of the Pukaskwa, Cascade, Bremner and Lurch watersheds. As one recalls:

> They didn't exactly trap in there. They used to come here to the height of the land, the whole bunch of them of them, eh, and from there they spread out. One bunch goes over there, another bunch this way and they all spread out. It was a sort of meeting pont they had there.

While specific locations such as Louis, Birch and Widgeon lakes were referred to as bases, generally the practice was that "Where the sun sets you camp there." One Pukaskwa trapper of long-standing commented on an interesting dimension of the groups life in the bush:

> ... the Indians all travel certain areas at certain times and they all kind of spread out from there. There's always one group here, and one group there, and somehow they managed to communicate with each other. They used to talk to each other. Even though they are distances apart they still communicate with each other ... they'll take a little branch and start tapping it and it'll carry the sound and somehow the other man that's on the other end senses that there is some kind of message going ... just like telegraph....

Other techniques referred to were building dead-fall traps ("mitcknegon"), fishing with lights ("jacklighting") and knowing how and when to kill a bear with an axe:

I have often heard from my grandfather how they used to do that, you know. You make a bedding outside a bear's den, a brush bedding. After you're all finished ... you sort of challenge the bear to come out and as he's coming out, you hit him over the head with the axe.... Anytime you go after a bear, you know there's a certain time. Just about the middle of winter, eh. They say the bear turns halfways in the season and in his hibernations, eh.... He'll lay one way one half of the winter and then he'll turn over. And just the time when he's turning over, that's the time you go after him. Because that's when its really, really fat, eh.

This somewhat exercise was said to yield some 80 pounds of bear fat that was rendered down into 10 pounds of tallow for cooking as well as a surge of adrenaline.

Early Euro-Canadian commercial trappers depended much upon this Native lore, especially in the days before registered traplines when they went "as far as you can until you see snowshoe tracks." Preparations for the season would start in September with "cruising" around looking for signs of game, cutting portages, leaving caches of traps and supplies so that:

... when the snow comes, well, they have run back and forth all fall, and by that time they know the country pretty well, eh. They knew where all the animal trails were and they were all set.

When the trapping season opened, traps would be visited every one or two weeks to check the catch and change the bait. Green poplar was used for beaver, beaver meat or fish for mink, marten and fisher, while anything would do for foxes and wolves. The uncertainty of the enterprise meant that the routine of tending a 50-mile trapping line was, of necessity flexible:

Maybe you go a week around this section of the lakes. You come back and you hit a corner and do the other section.... It's hard to judge the time. Some days you might go a piece and got a lot of skinning to do.... You can't say, "I'm going to start here and make that lake today." You may pass that lake if you don't get anything and you go to the next one. But if you get a bunch of fur, there's a lot of work. I never plan. I just get up in the morning, take my pack sack, and away I go. When it gets dark, I make my camp.

"Camps" were often a simple canvas or brush lean-to in the lee of a hill, some old-timers relying upon "snowshoe-rabbit robes" made of strips of skin woven together constituting the "original sleeping bag." The procedure was simple:

...build a balsam bed on top of the snow and a little brush lean-to, build a fire out in front and try to have enough wood to keep a fire going all night, and lay down in the balsam palms and the snowshoe rabbit robe, and freeze all night!

Apart from these overnight camps, trappers would often keep little cabins or trapping shacks along their lines, and if somewhat spartan, they must have been regarded as more permanent bases:

Four or five feet high, and big enough to have some balsam boughs thrown on the ground. Made out of crude logs and it didn't have a door. It had an opening that he hung a canvass screen over, but he always left it open when he was gone because a bear would tear it up if he didn't. And he left a few things in there, like some old tongs and a frying pan or two.

A way of life more than a profitable season, trapping from September to the end of February was a supplement to many who then moved into fishing in May. Looking back on the profitability of the activity, one recalled that "They were all bad years as far I am concerned. Never made a fortune yet," but concluded that "I ate good and never was on welfare. So it was not bad."

Others, often trappers also, prospected along the shore between the Pic and Pukaskwa rivers in the early 1900s. After asking other local trappers to "keep their eyes skinned for iron ore," they started staking out claims:

Our equipment consisted of a pocket compass with sights to guide, a straight-line, and axes. Donald [prospector] handled the compass and we, with the Indians, did any necessary cutting. We did not have any of the equipment that engineers would have. But in order that our lines would be straight, should a large tree get in the way of our sight, we would simply cut the tree down.

In this way, they marked out 10, four-sided claims, each side being one mile in length, with a post and sample at each corner. Another commented on such useful bush-lore as lighting a fire with a shoe-lace, stick, and dry birch bark, and using an "Indian smoke pole" to keep bugs away. While some travelled by canoe and small boat others preferred to be unencumbered:

No, we never had a boat with us at all. And the way to cross a river was, oh, you get a cedar of maybe eight, nine, or ten inches, fourteen feet long. Two of them, and tie them together with a rope. Lay between them and then paddle with your hands right across. It was a lot simpler than anything else. You don't have to carry them with you. Take your rope off and roll it up, put it in your packsack, and away you go.

Of course, much of this became irrelevant with the advent of the corporate scientific prospecting featuring aerial access, instrumental survey and external logistic support.

Those same developments that transformed prospecting also increased the tempo of tourism in the area and afforded another economic opportunity for those with bush skills. Rail, lake-steamers and motorized pleasure yachts brought increasing numbers of pleasure and adventure seekers into Pukaskwa, with the main activity concentrated in the harbours along the shore and the lower reaches of the main rivers. With the introduction of fly-in tourism after the 1950s, a new and more flexible pattern of visits became established. And again, several of the locals added guiding to their mixed portfolio of bush activity, if somewhat half-heartedly. One remarked, "I hated guiding. I'd sooner starve than guide." This becomes understandable after several of them recorded their routine in this activity:

Well, a guide has to be a man who knows the country and wouldn't get lost. That's the first thing. Then he had to know how to cook, and he had to know how to pack, and he had to know how to put up tents. But of course at that time, a tent was nothing to put up. There was only one way you could put up a tent. You cut a ridge pole and two cross pieces and hung her up there. That's all there was to it.

But the tent was perhaps the easiest part of the regimen:

On one particular trip on Lake Superior (now I am speaking off of Swallow River, Pukaskwa, Otter Cove, in that area) we had two boats, the *Mooswa* and the *Truant*, and we had eleven tourists. I would get up at 4:30

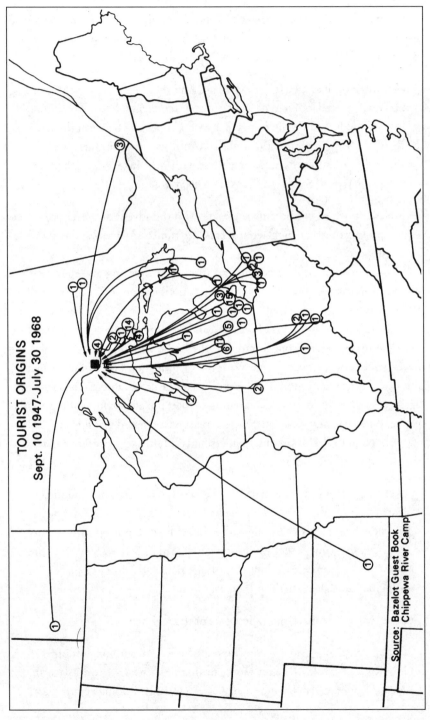

TOURIST ORIGINS
Sept. 10 1947–July 30 1968

Source: Bazelot Guest Book
Chippewa River Camp

in the morning, and cook breakfast for about fifteen people and they'd have to eat in shifts. And after each meal was done I would have to wash dishes and cook some more and by this time it was almost daylight. The tourists were getting a little bit edgey. They wanted to get going and the guides haven't eaten yet, so by the time we'd have our breakfast, you just threw it down, and then you had to pack lunch for eleven, fifteen people. And then you had to make your way to shore. You had to take two or three canoes and we walked two miles into Twin Lakes. And you paddles a canoe all day. Come in make a lunch at noon. Paddle again all afternoon. Pack your fish out. Pack your canoes out. And then turn around and peel vegetables and cook supper for that many people again. By the time we got down to our supper it would be 11:00 or 11:30 at night, and you're back up again at 4:30 in the morning. That's the way it went. So that was fishing.

Moose hunting was no less strenuous:

When they do knock one down then they all sit down and they rejoice and they have a really happy day. Well, then you've got to sit down and dress that thing out. It's not like sitting and dressing out a rabbit. You've got a few hundred pounds of meat to handle. And on one particular trip, three of us handled 1,525 pounds and that was for twelve miles. Now that was not all carrying. There's only one twenty minute portage; and another one over a bit of a lift; and another one on a forty-five degree about fifty feet up to the railway track. Now you've got canoes, tents, equipment, plus all this meat, and it's hard work. Every dollar you make, you earn it.

No wonder one concluded, "as far as guiding is concerned, it's a good life. It's tough. It's hard work.... You don't get to bed too early at night and you don't sleep in the morning, that's for sure." What emerges, therefore, is a whole cast of interesting characters. Two in particular have escaped anonymity because of the degree to which their escapades and idiosyncracies in the 1930s have been re-membered by so many who know Pukaskwa: Gus Weidman and Billy Newman.

Operating out of Otter Cove, Gus Weidman trapped the Pukaskwa water-shed and came to be a legend because of such feats of strength as lifting a 45-gallon barrel, fights and extrovert behaviour. Imagine the scene when large touring-yachts such as the *Sylvia*, *Seaforth* and *Seventeen* would anchor in Otter Cove:

> They would take him down, when they'd seen a moose coming into the water on one side or other of this cove. And as soon as it got swimming Gus would get on its back and he would swim all the way across the cove. like he would ride the moose and they would take pictures of him all the way across, eh.

Billy Newman was less flamboyant but no less interesting. Trapping in the region around Oiseau Bay, Newman is remembered for building 12-foot long, cedar, clinker-built skiffs and growing vegetables in a garden of sand fertilized with fish. But he was most renowned for his home-made fiddles. An itinerant fur-buyer recalls Newman's reaction to hearing the price for his furs:

> And he had twelve violins, all made and hanging up on his wall. And when I told him the price, he jumped up and played us a tune on every violin he had.... And he could play too. And beautiful violins. And he would tell you the story of every one, where the wood came from, and what it was, and where he got it up the beach. And, oh, he was tickled to death.

While many of the human activities in Pukaskwa were seasonal, sporadic and ephemeral, about a dozen individuals appear to have established themselves as permanent residents at several points, at least for short periods of time. Primarily trappers, in summer they fished and acted as guides for the occasional yacht-borne tourist. For some, prospecting or packing for prospectors, was integrated into the seasonal round of fishing, trapping and lumbering. In all these activities, the essential skills required were those derived from their bush-lore and an independent turn of mind that were common to all their various activities.

Conclusion: Lines on the Land, People in Place

Speaking of the life of her fisherman-trapper father, Bill Sayyea, Mrs Cormier referred to a rock outcrop near Simon's (Spruce) Harbour called Blushing Point where they used to watch the sailboats pass by. Noting that her parents had carved their names there and that "other people have done all kinds of pictures and things," perhaps this is the essential metaphor for all these transient lives that have left their impressions on Pukaskwa. Perhaps too much emphasis may be placed upon the isolated and wilderness character of areas such as the region bounded by the White and Pukaskwa rivers. Isolated they may have been, but for considerable numbers of people it was home, and for others a place of frequent visits and temporary residence.

But where are the region's Native peoples in all this? No, they are not mentioned as a particular category in this paper. I have left them out for two reasons. First, they don't need to be reminded of the ubiquitous presence of the shadows and essences of the past. This is central to their ontology. They are of nature, and nature is of them; their present recapitulates their past, and they intend to ensure that there is a continuity with their future. They know all about the invisible network of lines in their landscape that link them to other places and other times. Only we need to be reminded of that. And second, the Native peoples are everywhere in my conceptualization – if not explicitly. They showed their lands to the first French explorers; they already knew the habitats of the species sought out by the land-based trapping and water-based fishing economies; they worked in the lumber camps; they guided the tourists. My point is that to separate them out offends the purpose of this paper and, more importantly, does them a injustice. Indeed, they are the best evidence I have that the western construct of "wilderness" misrepresents the reality of what such areas have been to so many people.

I think my point is clear: even the most wild pieces of Canada's real estate possess a history. Like Chatwin's "songlines" or Lopez's "lays of the land," there are memories of past experiences of lived-in worlds everywhere. They constitute the rich, if ephemeral, dimensions of the "real geography" of the Pukaskwa region.

This is why I have no sympathy with Rupert Brook, in his "Letters from America," (1916), when he whined about the "horrid and solitary wilderness," the "empty land," and the absence of ghosts in the Canadian landscape. Noting that "the immaterial soil of England is heavy and fertile with the decaying stuff of past seasons and generations," he went on to compare the lot of the Canadian:

For his own forests and wild places are windswept and empty. That is their charm, and their terror. You may lie awake all night and never feel the passing of evil presences, nor hear printless feet... (1916: 196).

But he got it wrong! He wasn't looking or listening in the right way.

Endnotes

1. There are several classic statements on oral history methods and philosophy. Perhaps the best is still Thompson (1978), but for more recent discussions of new approaches in "interactive research" see Goodwin and Geritage (1990), Connelly and Clandinin (1990), and Eyles and Perri (1993).

2. All of the above quotations were taken from the Pukaskwa oral history project, (Revill Associates, 1980).

3. In 1976, an interpretive history of the area now comprised by Pukaskwa National Park identified the documented history of human interaction with the environment in the area, and recommended that an oral history should be undertaken to record personal recollections of the undocumented human content (Marsh, 1976). In 1980, an oral history reported on several of the more important themes of Euro-Canadian activities in Pukaskwa (Revill Associates, 1980). In this paper the following respondents have been quoted, though not identified as they were in the original report: Fishing (Lloyd Morden, Lyman Buck, Dolf King, Cecil Cress, Gib Gerow, Fred McCoy, Fred Legault, Ivan Purvis, Nap Michano, G. Depew); Lumbermen (Ivan Palmer, Nap Michano, T. MacCallum, Mark Gowan, Harry Bussineau, Graham Hurley, Patrick Kelly, Bud Harron); Trapping (H. Sabourin, Lyman Buck, George Coutu, John Calkins, Mrs. Cormier); Prospecting (G. Depew, Clem Downey, B. Murray, W. Richards); Guiding (Nap Michano, R. Bedard, George Ellis, John Calkins, G. Haight, H. Scott).

4. For perhaps the best account of the regimen in this particular region see Don MacKay (1978). He too interviewed many of the same people we interviewed in the Pukaskwa project.

References

Adams, G.F. and D.P. Kolinosky. (1974). *Out of the Waters: Ontario's Fresh Water Fish Industry*. Toronto: Commercial Fish and Fur Branch.

Baldwin, N.S. and R.W. Saalfeld. (1962). *Commercial Fish Production in the Great Lakes, 1867-1960*. Ann Arbour: Michigan.

Barnes, T.J. and J. Duncan. (1992). *Writing Worlds: Discourse, Text, and Metaphor in the Representation of Landscape*. London: Routledge.

Brook, Rupert. (1916). *Letters from America*. New York: Beaufort Books.

Connelly, F.M. and D.J. Clandinin. (1990). "Stories of Experience and Narrative Enquiry," *Educational Researcher* 19.5: 2-14.

Cosgrove, D. and S. Daniels. (1988). *The Iconography of Landscape*. Cambridge: University of Cambridge.

Eyles, John and E. Perri. (1993). "Life History as Method: An Italian Canadian Family in an Industrial City", *Canadian Geographer* 37.2: 104-119.

Fentress, James and Chris Wickham. (1992). *Social Memory: New Perspectives on the Past*. Oxford: Blackwell.

Goodwin, Charles and John Heritage. "Conversation Analysis," *Annual Review of Anthropology* 19: 283-87.

Jackson, J.B. (1984). *Discovering the Vernacular Landscape*, New Haven: Yale University.

Lopez, Barry. (1989). "Mapping the real geography," *Harper's Magazine* (November) 19-21.

Lowenthal, D. (1985). *The Past is a Foreign Country*. Cambridge: Cambridge University.

MacDonald, G.A. (1974). *East of Superior: A History of Lake Superior Provincial Park*. Toronto: Ontario Ministry of Natural Resources.

MacKay, Donald. (1978). *The Lumberjacks*. Toronto: McGraw-Hill Ryerson.

Marsh, J.S. (1976). *The Human History of the Pukaskwa National Park Area, 1650 to 1975: An Initial Study*. 2 Vols., Pukaskwa National Park, Marathon.

McCullough, Graham A. (1977). *The Commercial Fisheries of the Canadian Great Lakes*. Ottawa: Canadian Parks Service, Environment Canada.

Meinig, D.W. ed. (1979). *The Interpretation of Ordinary Landscapes: Geographical Essays*. New York: Oxford University Press.

Osborne, B.S. (1988). "The iconography of nationhood in Canadian art," in D. Cosgrove, D. and S. Daniels, *The Iconography of Landscape*. Cambridge: University of Cambridge, 162-178.

Osborne, Brian S. (1990), "Organizing the Lake Fisheries: Landscapes and Waterscapes," *Historic Kingston*. 38: 81-94.

—. (1992). "Interpreting a nation's identity: artists as creators of national consciousness," in A. R. H. Baker and G. Biger, *Ideology and Landscape in Historical Perspective*. Cambridge: Cambridge University Press, 230-54.

—. (1992a). "'The Kindling Touch of imagination': C. W. Jefferys and Canadian Identity," in Paul Simpson-Housley and Glen Norcliffe, *A Few Acres of Snow: Literary and Artistic Images of Canada*. Toronto: Dundurn Press, 28-47.

Porteous, D. (1990). *Landscapes of the Mind: Worlds of Sense and Metaphor*. Toronto: University of Toronto.

Revill Associates (1980). *Oral History of Pukaskwa National Park*. Parks Canada, Cornwall.

Sauer, C.O. (1963). "The Morphology of Landscape," in *Land and Life: A Selection from the Writings of Carl Ortwin Sauer*. Berkeley: University of California Press.

Shields, Carol. (1992). "Pioneers: Southeast Ontario," in *Coming to Canada: Poems*. Ottawa, Carleton University Press.

Shields, R. (1992). *Places on the Margin: Alternative Geographies of Modernity*. London: Routledge.

Short, J.R. (1991). *Imagined Country: Society Culture and Environment*. London: Routledge.

Stilgoe, J.R. (1982). *Common Landscape of America, 1850 to 1845*. Newhaven: Yale University.

Thompson, Paul. (1978). *The Voice of the Past: Oral History*. Oxford: Oxford University Press.

Tuan, Yi-Fu. (1974). *Topophilia*. Englewood Cliffs: Prentice Hall.

—. (1977). *Space and Place*. Minneapolis: University of Minnesota.

—. (1982). *Segmented Worlds and Self*. Minneapolis: University of Minnesota.

Werlen, Benno. (1993). *Society, Action and Space: An Alternative Human Geography*. London: Routledge.

Williams, Raymond. (1978). *The Volunteers*. London: Eyre Methuen.

Zelinsky, Wilbur (1988). *Nation into State: The Shifting Symbolic Foundations of American Nationalism*. Chapel-Hill: University of North Carolina.

WHERE HE DIDN'T SPEND HIS SUMMER VACATION: MARTIN LUTHER KING, RACISM AND FUNDY NATIONAL PARK

Alan MacEachern

Only in the last 20 years or so have national park historians begun to assess the uncomfortable fact that parks are a marriage of nature and culture. Parks, we think, should be expressly natural; people are only visitors, they do not belong there. We have begun to understand that national parks are as much cultural constructs as natural ones. They have historically been chosen to fulfil a certain landscape aesthetic, been maintained for specific economic needs, and been interpreted to reinforce a national identity. My paper makes the point that since parks while in operation are also susceptible to the day-to-day interaction of diverse peoples, park archival records can occasionally offer insights that have no direct connection to nature. Park histories, then, can be valuable not only in tracing our changing relationship to nature, but also in tracing our changing relationship to each other.[1]

My story takes place in 1960 at Fundy National Park, nestled along the Bay of Fundy in the southeastern corner of New Brunswick. It was a young park, the land bought only 10 years earlier by the provincial government and transferred to the Canadian National Parks Branch for administration. Offering few recreational opportunities, Fundy was being marketed as a quiet seaside spot for the whole family. It was beginning to justify its existence – that is, it was draw-ing American tourists who the federal and provincial governments hoped would boost the local economy. In 1959, over 40,000 Americans visited Fundy in July and August, up from 10,000 just six years earlier.[2]

In the spring of 1960, Harold DeWolf, a professor of theology at Boston University, wrote the owner of the Fundy Park Chalets to confirm a reservation for him and his wife. There was also, he added, a young couple he wished to invite along:

> Canada's history being what it is, we feel confident that you would treat them well, but we want to make sure, to avoid any possibility of embar-rassment. The friends of whom I speak are a fine Negro minister and his wife. They might want to take also their young children, but would more likely leave them with relatives. The young man is university-trained, with four degrees, an author and in every sense a cultivated gentleman. His wife is also a cultured person of superior character.[3]

DeWolf waited for a response throughout May and June, and finally re-ceived it just before leaving for New Brunswick at the beginning of July. Robert Friars, who had bought the bungalow court from the Parks Branch in 1957 and now managed it independently, confirmed the DeWolfs' reservation, but noted:

> With regard to the friends whom you mentioned ... I feel that I cannot accept the possibility of embarrassment which may arise from this situa-tion. Each day we have over one hundred guests at our site of which a great many are from the New England States, as well as those farther South. For this reason we feel that it would be better not to accommo-date your friends.[4]

Despite the rejection, the DeWolfs chose to travel, only without their young black friends, Dr. and Mrs. Martin Luther King, Jr.[5]

Harold DeWolf had been King's professor and mentor at the University School of Theology, and they had kept up their friendship after King received his PhD there in 1955.[6] It would seem that King periodically relied on DeWolf to help him get away from the rigours of the civil rights movement; King biog-rapher Stephen Oates recounts that in 1956, run down from a long speaking tour, King talked to DeWolf "about arranging a retreat for him in Boston, a sanctuary where he could be alone for 'spiritual renewal and writing.'"[7] In 1960, DeWolf again tried to help relieve his old friend of the stresses that came with being Martin Luther King. It was a very hectic spring for the young preacher. King was the inspirational leader of student sit-ins throughout the South seeking lunch counter desegregation. He had been arrested on trumped up charges of income tax fraud in February, and acquitted by an all-white jury in late May. In June, he met privately with presidential hopeful John F. Kennedy.

King never learned why the planned summer vacation to the Maritimes fell through. Harold and Madeline DeWolf travelled alone to Fundy, and while there tried to meet with Friars and the Park Superintendent, J.D.B. MacFarlane, but without success. So Harold DeWolf wrote the National Parks Branch at Ottawa upon his return and told of the offending correspondence, concluding, "...Mr. Friars' letter, when it came, while putting the blame on possible guests who might object – as is customary in discrimination practices – quite flatly declined to accept our friends at the Chalets."[8]

The flurry of letters that this complaint produced suggests something of the sociology of national parks departments, or perhaps any large, geographically extended bureaucracy. To their credit, the Parks Branch responded quickly and unequivocally. Chief B.I.M. Strong wrote Superintendent MacFarlane:

> The action of refusing accommodation on the basis of colour is certainly something we cannot condone.... I want you to make it clear to Mr. Friars that his arbitrary decision ... was certainly not in keeping with the democracy and freedom of which Canada is so justly proud. He should also be informed that if another incident of this nature comes to our attention corrective attention will be taken by the Department.[9]

The superintendent, perhaps feeling that the episode reflected poorly on him, defended Friars, noting that his rejection, though poorly worded, had only been intended to avoid embarrassment. As to Fundy National Park Chalets not permitting blacks, MacFarlane noted, "In fact it was just about this time that a Mr. and Mrs. Brown from Philadelphia (negroes) stayed at Mr. Friars' for several days."[10] MacFarlane's superiors were more than happy to have this incident interpreted for them as a misunderstanding. A handwritten note from within the Parks Branch on MacFarlane's letter reads, "This is much 'ado' about nothing. Prepare the usual 'will not happen' reply and thank the Supt for this."[11] Chief B.I.M. Strong sent DeWolf a mollifying note that both apologized for and rationalized Friars' letter. He wrote:

> Admittedly, Mr. Friars' statement ... was in bad taste but it was not by any means intended as a direct refusal to make accommodation available.... His action can only be attributed to overzealousness on his part to avoid possible embarrassment being precipitated by other patrons of his establishment. I am satisfied this will not happen again.[12]

Whether DeWolf accepted this explanation or not, he chose to pursue the matter no further.

Can we judge Friars's intentions with complete certainty? Most likely, Friars did tolerate the presence of blacks, but was quite willing to refuse entrance to an individual who sought permission beforehand. His slippery response to DeWolf was worded to let himself off the hook: "I don't discriminate, but others might." Less slippery is his conclusion: "it would be better not to accommodate your friends." As for the National Parks staff, they were quick to choose an interpretation of the episode that would allow it to be forgotten. What was important was to alienate no one, to make Fundy a park that everyone would feel comfortable in, blacks and racists alike. For this reason it was not considered necessary to draft a directive to all parks staff explicitly stating the Canadian National Parks' racial policy. The unpleasantness at Fundy was seen as strictly an isolated incident.

We can make the same mistake, and fail to ask what this isolated incident might possibly say about Canadian racial attitudes. As historians Robin Winks and James Walker point out, Canadians have traditionally felt a certain moral superiority to Americans on the basis of an allegedly more progressive stand on race relations.[13] A major reason for this, however, was that discrimination was always less visible, more anecdotal, since blacks here did not attain the population concentration that they did in the United States. When blacks were relegated to the balcony of a movie theatre, when a black family was refused housing, when blacks were discriminated against in a multitude of small and not so small ways, the offending parties were confronted individually, if at all, and there was little attempt to change general attitudes.[14] We might question how many such isolated incidents are silent parts of Canadian history, and how many will never become public because they do not concern Martin Luther King.

I cannot help thinking of the episode as a missed opportunity. What could have been a sweet moment in Canadian history never took place. One of the century's great men did not spend a short time in blissful anonymity on the banks of the Bay of Fundy, one thousand miles from the front line battle against discrimination, because he himself was the recipient of quiet discrimination here in Canada.

Endnotes

1. I wish to thank Jeannie Prinsen, George Rawlyk, Ian McKay, and Fitzhugh Brundage for their advice in writing this paper.
2. RG84 vol.1036 file F.121.13 vol.2, National Archives of Canada [henceforth, NAC].
3. Harold DeWolf to Robert H. Friars, 1 May 1960, RG84 vol.1025 file F.16.112.1 vol.3, NAC.
4. Friars to DeWolf, 24 June 1960, *Ibid.*
5. The Kings are never mentioned by name in the correspondence at the National Archives. I wish to thank Madeline DeWolf, widow of Harold DeWolf, for confirming that the Kings were the young couple referred to, and for her general recollections of the entire episode.
6. DeWolf's role as advisor on King's PhD has been closely examined since the 1990 discovery that much of the dissertation had ben plagiarized, some of it from a doctoral thesis on which DeWolf had been advisor only three years earlier. See "Becoming Martin Luther King, Jr. – Plagiarism and Originality: A Round Table," *The Journal of American History*, 78.1 (June 1991): 11-123.
7. Stephen B. Oates, *Let the Trumpets Sound: The Life of Martin Luther King, Jr.* (New York: Harper and Row Publishers, 1982), p. 101.
8. DeWolf to National Parks Branch, Department of Northern Affairs and Natural Resources, 21 July 1960, RG84 vol.1025 file F.16.112.1 vol.3, NAC.
9. Strong to MacFarlane, 29 July 1960, *Ibid.*
10. MacFarlane to Strong, 3 August 1960, *Ibid.*
11. Strong to a Mr. Kelly, 5 August 1960, *Ibid.*
12. Strong to DeWolf, 12 August 1960, *Ibid.*
13. Robin W. Winks, *The Blacks in Canada: A History* (Montreal: McGill-Queen's Press, 1981) and James W. St. G. Walker, *Racial Discrimination in Canada: The Black Experience* (Ottawa: Canadian Historical Association Historical Booklet #41, 1985).
14. This problem is discussed in Walker, 16-24, and Winks, especially 464-65.

Conservation, culture et identité : la création du Parc des Laurentides et du Parc de la Montagne Tremblante, 1894-1938

Yves Hébert[1]

L e mouvement de conservation a pris du temps à se développer au Québec. Bien que des influences américaine et canadienne-anglaise soient perceptibles dans l'apparition de ce mouvement, il n'en demeure pas moins que le Québec possède une histoire particulière en regard de la protection de la nature.[2] La création des deux premiers parcs provinciaux au Québec correspond, à n'en pas douter, à un moment significatif dans cette histoire. Toutefois, il s'avère essentiel de référer à des éléments de contextes plus larges pour mieux comprendre l'émergence de ces parcs au Québec :

1. le contexte de l'évolution du mouvement de conservation des ressources naturelles;
2. celui des tendances socio-culturelles des Canadiens français dans lesquelles émergent des représentations collectives liées à l'espace et des rapports à la nature particuliers.

Ces représentations, au même titre que les activités reliées à l'espace, concourrent dans une certaine mesure à façonner des paysages et à forger une identité, celle des Canadiens français.[3]

Le but de cet article est de tenter de comprendre pourquoi les Canadiens français n'ont pas été sensibles à la vocation première de ces premiers parcs à l'époque. Nous croyons que les sensibilités et les représentations du territoire des Canadiens français ont pris du temps à se transformer et à s'orienter graduellement vers les espaces montagneux éloignés du fleuve Saint-Laurent. Dans cette optique, l'influence du milieu anglophone et la situation politico-idéologique du Québec doivent être prises en compte dans l'explication des représentations et des rapports à la nature qu'entretiennent les Canadiens français.

Nous tenterons de démontrer que deux tendances culturelles, très dominantes à la fin du XIXe siècle, co-existent. 1) une tendance provenant du Canada anglais qui encourage la conservation, la création de parcs et le tourisme de villégiature; 2) une tendance visant à l'expansion géo-politique des Canadiens français sur le territoire s'exprimant d'abord et avant tout par la conquête de la nature.

I. La conservation des ressources naturelles et les premiers parcs provinciaux

Il est difficile de bien situer à quel moment le mouvement de conservation émerge au Québec. Au XIXe siècle, on perçoit davantage des initiatives isolées, l'absence d'une concertation et d'une réglementation précise en ce qui a trait à la protection des forêts et du milieu vivant. Bien qu'un certain nombre d'intellectuels et de fonctionnaires des gouvernements provincial et fédéral cherchent à faire adopter des mesures de protection de la forêt et du gibier à différents moments, la croyance aux ressources inépuisables et au territoire à conquérir perdure jusqu'au début du XXe siècle.[4]

Selon Peter Gillis, on s'accorde à situer les origines du mouvement de conservation au Québec dans les années 1880.[5] En effet, suite au congrès de l'Association forestière américaine tenu à Montréal en 1882, des grands principes de base furent adoptés pour mieux conserver la forêt et l'exploiter. D'après William Lynch, commissaire des terres de la Couronne :

La valeur de nos richesses forestières, la rapidité avec laquelle elles sont exploitées et avec laquelle disparaissent celles des contrées qui nous avoisinent, nous imposent comme devoir impérieux l'obligation de veiller à leur conservation et à leur exploitation de la manière la plus judicieuse possible.[6]

Parmi les mesures évoquées lors de ce congrès, l'idée de créer des réserves forestières est mise de l'avant. Ces réserves qui seraient définies en fonction de territoires non colonisables et en vue de besoins futurs pour l'exploitation permettraient une gestion plus rationnelle des ressources forestières.

En 1883, une première réserve forestière apparaît à l'est de la rivière Outaouais, mais elle fut « abolie en 1886 par le Parti National à la suite de l'opposition des intérêts de la colonisation de cette région ».[7] Alors qu'une loi fut adoptée pour la création d'autres réserves forestières, le gouvernement d'Honoré Mercier crût bon de l'abolir en 1888 pour favoriser les colonisateurs.[8] Il faut comprendre ici que ce sont les marchands de bois qui ont été les premiers à promouvoir le principe des réserves forestières à l'époque.[9]

Ces réserves forestières répondaient au problème du déboisement important que connaissait le Québec au cours du XIXe siècle.[10] C'est pourquoi, elles furent créées de nouveau sous les régimes de Lomer Gouin et de Simon-Napoléon Parent.[11] Elles répondaient certes aux besoins d'une gestion plus rationnelle des ressources naturelles mais possédaient leur part de contradictions quant aux objectifs poursuivis. Elles s'inscrivent dans la "doctrine of usefulness" qu'analyse Robert Craig Brown dans une étude sur les Parcs nationaux canadiens.[12]

II. Les premiers parcs provinciaux au Québec

L'histoire des parcs provinciaux au Québec peut être définie en trois grandes périodes : 1895-1938; 1938-1977; 1978-1993. Entre 1895 et 1938, on assiste à la création de quatre Parcs dits nationaux : le Parc des Laurentides, le Parc de la Montagne Tremblante, le Parc de la Gaspésie et le Parc du Mont Orford. Chacun possède en fait sa propre législation. Il n'existe pas encore à cette époque de véritable politique d'ensemble qui intégre les objectifs de ces parcs. De fait, chacun de ces parcs possède une histoire qui lui est propre. Cette histoire nous révèle cependant l'ambiguité qui existe entre les notions de Parc National et de réserve forestière.

Durant la période de 1939 à 1977, aucun parc ne fut créé dans la province. Le gouvernement préféra consolider ceux qui existaient et organiser des réserves de chasse et de pêche. La période de 1977 à nos jours est caractérisée par l'implantation d'un véritable réseau de réserves fauniques à l'intérieur desquelles se retrouvent des parcs de conservation. Par exemple, l'ancien Parc National des

Laurentides, nom changé pour réserve faunique des Laurentides, comprend aujourd'hui le Parc de la Jacques Cartier et le Parc des Grands Jardins. Attardons nous maintenant à l'histoire de la création du Parc de la Montagne Tremblante et du Parc national des Laurentides.

Le Parc de la Montagne Tremblante

Les origines du Parc de la Montagne Tremblante demeurent singulières.[13] En effet, c'est le projet de créer un sanatorium sur la montagne Tremblante, soutenu notamment par le docteur Camille Laviolette de l'Hôpital Notre-Dame de Montréal, qui soutenait l'idée de constituer une réserve forestière sur ce territoire. Croyant aux vertus thérapeutiques de l'air frais et sec indispensable à la guérison des maladies pulmonaires, le docteur Laviolette encouragea vivement le gouvernement à lui concéder des terres sur le versant sud de la montagne.[14] Le 20 mars 1894, le docteur Laviolette faisait donc parvenir sa requête au gouvernement. Après de multiples démarches, le commissaire des terres de la Couronne, Edmund James Flynn, proposa un projet de loi au gouvernement. Puis, suite à un rapport de l'agent des terres de la division de Greenville, A. B. Fillion, le gouvernement adopta le texte de loi créant le 3 janvier 1895 le Parc National de la Montagne Tremblante. Elle fut sanctionnée par le Lieutenant Gouverneur le 12 janvier 1895.[15]

Pour le gouvernement, la création d'un parc dit national répondait à des objectifs précis : créer une réserve forestière et permettre l'établissement d'un sanatorium :

> Que la mise en réserve d'une grande étendue de forêt attenanteau, etenserrant de toute part le site d'un hôpital de ce genre, est une des conditions essentielles de la réussite d'un tel projet tout en permettant l'accomplissement de ce qui se fait déjà ailleurs dans plusieurs Etats et provinces qui nous avoisinent, c'est à dire l'aménagement de la forêt même, la protection du gibier qui l'habite et celle du poisson qui l'abonde dans les lacs et les rivières qui la silllonnent.[16]

Or, dès 1897, la volonté de redéfinir les objectifs du Parc en fonction de ceux adoptés pour le Parc National des Laurentides se fit sentir.[17] En fait, les règlements du Parc des Laurentides touchaient un peu plus la protection du gibier et des forêts. On structura davantage la législation du Parc, et le projet du docteur Laviolette échoua complètement en dépit des nombreux efforts de la Ligue Anti-tuberculeuse de Montréal. En 1924, le ministère des Terres et forêts, par un Arrêté en Conseil, modifia le statut du Parc en fondant des « Réserves forestières permanentes » avec les Parcs existants. Suite à deux autres amendements modifiant la loi et ajoutant des préoccupations liées à la protection de la faune, on retrouvait en 1925 deux entités distinctes :

le Parc de la montagne Tremblante (60 km²) sous la juridiction du ministère de la colonisation, des mines et des Pêcheries, et la réserve forestière de la Montagne-Tremblante (3,1008 km²) sous l'autorité du ministère des Terres et forêts[18].

La création du Parc de la Montagne Tremblante heurta également les intérêts des marchands de bois. Bien que des législations avaient clairement été établies, il n'en demeure pas moins que les compagnies forestières obtinrent des concessions dans les limites de la réserve. La Canadian International Paper, une filiale de la société américaine International Paper devenait propriétaire en 1925 d'une concession à l'ouest du Parc. De plus la compagnie E. B. Eddy de Hull exploita à partir de 1926 le bassin supérieur de la Rivière Rouge pour le bois de pulpe.[19] Au début du xxe siècle, selon Marcel Fournier, une quarantaine de compagnies se partagent le territoire du Parc ainsi qu'une trentaine de Clubs de chasse et pêche.

La création du Parc de la Montagne Tremblante nous apparaît entrer dans des stratégies contradictoires qui tendent à soutenir à la fois les intérêts des marchands de bois et les intérêts de Clubs de chasse et de pêche. Pour certains, dont le député de L'Islet F. G. M. Deschênes, « ces parcs ont pour but de donner des parcs d'amusement aux amis des ministres et d'accroître les dépenses de la province ».[20] La notion de Parc à l'époque ne semble donc pas englober la préservation de la faune et de la flore. Elle sous entend encore moins l'ouverture du territoire aux vacanciers qui recherchent la nature comme lieu de délassement. Ce n'est qu'en 1958 que le Parc du Mont Tremblant sera ouvert au public.

Le Parc National des Laurentides

Le Parc National des Laurentides, actuellement connu sous le nom de Réserve faunique des Laurentides, est situé à une cinquantaine de kilomètres au nord de la ville de Québec. Une route, le boulevard Talbot, traverse le Parc et mène jusqu'à Chicoutimi. Ce territoire montagneux, parsemé de lacs et de rivières, était autrefois considéré comme un vaste réservoir de chasse et de pêche pour les Montagnais. Dès le régime français, une route de Portage appelé "Chemin des Jésuites" traversait le territoire jusqu'au poste de traite de Metabetchouan. Utilisé jusqu'en 1700, ce chemin était abandonné suite à la fermeture du poste de traite. Vers la fin du siècle, une poignée de bourgeois citadins de Québec y organisent un petit nombre de Clubs de chasse et de pêche.

L'idée de créer un parc national retrouve ses origines dans des tractations politiques. En effet, selon Marcel Fournier, l'adoption d'un projet de loi créant le Parc de la Montagne Tremblante soulevait un favoritisme évident pour la région de Montréal. C'est pourquoi le projet de fonder un deuxième parc au nord de Québec apparut comme une solution à ces "jeux de coulisses."[21] C'est en effet Edmund James Flynn, député de Gaspé à l'Assemblée nationale et commissaire des terres de la Couronne, qui contribua le plus à définir les grands objectifs de ce parc et son territoire. Selon Flynn, le moment était opportun d'imiter les Etats-Unis, qui avait fondé le Parc Yellowstone et l'Ontario qui venait tout juste de créer le Parc Algonquin. En fait, il s'agissait d'organiser une réserve afin de protéger les vieilles forêts et tout à la fois protéger le gibier et le poisson.

Le territoire prévu pour le Parc comprenait les sources des rivières Montmorency, Jacques Cartier, Sainte-Anne-de-la-Pérade, Batiscan, Metabetchouan, Upikkauba, Upika, Chicoutimi, Boisvert, à Mars, Ha! Ha!, Murray et Sainte-Anne. Il était constitué aussi d'une grande partie des terres vacantes de la Couronne des comtés de Montmorency, Québec et Charlevoix, le tout formant une superficie de 2531 mille carrés.

Les résolutions qui devaient être considérées pour organiser ce parc diffèrent de celles du Parc de la Montagne Tremblante et touchent davantage la protection du poisson et du gibier et des vieilles forêts.

Attendu qu'il est d'intérêt public d'établir une réserve forestière et parc national dans cette province de manière à protéger ses forêts, le poisson et le gibier, de conserver une réserve d'eau constante et d'encourager ll'étude et la culture des arbres forestiers

[...]

Que ce territoire sera mis à part comme réserve forestière, endroit de pêche et de chasse, parc public et lieu de délassement sous le contrôle du commissaire des Terres de la Couronne, pour les citoyens de la province de, sujet aux dispositions de la loi à être basée résolution et aux règlements qui seront faits en vertu d'icelle, et sera connu sous le nom de "Parc national des Laurentides."[22]

Le 12 janvier 1895, deux textes de lois, forts différents d'ailleurs, furent adoptés par la législature afin de créer les Parcs de la Montagne Tremblante et le Parc National des Laurentides. Dans le texte de loi du Parc des Laurentides, un certain nombre de clauses peuvent être amendées par le Lieutenant gouverneur en conseil pour répondre à des fins de gestion de la faune, de la coupe du bois et de l'exploitation de la forêt. On vise la conservation et la protection du gibier et des oiseaux en général et de tous les animaux sauvages du parc à l'exception des loups, ours ou tout autre animal nuisible ou destructeur. De plus, une clause prévoit l'émission de licenses ou permis d'occupation pour l'exploitation des mines et l'exploitation forestière sous certaines conditions. Bref, la législation qui touche l'organisation du Parc des Laurentides est très similaire à celle qui instaura le Parc Algonquin en Ontario.[23] On est encore loin des préoccupations liées à la préservation des ressources naturelles.

Il est évident que la constitution du Parc des Laurentides n'empêcha jamais l'exploitation forestière. Près de 93% de son territoire était sous concession au tournant du siècle. Cette exploitation n'empêcha pas la fondation de Clubs de chasse et de pêche. Elle eut comme effet positif la construction de chemins qui favorisèrent dans les années qui suivirent la structuration du Parc comme lieu de délassement pour les citoyens de la province. En définitive l'action du gouvernement n'était pas étrangère à la fréquentation de plus en plus croissante du Parc par les citadins.

C'est l'analyse des rapports du surintendant du Parc National des Laurentides qui nous permet de saisir l'implication de l'Etat dans le développement du Parc; elle nous permet également d'appréhender des savoirs et des pratiques quant à la gestion de la faune habitant le Parc. Nous croyons que l'histoire du Parc des Laurentides est similaire à celles d'autres parcs provinciaux puisque leurs gestionnaires ont vécu des problèmes identiques et surtout qu'ils ont perçu et organisé de manière semblable la faune de ces habitats.[24] Jusqu'à la fin des années trente, les grandes préoccupations du Surintendant touchent surtout la gestion de la faune. Mais on ne perçoit pas encore certaines contradictions qui existent quant à l'utilisation du Parc des Laurentides.

On chercha dès lors à protéger le caribou, l'orignal et les cours d'eau susceptibles d'intéresser les "sportsmen" de Québec et des environs. La question du caribou, qui était centrale dans la gestion du parc, souleva des spéculations quant à sa disparition du territoire. Dès la création du parc, l'inspecteur nota une croissance de l'orignal. Avec les années, le nombre d'orignaux et de castors s'accrût. On constata par contre une importante diminution du caribou et sa disparition graduelle du parc. Quant à expliquer le déclin de cette espèce, c'est surtout à des spéculations qu'on a affaire. Le nombre de loups gris augmenta et la quantité de prises pour la chasse aussi. De plus l'exploitation forestière ne fut pas sans conséquences sur l'espèce.

Dans les représentations, le caribou symbolise la nature sauvage et pour plusieurs, il faut le protéger au détriment d'autres espèces. Thomas Fortin, inspecteur du Parc, estimait sa population à plus de 10,000 avant que le Parc des Laurentides ne soit créé. Selon lui, l'espèce est disparue du territoire suite à une migration importante. Par ailleurs, la consanguinité dans le troupeau était considérée comme un facteur négatif par Fortin.[25] Si en 1872, James MacPherson Lemoine encourageait les chasseurs à défier le caribou, quarante ans plus tard, le discours est bien différent[26]. Selon l'ethnologue Paul-Louis Martin, en moins de quinze années, plus de 10,000 caribous disparurent.[27]

La disparition du caribou souleva un problème de taille et parmi les suspects figuraient les chasseurs mais surtout le loup et le castor. Il est vrai que les moyens utilisés pour exterminer le loup étaient discutables pour l'époque. En 1910, W.J.C.Hall, le surintendant du Parc, croyait à l'efficacité d'appâts qu'on fixe sur des crochets d'os de baleine et ne conseillait pas l'utilisation de poison. Deux ans plus tard, il soutient que le poison s'est avéré somme toute très efficace puisque plus d'une vingtaine de loups périrent grâce à ce moyen drastique[28]. Thomas Fortin, pour sa part, plaçait des boulettes de poison sur la glace des lacs et pour piéger le loup il parsemait l'endroit avec des têtes de "volailles."[29] La diminution du loup sur le territoire du Parc des Laurentides n'est sans doute pas étrangère à l'augmentation de la prime pour chaque tête que le gouvernement versait depuis 1861 afin de limiter les ravages de cet animal dit nuisible. En 1906, justement, la prime passa de 5$ à 15$ puis elle fut augmentée à 25$ par tête en 1931.[30]

Le castor figure aussi au banc des accusés quant à la disparition du caribou. En effet, on croit que la croissance du castor aux abords des lacs du Parc des Laurentides a pour effet de relever le niveau de l'eau et de refouler vers d'autres régions le caribou[31]. C'est pourquoi, à partir de 1906, le surintendant permettait la prise des castors "dans certaines eaux peu profondes, où ils détruisent le poisson et le gibier."[32] On chercha aussi à l'éloigner des Clubs de chasse et de pêche en 1912. La gestion de la faune qui se faisait donc à l'époque était intimement liée aux intérêts des Clubs de chasse et de pêche.

Cette gestion au fil des ans évolua et dépassa le cadre des intérêts individuels pour atteindre cette fois une dimension plus écologique. Avec la parution d'ouvrages spécialisés, notamment par la Commission géologique du Canada, sur la botanique et la faune, on comprenait relativement mieux les liens écologiques entre la faune et la flore.[33] De fait, en 1915, le surintendant du Parc National des Laurentides semble plus attentif au problème de la protection des oiseaux insectivores. Au ministre des Terres et forêts W. J. C. Hall écrit :

> Quant aux oiseaux insectivores, vous avez approuvé ma recommandation d'établir une saison de prohibition perpétuelle dans le Parc, et avez de plus défendu de molester ces oiseaux, à cause de leur valeur économique. Cela sera incorporé dams les règlements revisés du Parc et nous pouvons dire au moins que nous avons fait notre part.
>
> [...]
>
> C'est donc une obligation évidente pour tout pays d'aider à perpétuer la vie des oiseaux, et c'est aussi son intérêt direct. Faisons donc notre bonne part en ce sens, dans la province de Québec. Examinons nos lois avec soin et voyons s'il n'y aurait pas des modifications à y faire; s'il s'y trouve des lacunes, qu'on y supplée, et que l'on fasse tous les efforts possibles pour que ces lois soient strictement observées.[34]

On connaît peu le dévelopement du Parc National des Laurentides entre 1914 et 1930. A partir des années 1920, le ministère des Terres et forêts se préoccupa davantage de sa gestion. On chercha dès lors à le structurer et à lui donner une plus grande fonction récréative. En 1920, le Parc des Laurentides ne compte ni chemins, ni camps, ni organisation en tant que telle. A partir de 1920, Joseph-Edouard Perrault, député d'Arthabaska décida "que l'heure était arrivée de faire du Parc National 'un lieu de délassement.'"[35] Tout était donc à faire et le budget était du même coup insuffisant. C'est à partir de cette période que le gouvernement décida d'investir les quelques revenus provenant des droits de chasse et de pêche pour l'améliorer. Un premier camp, le Camp Mercier, apparut en 1920. Il s'agissait d'une petite hôtellerie agréable pour un début. On raconte que le Gouverneur Général du Canada et Lady Wellington y firent un séjour dès son ouverture. Par la suite d'autres camps s'ajoutèrent au Parc. Bref, en une décennie, une vingtaine de camps furent contruits ou aménagés à partir de constructions déjà existantes. En 1928, le gouvernement décida d'interdire complètement la chasse sur le territoire. Il s'orienta avec les années vers des objectifs qui se rapprochaient davantage de la préservation de la flore et de la faune.

En somme, on peut dire que le gouvernement se préoccupa davantage de la préservation des ressources du Parc à la fin des années 1920. Cela coïncidait avec la montée du mouvement de préservation qui émergeait un peu partout en Amérique du Nord. Ce qu'il faut retenir de l'histoire du Parc des Laurentides, c'est la présence d'une double perception du concept de parc. Le Parc est à la fois considéré comme réserve forestière où l'on protège la forêt pour les besoins futurs et comme réserve de chasse et de pêche. On se représente le Parc aussi comme un lieu symbolique qui permet la survie de certaines espèces comme le caribou. Les ingénieurs forestiers de la province de Québec ont coutume de caractériser le Parc de la Montagne Tremblante et le Parc National des Laurentides comme étant des Réserves forestières polyvalentes.[36]

III. Représentations de l'espace et rapports à la nature des Canadiens français

L'histoire des premiers Parcs de conservation au Québec est représentative d'une manière de percevoir la nature sauvage et les vastes territoires non occupés par l'être humain. Elle correspond à l'univers cognitif d'un petit groupe d'hommes d'affaires, de marchands et de membres du gouvernement provincial.[37] Mais qu'en est-il des représentations de l'espace des Canadiens français, de leur imaginaire et de leurs rapports à la nature ? A l'instar de Jacques Mathieu et de Jacques Lacoursière, nous croyons que l'imaginaire relatif à l'espace renvoie à un ensemble de représentations, de symboles et de mythes qui contribuent en définitive à définir l'identité québécoise. Ces représentations déterminent dans une bonne mesure les rapports qu'entretiendront les Canadiens français avec la nature.

L'histoire du Québec fait apparaître deux manières de se représenter l'espace et la nature. D'une part, considérant l'évolution historique du Québec et les courants d'idées dominants, notamment influencés par l'Eglise catholique, on perçoit l'espace et la nature dans la perspective de la conquête et du défi. D'autre part, une tendance à vouloir apprivoiser la nature émerge. Cette manière de se représenter l'espace, les paysages et la nature trouve ses origines dans une nouvelle sensibilité culturelle, influencée notamment par ce qu'on appelé le sentiment du pittoresque. Cette nouvelle sensibilité à la nature s'inscrit désormais dans la manière d'organiser l'espace de vie. Mais ces deux grandes tendances ne sont pas uniques au Québec.[38]

La conquête du territoire

On a longtemps perçu le Québec comme un territoire à conquérir. Cette représentation est la base de deux idéologies : 1) l'idéologie clérico-nationaliste qui prône l'attachement à l'agriculture et la sauvegarde des acquis culturels des Canadiens français; 2) le libéralisme qui valorise l'exploitation intensive des ressources naturelles pour le bien être de la collectivité.

Fortement influencée par le clergé catholique canadien-français, l'idéologie clérico-nationaliste cherche surtout à contrer l'émigration des Canadiens-français aux Etats-Unis et l'exode vers les villes. Cette idéologie vise entre autres la colonisation des terres neuves. Au cours du XIXe siècle, les terroirs de la vallée du Saint-Laurent ne suffisent plus aux besoins de la population en croissance, et toute la propagande idéologique sur la colonisation est dirigée vers les anciennes paroisses rurales. L'analyse de cette idéologie nous montre qu'elle repose sur un ensemble de mythes et de symboles qui valorisent le nord et la conquête des terres neuves. On retrouve ainsi un mythe du Nord et un mythe de la terre promise qui symbolisent la conquête du territoire.

Le mythe du nord a nourri l'idéologie de la survivance culturelle des Canadiens français. Ce mythe, nous dit Christian Morissonneau, est consolateur et régénérateur. "L'espace et les ressources illimitées engendrent des espoirs et des promesses toujours entretenues sinon toujours fondées."[39] Face à l'expansion du monde anglo-saxon, celle-ci étant perçue comme une menace, et face à un sentiment de perte du continent, on a donc dirigé les Canadiens français vers le nord, vers la terre promise.[40] Les mythes qui leur sont associés correspondent à des représentations du territoire qui ont surtout été exprimées par une certaine élite du Québec qui voyait surtout la colonisation comme une réponse à l'émigration aux Etats-Unis. Certains, comme Ivanhoë Caron, missionnaire-colonisateur en Abitibi de 1912 à 1923, vantent le nord mais aussi ses ressources naturelles à exploiter. Le nord est désormais perçu comme un territoire à conquérir pour un projet collectif bien déterminé.[41]

Pour sa part, le mythe de la terre promise, finement étudié par Morissonneau, renvoie à une imagerie biblique inspirée. Mais ce mythe "doit être entendue comme la dialectique entre le repli sur soi et le désir de l'expansion."[42] Dès lors, c'est le nord qui doit être entendue comme la terre promise.

Mais quelle est la place de la nature dans ces représentations ? De quelle manière ces représentations agissent t'elles sur les rapports concrets à la nature ? Il est vrai que le projet colonisateur entretenait des contradictions quant à la manière de percevoir la nature. Ainsi, on cherche à dominer la nature et à permettre l'établissement des colons. En revanche, une fois la prise de possession du territoire, on valorise cette nature. La plus belle illustration de cette affirmation se retrouve dans *l'Abatis* de Félix-Antoine Savard, écrivain et ancien missionnaire-colonisateur en Abitibi. D'ailleurs la nature est l'inspiration du poète qui ne tarit pas d'éloges devant le travail acharné des colons de l'Abitibi. "On n'échappe pas à la nature" dit-il dans cet ouvrage considéré comme un des classiques au Québec.[43] Ainsi, pour F. A. Savard la colonisation est d'abord une nécessité pour instaurer la paix sociale. Il faut coloniser, maîtriser la nature puis ensuite louanger cette nature.

Il n'a fallu qu'un peu plus de cinquante ans pour occuper à peu près toutes les terres colonisables de la province. On a gagné ainsi de nouvelles régions, le Saguenay-Lac Saint-Jean, le Témiscamingue, l'Abitibi et les terres intérieures de la Vallée du Saint-Laurent. La prise de possession de ces vastes territoires se faisait par vagues successives de peuplement organisé surtout par les Sociétés de colonisation. La colonisation et l'exploitation forestière sous-entendent il est vrai des rapports à la nature déterminants, caractérisés par le recul du couvert végétal et par le refoulement de la faune vers des régions sauvages. On a pendant longtemps déploré les coupes abusives opérées par les colons qui délaissent leur lots.[44] De plus, certaines pratiques de chasse et de pêche ont été condamnées par plusieurs dans les zones de colonisation. Au Saguenay-Lac Saint-Jean, nous dit l'historien Russel Bouchard, la perdrix blanche et le lagopède des saules subirent les assauts de chasseurs peu scrupuleux.[45] L'explication à ces pratiques réside sans doute dans l'absence de réglementations et de législations du gouvernement en matière de gestion de la flore et de la faune. La colonisation entretenait donc des rapports de domination avec la nature.

Pour sa part, le libéralisme sous-entend le même type de rapports à la nature. Certes on connait bien les postulats du libéralisme économique. Nous savons qu'il vise l'exploitation des ressources naturelles pour le bien être de la collectivité. Au Québec, les tenants du libéralisme se retrouvent surtout dans les milieux d'affaires francophones et anglophones des villes et des "grosses paroisses" au tournant du siècle. Gagnés par l'individualisme, les marchands et les membres des professions libérales soutiennent que le bonheur est conditionnel à l'épanouissement de l'individu et de sa propriété.[46]

La conquête du territoire s'est donc opérée à la manière des tenants du clérico-nationalisme prônant la colonisation et à la manière des hommes d'affaires qui ont adopté les principes du libéralisme économique. Au cours du XIXe siècle et jusque vers la crise, on s'est donc représenté le Québec comme un territoire et des ressources à conquérir. A l'instar de Jacques Mathieu et de Jacques Lacoursière nous croyons que :

> le rapport de la collectivité québécoise à l'espace aurait servi à compenser une réalité historique difficile à supporter. Elle aurait produit un discours valorisant ses forces et ses aptitudes face à la nature. Les constants recommencements que révèle l'exploitation du territoire auraient également touché les sensibilités. Dans ce pays neuf, chacun aurait dû en quelque sorte, se faire pionnier, conquérir sa part de territoire, pour s'aménager un espace de vie.[47]

Un territoire et une nature à apprivoiser

Au cours du xixe siècle, une nouvelle sensibilité à l'égard de la nature commence à poindre au Québec. Elle s'inscrit notamment dans la littérature, la peinture et les récits de voyageurs. Elle se retrouve aussi dans les usages sociaux de la nature. Par la villégiature et le tourisme de plein air on cherche dès lors à apprivoiser la nature et à apprécier les paysages uniques.

Ce sentiment de la nature prend notamment ses origines dans le courant romantique dans lequel émergent deux doctrines esthétiques qui prévalaient au cours du xixe siècle : le pittoresque et le sublime. Inspiré par les écrits des anglais Uvedale Price et William Gilpin à la fin du xviiie siècle, le pittoresque repose sur la connaissance qu'on acquiert grâce aux perceptions sensibles par opposition à la raison et au cartésianisme qui dominaient au xviiie siècle.[48]

Au Québec, le courant pittoresque a été bien implanté. Il a davantage été exprimé par des bourgeois anglophones résidants dans les villes du Québec et par des membres de la bourgeoisie canadienne-française dans les régions. Dans cette ligne de pensée, la nature est perçue de manière plus sensible de la part de ce groupe d'individus. On recherche donc des lieux et des paysages qui provoquent des sentiments de nostalgie et de mélancolie. Ainsi, la nostalgie du paradis perdu, la mélancolie provoquée par le passé et par les paysages bucoliques s'entremêlent et incitent à la création artistique sinon à un usage plus respectueux de la nature. Le pittoresque apparaît donc comme l'évocation d'une nature à retrouver et d'un passé à valoriser.[49] Son expression se retrouve surtout dans la villégiature et le tourisme.

Au xixe siècle, le courant romantique a surtout été défini et reproduit par la bourgeoisie d'affaires et par les membres des professions libérales. Au Québec, les premiers lieux de villégiature furent créés par cette bourgeoisie. C'est surtout en bordure du Saint-Laurent et des grands lacs, comme le lac Memphremagog, que ces premiers sites apparurent. De fait, entre 1850 et 1920, le tourisme se développa rapidement aux abords du fleuve et près du fjord du Saguenay.

Le fleuve Saint-Laurent a occupé une place importante dans les représentations et dans la culture. Il ne faut surtout pas oublier que le fleuve a d'abord été le facteur principal de cohésion du développement du pays et facteur d'intégration et de dynamisation des socio-économies.[50] Dans l'imaginaire collectif, le fleuve symbolise la peur, le défi et l'émerveillement. Il symbolise aussi un passé glorieux avec ses premiers explorateurs.[51]

La conjugaison de milieux montagneux et des abords du fleuve constituaient des sites exceptionnels pour le développement du courant pittoresque. Les plus célèbres se retrouvent dans Charlevoix, en Gaspésie et dans Kamouraska.[52] On recherche la beauté des lieux, la nature vierge et l'air salin. Adolphe Basile Routhier, juge, auteur, chroniqueur et auteur du O'Canada, se vante même d'avoir fondé à Saint-Irénée les Bains, la plus belle place d'eau en Amérique du nord.[53] Dans Kamouraska, notamment à Rivière Ouelle et à Rivière-du-Loup les membres de la bourgeoisie canadienne-française ainsi que des auteurs tels qu'Arthur Buies se retrouvent aux abords du fleuve dans des villas cossues.[54] Au début, les attitudes des résidents des vieilles paroisses du comté de Kamouraska à l'endroit des "étrangers" venus apprivoiser les rivages révélaient, selon Horace Miner, un conflit entre les mœurs traditionnelles et les manières urbaines. Les villageois durent ainsi s'adapter à cette vogue grandissante liée aux loisirs de la plage et ce en dépit des sermons des curés.[55]

L'expression du pittoresque se retrouve désormais dans le paysage. C'est dans l'architecture qu'il faut remarquer des influences de ce courant. D'ailleurs, l'apparition des villas marque l'émergence de nouvelles manières de percevoir et d'aménager la nature. Ces "cottages," qu'on retrouve en bordure du fleuve et dans les villes qui possèdent de grands boisés, s'inspirent surtout de l'architecture néo-classique. On cherche désormais à créer une harmonie entre la maison, le site et le jardin. Inspirée grandement par l'héritage anglais et américain, cette manière d'aménager la nature gagna peu à peu les régions rurales.[56]

Les Canadiens français ont été sensibles à ces nouvelles valeurs et les usages sociaux de la nature se transformèrent à partir des années 1930. Ils empruntèrent au courant pittoresque et grâce à l'expansion du réseau routier, le tourisme gagna les régions et surtout la Gaspésie. Sur la Côte-du-Sud, dans le Bas Saint-Laurent et en Gaspésie on apprivoise le fleuve. Ainsi, au début du siècle toute une ligne de petits chalets se développe en bordure de l'affluent. L'attrait pour les Iles se fait également sentir. L'Île-d'Orléans, et l'Île-aux-Coudres sont recherchés par les villégiateurs. A partir des années 1930 et plus particulièrement après la seconde guerre mondiale, les citadins redécouvrent la campagne grâce aux campagnes publicitaires du gouvernement en faveur du tourisme.

Cette nouvelle sensibilité gagna t'elle les paysages montagneux éloignés du fleuve? Nombreux sont les textes qui démontrent que la montagne est à craindre. Le pays montagneux est dur, inaccessible et représente l'isolement de l'être humain[57]. Ce nord montagneux est déchiré par des gouffres béants et des gorges profondes. Considéré comme un milieu obscur et ténébreux cette partie du pays n'est qu'une terre de torrents et de convulsions.[58] Cette vision négative de l'espace montagneux aurait peut être contribué à renforcer le mythe du nord qui vise la conquête et la maîtrise de la nature.[59] Bien que ces descriptions soient empruntées à des hommes de lettres, il n'en demeure pas moins que les contrastes qu'on observe dans la géographie du Québec ont contribué à créer des représentations positives et négatives qui marquèrent l'imaginaire des Canadiens français. Ajoutons que c'est par la médiation des rites religieux que se vivaient les appréhensions et les peurs à l'égard de cette nature.[60] Les années 1930 et suivantes peuvent être caractérisées par une nouvelle perception des paysages et par l'apparition de nouveaux usages sociaux de la nature. On apprivoise graduellement les montagnes du Québec et les Parcs provinciaux grâce à l'évolution des loisirs de plein air mais surtout grâce à l'expansion du réseau routier du Québec.

* * *

Revenons donc à notre point de départ. Comment expliquer que les Canadiens français n'ont pas été sensibles à la création des premiers parcs provinciaux dès leur création ? Comment expliquer le fait qu'ils ont tardé à jouir de ces espaces sur le plan esthétique et sur le plan des loisirs de plein air ? Les réponses à ces questions sont multiples.

La première raison pourrait se trouver dans le fait que les premiers parcs provinciaux du Québec furent créés par un petit groupe d'hommes d'affaires et d'hommes politiques qui cherchaient d'abord et avant tout à protéger leurs intérêts. Ainsi, les premières réserves forestières, conçues pour éloigner les colonisateurs, permirent aux marchands de bois de conserver la matière ligneuse pour les besoins futurs. En créant le Parc National des Laurentides, et en protégeant le poisson et le gibier le gouvernement favorisa du même coup les Clubs de chasse et de pêche. Ainsi, ces parcs furent peu accessibles aux Canadiens français.

En deuxième lieu, nous croyons que les représentations du territoire des Canadiens français et de leurs rapports à la nature ne sont pas homogènes. Ces représentations et ces rapports à la nature sont différenciés dépendant des espaces ou des paysages perçus. On perçoit les espaces vierges, notamment le Nord du Québec comme des territoires à conquérir et ce dans l'optique de la survivance de la nation. Les rapports à la nature qui font suite à ces représentations sont caractérisés par l'exploitation intensive de la forêt et des ressources naturelles. Dans cette perspective, la constitution de parcs provinciaux est un frein à l'expansion colonisatrice.

Par ailleurs, au XIXe siècle, les Canadiens français se représentent le fleuve et ses rives de manière différente. Les paysages bucoliques de la vallée du Saint-Laurent, les paysages contrastés de Charlevoix et de la Gaspésie marquèrent les représentations d'une manière plus positive avec le temps. Les rapports à la nature en bordure du fleuve sont intimement liés aux activités économiques et aux modes de production des populations qui vivent de la pêche et de l'agriculture. Ils nous apparaissent plus harmonieux. Les Canadiens français auraient donc privilégié les paysages du fleuve au détriment des Parcs provinciaux.

En définitive les représentations des Canadiens français ont joué un rôle déterminant dans la manière d'occuper l'espace et dans les rapports à la nature. La création des premiers parcs provinciaux constituent à notre avis un épiphénomène dans la constitution de ces représentations. Il faut donc attendre les années 1930 pour observer des changements dans les usages sociaux de la nature et ce par le biais du tourisme et de la villégiature. Rappelons que l'influence anglo-saxonne aura été déterminante dans l'articulation de ces changements.

Notes

1. L'auteur est historien-consultant. Il a été chercheur à l'Institut québécois de recherche sur la culture et au Dictionnaire biographique du Canada. Il se spécialise en histoire régionale et en histoire environnementale. Il est co-auteur d'une *Histoire de la Côte-du-Sud* à paraître à l'IQRC.

2. En ce qui concerne l'étude des influences étrangères sur le mouvement de conservation en général voir : Michel F. Girard. "Conservation and the Gospel of Efficiency : un modèle de gestion de l'environnement venu d'Europe," *Histoire sociale/Social History*, 23,45 (mai 1990) : 63-79.

3. Jacques Mathieu et Jacques Lacoursière. *Les mémoires québécoises*. Sainte-Foy, Les Presses de l'université Laval, 1991. p. 59.

4. Yves Hébert. "La genèse de la pensée écologique au Québec, 1800-1940," Dans *To see ourselves/to save ourselves Ecology and Culture in Canada/Conscience et survie, Ecologie et culture au Canada, Canadian Issues/Thèmes canadiens* 13 (1991): 33.

5. Peter Gillis "Canadian Federal Forest Reserves, 1883-1933 : A Parallel Experiment," dans Harold K. Steen. *Origins of the National Forests: A Centennial Symposium.* Durham, Forest History Society, 1992. p. 46.

6. Rapport du Commissaire des terres de la Couronne, William Lynch, *Documents de la Session de la province de Québec*, 1881-82. p. VI.

7. Michel F. Girard. *La forêt dénaturée : les discours sur la conservation de la forêt québécoise au tournant du xxᵉ siècle.* Thèse de maîtrise (Histoire), Université d'Ottawa, 1988. p. 129.

8. Thomas R. Roach et Peter Gillis. *Lost Initiatives: Canada's Forest Industries, Forest Policy and Forest Conservation.* New York, Greenwood Press, 1986. p. 112.; Bruce Hodgins et al. "The Ontario and Quebec Experiments in Forest reserves", *Journal of Forest History* (janv. 1982): 24.

9. Robert Peter Gillis. "The Ottawa Lumber Barons and the Conservation Movement, 1880-1914," *Journal of Canadian Studies /Revue d'études canadiennes*, 9, 1 (février 1974): 21.

10. Au XIXe siècle, le Québec participa à l'effort canadien d'approvisionner l'Angleterre en bois de construction. L'exploitation de la forêt sur le plan économique répondait d'abord à la demande de l'Angleterre victime d'un blocus continental, ensuite aux intérêts des marchands du Québec. Linteau, Durocher, Robert. *Histoire du Québec contemporain, de la confédération à la crise.* Montréal, Boréal Express, 1979. pp. 131-133.

11. C'est près de 165,109 milles carrés qui ont été alloués à la création des réserves forestière suivantes : Labrador, Saint-Maurice et Ottawa, Bonaventure, Rimouski, Rivière Ouelle, Témiscouta, Chaudière, Barachois. Bruce Hodgins. p. 27.

12. Robert Craig Brown. "The Doctrine of Usefulness: Natural Resource and National Park Policy in Canada, 1887-1914," in J. C. Nelson and R. C. Sace. *The Canadian National Parks. Today and Tomorrow.* Calgary, National and Provincial Parks Association of Canada, 1968. pp. 95-108.

13. Le Parc de la Montagne Tremblante est situé à environ 80 kilomètres au nord de Montréal.

14. Marcel Fournier. *Histoire du parc du Mont Tremblant, des origines à 1981.* Montréal, ministère du Loisir, de la chasse et de la pêche, direction régionale de Montréal, 1981. p. 14.

15. Québec, *Statuts du Québec 1895*, Loi établissant le Parc de la Montagne Tremblante (58 Victoria, chapitre 23); Marcel Fournier, *Op.cit.*, p. 78.

16. *Débats de l'Assemblée législative de la province du Québec*, (1896): 206.

17. Marcel Fournier, p. 22.

18. *Ibid.* p. 29.

19. *Ibid.* p. 32.
20. *Débats de l'Assemblée législative de la province de Québec*, (1896). p. 263.
21. *Ibid.* p. 19.
22. *Débats de l'Assemblée législative de la province de Québec*, (1894): p. 219.
23. Corporation professionnelle des ingénieurs forestiers du Québec, *Parcs, territoires et zones analogues. Plein air et conservation au Québec.* s.l., La Corporation, 1974. p. 8; Jean Luc Bourdages. *Les parcs naturels du Canada et du Québec.* Montréal, Université de Montréal, Faculté des Arts et des sciences, 1984. p. 55. Ontario, Agonquin National Park, Chapter 8, 56 Victoria.
24. Thomas R. Dunlap. "Ecology, Nature and Canadian National Park Policy: Wolves, Elk,and Bison as a Case Study," in *To see Ourselves/To save ourselves, Ecology and culture in Canada/Conscience et survie, Ecologie et culture au Canada, Canadian issues/ Thèmes canadiens (Association d'études canadiennes/Association for Canadian Studies*, 13 (1991): 141.
25. Damase Fortin. *Thomas Fortin, le dernier de nos coureurs des bois, le Parc National des Laurentides.* Québec, les Éditions Garneau, 1945. pp. 110-111.
26. James MacPherson Lemoine est surtout connu comme chroniqueur et homme de lettres à Québec à la fin du XIXe siècle. Voir : *L'album du touriste, archéologie, histoire littérature, sport.* Québec, Imprimé par Augustin Côté, 1872. pp. 200-203.
27. Paul Louis Martin. *Histoire de la chasse au Québec.* Montréal, Boréal, 1980. p. 167.
28. W. C. J. Hall. "Rapport concernant le Parc National pour l'année 1912," *Documents de la Session de la province de Québec*, Tome 2, no. 46 (1912): pp. 60-61.
29. Damase Fortin. pp. 88-89.
30. Daniel Banville. *Le contrôle des prédateurs du gros gibier au Québec de 1905 à 1980.* Québec, Ministère du loisir, de la chasse et de la pêche, Direction générale de la faune, 1981. (Document non publié, conservé au ministère). p. 12.
31. W. C. J. Hall. "Rapport sur le parc des Laurentides," *Documents de la Session de la province de Québec*, Tome I,(1906) Rapport du ministre des Terres et forêts, Appendice no. 30. pp. 130-131.
32. W. C. J. Hall. "Rapport sur le parc National des Laurentides," Rapport du ministère des terres et forêts, *Documents de la Session de la province de Québec*, (1906-1907): 93.
33. Nous faisons allusion ici à la publication de John Macoun et James M. Macoun. *Catalogue des oiseaux du Canada.* Ottawa, Ministère des mines, Commission géologique du Canada, 1915.
34. W. C. J. Hall. "Rapport sur le Parc National des Laurentides pour l'année 1914-15," Rapport du ministère des terres et forêts, *Documents de la Session de la province de Québec*, Tome 1 (1916). Appendice no. 18. p. 33.
35. L. A. Richard. "Le Parc National des Laurentides," Rapport du ministère de la colonisation, de la chasse et de la pêche, *Documents parlementaires de la province de Québec*, Tome (1931). p. 528.
36. Jean Luc Bourdages, p. 56.

37. L'univers cognitif renvoie ici à la manière de percevoir l'environnement et au bagage culturel et scientifique, ainsi qu'aux attitudes, valeurs et stéréotypes qui déterminent l'action. Voir Irwin Altman et Martin Chemers. *Culture and Environment*. Monterey, Brooks / Cole, 1980. p. 45.

38. Voir à ce sujet l'ouvrage du sociologue Jean-Paul Bozonnet.*Des monts et des mythes. L'imaginaire social de la montagne*. Grenoble, Presses universitaires de Grenoble, 1992.

39. Christian Morrissonneau. *La terre promise : le mythe du nord québécois*. Montréal, Hurtubise HMH, 1978. p. 176.

40. Dean R. Louder, Christian Morissonneau et Eric Waddell. "Picking Up the Pieces of a Shattered Dream: Quebec and French America," *Journal of Geography*, 4,1 (Fall/ Winter 1983): 48.

41. Andrée Héroux et Yves Hébert. "Ivanhoë ... un géographe utile", *Géographes* (Société des professeurs de Géographie du Québec / Association des géographes profession- nels du Québec), 2 (nov. 1992): 64-65.

42. Morissonneau, p. 80.

43. Félix-Antoine Savard. *L'Abatis*. Montréal, Fides, 1943. p. 11.

44. Normand Séguin. *La conquête du sol au 19e siècle*. Sillery, Boréal Express, p. 134.

45. Russel Bouchard. "La faune menacée... un vieux problème au Saguenay". *Saguenayensia*, 29,4 (oct.-déc. 1987): 14.

46. Fernande Roy. *Progrès, harmonie, liberté. Le libéralisme des milieux d'affaires francopho- nes à Montréal au tournant du siècle*. Montréal, Boréal, 1988. p. 269.

47. Lacoursière et Mathieu, p. 92.

48. France Gagnon Pratte. *L'architecture et la nature à Québec au dix-neuvième siècle : les villas*. Québec, ministère des affaires culturelles, Musée du Québec, 1980. p. 89.; Patricia Jasen. "Romanticism, Modernity, and the Evolution of Tourism on the Niagara Frontier, 1790-1850," *Canadian Historical Review*, 72, 3 (1991): 283-288.

49. Jane Wright. *L'architecture pittoresque au Canada*. Ottawa, Parcs Canada, Environne- ment Canada, 1984. p. 14.

50. Serge Courville, Jean-Claude Robert et Normand Séguin. "Le Saint-Lauent, artère de vie : réseau routier et métiers de la navigation au xixe siècle," *Cahiers de géographie du Québec*, 34, 92 (sept. 1990): 181,194.

51. Mathieu et Lacoursière, pp. 46-48.

52. Yves Beauregard et Alyne Lebel. "Quelques plages au bord du majestueux", *Cap-aux- Diamants*, (Numéro spécial sur le Saint-Laurent), 22 (été 1990).

53. Yves Hébert. "Adolphe Basile Routhier," *Dictionnaire biographique du Canada* Vol 13. A paraître. Voir aussi : Philippe Dubé. *Deux cent ans de villégiature dans Charlevoix, l'histoire du pays visité*. Québec, Presses de l'Université Laval, 1986.

54. Kamouraska peut être considéré comme le premier site de villégiature au Québec. Voir Roger Brière. "Les grands traits de l'évolution du tourisme au Québec," *Bulletin de l'Association des géographes de l'Amérique française*, 11 (sept. 1967): 86.

55. Horace Miner. *Saint-Denis : un village québécois*. Montréal, Hurtubise, HMH, 1985.

56. "Cette attention accordée à l'aménagement de la nature environnant les résidences s'inscrit dans une révolution de la relation maison-jardin, concept romantique véhiculé par l'architecte paysagiste William Kent en Angleterre et repris à traveres le monde par la suite." France Gagnon Pratte. p. 88.

57. Léopold Lamontagne éd. *Arthur Buies (1840-1901)*. Montréal et Paris, Fides, p.59.

58. George Monro Grand, D.D. *Le Québec pittoresque*. Ouvrage présenté par Robert Lahaise, Montréa, Hurtubise, HMH, 1985. p. 231.

59. Le sociologue Jean-Paul Bozonnet a observé cette tendance pour la France. Dans l'imaginaire social, selon lui, les zones de montagnes qui offrent un paysage désordonnée "s'offrent logiquement comme espace à conquérir, domestiquer et à coloniser". Jean-Paul Bozonnet. *Des monts et des mythes*. p. 25.

60. Benoit Lacroix. "Que racontaient nos ancêtres ?" dans *Ecologie et environnement*, Cahiers de recherche éthique, no. 9 Montréal, Fides, 1983. pp. 44-49.

At the Foot of the Mountain:

Preliminary Thoughts on

The Alpine Club of Canada,

1906-1950

PearlAnn Reichwein

The Alpine Club of Canada (ACC) was established in 1906 to put Canadians on the mountaineering map.[1] Despite the popularity of the Canadian Rockies as a tourist destination among foreign travellers in the late-nineteenth century, Canadians were largely indifferent to their mountains.[2] Thus alpinists from Britain, the United States and Europe were free to explore the Canadian Rockies and claim the prestige of many discoveries and first ascents. Early railway tourism had steamed through the Rockies in the 1880s with the advance of the Canadian Pacific Railway (CPR). Wilderness beauty – combined with natural wonders such as glaciers, hot springs and ice caves – evoked the awe and curiosity of many Victorian rail travellers enticed to visit the "Canadian Alps."[3] Fostered by transcontinental railway expansion, the first Dominion park was created in 1885 when Ottawa designated the Banff Hotsprings Reserve, renamed Rocky Mountains Park in 1887, the precursor of today's Banff National Park. From the 1890s to 1920, national parks along the railways offered relatively easy access to exciting prospects during Canada's golden age of mountaineering. The ACC played a central role in bringing this new frontier to the attention of Canadians and the world.

In March 1906, Arthur Wheeler (1860-1945), a Dominion Lands surveyor, and Elizabeth Parker (1856-1944), the literary editor of the *Manitoba Free Press*, called a small circle of delegates to Winnipeg for the founding meeting of the Alpine Club of Canada.[4] Intent on promoting alpinism and the Canadian "mountain heritage," the ACC assumed Canada's mantle in the world of mountaineering. As a distinctly Canadian alpine club, the ACC manifested both organisational nationalism and the values of a socially active Canadian middle class. From its inception, the club became the organisational backbone of Canadian alpinism, and an influential partner in the management of the national mountain parks. In this context, the following paper is a preliminary discussion of the Alpine Club as a key stakeholder in national park development from 1906 to 1950, drawing on primary research conducted at the National Archives of Canada and the Whyte Museum of the Canadian Rockies Archives.

In 1906, the founders of the Alpine Club built much more than a simple sport club for climbers. Institutionally modeled after "The Alpine Club," Britain's queen of alpine clubs founded in 1857, the ACC was a sophisticated alpine organisation designed to pursue several objectives. The articles of the 1906 ACC constitution reflected aims specifically tailored for Canadian circumstances:

- The promotion of scientific study and exploration of Canadian alpine and glacial regions.
- The cultivation of art in relation to mountain scenery.
- The education of Canadians to an appreciation of their mountain heritage.
- The encouragement of the mountain craft and the opening of new regions as a national playground.
- The preservation of the natural beauties of the mountain places and of the fauna and flora in their habitat.
- The interchange of literature with other alpine and geographical organisations.[5]

Since creating this charter almost 90 years ago, the ACC has maintained extraordinary continuity as witnessed by the *Canadian Alpine Journal*, published annually with few exceptions since 1907. Conceived with a wide-ranging agenda beyond the scope of a simple mountaineering club, the ACC has remained an agile and long-lived national organisation.

Paradoxically, the ACC adopted a constitution that incorporated both the use and preservation of Canada's mountain regions. This seeming contradiction corresponded to the Dominion parks legislation. The same dual mandate was inscribed in the Rocky Mountain Parks Act (1887), the Dominion Forests Reserves and Parks Act (1911), and the Dominion Forests Reserve and Parks Act (1927), governing the Dominion parks prior to the proclamation of the National Parks Act (1930). References to the "heritage" of the Canadian Rockies as a "playground" and "national asset" cropped up in the ACC lexicon much as they did in national parks rhetoric.[6] Like playgrounds, the national parks – in the minds of early ACC members – were outdoor areas for public enjoyment and recreation, but they were also public trusts to be protected in their natural state for future generations; herein lurked the shadows of conflict. Thus, as Canada joined the ranks of mountaineering nations, both alpinism and the national parks embodied a dialectic powered by the contending imperatives of human use and nature preservation.

The ACC quickly spread across the country and abroad as the organisation grew to become Canada's pre-eminent authority on mountaineering, especially in the Rocky Mountain national parks, which set the stage for the development of the Canadian national park system later in the twentieth century. Local ACC branches, called sections, met in cities including Victoria, Vancouver, Calgary, Edmonton, Saskatoon, Winnipeg, Toronto, New York and London, England. Membership enrolment climbed from 79 in the ACC's first year to 200 early in 1907, 400 in 1908, and more than 650 in 1911.[7] Today members number over 5,000 strong.[8] Contrary to British tradition, the ACC always admitted both women and men, in this respect emulating the pattern of North American mountaineering clubs. One third of ACC memberships in 1907 were held by women; by 1917, women held close to one half.[9] Beyond the borders, the ACC was linked to an international mountaineering fraternity through association with other national alpine clubs.

Membership encompassed the spectrum of anglo-Canadian society from the distinguished Sir Sandford Fleming (1827-1915) to the hundreds of city dwellers who travelled to the ACC summer camps mushroomed annually at the foot of the mountains in the towering Canadian Rockies. Occupationally the ACC was drawn in the main from white collar professionals with a heavy representation of school teachers, university staff and faculty, a number of barristers, engineers, doctors, nurses, and a sprinkling of artists, businessmen, civil servants and clerics.[10] Among the mass membership shone the celebrated illuminaries of the alpine world – summiteers, explorers, scientists and literati. This well-educated, articulate constituency shared an avid interest in natural history, the mountains and climbing.

Club life centred around the annual camp held each summer in the Canadian Rockies. When the flags were at last raised over the campsite prepared by outfitters and club organizers, most camps could accommodate more than a 100 people in canvas tents for up to two weeks. Organised climbs were the order of the day. New members were expected to fulfil the requirements of a graduating "ascent of at least 10,000 feet above sea level,"[11] and seasoned mountaineers headed off to test the routes up the surrounding peaks. At rough hewn tables and benches, campers dined together in an open air club atmosphere. The evening campfire – "altar and hearthstone of the Club" – was a forum for alpine lectures, music, mirth and recounting the day's vigorous climbing ventures.[12] Sunday mornings around the campfire, climbing clergymen exhorted all eyes to lift to the mountains, no doubt praying for their safe return. The sheer logistics of carrying off such a large annual event located on a different remote site each year, attested to the strength of organisation behind the ACC, which was in this respect not unlike a military encampment or Boy Scout jamboree, and to the co-operation between the club and parks department.

The ACC constructed several bases of operation in the national parks through the Rocky Mountains and Selkirks. In 1909 the ACC's landmark Banff Clubhouse was built on the side of Sulphur Mountain "giving permanent visibility to national mountaineering in Canada."[13] The Fay Hut, built in 1927 to provide shelter in Kootenay National Park, was the first ACC backcountry hut. Gradually, the club extended its property holdings within the parks to include a series of these alpine huts. From Banff, west to Yoho and Glacier, and north to Jasper, the ACC stationed a physical presence in the national parks.

The ACC was at the forefront of twentieth-century tourism in the mountain parks and, according to its constitution, provided for "the opening of new regions as a national playground." Alpinism, as it originated in nineteenth-century Europe, was by definition an expansionary form of scientific and imperial conquest. Canadian alpinism, too, was by its very origins an expansionary activity. Mountaineering pushed back the frontiers, always on the search for new climbs and "unnamed" peaks as it radiated out from the railway lines and reached farther into the backcountry.

Up until the end of the First World War, the ACC was content to operate primarily along the CPR line through Rocky Mountains, Yoho and Glacier National Parks. By today's standards, the 1916 camp was held relatively close to Banff townsite, as Arthur Wheeler estimated "the locality is very fine and well deserves advertising."[14] By 1922 Thomas Moffat (1870-1939), leader of the ACC

Calgary Section, warned the Superintendent of Rocky Mountains Park that without continued federal support for Wheeler's ACC-affiliated backcountry tour operation, the club would take their business elsewhere:

> We as a Club, have exhausted the near-in points such as Yoho, O'Hara, Paradise, etc., and we must reach out to points further in the heart of the Rockies ... failing this we will have to transfer our activities to the Mt. Robson district.[15]

After World War II, familiar districts once again dulled the senses. As ACC President Brigadier Sir Oliver Wheeler (1890-1962) – Arthur Wheeler's son, accomplished mountaineer, and distinguished Surveyor General of India – explained: "There is a great urge, particularly from our younger members, for new ground." He advised Ottawa to open up the "virtually unknown" Fortress Lake region for the 1953 camp by laying a road through the recesses of Jasper National Park:

> Given a road to that point, the Alpine Club of Canada could popularize one of the finest scenic and climbing areas in the main Rockies and could – would – introduce many, many tourists and members of other organized clubs.[16]

The move away from the CPR mainline north to the Jasper district illustrates how over time the ACC persistently pushed back the unknown frontiers of the Rocky Mountain parks.

As a pioneer user, the club assailed the boundaries of recreation in the parks and ventured into areas subsequently subjected to frequent tourist traffic. The consecutive annual Alpine Club summer camps carried revenue into the parks and publicized the wilderness mountain playgrounds beyond the mountaineering constituency to a mass public of potential tourists and recreationists. Thus each generation of ACC presidents claimed: "The tourists bring the large money, but the Alpine Climber opens up the region for the tourist."[17]

ACC campsites were in many cases the precursors of twentieth-century mass tourism in the mountain parks as the auto age placed these national playgrounds within easier reach of a growing population of leisure seekers. For example, four ACC camps were staged in Paradise Valley before 1945.[18] The first ACC reports extolled the remote wilderness virtues of Paradise Valley, which is today considered a day hike from the Moraine Lake Road not far from the camera-congested shores of Lake Louise. In this respect, the ACC acted as the thin edge of the wedge for commercial tourism in the parks and public access to remote mountain areas.

Parks officials were keen to encourage the club's activities as if realizing that when it came to tourist visitors in the mountain parks, the rest would follow the best of the alpine world. The role of the ACC in publicity was continually highlighted as a rationale for close co-operation between the department and the club, as indicated for example by Howard Douglas, chief superintendent of Dominion Parks, in 1914:

> The Alpine Club is doing splendid work in connection with the opening up and advertising of mountains within the Parks boundaries as well as outside and anything that we can do to facilitate their operations I think should be carried out.[19]

In 1916 Dominion Parks Commissioner James Bernard Harkin (1875-1955) stated "it is the policy of the department to co-operate in every way possible with the Alpine Club" and throughout his long tenure exactly this policy was animated by the department.[20] After Harkin's retirement in 1936, the department continued this preferential policy into the post-war period. Roy A. Gibson, Ottawa director of the National Parks, noted to his deputy minister in 1949: "The mountain parks receive splendid advertising from the activities of the Alpine Club. We have always considered this justification for special treatment.[21]

The ACC was thus poised as a prominently placed client-user group during the formative period of national park development. During the Edwardian era, the ACC explored and mapped many areas in the Rockies, circulated information about the parks, and in the early 1900s contributed directly to the Dominion Parks section of the Department of the Interior Annual Report.[22] The club rendered itself an indispensable partner in the early days of park management when the whole of the parks administration might have fit into a one-room office. As time went on, the ACC buttressed parks conservation policies, and assisted the restoration of mountain areas "despoiled by tourists and others."[23] A long history of co-operation between the club and government administration was built on this foundation, and to some degree it shaped the evolution of the national parks in concept and reality.

A reciprocal relationship developed between the club and the parks administration, whereby the ACC called on the department for operational services, an annual federal grant to sponsor activities, and access privileges within the parks; the national parks authorities in turn recognized the ACC as the national mountaineering authority, referred the public to the club for information, and relied on the ACC for expertise and free publicity. The two parties shared an interest in the aims of the national parks and mutually encouraged each other's activities as related to conservation, tourism and mountaineering.

The most effective ACC executives and parks administrators fostered this reciprocity to mutual advantage, frequently employing informal channels or an internal collegial network to carry on contacts. A prime example of this rapport is that Commissioner Harkin and longstanding ACC leader Arthur Wheeler both worked for the Department of the Interior. From 1911 to 1936, they interacted in person and via a sustained correspondence regarding matters of concern to the ACC and the parks. Harkin even used this conduit to spur the club's defence of the national parks against the incursion of resource developments, for example calling on "alpinists to present the other side publicly" during the 1922 Waterton Lakes irrigation debate.[24] This opportunity for dialogue opened up communications and strengthened the partnership between the club and senior administration, although sometimes at the expense of park superintendents circumvented by Wheeler's inclination to deal with the top man in Ottawa.

Generally superintendents worked to service the on-the-ground needs of the club – sending wardens to assist at the summer camps, installing telephone communications lines, electrifying the Banff Clubhouse, getting the trails in shape – in accordance with the daily operational demands of park management. Some forged closer ties with the ACC, such as Jasper Superintendent Maynard Rogers who encouraged ACC publicity of his park through the *Canadian Alpine Journal* and responded favourably to invitations to informal gatherings of the Edmonton Section during the interwar period.[25] In the 1940s, Homer Robinson, associate superintendent of Parks and Resources Information in Ottawa, reinforced liaisons with the club to profit from the added glamour of mountaineering in park advertising and monitor the inside workings of the organisation.[26]

The reciprocal relationship between the national parks administration and the club also showed up in the process of public policy formation. Often the ACC served to stimulate parks policy, for example regarding regulating the use of fire trails, licensing procedures for club huts, or mountaineering registration, as the department coped with the daily realities of managing user demands. While ACC president in the 1950s, Oliver Wheeler requested the national parks to undertake long range planning of trail projects in order to accommodate the club's advance selection of campsites. This request snapped down the chain of command from Ottawa, out to park superintendents, down to wardens in the field, and back up the administrative ladder. Thus the national parks hierarchy set planning in action designed not "to put in trails to any location where the Alpine Club might wish to plan to locate," but to co-ordinate ACC demands within an overall policy framework for regular trail development.[27] In other cases, the department approached the ACC for specialized input in the areas of safety, ski mountaineering, the training and regulation of mountain guides and on-the-ground alpine expertise. Regarding backcountry skiing, Harkin noted in 1933: "It is considered that the Alpine Club being the pioneer organisation supporting such recreation throughout the Parks will be in a position to offer suggestions."[28] Thus, policy making for the national mountain parks was an interactive process that involved both user and state.

A strong collective identity pervades the history of the ACC. As regards the national parks, the club's executive and general membership held that the ACC represented a distinct "class of visitors," a group with particular needs and interests.[29] From the club perspective, the ACC was a selfless institution and first among groups deserving preferential treatment in the parks. This canon was passed in continuity from one club generation to the next as the ACC celebrated its achievements.

Arthur Wheeler was one of the first to expound on "the wants of the Alpine Club and the large class they represent." He sounded a populist note against a backdrop of affluent tourism in the mountain parks: "Canadians of moderate means who desire to travel in the hills have as much right to enjoy the privileges and beauties of their mountain heritage as wealthy outsiders, or wealthy motorists."[30]

Members were quick to point out that many middle-class professionals owed their experiences of the national parks to the ACC, as F.W. Waterman declared in 1922: "I trust that it can be made clear to the proper authorities that so far as the membership of the Club is concerned, it is *the Club that brings us to the mountains*."[31]

In the 1950s, Oliver Wheeler argued that the club deserved special consideration in the national parks:

I think this Club should be treated somewhat differently from an ordinary (commercial etc.) concessionaire. The Club is a permanency and in its 47 years of existence has done more than any other single institution to open up our mountains and bring revenue to the Parks and to Canada, both as a Club as such and from the explorations of its individual members, Canadian, British and American.[32]

The same rationale was used as late as 1965 to draw the line between the ACC and "tourists, speed hounds and determined sightseeing dowagers" in defence of retaining the club's backcountry huts where mountaineers could meet "with their own kind":

Without the past efforts in exploration of members of the club, beautiful routes and marvellous places would be unknown. The members of the Club have been foremost in telling the world about our mountains. The Alpine Club is not and never has been a clique seeking to retain part of our Canadian heritage for its own enjoyment. The members have consistently published by writings and speeches the beauties of the remote places.[33]

From the outset, the ACC conveyed a clearly defined group identity and acted as a self-conscious stakeholder group ready to promote its own agenda in the development of the mountain parks.

Parks officials, to a large extent, recognized the ACC as the organisational animus of the Canadian mountain world and perpetuated the special relationship with the club even as new user groups – the BC Mountaineering Club, Trail Riders of the Canadian Rockies, and the Calgary Ski Club to name a few – emerged on the scene. By the 1950s, Ottawa National Parks Director James Smart acknowledged this long-standing rapport: "The Alpine Club of Canada, in years past has been given strictly preferential treatment, especially in so far as rentals and license fees are concerned."[34] To a large extent, the acc was a very stable national organisation, perhaps more so than the continually reorganised government structure housing the national parks administration. In part the club's longevity recommended it as a national user group with self-perpetuating preferential status.

Margaret Johnston and John Marsh have commented that from 1906 to 1930 the ACC actively promoted a "wise use" conservation ethic through efforts to support national and provincial parks in Alberta and British Columbia, and to oppose hydro developments proposed in the 1920s for Waterton Lakes and Rocky Mountains national parks. Involvement in conservation issues then declined until the 1960s.[35] While this overall pattern is certainly accurate, it seems likely that various discourses in conservation thought – ranging from utilitarian "scientific management" to aesthetic preservation – were at play within the club, and even within the minds of the individual members.

For example, ACC co-founder Elizabeth Parker espoused an ethic of aesthetic preservation steeped in literary romanticism, and was in some senses comparable to John Muir, father of the Sierra Club. It was Parker who instilled the ACC with a mission to champion the all-encompassing Canadian "mountain heritage":

> By virtue of its constitution, the Alpine club is a national trust for the defence of our mountain solitudes against the intrusion of steam and electricity and all the vandalisms of this luxurious, utilitarian age; for the keeping free from the grind of commerce, the wooded passes and valleys and alplands of the wilderness. It is the people's right to have primitive access to the remote places of safest retreat from the fever and the fret of the market place and the beaten tracks of life.[36]

That Parker was disillusioned in later life with the havoc wrecked by modern tourism in her beloved mountains attests to the idealism of her conservation sentiments. She saw too late tourism's clash of values in the parks and the inevitable sublimation of true wilderness to the forces of human infiltration.[37]

Mary Schäffer (1861-1939), well-known explorer, artist, and ACC founding member, lamented the passing of Canada's mountain parks from true wilderness to managed public playgrounds, but readily adopted a pragmatic avenue to safeguard her favourite haunts. In 1911 she surveyed Maligne Lake under the auspices of the Geographic Board of Canada and promoted the tourism value of the area in order to have the region drawn back under the aegis of Jasper National Park.[38] Schäffer's politic approach to utilitarian conservation bridged the transition from wilderness to modern managed parks. For Schäffer, the ends justified the means.

Different streams of thought could flow together regarding the conservation and use of the national parks. Arthur Wheeler, for instance, had no illusions about the future of wilderness within the parks:

The preserving of Lake O'Hara for all time in its primitive wilderness and grandeur is idealistic but impossible.... The best that can be done is to control commercial desecration as much as possible, and this is being done now under government supervision.[39]

As a land surveyor, he knew the long-range implication of opening the wilderness was to tame it. None the less Wheeler's pragmatic realism on this point co-existed with a strong stand for the preservation of alpine flowers. He railed against the destructive practices of people "digging up the wild flowers" and warned that the flora would "cease to exist." Thus he urged the Canadian parks administration to follow the American lead and adopt a strict wildflower protection policy.[40] Essentially, control was the key to preservation. Thus management was vital to any conservation strategy. In the case of Don Munday (1890-1950), photographer and prominent ACC member, it did not seem contradictory to advocate the creation of parks on the west coast in 1928; then in 1948 recommend the national parks administration improve the view along the highway through Banff Park by slashing back the forest – a drastic measure, to say the least, not usually associated with conservation.[41]

In the end, the club's approach to conservation was as varied as its individual members and streamed together a number of different ethics moulded by contemporary influences. This elasticity created an inner tension within the group, dynamically drawing it back and forth between preservation and use, but commonly settling for a middle ground. Thus the inner tension generally operated within the bounds of the ACC's preferred status with the national parks administration in Ottawa.

The ACC's overt public lobbying for conservation in the national parks definitely peaked during the 1920s, led on by the aforementioned resource use conflicts over the Waterton and Spray Lakes. These conflicts centred around a proposed irrigation diversion from the Waterton Lakes on the Alberta-Montana border, and a massive hydro-electric conversion involving the Spray Lakes chain south of Canmore, Alberta. As a result of the latter conflict, the Spray Lakes were excised from national park territory and transferred to Alberta in 1930. Eventually this area became the "multiple-use" Kananaskis Provincial Park. During this period Wheeler, encouraged by Harkin, propelled the ACC as a proto-conservation lobby group allied with the department against forces – including the Calgary Power Company, the Government of Alberta, and R.B. Bennett – set on marauding national park lands. After 1930 the club grew more concerned with maintaining an expanding four-season roster of sport activities, including ski mountaineering and innovations in technical climbing, during the Depression and wartime. Public conservation advocacy faded from the ACC agenda.

By 1945, the ACC's focus had shifted in keeping with the general post-war trend to capital investment in national parks infrastructure. Galvanised by a push to make the mountains accessible to auto-age tourism, the ACC submitted formal proposals to the federal government for post-war development of the national parks calling for "the development and greater utilization of the National Parks of Canada by the general public."

Recommendations centred on construction of roadways, trails, and facilities to increase access to "the inner recesses of the Parks."[42] Conservation was conspicuous by its absence from these proposals, as was the ACC when it came to renewed hydro-development clashes in the 1940s. The internal pendulum of the organisation had swung from preservation to utilization as a new generation of Alpine Club men and women moved to the fore in an era of post-war expansion.

None the less, just as Banff was the birthplace of the national parks system, the ACC was parent to a legacy of national parks public advocacy bodies. In 1923 amid the Calgary Power Spray Lakes hydro-development controversies, the ACC sponsored the organisation of the Canadian National Parks Association, later known as the National Parks Association of Canada (NPAC). This group became an influential advocate of national parks urging "the conservation of the Canadian National Parks for scientific, recreational and scenic purposes, and their protection from exploitation for commercial purposes."[43] This mandate bore striking similarity to the original objectives set 16 years earlier in the ACC constitution. Increased emphasis on political action to forestall immoderate resource development was the new keynote. In essence, the ACC fostered the NPAC through its early years and the two groups shared overlapping memberships. W. J. Selby Walker (1879-1952), an active ACC man, was also the long-time Calgary-based guiding spirit of the NPAC, which played a national role in parks advocacy for several decades. The National Parks Act (1930) to a large extent reflected an enhanced emphasis on conservation and protection resulting from the battles led by the Alpine Club during the 1920s.

Through the creation of this more specialized group, it seems the ACC was able to delegate a fair degree of responsibility for citizen conservation advocacy away from its own activities. Organisationally and philosophically the Alpine

Club of Canada served as the precursor to the National Parks Association of Canada, succeeded in 1963 by the National and Provincial Parks Association of Canada, and renamed the Canadian Parks and Wilderness Society in 1986. Thus the ACC transmitted its early national parks ethic to new generations of conservation-minded Canadians, generations that would ultimately stress environmental protection and wilderness preservation as the primary purposes of the national parks.

Although the nature of this analysis is tentative, it suggests the ACC was a long-lived organisation that played an active role in the development of Canada's mountain parks as a pioneer and longtime park user. Year after year, the ACC faithful travelled for miles to indulge and delight in the splendour of the western mountains. What drove these people to the summits far from the bright lights of urban, industrial city life? Did they follow the ACC motto *"sic itur ad astra"* – this way unto the stars – reaching for new heights known only in the company of climbers and nature? Did they seek an escape, or were the national parks by extension the natural mountain playgrounds of the city, a welcome wilderness once nature had been elsewhere tamed? Whatever the case, the ACC stood with ice axe ready to open up the national parks for public recreation.

Two main themes are suggested from this discussion. First, the longevity of the ACC represents an organisational success story. Based on the collective culture of anglo-Canadian, middle-class alpinism, the ACC maintained national and local levels of specialized club activity. Camping and climbing in the mountains were the heart of the ACC. Essentially the club stuck to this central project even as it changed with the times, adapting to innovations in mountain recreation, reaching abroad on expeditions, and shifting its internal pendulum between preservation and use of the national parks. This specialization was the keynote of alpinism and the basis for a strong group identity among club members who readily distinguished between themselves and other park visitors, and even other mountaineering groups. Continuity within the club was likely reinforced by family associations. Mountaineering in the ACC tradition ran through families like the Wheelers from father, to son, to grandson; the Parkers from mother, to daughter; and the Mundays between wife and husband. As its founders had predicted, the Alpine Club "gathered to itself a noble succession of Canada's good men in every high and useful vocation of life" and "added a worthy something to Canadian literature, art and science."[44]

Second, analysis of the relationship between the club and the national parks administration suggests that the ACC was an articulate and politically alert body

with a pro-active commitment to public-policy formation. The ACC participated in national parks public-policy making through direct channels such as
official statements on park policy, and indirect means such as the *Canadian
Alpine Journal*. Possibly the influence of the ACC extended beyond the size of its
membership, no doubt because of the nature of its well-connected, highly motivated constituency. The club had pull over the long haul. Today the ACC is
considered a partner NGO – the current idiom for a co-operating non-government
organisation – and it continues to exert a certain preferential user status.

Throughout the course of the twentieth-century growth of the national park
system, the ACC was an extremely stable structural entity with a foothold in the
mountain parks. It forged a partnership with the national parks administration
at an important juncture, and established a critical physical presence in the
parks with its huts and Banff Clubhouse.[45] This rapport persisted into the post-
war era. As late as 1967, there was no other citizen group comparable to the ACC
in terms of their backcountry building program in the national parks.[46] Thus
the ACC stood out as a national institution among the crowds of post-war park
users and retained its preferential status.

Canada's expanding system of national parks evolved inside a thunderhead
of public and private interests. The value and function of the mountain parks –
Canada's first national parks – were variously conceived over time by contending forces. The parks were the commercial playgrounds of the "doctrine of usefulness."[47] They were a resource to be carefully tapped for the greater good of
the greatest number in keeping with "wise-use conservation." According to "scientific management" and business progressivism, parks were a laboratory for
systematic manipulation by planners. As ecology emerged as a professional science, emphasis was placed on the "biocentric" value of parks. To nature preservationists and transcendentalists, parks were sanctuaries of nature and the soul.
The dual mandate of the national parks, use and preservation, generated ongoing friction as these national park visions surfaced, collided and transformed in
policy and legislation.

Against this backdrop, the ACC is a prism through which to observe the
changing conceptual weather patterns of the national mountain parks. Like the
national parks themselves, the ACC was influenced by an inner tension between
preservation and use. The ACC vision of the parks transmuted over time, and
ultimately transformed the parks. Parks were shaped by park users as well as by
government and commerce. In this process, the ACC played a key role spanning
almost ninety years in the maturation of the Canadian national park system.

The Alpine Club of Canada in essence painted a vision of itself onto the mountain park backdrop, fulfilling Elizabeth Parker's invocation: "May the Alpine Club live as long as the mountains of Canada."[48]

Endnotes

1. This article is dedicated in memory of Ronald William Maslin (1930-1993), Parks Canada administrator and planner.

2. In popular usage, the term "Rockies" collectively identifies the Rocky Mountain main ranges together with the Columbia Mountains and their Selkirk Range to the west in BC, although properly speaking the Rocky Mountain Trench divides the main ranges from the latter formations. Popular convention is observed in this paper.

3. Comparing the Canadian Rockies to the Swiss Alps was one of many tactics used in the CPR's active tourism marketing campaigns, see: E. J. Hart, *The Selling of Canada: The CPR and the Beginnings of Canadian Tourism* (Banff: Altitude, 1983).

4. See Arthur O. Wheeler, "Origin and Founding of the Alpine Club of Canada, 1906," and Elizabeth Parker, "The Approach to Organization," *Canadian Alpine Journal* (hereafter CAJ) (1938) 82-96. Wheeler served as ACC President from 1906 to 1910, Director from 1910 to 1926, Hon. President from 1926 to 1945, and CAJ Editor from 1907 to 1927. Parker was the national Secretary from 1906 to 1910, a dedicated CAJ contributor, and one of the first honorary ACC members elected in 1906.

5. "Constitution," CAJ (1907) 178.

6. Margaret Johnston and John Marsh, "The Alpine Club of Canada, Conservation and Parks, 1906 to 1930," CAJ (1986) 17. Johnston and Marsh observed: "Many of the statements regarding the Club's philosophy coincide with statements used contemporaneously to promote the national parks."

7. Elizabeth Parker, "Report of the Secretary," CAJ (1907) 164; "Report of Secretary" CAJ (1908) 320; "Report of the 1911 Camp," CAJ (1912) 146.

8. Kevin Lohka, "The Heart of the Club" *The Newsletter*, 15 April 1994, 2.

9. Gina LaForce, "The Alpine Club of Canada, 1906-1929: Modernization, Canadian Nationalism, and Anglo-Saxon Mountaineering" MA Thesis, University of Toronto, 11 July 1978, 6; Cyndi Smith, *Off the Beaten Track: women adventurers and mountaineers in western Canada* (Jasper: Coyote Books, 1989) 18.

10. Whyte Museum of the Canadian Rockies Archives, AC 90 F97.

11. Parker, CAJ (1907) 165.

12. Parker, "Report of the Hon. Secretary," CAJ (1910) 207.

13. Parker, "Report of Hon. Secretary," CAJ (1909) 146.

14. National Archives of Canada (hereafter NAC), RG 84, vol. 1, file R62, part 2, A. Wheeler to Harkin, 9 May 1916.

15. NAC, RG 84, vol. 102, file U36-1, part 2, Moffat to Stronach, 25 March 1922.

16. NAC, RG 84, vol. 2019, file U36-1, part 6, O. Wheeler to Smart, 20 Oct. 1951. Sir

Edward Oliver Wheeler was known for his 1921 survey reconnaissance of Mt. Everest, and served as ACC National President from 1950 to 1954.

17. NAC, RG 84, vol. 2243, file Y16-3, part 1, O. Wheeler to Hutchinson, 18 April 1953.

18. ACC camps were held in Paradise Valley in 1907, 1918, 1933, and 1944; ACC, *List of Members*, 1976, 150.

19. NAC, RG 84, vol. 2243, file Y16-3, part 1, Douglas to Harkin, 21 Feb. 1912.

20. NAC, RG 84, vol. 1, file R62, part 2, Harkin to Rocky Mountains Park Superintendent, 25 May 1916.

21. NAC, RG 84, vol. 189, file U36-1, part 1, Stronach to Smart, 13 April 1949, see note to Deputy Minister, 16 April 1949.

22. See for example: *Annual Report of the Department of the Interior*, 1912, 8, 39-40.

23. Parker, "The Approach to Organisation," CAJ (1938) 97.

24. NAC, RG 84, vol. 102, file U36-1, part 2, Harkin to A. Wheeler, 6 April 1922.

25. NAC, RG 84, vol. 102, file U36-1, part 2, Rogers to Mitchell, 31 Oct. 1923; NAC, RG 84, vol. 102, file U36-1, part 5, Rogers to Wates, 28 Nov. 1932.

26. NAC, RG 84, vol. 189, file U36-1, Robinson letters 1946-48.

27. NAC, RG 84, vol. 189, file U36-1, part 1, O. Wheeler to Smart, 19 March 1951; *Ibid.*, Smart to Wheeler, 28 March 1951; *Ibid.*, Smart to Supts., 28 March 1951; *Ibid.*, Coleman to Smart, 4 May 1951.

28. NAC, RG 84, vol. 102, file U36-1, part 5, Harkin to A. Wheeler, 22 Sept. 1933.

29. NAC, RG 84, vol. 102, file U36-1, part 2, Resolution, General Meeting ACC, Victoria, 11 Feb. 1922.

30. NAC, RG 84, vol. 102, file U36-1, part 2, A. Wheeler to Harkin, 19 Oct. 1921.

31. *Ibid.*, Waterman to A. Wheeler, 14 Jan. 1922. Original underlined.

32. NAC, RG 84, vol. 2248, file Y16-26, O. Wheeler to Steeves, 31 Jan. 1953.

33. NAC, RG 84, vol. 2019, file U36-1, part 8, Green to Davis, 24 May 1965.

34. NAC, RG 84, vol. 2249, file Y16-40, part 1, Smart to O. Wheeler, 18 Feb. 1953.

35. Margaret Johnston and John Marsh, "The Alpine Club of Canada, Conservation and Parks, 1906 to 1930," CAJ (1986) 16-19.

36. Elizabeth Parker, "The Alpine Club of Canada," CAJ (1907) 5.

37. P. A. Reichwein, "Guardians of a Rocky Mountain Wilderness: Elizabeth Parker, Mary Schäffer, and the Canadian National Park Idea, 1890-1914," MA Research Essay, Carleton University, 1990.

38. *Ibid.*.

39. NAC, RG 84, vol. 2243, file Y16-3, part 1, A. Wheeler to Wilcox, 22 Jan. 1914.

40. Banff National Park, box 80, file 6.2/5-L3.1/A-11, vol. 2, A. Wheeler to Stronach, 26 June 1923; *Ibid.*, Stronach to Wheeler, 6 July 1923.

41. NAC, RG 84, vol. 102, file U36-1, part 4, NAC, RG 84, vol. 189, file U36-1, part 1, Munday to Harkin, 31 Aug. 1928; *Ibid.*, Smart to Robinson, 9 Dec. 1948.

42. "Post-war Development of National Parks," CAJ (144-45) 168-74.

43. Cited in Leslie Bella, *Parks for Profit*, (Montreal: Harvest House, 1987) 51.

44. Parker, CAJ (1908), p. 323.

45. One question beyond the scope of this paper is how Parks Canada, with the complicity of certain ACC members, destroyed the historic Banff Clubhouse early in the 1970s. Ironically, the same building would today be considered one of the park's leading heritage structures and a cultural resource worthy of conservation.

46. NAC, RG 84, vol. 2019, file U36-1, part 8, Kun to Reeve, 10 Aug. 1967.

47. R.C. Brown, "The Doctrine of Usefulness: Natural Resource and National Park Policy in Canada, 1887-1914," in *The Canadian National Parks: today and tomorrow*, eds. J.G. Nelson and R.C. Scace, (Calgary: University of Calgary, 1968) 94-110.

48. Elizabeth Parker, "In Memoriam: Stanley Hamilton Mitchell," CAJ (1939) 105.

The EVOLUTION OF WORLD HERITAGE

IN CANADA

Nancy Elliot

World Heritage Sites are recognized internationally for their unique and superlative properties. Canada currently has 10 designated World Heritage sites. Three sites, the newly established Tatshenshini-Alsek Wilderness Park in British Columbia, Waterton Lakes-Glacier National Parks, and Miguasha Provincial Park (Quebec), are being reviewed during 1994 and may be designated at the World Heritage meeting in December 1994. This article provides some findings from a master's thesis on the past, present and future application of World Heritage in Canada. By addressing the evolution of World Heritage in Canada, I will present some conclusions from a chapter of this thesis that discusses patterns evident from the history behind the nomination process.

These findings may have relevance to protected areas in general, as this work analyzes the political dynamics which determine which sites receive international recognition.

What is World Heritage?

The United Nations Educational, Scientific and Cultural Organization's (UNESCO) *Convention for the Protection of the World Cultural and Natural Heritage* (Canada 1979), commonly called the World Heritage Convention, recognizes the protection of the world's heritage as an international responsibility. World Heritage sites are recognized at the international level as having outstanding natural and/or cultural features. Designation under the convention implies that governments will make a strong commitment to protecting sites located within their geographic borders. In addition, the World Heritage designation may increase the profile and prestige of a site.

Origins of Canadian World Heritage Sites

Since the inception of the World Heritage Convention, 11 sites in Canada have been designated to the World Heritage List, including the Burgess Shale, designated on its own in 1981, and expanded to the Canadian Rocky Mountain Parks Site in 1984. Canada also submitted nominations for three sites in 1993, which were to be reviewed at the 1994 World Heritage Committee meeting. These were: the newly established Tatshenshini-Alsek Wilderness Park in British Columbia; Waterton Lakes-Glacier National Parks, a joint nomination between Canada and the United States; and Miguasha Provincial Park in Quebec. In addition, a number of other heritage areas were being considered for future nominations, including the Town of Lunenburg in Nova Scotia, the Rideau Canal in Ontario, and the Red Bay basque whaling site in Newfoundland.

A few patterns are evident from the historical descriptions of the nominations of Canadian World Heritage sites. These are identified and discussed below.

1. Government or bureaucratic origins of early sites.

Most of the Canadian sites nominated and designated to the World Heritage list were chosen by the bureaucracy. Parks Canada is the agency responsible for administering World Heritage in Canada, and thus many of the nominations originated within the agency. Several lists of candidate sites exist, including the official tentative list, submitted on 14 July 1980 at the request of the World Heritage Committee (Bennett 1980b). Tentative nomination lists aid the Committee and its advisory organizations, the International Council of Monuments and Sites (ICOMOS) and the World Conservation Union (IUCN), in the formidable task of comparing sites that have similar qualities and features. In addition to the official tentative list, three other lists of tentative sites, dating from late 1977 to 1979, exist (Hardie 1977; Faulkner 1978; Bennett 1979b). These represent various examples of "working" attempts to determine which Canadian sites may qualify as having internationally superlative and unique characteristics. In addition, the IUCN published an inventory of potential World Heritage Sites in 1982, produced after several meetings of natural area experts (*International* 1982). These various lists named the following designated sites as potential candidates to the World Heritage list:

- Ninstints, South Moresby Island
- Kluane National Park Reserve
- Dinosaur Provincial Park
- L'Anse Aux Meadows National Historic Site
- Nahanni National Park
- Rocky Mountain National and Provincial Parks
- Head-Smashed-In Buffalo Jump
- Wood Buffalo National Park
- Gros Morne National Park

Civil servants dominated the selection process. Those who were most famil-iar with the attributes of each site were likely the most competent at suggesting candidate nominations. Furthermore, since the World Heritage Convention stipulates that a site must be protected before it is designated, all sites nomi-nated in Canada have some connection with and familiarity to bureaucrats, since it is the provincial or federal employees who manage and promote the sites on a day-to-day basis.

Civil servants have also been the most competent in identifying barriers to nomination. Because of their familiarity and experience with the convention itself, civil servants determined that potential nominations would or would not satisfy the conditions of the convention, particularly with reference to the con-dition of integrity. This point was demonstrated in the late 1970s and early 1980s during discussions over the potential of nominating Niagara Falls as a joint US-Canada nomination. The nomination of Niagara Falls, although at one time given serious consideration, lost its favour as a candidate because of concerns that it would not satisfy the integrity component of the convention. The Operational Guidelines of the World Heritage Convention, paragraph 36 (iii), state:

The sites described ... should contain those ecosystem components re-quired for the continuity of the species or the other natural elements or processes to be conserved. This will vary according to individual cases: for example, the protected area of a waterfall would include all, or as much as possible, of the supporting catchment area...(UNESCO 1992).

As early as 1978, Peter Bennett, Special Advisor to the Assistant Deputy Minister on the World Heritage Convention, expressed concern that the upstream portion of the Niagara River was not adequately protected (Bennett 1978). The Americans were also reluctant to pursue such a nomination, possibly because of the negative publicity an international profile might generate. Although the nomination was pursued for several years in a row, the Americans did not change their minds, especially in light of the problems at Love Canal, which the Americans saw as an inextricate part of the whole Niagara complex (Bennett 1980c).

2. Government Influence

The influence of the federal government on the nomination process is not as direct today as it was during the early years of the convention. It is clear that the federal government was active in each nomination. As the agency responsible for World Heritage in Canada, Parks Canada continues to participate actively in the nomination process; however, the influence of the federal government is not as direct as it has been in the past. The nomination of the Historic District of Quebec and Tatashenshini-Alsek Park, as well as the potential nominations of the Rideau Canal and the Town of Lunenburg, support this assertion. This subtle shift may reflect decreasing budgets and the decentralization of power within Canada during the 1980s.

Quebec City

The proposal to nominate Old Historic Quebec to the World Heritage List did not appear in earlier documentation from Parks Canada. In part, this was because of Quebec's desire to nominate its own sites directly to the World Heritage List, as opposed to being nominated through the federal government (Fraser 1986). In addition, the federal government may have had reservations over entering into heritage discussions with the province of Quebec, given that constitutional powers over cultural and natural resources rest with the provinces. As a result, the nomination of Historic Quebec City is the closest of all the early nominations to being a "grassroots" initative, having originated with one man.

Jacques Dalibard, currently Executive Director of Heritage Canada, started the effort to generate support for a Historic Quebec City World Heritage designation in 1979. Dalibard has had a long time interest in Historic Quebec City. In 1968, as Chief Restoration Architect for Parks Canada, he became involved in the restoration of the fortified walls and Artillery Park. In this role, he gained firsthand appreciation of the potential loss of the city's historic resources, as demolition and construction threatened to modernize the city's historic face. A few years later, in 1978, while teaching at Columbia University in New York, he began to see the historic city in an international perspective, and thought that the city might quality for the World Heritage List. Returning to Ottawa in late 1978 to become executive director for Heritage Canada, he suggested to Parks Canada that it might be possible to nominate the historic district to the World Heritage List. He also personally supported the nomination against initial resistance from federal, provincial and municipal officials. Even ICOMOS initially rejected the idea of a World Heritage designation for Quebec City, since the organization was very Eurocentric in its consideration of significant culture. One argument that proved successful in swaying international opinion was the portrayal of Quebec as the cradle of French civilization in the New World (Dalibard 1993).

Tatshenshini-Alsek Wilderness Park
In July 1993, Premier Mike Harcourt of British Columbia announced the creation of a protected area in the northwestern portion of the province. Accompanying this announcement was the declaration that the park would be nominated to join Wrangell-St. Elias-Glacier Bay Parks in Alaska and Kluane National Park Reserve in the Yukon, on the World Heritage List. This nomination reflects the efforts of grassroots organizations to protect the Tatshenshini and Alsek Rivers. The establishment of this area as a protected area in this areas raised controversy since it eliminated the possibility of Geddes Resources Ltd. of Vancouver developing the Windy-Craggy copper mine.

Although both the international community and the American and Canadian parks agencies supported the formation of a protected area, the influence of NGOs is quite evident in the struggle to have the area protected and nominated. Since October 1991, Tatshenshini International, representing over 50 environmental groups, has been pressuring the Canadian and American governments to protect the area. In 1992, American Rivers announced that the Tatshenshini was the second most-threatened river in North America. Reportedly, American Rivers has a direct "pipeline" into the office of (then) Senator Al Gore; in April 1992, Gore introduced a resolution in the American Senate calling for protection of the Tatshenshini-Alsek Watershed and its nomination as a World Heritage Site, an act which gave the issue a higher profile (Careless 1993; McNamee 1992; Murtha 1993). It is rumoured that during the Yeltsin-Clinton summit meeting in the spring of 1993, President Clinton asked Prime Minister Mulroney to assist in the protection of the area by seeking the co-operation of the British Columbia government (Careless 1993; Murtha 1993). In analyzing the events which lead to the establishment of the Tashenshini-Alsek Wilderness Park and its nomination as a World Heritage Site, it is evident that the public, through lobby groups, was extremely influential at encouraging international organizations, the American and Canadian federal governments, and the provincial government to support the creation of the park and its nomination of a World Heritage Site.

Rideau Canal
Interest in nominating the Rideau Canal was mentioned as early as 1989 in a letter from the Director General, Parks Canada Ontario Region to Harold Eisvik, Senior Policy Advisor, Canadian Parks Service (Rozsell 1989). Although in the past discussions were internal, recent interest in the site has been spearheaded by the "Friends of the Rideau," a co-operative agency whose members represent the general public (Joanisse 1992; Turner 1992).

Town of Lunenburg
In September 1992, the historic district "Old Town," of the Town of Lunenburg was designated a National Historic district. The Town of Lunenburg is presently pursuing the possibility that the historic district may qualify as a World Heritage Site. This nomination is being carried forward by the town council and members of the community (Mawhinney 1993).

3. The role of individuals closely tied with the resource influenced the decision to nominate World Heritage Sites.
Within the provincial and federal bureacracies, there is evidence that key individuals influenced which sites were nominated. At the federal level, Peter Bennett showed particular sentiment towards the selection of L'Anse-Aux-Meadows as a World Heritage Site. Although it was not clear why this site was selected to be Canada's first cultural nomination, Bennett's personal familiarity with the site may have influenced the decision to nominate L'Anse Aux Meadows. Making a speech in 1979, Bennett expressed his personal sentiment:

> Let me at the outset of this paper, make one important disclaimer, I am neither a professional historian nor a professional archaeologist. I am

merely a generalist, an administrator with a love of history, who was fortunate to be in a key position in Parks Canada in Ottawa at the time when the immense significance of the L'Anse-aux-Meadows site first came to be generally realized (Bennett 1979a).

With three provincial sites, Old Historic Quebec City, Head-Smashed-In Buffalo Jump Provinical Historic Site, and Dinosaur Provincial Park, it is apparent that the nominations were directed by individuals who personally felt that the heritage resources of the sites were internationally significant. Jacques Dalibard's influence on the Old Historic Quebec nomination was discussed above. In Alberta, there is evidence that individuals within the government personally promoted the concept of nominating Head-Smashed-In and Dinosaur.

In the case of Head-Smashed-In, the lobby was strong from "in system" archeologists, who had worked at the site and recognized that its superlative qualities were internationally significant (Brink 1992; Byrne 1993; Manyfingers 1993). At Dinosaur, provincial civil servants played an instrumental role in promoting the site for nomination. The nomination originated within the Alberta recreation and parks department, with the primary motivation being the desire to recognize that there are some places within provincial jurisdiction that are internationally significant (Butler 1993; Byrne 1993; Thesen 1993). Although the federal government submitted the application at the international level, the "impetus came from within the government departments responsible for the administration and protection of the resource" (Thesen 1993).

4. The emergence of NGOs in pressing for the nomination of sites.

NGOs have become more active in promoting World Heritage. The Tatshenshini-Alsek, the Rideau Canal and the Town of Lunenburg all illustrate the development of NGO activity supporting World Heritage in Canada. In each case, the perception that designation to the World Heritage List brings recogniton and added protection to the site may have been a central motivation for pursuing designation.

5. Tourism opportunities played a limited role in influencing the establishments of sites.

The opportunity for tourism played a secondary role in the overall pattern of nominating sites for World Heritage. At Head-Smashed-In Buffalo Jump, there is some evidence to indicate that the marketable properties of the site may have influenced individuals to pursue the designation in an effort to secure funding. The designation of the site to the list was a catalysct in securing funding for the interpretive development of the site. At the centre of the interpretive program is a $10-million-dollar visitor centre. Funding was secured by the increased recognition and profile the site received within the government because of the international profile (Brink 1992). The Town of Lunenburg indicates that some of their interest in acquiring international recognition rests with the tourism potential and benefits that such a designation would create (Mawhinney 1993).

In at least one instance, however, the potential increase in tourism played a part in discouraging nomination of a site. This was shown during the early 1980s when the Old Crow band was approached with the idea of nominating a Bering Land Bridge site in the Yukon. Although the federal government approached the band council at least twice, the council passed resolutions turning down the idea of estasblishing a World Heritage site within their traditional lands. The band was cautious over concerns that their lifestyle would be affected by the attention such a designation would bring, particularly by the potential influx of tourists to the area (Old Crow 1980).

6. There has been a significant period of inactivity where no Canadian sites were submitted for nomination.

Parks Canada was most active in the nomination of sites during the late 1970s and early 1980s. Even the nomination of Old Historic Quebec, designated in 1985, and Gros Morne, in 1987, were conceptualized and begun during the earlier period. No sites were nominated between 1986 and 1993.

This period of inactivity reflects the recognition that Canada is over represented on the World Heritage List. In January 1993, there were 134 signatory nations to the World Heritage List. As Canada currently has 10 sites, if distribution of designations was equal amongst nations, the World Heritage List would have 1,340 sites on the list. Thus, it has been recognized that Canada, with its ten sites, is well represented on the list. Since the World Heritage Committee can only process 35 or 40 nominations per year, Canada "has been reluctant to 'hog' the process" (Cameron 1991), and thus has not submitted any new nominations for a few years. Canada's recent activity, however, reflects the belief that enough time has passed to have allowed some other nations to have had an opportunity, and that Canadian sites can now be submitted for consideration (Cantin 1993).

7. Native peoples have been involved with World Heritage at varying levels.

Communication and consultation with the Old Crow band council demonstrated early commitment on the part of Parks Canada to consult with Native groups over the potential nomination of a World Heritage Site.

The nomination for Ninstints emerged as part of the Anthony Island Planning Task Force, formed in June 1980 with representatives from the Province of British Columbia and the Skidegate Indian Band. In the minutes of the Task Force meeting of 6 June 1980, the members discussed the proposal for World Heritage status, noting that the Skidegate Band was in support of the proposed nomination (Anthony 1980). The designation was supported by the council of the Skidegate Band in a Band Council Resolution, on 27 August 1980. It has been suggested that one reason the actual nomination was pursued was to improve relations between the provincial government and the Haida nation, by recognizing that Haida heritage is internationally significant (Frey 1993).

Native peoples did enquire about the implications of the designation of Wood Buffalo. They indicated that they were surprised that the park had been designated to the World Heritage List, and expressed concern that the status would restrict their use of the resources:

> Our concern about the designation of Wood Buffalo National Park as a World Heritage Site, arises from the fact that we who live off of the natural resources of this area ... were never consulted or informed of this event while the nomination was in its formative stages. Instead we were to find out about this through the median over two years down the road when the time was announced for the unveiling of a plaque commemorating the event.
>
> As you can see, this was a surprise to us and inevitably our concerns arose as to the possible alienation of some of our areas of harvest.... What we require ... is ... assurance that the new status of Wood Buffalo National Park will not decrease our activities of harvest or enfringe on our rights as hunters and trappers and fishermen (Kurszewski et al. 1985).

In reponse, the Minister of the Environment Tom McMillan assured the natives that their access to resources would not be affected by the designation:

I regret that you were not informed that the park was to be nominated as a World Heritage Site.... It is a very distinctive honour, but it gives no legal authority to UNESCO. Please be assured that Wood Buffalo's new status will not reduce your harvesting, hunting, trapping or fishing rights. These activities will continue to be guided by the National Parks Act and appropriate regulations (McMillan 1985).

More recently, controversy has emerged over the lack of consultation with the Champagne-Aishihik band during the nomination of the Tatshenshini-Alsek park. This issue, still unresolved, has received much prominence; former Prime Minister Kim Campbell requested that the nomination be delayed until the band were fully consulted ("PMs Letter" 1993; "PM Seeks" 1993).

Conclusion

Although the selection of World Heritage nominations was dominated in early years by civil servants, other influences are evident. These include support from individuals connected with the sites, opportunities for tourism, grassroot NGOs, and native groups.

References

Anthony Island Task Force. 1980. Minutes of 6 June 1980.

Bennett, Peter H. 1978. Special Advisor to Assistant Deputy Minister, Parks Canada, on UNESCO World Heritage Convention. Memo to file. 23 November 1978.

—. 1979a. Special Advisor to Assistant Deputy Minister, Parks Canada, on UNESCO World Heritage Convention. Letter to Mr T.A. Drinkwater, Deputy Minister, Department of Recreation, Parks and Wildlife, Government of Alberta. 26 February 1979.

—. 1979b. Special Advisor to Assistant Deputy Minister, Parks Canada, on UNESCO World Heritage Convention. Letter to Mr N. Faulkner, Executive Director, Office of Native Claims. 17 May 1979.

—. 1980a. Special Advisor to Assistant Deputy Minister, Parks Canada, on UNESCO World Heritage Convention. Memo to file. 8 July 1980.

—. 1980b. Special Advisor to Assistant Deputy Minister, Parks Canada, on UNESCO World Heritage Convention. Letter to the Secretariat, World Heritage Committee. 14 July 1980.

—. 1980c. Special Advisor to Assistant Deputy Minister, Parks Canada, on UNESCO World Heritage Convention. Letter to John Lewis, Director, Ontario Region. 28 July 1980.

Brink, Jack. 1992. "Blackfoot and Buffalo Jumps." *Alberta.* 3.1: 19-43.

Butler, Jim Dr. 1993. Professor, Parks, Wildlife and Conservation Biology, Forest Science, University of Alberta. Telephone Interview. 19 March 1993.

Byrne, Dr. William J. 1993. Assistant Deputy Minister, Historical Resources Division, Alberta Community Development. Telephone Interview. 22 March 1993.

Cameron, Christina. 1991. Chairperson, World Heritage Committee. Interoffice Memorandum to John A. Carruthers. 17 September 1991.

Canada. 1979. *Convention for the Protection of the World Cultural and Natural Heritage.* Treaty Series 1976 No. 45. Ottawa: Ministry of Supply and Service.

Cantin, Gisèle. 1993. Chief, Intergovernmental Affairs, Canadian Parks Service. Personal Interview. 16 November 1993.

Careless, Ric. 1993. Tatshenshini International. Telephone Interview. 19 October 1993.

Dalibard, Jacques. 1993. Executive Director of Heritage Canada. Personal Interview. 23 February 1993.

Faulkner, J. Hugh. 1978. Minister of Indian and Northern Affairs. Letter to Mr. James Morgan, Ministry of Tourism, Newfoundland. 7 March 1978.

Fraser, Barbara K. 1986. *The Efficacy of the World Heritage Convention as a Planning Tool for the Rigorous Protection of Natural Sites.* MSc Thesis. University of British Columbia.

Frey, Patrick. Heritage Conservation Branch, Province of British Columbia, Ministry Responsible for Culture and Tourism. Telephone Interview. 25 March 1993.

Hardie, Duncan. 1977. *Canada World Heritage Natural Area Candidates.* Ottawa: Parks Canada.

International Union for Conservation of Nature and Natural Resources Commission on National Parks and Protected Areas (CNPPA), 1982. *The World's Greatest Natural Areas – An Indicative Inventory of Natural Sites of World Heritage Quality.* Switzerland: International Union for Conservation of Nature and Natural Resources Commission on National Parks and Protected Areas.

Joanisse, Carole. 1992. ADM Secretary. Letter to Christina Cameron, Director General, National Historic Sites. 25 February 1992.

Kurszewski, George, Fort Smith Joint Leadership Group, Raymond Beaver, Chief, Fitz-Smith Native Band, and Allen Heron, President, Fort Smith Metis Local #50. 1985. Letter to the Honourable Tom McMillan, Minister of the Environment. 24 September 1985.

Manyfingers, Kirby. 1993. Interpretation Officer, Head-Smashed-In Buffalo Jump. Personal Interview. 8 September 1993.

Mawhinney, D. Laurence. 1993. Mayor, Lunenburg, Nova Scotia. Letter to Gisèle Cantin, Chief, Intergovernmental Affairs, Canadian Parks Service. 20 May 1993.

McMillan, Tom. 1985. Minister of the Environment, Government of Canada. Letter to George Kurszewski, Fort Smith Joint Leadership Group, Raymond Beaver, Chief, Fitz-Smith Native Band, and Allen Heron, President, Fort Smith Metis Local #50. 14 November 1985.

McNamee, Kevin. 1992. "Environmentalists Fight for Wilderness Preserve". *Nature Canada*. Vol. 21(4), pp. 40-1.

Murtha, Mike. 1993. Planner, British Columbia Ministry of Environment, Lands and Parks. Telephone Interview. 29 September 1993.

Old Crow Band. 1980. Resolution. 21 April 1980. "PM's letter undermines her own mining minister". 1993a. *Vancouver Sun*. 22 September 1993.

"PM seeks heritage review". *Globe and Mail*. 22 October 1993.

Rozsell, Jane. 1989. Director General, Canadian Parks Service. Memorandum to H.K. Eidsvik, Senior Policy Advisor, 25 September 1989.

Thesen, Cliff. 1993. Chief Park Ranger, Dinosaur Provincial Park. Personal Letter. 19 February 1993.

Turner, Larry. 1992. Friends of the Rideau. Letter to Christina Cameron. 12 March 1992.

United Nations Educational, Scientific and Cultural Organization. 1992. *Operational Guidelines for the Implementation of the World Heritage Convention*.

The Creation of National Parks and Equivalent Reserves in Ontario and the Antipodes: A Comparative History and Its Contemporary Expression

John Shultis

With the creation of Algonquin National Park in 1893, the province of Ontario became the first regional government in North America, and among the first in the world, to establish a national park or equivalent reserve. The movement to establish such reserves in the public domain began in New World, British colonies and ex-colonies during the mid- to late-nineteenth century. Each of these early national parks had similar histories and served equivalent functions, in large part because they emanated from common social, cultural, economic and political antecedents found in each of these countries.

This paper provides an analysis of these common factors that lead to the proliferation of national parks and equivalent reserves in the second half of the nineteenth century, focusing on the experiences of Ontario and the Antipodean countries of Australia and New Zealand. The prototypes of national parks will be reviewed, and the principal reasons behind the establishment of early national parks, beginning with the United States – the first country to establish a national park – will be documented. Next, commonalities and differences between the Antipodean and North American establishment of national parks and equivalent reserves will be identified. Finally, the paper will gauge the contemporary impact of nineteenth-century national park establishment.

Prototypical Protected Areas

Long before the establishment of protected areas in non-urban locations, commons, parks, gardens, and rural cemeteries[1] were often found in or near urban areas. The concept of the urban park had been transplanted by settlers emigrating from the Old World, where such protected areas had been established since at least the Mesopotamian civilization.[2] Cities in Europe began to establish public parks (normally termed "public walks") from the sixteenth century: "virtually every town of any social pretension became prepared to vote money for a walk or avenue where local beaux and belles might stroll up and down under the trees to display their best clothes and exchange gossip, as a sort of outdoor assembly room."[3] Urban parks created in the nineteenth century were a product of the reform movement, generated largely by the economic and social impacts of the Industrial Revolution.[4] They served a variety of social, recreational and public health functions: not only did they serve as areas for public recreation, they produced considerable civic pride. Urban parks were also designed to control working and middle classes" leisure behaviour through the provision of rational recreation opportunities deemed suitable by the ruling class.[5] The popularity of the urban park concept, first in the Old World, then in the New World, had an critical role in the development of the national park concept.

There were also a number of non-urban protected areas commonly found in Britain and, somewhat less frequently, on the Continent. These protected areas – royal forests, chases, parks and warrens – had been established from the late Medieval period (c. 1100 AD).[6] By the nineteenth century, private parks were typically composed of enclosed, "unimproved" lands located beyond the open fields surrounding the manor.[7] These protected areas were used by the upper classes for consumptive and non-consumptive recreation, utilitarian purposes (e.g., food and wood) and as expressions of their wealth, status and power within society and over the natural environment.[8] Again, the appearance and functions of private gardens and parks would be emulated in early public, non-urban parks in the New World.

Early Protected Areas in the United States

The first federal reservation of land in the United States was that of Arkansas Hot Springs in 1832. This designation stemmed largely from the government's perception that private development of the area was proceeding in an unacceptably exploitative manner.[9] The popularity and status of Old World spas such as Bath and Baden Baden, and the perceived health benefits deriving from the use of such areas were also important prerequisites. Also, international outrage at the crass commercialism demonstrated by the private sector at Niagara Falls, the most famous of all natural attractions in North America in the nineteenth century, was a source of acute embarrassment for both the American and Canadian governments.[10] The portentous example of Niagara Falls influenced the decision to protect the Arkansas Hot Springs from unscrupulous private development, and for the federal government to restrict future "improvement" of the area to that which it considered to be in the national interest. This first reservation of public lands was significant in that it was a conspicuous departure from the normal *laissez-faire* policies of this era that championed individualism and equated the public good with free market forces.[11]

The establishment of Yosemite Park in 1864 created the first public, non-urban protected area in the world; however, as the park was deeded to the state of California, Yellowstone Park, legislated in 1872, is normally considered the first national park equivalent in the world.[12] The establishment of Yosemite and Yellowstone Parks was to have far-reaching effects; as noted in the following sections, politicians and bureaucrats in Australia, New Zealand and Ontario soon became aware of the existence, notoriety and function of these archetypal national parks.

There are a number of common reasons behind the establishment of Yosemite and Yellowstone parks. Perhaps most importantly, at this stage in its cultural development, the United States was searching for a national icon which would deflect caustic British remarks on the lack of culture and "civilization" in their adolescent country. The Americans were taunted by comments suggesting that America had "done absolutely nothing for the Sciences, for the Arts, for Literature, or even for the statesman-like studies of Politics or Political Economy."[13] The same author went on to suggest that Americans "should make it their chief boast, for many generations to come, that they are sprung from the same race with Bacon and Shakespeare and Newton."[14]

Perry Miller[15] has best linked burgeoning national pride in the United States in the nineteenth century with the creation of a new symbolism and appreciation of wilderness.[16] America's writers, painters and philosophers came to use the American wilderness to portray what all Americans felt was the manifest destiny of their country:

Into undefiled Nature went the characters of Romance; within it the dark forces were exorcised, and out of it the creatures of light, male and female, emerged – strengthened, purified, exuding a native virtue that not only needed no instruction from European sophistication but could proudly scorn the culture of the Old World as a mask of depravity.[17]

Such was the hope, and eventually the belief, of the intelligentsia in the United States.

With the linking of American culture and wilderness, urban-based intellectuals slowly began to respond to the ever-increasing destruction of the wilderness. While very few, if any, did not strongly condone the settlement of "uncivilized" wilderness, increasing levels of devastation were soon met with calls for at least some minimal degree of public preservation. A few, including George Catlin, felt that as the private sector was focused on the exploitation of natural resources, the federal government, "by some great protecting policy," should undertake the provision of a *"nation's Park."*[18]

When the federal government finally acted on the increasing number of similar suggestions[19] by creating Yosemite and Yellowstone Parks, it was only the most spectacular, monumental landscapes that were to be "set aside" from the normal forms of land use (principally logging, mining and agriculture). This maximised both national and international pride in the American landscape and the potential for revenue generation as tourist destinations. Furthermore, the *type* of landscape was also critical: only those landscapes that best fit the aesthetic sensibilities of the times – primarily the sublime, romantic landscape found in the Rocky Mountains – were protected. These areas were also considered "worthless lands"[20] in the sense that the traditional economic activities of agriculture, logging and mining were unsuitable in these areas. As numerous transportation company officials and politicians were well aware, however, these parks had a formidable latent worth in terms of their tourist potential. Railroad companies in particular placed their extremely influential support behind the creation of many of the national parks in the United States (and, later, in Australia and Canada) in the nineteenth and early-twentieth century.[21] As at Niagara Falls and the Arkansas Hot Springs, the fear that private speculators would disfigure these spectacular landscapes in the name of crass commercial gain was also expressed by politicians and writers. As a result, the federal government was encouraged to take over development of these areas.

Finally, early national parks in the United States were created in order to provide recreational opportunities and to provide areas where jaded urban dwelling visitors could regain their physical and emotional health and revel in the awe-inspiring scenery and uncontaminated air of the western mountain ranges: the notion of wilderness as health resort was well established by the third quarter of the nineteenth century.[22] As John Muir noted in 1898:

> Thousands of tired, nerve-shaken, over-civilized people are beginning to find out that going to the mountains is going home; that wildness is a necessity; and that mountain parks and reservations are useful not only as fountains of timber and irrigating rivers, but as fountains of life. [23]

The Australian National Park Movement

During the early exploration of the American western frontier, American writers and artists had found it difficult to describe adequately the new landscapes they found in their country: the normal associations and literary conventions passed down from the Old World (principally Britain) did not always comfortably conform with these new landscapes.[24] In Australia, discomfort with the indigenous landscapes was amplified by the even more alien appearance of the indigenous Australian flora and fauna. The emotional and geographical distance from the old country contributed to a flurry of acclimatization (introduction of foreign plants and animals) and an initial feeling of unfamiliarity and antipathy toward Australia's natural features.[25] By the middle of the nineteenth century, however, with the continued growth of urban areas on the south-eastern coast, and the resulting development of an urban elite, coupled with an increased familiarity with Australian landscapes, more positive (and utilitarian) attitudes began to surface. In 1866, for example, a small area of the Fish River (Jenolan) Caves district in New South Wales was protected by legislation intending to preserve "a source of delight and instruction to succeeding generations and excite the admiration of tourists from all parts of the world."[26]

The reserve generally regarded as the first national park equivalent in Australia was "The National Park," an area of 7,284 hectares located only 22 kilometres from Sydney in New South Wales. The park was established in 1879, only seven years after the creation of Yellowstone Park. The establishment of The National Park (now Royal National Park) was primarily due to contemporary concerns with environmental conditions and public health in Sydney. The riparian landscape reserved was state-owned, still available for reservation as "a consequence of the poor quality of much of it and of the Georges River between it and the expanding Sydney."[27]

In the 40 years following the designation of The National Park, South Australia (1891), Victoria (1892), Western Australia (1895), Queensland (1908) and Tasmania (1916) were all to establish similar reserves.[28] In Victoria, Western and South Australia, the first national parks were established in the immediate hinterland of the state capitals, easily accessible by rail, and specifically designed for mass recreation. These early Australian national parks represent the strongest link among the first four countries to create national parks – the United States, Australia, Canada and New Zealand – between the ensconced urban park concept and the nascent national park concept. The South Australian national park, for example, was "seen essentially as a 'peoples' playground," a bigger, boskier, more relaxed version of a municipal park."[29] Even the first national parks of Queensland and Tasmania, while established in relatively rugged terrain more in keeping with their predecessors in the United States, were primarily designed to cater for recreation and tourism. Indeed, it was not until the 1930s that Australians, led by Miles Dunphy in New South Wales, began to lobby for government provision of wilderness areas designed for the preservation of relatively undisturbed lands and indigenous species.[30]

The role of the earlier American national parks in the development of the early Australian national parks has been a matter of some debate in the limited literature on the history of Australian protected areas. Geoff Mosely suggested that "the movement which led to the declaration of Royal National Park was completely local and indigenous" and proudly points out that The National Park of New South Wales was the first park in the world to be officially termed a "national park" in the government policy through which it was dedicated.[31] Pettigrew and Lyons[32] were more cautious, suggesting that while members of Sydney's amateur naturalists were familiar with the Yellowstone reservation (a Royal Society of New South Wales meeting in 1878 had included a description and illustrations of Yellowstone Park), it was more likely that Robertson had modelled the park after the urban parks present in Britain at this time. The first public presentation raising the possibility of a national park in Queensland in 1896 was also based upon first-hand knowledge of Yosemite, Sequoia and General Grant National Parks obtained during a visit to California in 1878.[33] It seems likely, therefore, that at least some of those actively lobbying the government to create "The National Park" in New South Wales and other states were cognizant of the American precedents.

In Australia, from the beginning of European settlement in 1788, each separate "colony" (i.e., state) possessed jurisdiction over its natural resources. The federation of the Australian colonies in 1901 to form the Commonwealth of Australia retained state control over natural resources. Therefore, as in Ontario, which also had jurisdiction over its natural resources, each state created its own "national" park system.

Regional governments in Australia (as well as those in the United States and Canada[34]) continue to display a rather uneven system of legislative and managerial structures dealing with the creation and management of protected areas.[35] The Australian (i.e., federal) National Parks and Wildlife Service was formed by an Act of Parliament in 1975, making Australia the last of the four countries to establish a federal, legislated agency specifically dealing with national parks.[36]

Protected Areas in Aotearoa/New Zealand

Organized European colonization of Aotearoa/New Zealand began in 1840, the year that many Maori chiefs and representatives of Queen Victoria signed the Treaty of Waitangi. The signing of this treaty paved the way for increased British settlement through the systematic acquisition of Maori land. As in other British colonies, earlier forms of protected areas including urban parks appeared soon after the settlement of Aotearoa/New Zealand began.

The relatively late settlement of New Zealand often led to an increased awareness of the importance of providing protected areas, principally in urban areas; by this time, people were well aware of the usefulness of urban parks in improving social and environmental conditions.[37] For example, the surveyor of the town of New Plymouth was requested to provide open space for recreational purposes, as:

> Many of the vices and diseases of old countries may be traced to the absence of provisions for this purpose, and there can be no excuse for the founders of new colonies who neglect to profit by the sad experience which history affords them.[38]

Unhappily, the overriding political concern in New Zealand to facilitate settlement at all costs[39] did not allow for a similarly foresighted attitude with regards to non-urban protected areas. The first bill introduced into the New Zealand parliament involving the conservation of natural resources was Prime Minister Julius Vogel's New Zealand Forests Bill of 1874. The bill, which in part attempted to create forest reserves totalling two per cent of each province's land area, was only passed after great debate in a considerably weakened form, and was repealed two years after the act was passed.

One of the principal reasons for the failure of this act appears to have been provincial concern that the federal government would usurp jurisdiction over the exploitation of natural resources, which at the time was the prerogative of the provincial governments. The provinces, which had been established in 1852, were not the least bit interested in relinquishing this provincial authority, as it was absolutely vital to the social and economic development of each province. In 1876, however, the provincial governments were abolished, replaced with a single, centralized government. The federal government appeared more willing to act on issues involving conservation; the Forest Conservation Act of 1883, the New Zealand State Forests Act of 1885, and subsequent bills dealing with conservation and preservation proved more successful.[40]

As in the United States and Canada,[41] the tourism potential of hot springs as spas and resorts served as the catalyst for the creation of the first protected areas. In 1874, outgoing Premier Fox wrote a memorandum suggesting to his successor that parts of the central North Island be protected for their "sanitary purposes."[42] Fox commended the earlier actions of the United States government in reserving the Yellowstone area, and expressed the seemingly common fear that these magnificent natural areas would be impoverished by private development:

> that they should be surrounded with pretentious hotels and scarcely less offensive tea gardens; that they should be strewed with orange-peel, with walnut shells, and the capsules of bitter beer bottles (as the Great Pyramid and even the summit of Mount Sinai are), is a consummation from the very idea of which the soul of every lover of nature must recoil.[43]

Fox was also careful to note that the proposed area was "almost worthless for agricultural or pastoral, or any similar purposes; but when its sanitary resources are developed, it may prove to be a source of great wealth to the colony."[44] Fox's efforts led to the passing of the Thermal Districts Act in 1881, legislation echoing that of Arkansas Hot Springs (1832), Yosemite (1864), Yellowstone (1872) and foreshadowing the creation of Rocky Mountain (Banff) Park (1887) by the federal government of Canada and Algonquin National Park (1893) in Ontario.

New Zealand followed these early efforts at federal protection of lands with the establishment of the world's fourth national park. Tongariro National Park was first deeded to the New Zealand government by Maori chief Te Heuheu Tukino in 1887; however, due to political uncertainty over the national park concept and the need to ensure that the area was not suitable for settlement or logging, legislation to create officially Tongariro National Park was delayed until 1894.[45]

New Zealand, then, was the first nation to establish a national park in co-operation with its indigenous people. The purpose of this first national park was virtually identical with those of the United States, Canada and Ontario: politicians saw these areas as places which, through their scenic attributes, would become world famous tourist attractions, creating revenue and status for their country/province. For example, John Ballance, the minister of Lands, predicted that Tongariro "would be a great gift to the colony: I believe it will be a source of attraction to tourists from all parts of the world and that in time this will be one of the most famous parks in existence."[46] Until well into the twentieth century, national parks in were seen as large, scenic reserves established primarily for the provision of recreation and tourism opportunities rather than for the preservation of wilderness or indigenous species.[47]

Ontario's Protected Areas

The first provincial reservation of land in Ontario occurred in 1887 with the creation of Queen Victoria Niagara Falls Park. As in Australia, New Zealand and the United States, this first public reservation owed much to the well-established urban park concept; there was also the seemingly common perception that the area "was gradually being destroyed by the artificial means adopted for money-making purposes" and that "it would be better and more satisfactory to the people for the province to undertake the work."[48] Internal memorandum written to Premier Mowat on the issue referred to the existence of Yosemite and Yellowstone parks in the United States, and suggested that it was now a recognized duty of government to protect natural wonders from unscrupulous development.[49]

The Ontario government followed this initial effort with the establishment of Algonquin Park in 1893. Ontario followed in the footsteps of several states in Australia by initially identifying the park as Algonquin *National* Park; the name was not changed to Algonquin Provincial Park until the passing of the Provincial Park Act in 1913.[50] The reason behind naming these areas "national" as opposed to provincial or state parks appears similar: each government considered their parks worthy of national park status (as exemplified by Yosemite,

Yellowstone and Banff) in terms of their status, size and function. Quebec's first two provincial parks (Mont Tremblant and Laurentides), established in 1894 and 1895 respectively, were also classified as national as opposed to provincial parks.[51]

Ontario also followed the lead of the United States, Australia, Canada and New Zealand in establishing the area for its "health resort and pleasure ground" purposes, to encourage revenue generation through the "improvement" of the wilderness and to apply conservation practices (e.g., protection of watershed, timber and wildlife for utilitarian purposes) for the "benefit, advantage and enjoyment of the people."[52] Concern over fish and game populations in the province, as outlined in the Royal Commission on Game and Fish's report tabled in 1892, was also instrumental to the creation of Algonquin National Park.[53]

The establishment of the third provincial park, Rondeau Provincial Park, was generated by distinctly different pressures, illustrating the haphazard, ad hoc manner in which all governments approached park creation at this time. While Queen Victoria Park and Algonquin National Park had chiefly been initiated by members of the Ontario bureaucracy, petitions from residents of Chatham and Kent County in southern Ontario provided the impetus for the designation of Rondeau.[54] Algonquin and Rondeau were to become the prototypes of two different types of provincial parks: Algonquin, a national park equivalent, was a large park located on the periphery of settlement, designed primarily for watershed, forest and game protection, the conservation (i.e., "wise-use") of these resources and tourism; Rondeau was a small park close to population centres, created and managed to provide recreational opportunities to local residents.[55]

Common Factors in National Park Establishment

Early non-urban, public park establishment in Australia, Canada, New Zealand and the United States followed a similar pattern, based largely upon these countries' common social and cultural backgrounds. While each country had, and continues to have idiosyncratic social, economic and political characteristics, commonalities present in the mid- to late-nineteenth century led to, *inter alia*, the rapid hierarchical diffusion of the national park concept.

Through the comparison of national park establishment in these four countries, eight indicative social characteristics shared by Australia, Ontario, New Zealand and the United States may be identified:

1. colonial legacy;

2. availability of natural resources and public land;

3. mismanagement of existing natural attractions;

4. feelings of national/cultural inferiority;

5. desire for revenue generation;

6. concern over "worthless lands";

7. increasing destruction of wilderness and indigenous species; and

8. calls for public recreation areas.[56]

The first common characteristic, the shared colonial legacy, refers to the fact that Australia, Canada (i.e., Ontario), New Zealand and the United States were all British colonies (or, in the case of Canada and the United States, ex-colonies). As adolescent countries, the exploitation of natural resources and the advancement and settlement of the frontier were essential to economic and social development. Indeed, these issues were the dominant preoccupations of each area's government(s).

Another result of this common colonial legacy was the fact that each country/region had what seemed to most observers as limitless expanses of wilderness filled with immeasurable amounts of natural resources. Moreover, as opposed to Britain and other Old World countries, the vast majority of these areas were held by the public rather than the private sector. Governments would not have to consume precious finances to purchase or otherwise obtain land.

Each country had also been subjected to sometimes severe criticism over the despoliation of natural tourist attractions by the private sector. The management of Niagara Falls, the most famous natural attraction in the New World, had been subjected to the most criticism in this regard, but other areas, such as the Pink and White Terraces in New Zealand, had also been sources of embarrassment. National and regional governments alike were grudgingly coerced into accepting responsibility for the legislative protection of these landscapes.

The governments' acceptance of this relatively new responsibility was based in part on colonies/nations in the New World's fear of being inferior to Old World nations. Australia, Canada, New Zealand, and even the United States, which already had a sizable population and well-established economy, were well aware of the their lack of cultural achievements compared to the Old World. Each country seized upon the provision of protected areas as a means of assuaging these feelings of cultural inferiority.[57] National parks in particular were utilized by New World politicians and intelligentsia to increase their country's or region's national pride and status, much like earlier private parks had been utilized in Britain to improve their owner's standing and prestige. For example, in an attempt to prod the commissioner of Crown Lands of Ontario into creating Algonquin National Park, the Canadian Institute suggested in 1892 that "The establishment of national parks will conduce to the fostering of a patriotic spirit and be a means of increasing interest in Canada abroad."[58]

As the above quote suggests, the status of these national parks served to enhance their function as tourist attractions. Politicians in the Australia, Canada, New Zealand and the United States all emphasized the importance of revenue generation as one of the primary functions of these newly created tourist destinations. The wilderness conditions found in these national parks were to be only a secondary attraction; however, wilderness was to be "improved" through the development of genteel attractions such as spas, hotels, roads, zoological displays and picnic facilities. For example, N.P. Langford, one of the most influential early sponsors of Yellowstone Park, suggested that islands in Yellowstone Lake be beautified "with the attractions of cultivated taste and refinement."[59] An impatient member of the New South Wales government spoke for the vast majority of politicians in all four countries when he asked "is [The National Park] to remain a wilderness?... Certainly it ought not to remain a wilderness with no effort whatever to improve it."[60] Revenue was not only to be generated through tourism, but also through the utilization of the natural resources of the areas: national park and equivalent reserves reflected conservationist rather than preservationist principles.

In a similar vein, government officials in each country/region had to be fully convinced of the unsuitability of the proposed land for settlement, agriculture, forestry and mining potential. Only if the proposed park could be considered so-called worthless land[61] with regards to these traditional uses of the land would politicians (and the public) agree to support park establishment.

There were other compelling forces at work which helped convince politicians of the need for protected areas. In each country, increasing settlement and advancing technology (particularly the development of the railroad) was causing increasing destruction of the wilderness and its inhabitants. While this was a source of great pride to each country, by the third quarter of the nineteenth century, it had also simultaneously become a cause of increasing concern to a small number of influential citizens. The social dissonance created by the simultaneous desire to both subdue the wilderness and protect the most spectacular yet economically worthless of each nation's wilderness provided the impetus for an increasing number of writers, artists and bureaucrats to appeal to their governments to create what became known as national parks.

Finally, the provision of national parks was a response to increasing requests for recreational areas. Support of the concept of national parks were geared to and derived from the middle and upper classes, the leisured, educated classes able to appreciate and access natural environment far outside the urban centres. The appreciation of the picturesque and sublime had become popular by the beginning of the nineteenth century,[62] and, together with Romanticism and Transcendentalism, had popularized the appreciation of wilderness. The idea that mere contact with nature, particularly wild nature, healed physical and moral ills spread throughout Western society. The success of the urban park concept in the mid-nineteenth century suggested that public, non-urban parks would be a logical and successful progression. Indeed, the United States (Arkansas Hot Springs), New Zealand (Thermal Districts) and Ontario (Queen Victoria Park) each established an urban national park equivalent before creating a non-urban national park.

It is significant that the national park systems created by regional as opposed to federal governments (i.e., Ontario and the Australian states) were more likely to create national parks near urban areas. With the exception of Algonquin, and the first national parks in Queensland and Tasmania, regional governments reacted to local public pressure to create protected areas. Each federal government in Canada, New Zealand and the United States, and each regional government in Australia and Ontario, however, created national parks due to the common social characteristics outlined above. As a result, national parks in each of these areas served almost identical, utilitarian purposes: a combination of social, tourism, conservation and recreation functions.

For many years, the parks served these objectives efficiently. From the beginning, they served as status symbols to young nations/colonies desperately trying to achieve their perceived manifest destiny. The wilderness would be conquered, but remnants would be protected from the inexorable exploitation of these times. They would continue to be utilized, as sources of wood, food, water and tourism revenue, but would also be places of emotional and physical healing for those sufficiently educated and affluent to access and enjoy the wilderness.

The Contemporary Expression of National Park History

While many park boundaries have been altered since their establishment, there has been little significant change in their basic form. That is, national parks' optimal use, in terms of their prevailing form and design, is still based on utilitarian principles and the provision of tourism and recreation opportunities, not on the preservation of ecological integrity. This is a crucial historical certainty: while national parks now normally reflect preservationist values, the national parks' current configuration can not serve these functions adequately in the long term.[63] For example, in 1988, the Canadian federal government amended the National Parks Act to state that the "maintenance of ecological integrity ... shall be the first priority" when creating management plans for national parks.[64] Provincial and state governments in Australia, Canada and the United States have not pursued the preservationist agenda to the same extent: provincial/state legislation and policies continue to reflect conservationist objectives. In Ontario, for example, a recent policy statement declares that the new overriding goal of the Ontario Ministry of Natural Resources (OMNR) is "To contribute to the environmental, social and economic well-being of Ontario through the sustainable development of natural resources,"[65] a goal which reflects conservationist rather than preservationist principles. Similarly, the primary goal of the Ontario provincial park system is the provision of a variety of recreation opportunities for residents and non-residents of Ontario.[66]

Conclusion

Popular concepts in society translate and crystallize the attitudes and values of the time to form an appropriate resolution. In the mid- to late-nineteenth century, a number of changing social attitudes and values within the middle and upper classes consolidated to form the national park concept. Soon after the United States created the world's first national park, the concept quickly diffused throughout temperate, British colonies and ex-colonies. The concept of the national park was able to diffuse so quickly because of the presence of common cultural, social, economic and political conditions in Australia, Canada (i.e., Ontario), New Zealand and the United States. The common possession of antecedent protected areas – particularly urban parks – was also instrumental in the popularity and diffusion of the national park concept. These commonalities also had significant impacts upon the structure and function of these new protected areas. By and large, the early national parks in the United States, Australia, Canada, New Zealand and Ontario were created to protect the environment from overexploitation by the private sector and overzealous settlers, and to provide tourism and recreational opportunities for the middle and upper classes.

Australia's early national parks were different in that they were an amalgam of the earlier urban park and the new national park ideals: they were intended more for the provision of mass recreation opportunities than were the national parks of the United States, Canada and New Zealand. Ontario, the other regional government included in this study, was also to concentrate on the provision of parks near urban centres after the establishment of Algonquin National Park.

While national parks established in the nineteenth century were to perform their functions admirably for a number of years, the recent redirection of the national park concept to fulfil preservationist objectives, based largely upon ecological principles, has been problematic. As the purpose and functions of the national parks and equivalent reserves evolve, it may be necessary to reconfigure their contemporary form to better reflect and enable preservationist objectives.

Notes

This paper was first presented at the Changing Parks Conference in Peterborough, Ontario, April 1994. An altered version was later published in *Forest and Conservation History* 39.3 (July 1995): 121-29.

1. Huth, H. *Nature and the American Mind: Three Centuries of Changing Attitudes* (Berkeley and Los Angeles: University of California Press, 1957); French, S. "The Cemetery as Cultural Institution: The Establishment of Mount Auburn and the 'rural cemetery' movement," *American Quarterly* 26 (1974): 37-59.

2. Chadwick, G. F. *The Park and the Town* (New York: Frederick A. Praeger, 1966); Bailey, P. *Leisure and Class in Victorian England: Rational Recreation and the Contest for Control* (London, Routledge and Kegan Paul, 1978); Newton, N. T. *Design on the Land: the Development of Landscape Architecture* (Cambridge, MA: Belknap, 1971).

3. Thomas, K. *Man and the Natural World: Changing Attitudes in England 1500-1800* London, Allen Lane, 1983) 205.

4. Stormann, W. F. "The Ideology of the American Urban Parks Movement: Past and Future," *Leisure Sciences* 13 (1991): 137-151.

5. Malcolmson, P. *Popular Recreations in English Society 1700-1850* (London: Cambridge University Press, 1973); Bailey, *Leisure and Class in Victorian England*; McFarland, E. M. "The Beginning of Municipal Park Systems" in G. Wall and J. S. Marsh, eds., *Recreational Land Use: Perspectives on its Evolution in Canada*, (Ottawa: Carleton University Press, 1982), pp. 257-271.

6. Cantor, L. M. and Hatherly, J. "The Medieval Parks of England," *Geography* 64 (1979): 71-85; Rackham, O. "Trees and Woodland in a Crowded Landscape – the Cultural Landscape of the British Isles," in H.H. Birks, H.J. Birks, P.E. Kaland and D. Moe, eds., *The Cultural Landscape: Past, Present and Future*, (Cambridge: Cambridge University Press, 1988), pp. 53-78.

7. Prince, H.C. *Parks in England* (Isle of Wight: Pinhorns, 1967); Darby, H.C. *Domesday England* (Cambridge: Cambridge University Press, 1977); Young, C.R. *The Royal Forests of Medieval England* (Leicester, Leicester University Press, 1979); Cantor, L.M. "Forests, Chases, Parks and Warrens" in L.M. Cantor, ed., *The English Medieval Landscape*, (London: Croom Helm, 1982), pp. 56-85.

8. Williams, R. *The Country and the City* (London: Chatto and Windus, 1973).

9. Ise, J. *Our National Park Policy: A Critical History* (Baltimore: Johns Hopkins Press, 1961).

10. Huth, *Nature and the American Mind*; Killan, G. "Mowat and a Park Policy for Niagara Falls 1873-1887" *Ontario History* 70 (1978): 115-135; Runte, A. "National Parks: the American Experience" (Lincoln: University of Nebraska Press, 1987).

11. The United States was strongly influenced by the British economic tradition espoused by Adam Smith and his advocates: see Dorfman, J. *The Economic Mind in American Civilization 1606-1865* (New York: Viking, 1946); Speigal, H.W. *The Rise of American Economic Thought* (New York: Augustus M. Kelly, 1960); Evans, E.J. *The Forging of the Modern State: Early Industrial Britain 1783-1870* (London: Longman, 1983).

12. Nash, R. "The American Invention of National Parks," *American Quarterly* 22 (1970): 726-735; Nash, R. *Wilderness and the American Mind,* 3rd ed. (New Haven: Yale University Press, 1982); Runte, *National Parks*. The term national park equivalent is utilized because the legislation creating both Yosemite and Yellowstone designated these areas as "Parks" rather than "National Parks." Yellowstone was termed a national park in text of the Sundry Civil Bill of 1883 and the Wyoming Act of 1890, and in the title of Chapter 72 of the Lacey Act and Chapter 198 of the Hayes Act in 1894. The Yosemite National Park Act, which deeded the park back to the federal government, was passed in 1890.

13. Smith, S. "Review of 'Statistical Annals of the United States of America,'" *Edinburgh Review* 33 (1820): 79.

14. *Ibid.*

15. See, for example, Miller, P. *Errand into the Wilderness* (Cambridge: Belknap, 1956); Miller, P. *Nature's Nation* (Cambridge: Belknap, 1967).

16. See also Foster, E. H. *The Civilized Wilderness: Backgrounds to American Romantic Literature 1817-1860* (New York: The Free Press, 1975); Allen, J.L. "Horizons of the Sublime: the Invention of the Romantic West," *Journal of Historical Geography* 18 (1992): 27-40; Bowden, M. J. "The Invention of American Tradition" *Journal of Historical Geography* 18 (1992): 3-26.

17. Miller, P. "The Romantic Dilemma in American Nationalism and the Concept of Nature" in Miller, *Nature's Nation*, p. 252.

18. Catlin, G. *Letters and Notes on the Manners, Customs, and Conditions of North American Indians* (New York: Dover, [1844] 1973), Volume I, pp. 261, 262.

19. Similar statements can be found in Thoreau, H. D. "Journal Entry 305: January 3, 1861" in B. Torrey and F. H. Allen, eds., *The Journal of Henry D. Thoreau*, Volume 14 (New York: Dover, 1962) 156; Marsh, G. P. "Earth As Modified By Human Action," cited in Passmore, J. *Man's Responsibility for Nature* (London: Duckworth, 1974) 104.

20. Runte, *National Parks*.

21. Brown, R. C. "The Doctrine of Usefulness: Natural Resource and National Park Policy in Canada" in J. G. Nelson and R. C. Scace, eds., *The Canadian National Parks: Today and Tomorrow* (Calgary: University of Calgary Press, 1968); Haines, A. L. *The Yellowstone Story: A History of Our First National Park* (Yellowstone National Park, WY: Yellowstone Library and Museum Association and Colorado Associated University Press, 1977); Nash, R. *Wilderness and the American Mind*; Bella, L. *Parks for Profit* (Montreal: Harvest House, 1987); Runte, *National Parks*; McNamee, K. "From Wild Places to Endangered Places: A History of Canada's National Parks" in P. Dearden and R. Rollins, eds., *Parks and Protected Areas in Canada: Planning and Management* (Toronto: Oxford University Press, 1993) 17-44.

22. Thompson, K. "Wilderness and Health in the Nineteenth Century" *Journal of Historical Geography* 2 (1976): 145-161; Hyde, A. F. "An American Visitor: Far Western Landscape and National Culture, 1820-1920" (New York: New York University Press, 1990). William H. H. Murray's *Adventures in the Wilderness; or, Camp Life in the Adirondacks*, first published in 1869, was a popular call to arms for those desiring a wilderness 'cure'.

23. Muir, J. "The Wild Parks and Forest Reservations of the West" in J. Thaxton, ed., *The American Wilderness* (New York: Barnes and Noble, 1993).

24. Nash, *Wilderness and the American Mind*.

25. Heathcote, R. L. "Visions of Australia, 1770-1970" in R. Rapoport, ed., *Australia as Human Setting: Approaches to the Designed Environment* (Sydney: Angus and Robertson, 1972) 77-98; Bolton, G. *Spoils and Spoilers* (Sydney: George Allen and Unwin, 1981); Hughes, R. *The Fatal Shore* (New York: Knopf, 1987); Dunlap, T. R. "Australian Nature, European Culture: Anglo Settlers in Australia" *Environmental History Review* 17 (1993): 25-48.

26. Powell, J. M. *Environmental Management in Australia 1788-1914* (Melbourne: Oxford University Press, 1976), p. 114.

27. Pettigrew, C. and Lyons, M. "Royal National Park: A History" *Parks and Wildlife* 2 (1979): 17.

28. Mosely, G. "A History of the Wilderness Reserve Idea in Australia" in G. Mosely, ed., *Australia's Wilderness: Conservation, Progress and Plans: Proceedings of the First National*

Wilderness Conference, Canberra, 1977 (Canberra, Australian Conservation Foundation, 1978).

29. Whitelock, D. *Conquest to Conservation: History of Human Impact on the South Australian Environment* (Netly: Wakefield, 1985) 124.

30. Groome, A. *One Mountain After Another* (Adelaide: Angus, 1949); Dunphy, M. "The Bushwalking Conservation Movement, 1914-1965" *Parks and Wildlife* 2 (1979): 54-64; Strom, A.A. "Impressions of a Developing Conservation Ethic, 1870-1930" *Parks and Wildlife* 2 (1979): 45-53; Frawley, K.J. "The History of Conservation and the National Park Concept in Australia: A State of Knowledge Review" in K.J. Frawley and N. Semple, eds., *Australia's Ever Changing Forests: Proceedings of the First Conference on Australian Forest History* (Cambell, ACT: Department of Geography and Oceanography, Australian Defence Force Academy, 1988) 395-417.

31. Mosely, G., *A History of the Wilderness Reserve Idea in Australia*, 27.

32. Pettigrew and Lyons, *Royal National Park*.

33. Groome, *One Mountain After Another*.

34. Cox, T. R. "From Hot Springs to Gateway: The Evolving Concept of Public Parks, 1832-1976" *Environmental Review* 5 (1980): 14-26; Myers, P. "State Parks in a New Era: Volume 1 – A Look at the Legacy" (Washington, D.C.: Conservation Foundation, 1989); Dearden and Rollins, *Parks and Protected Areas in Canada: Planning and Management*.

35. See, for example, Nelson, H. "Policy Innovation in the Australian States" *Politics* 20 (1985): 77-88; Davis, B. "Wilderness Conservation in Australia: Eight Governments in Search of a Policy" *Natural Resources Journal* 29 (1989): 103-114.

36. Canada was the first of these countries to establish a federal agency specifically created to administer national parks (Dominion Parks Branch, established under the Dominion Forest Reserves and Parks Act, 1911), followed by the United States (National Parks Service, National Parks Service Act, 1916) and New Zealand (National Parks Authority, National Parks Act, 1952).

37. Hamer, D. "150 Years of Auckland and Wellington Cities" in D. Green, ed., *Towards 1990: Seven Leading Historians Examine Significant Aspects of New Zealand History* (Wellington: GP Books, 1989) 32-48; Hamer, D. "Towns in New Societies" in J. Phillips, ed., *New Worlds?: The Comparative History of New Zealand and the United States* (Wellington: GP Books, 1989) 77-95; Shultis, J.D. "Natural Environments, Wilderness and Protected Areas: An Analysis of Historical Western Attitudes and Utilisation, and Their Expression in Contemporary New Zealand" (Doctoral Thesis, Department of Geography, University of Otago, Dunedin, 1992).

38. Anon., "Extracts From the Instructions of the Directors of the Plymouth Company of New Zealand, to Their Chief Surveyor, Mr. F. A. Carrington" *New Zealand Journal* 1 (1840): 193.

39. Steven, R. "Land and White Settler Colonialism: The Case of Aotearoa" in D. Novitz

and B. Wilmott, eds., *Culture and Identity in New Zealand* (Wellington: GP Books, 1989) 21-34; Shultis, *Natural Environments, Wilderness and Protected Areas*.

40. Roche, M. M. *Forest Policy in New Zealand: An Historical Geography 1840-1919* (Palmerston North: Dunmore, 1987).

41. In 1885, a 10 square mile reserve surrounding recently discovered hot springs was reserved by the federal government; this area, legislated as Rocky Mountains Park in 1887, was the nucleus of what is now Banff National Park. For information regarding the importance of the development of spa resorts in Canadian National Park history, see Brown, *The Doctrine of Usefulness*; Marty, S. *A Grand and Fabulous Notion: The First Century of Canada's Parks* (Toronto: NC Press, 1984); Bella, *Parks for Profit*; Lothian, W. F. *A History of Canada's National Parks* (Ottawa: Minister of Supply and Services, 1976).

42. *Appendices to the Journal of the House of Representatives* (hereafter AJHR), 1874, Appendix H-26 (Wellington, New Zealand Government), p. 1.

43. AJHR, 1874, H-26, p. 4.

44. *Ibid.*

45. Harris, W. W. "Three Parks: An Analysis of the Origins and Evolution of the New Zealand National Park Movement" (Master's Thesis, Department of Geography, University of Canterbury, Christchurch, 1974); Shultis, J. D. "National Parks and National Development: The Establishment of National Parks in the United States, Australia, Canada and New Zealand" in R. Welsh, ed., *Geography in Action: Proceedings of the Fifteenth New Zealand Geographical Society Conference, Dunedin* (Wellington, New Zealand Geographical Society, 1990).

46. New Zealand Parliamentary Debates, 1894, Vol. 86, 579.

47. See, for example, Turner, E. P. "Scenic Reserves and National Parks" *Journal of the New Zealand Society of Horticulture* 6 (1936): 1-5.

48. "Ontario Legislature," *Globe* (Toronto), 1 April 1887, 5.

49. Killan, G. *Protected Places: A History of Ontario's Provincial Parks System* (Toronto, Dundurn, 1993).

50. *Ibid.*

51. *Ibid.*

52. Statutes of the Province of Ontario, 56 Victoria, Chapter 8, 32.

53. Ontario Sessional Papers, "Report of the Commissioners Appointed to Collect Information upon the Game and Fish of the Province of Ontario," Part VI, no. 79 (1892).

54. Killan, G., "Ontario's Provincial Parks, 1893-1993: 'We Make Progress in Jumps'" in L. Labatt and B. Litteljohn, eds., *Islands of Hope: Ontario's Provincial Parks System* (Toronto: Firefly Books, 1992) 20-45; Killan, *Protected Places*.

55. Lambert, R. and Pross, P. *Renewing Nature's Wealth: A Centennial History of the Public Management of Lands, Forests and Wildlife in Ontario 1763-1967* (Toronto: Dundurn Press, 1967); Morrison, K. "The Evolution of the Ontario Park System" in Wall and Marsh, *Recreational Land Use*, 102-121.

56. These eight commonalities also include the Canadian federal government's development of the national park concept; see Shultis, *Natural Environments, Wilderness and Protected Areas.*

57. Miller, *Nature's Nation*; Nash, *Wilderness and the American Mind.*

58. Cited in Killan, *Protected Places,* p. 13.

59. Cited in McCool, S. F. "The Challenge of Managing Wilderness in an Era of Change" in A. H. Watson, ed., *Outdoor Recreation Benchmark 1988: Proceedings of the National Outdoor Recreation Forum* (Asheville, NC: USDA Forest Service General Technical Report SE-52, 1989) 385.

60. Cited in Mosely, *A History of the Wilderness Reserve Idea in Australia,* p. 27.

61. Runte, *National Parks*; Sellars, R. W. et al., "The National Parks: A Forum on the "Worthless Lands" thesis" *Journal of Forest History* 27 (1983): 130-45.

62. Monk, S. *The Sublime: A Study of Critical Theories in XVIII-Century England* (Ann Arbor: University of Michigan Press, 1960); Hussey, C. *The Picturesque: Studies in a Point of View* (Hamden, CT: Archon Books, 1967); Andrews, M. *The Search for the Picturesque: Landscape Aesthetics and Tourism in Britain, 1760-1800* (Aldershot: Scholar Press, 1989); Allen, *Horizons of the Sublime.*

63. See Simberloff, D. S. "Design of Nature Reserves" in M. B. Usher, ed., *Wildlife Conservation Evaluation* (London: Chapman and Hall, 1986) 315-369; Chase, A. "Playing God in Yellowstone: The Destruction of America's First National Park" (New York: Harvest/Harcourt Brace Jovanovich, 1987); Newmark, W.D. "A Land Bridge Island Perspective on Mammalian Extinctions in Western North American Parks" *Nature* 325 (1987): 430-432; Shafer, C.L. *Nature Reserves: Island Theory and Conservation Practice* (Washington: Smithsonian Institution, 1990).

64. Bill C-30, "An Act to Amend the National Parks Act" (Ottawa: Supply and Services Canada, 1988).

65. OMNR, "MNR: Direction '90s" (Toronto: OMNR, n.d., mimeographed) n.p.

66. OMNR, Provincial Parks and Natural Heritage Branch, "Ontario Provincial Parks Policy" (Toronto: OMNR, n.d., mimeographed) n.p.

The Elusive Scottish Park System

Louise Livingstone

Although there are obvious dangers in drawing too close a parallel between one country and another, there is value in looking at how Scotland, a small country on the periphery of Western Europe lying at the same latitude as Hudson Bay, protects its special areas. Certainly in Scotland both the Canadian national park system and the Ontario Provincial Parks are held in very high esteem and much has been learnt from North American park planning as well as interpretation methodology. At present there is a great deal of thought and discussion in Scotland about the future for wild mountain areas and the whole question of how this relates to sustainable development. (The Countryside Commission for Scotland produced a discussion paper, *The Mountain Areas of Scotland: Conservation and Management* (1990) and the Secretary of State's, Cairngorm Working Party published their *Public Consultation Paper* in 1992 about the future of the Cairngorms).

It is interesting to see how John Muir is now being commemorated in Scotland. He went to North America as a young man, was closely involved with the early National Park movement and the call for the protection of wilderness. A charitable organization set up in his memory is buying up large areas of land in Scotland to manage as wild land for conservation and a country park, near his home town of Dunbar, is called after him.

The Lack of National Parks in Scotland

Although the mountains of the Highlands of Scotland are internationally known for their beautiful landscapes and are described by some as the last wil-

derness of Europe, there are no Scottish national parks. There are unique ecosystems: such as the "Flow Country" or blanket peat land of Caithness and
Sutherland with its rich communities of wading birds; the West Coast sea lochs
and islands with their marine mammals, such as sea otters, seals, dolphins and
whales as well as sea birds and fish communities; and the arctic tundra of the
Cairngorm mountains, where winds and freezing temperatures make weather
conditions as severe as anywhere.

Even though much of Scotland has landscapes of great beauty and scientific
nature conservation importance, there are no Scottish national parks despite,
at least, 50 years of debate. At the same time as the Dower Commission reviewed the establishment of national parks in England and Wales, the Ramsay
Commission (1945) produced a report calling for national parks for Scotland.
The report identified a number of areas that should be designated, such as the
Cairngorms, Wester Ross, Loch Lomond, Glen Coe and Glen Affric. In England and Wales there was a great public pressure for national parks. There had
been a number of famous conflicts between walkers from the industrial cities
and landowners over access, and much land was already in public ownership,
for example in the Lake District where the National Trust safeguarded key areas.

The National Parks and Access the Countryside Act (1949) introduced national parks to England and Wales. In Scotland, with its low population there
was not the same amount of recreational pressure nor such a well developed
amenity lobby. In addition, the land owners were keen to retain the status quo
and did not feel the need to support a movement towards national parks. It is
also interesting to see how England and Wales formalized "rights of way" that
now provide the main system of access to the countryside whereas in Scotland
it was felt that this could, in effect, reduce access. Again the land owners did
not wish to give up control of their land. The act, as well as establishing the legislation for national parks, set up a new government body to promote nature
conservation, the Nature Conservancy. There had been considerable pressure
from the scientific community, with the British Ecological Society in the forefront, for the government to create a biological service responsible for nature
conservation and a comprehensive system of nature reserves in the UK. Its functions as summarized in the charter were "To provide scientific advice on the conservation and control of natural flora and fauna of Great Britain; to establish,
maintain and manage nature reserves in Great Britain, including maintenance of
physical features of scientific interest; and to organize and develop research and
scientific services related thereto" (*Nature Conservation in Great Britain* 1984).

Effort within the new Nature Conservancy, in its early years, went towards the development of a system of protecting scientifically important areas by setting up a number of National Nature Reserves that either they owned or managed through agreement with the owners. National Nature Reserves had a much lower public profile than national parks but had clear objectives to safeguard scientific interest. In addition to establishing National Nature Reserves the NC had the duty to notify planning authorities of Sites of Special Scientific Interest (SSSIs). Development rather than agricultural or forestry change was seen as the most likely way these areas could be damaged.

The potential Scottish national park areas identified by the Ramsay Commission were highlighted and special protection given in the new town and country planning legislation. National Nature Reserves were established in parts of the areas and later on, the Countryside Commission delegated them as well as other areas as National Scenic Areas because of their landscape significance. The Countryside Commission of Scotland (CCS) was set up in 1967 under the Countryside (Scotland) Act 1967 to promote the enjoyment of the Scottish countryside and the protection of its beauty. A sister organization, the Countryside Commission in England and Wales, was established in the following year.

The CCS ran parallel to the scientific Nature Conservancy (latterly the Nature Conservancy Council for Scotland) until they were joined in 1992 as the Scottish Natural Heritage. This meant that there was one government body promoting access and recreation in the countryside and one body attempting to promote science-based nature conservation. How did the proposed national parks fit in? The parts of the country identified were important both scientifically and for their landscape beauty, tourism and recreation potential. The national parks that were designated in England and Wales were very much cultural landscapes with smaller areas of nature conservation interest within them.

Before describing the work of the CCS to establish a comprehensive park system for Scotland, it is necessary to put the whole issue into some sort of historical context, if somewhat over simplified. (T.C. Smout's *The History of the Scottish People 1560–1830* and *A Century of the Scottish People 1830–1950*, 1986 make the most comprehensive and readable introduction to the history of Scotland).

Scotland in Context

The view from this side of the Atlantic is that the UK is a densely over-populated island. But this is not the case in Scotland. Scotland is a little bigger than eastern Ontario. The mainland from north to south is about 500 kms. The two island groups of Orkney and Shetland stretch a further 200 kms north. The mainland and the Inner and Outer Hebrides are very approximately 300 kms wide. Scotland, like southern Ontario, is highly urbanized. Nearly three of its four million people live in the old industrial heartland of the Central Belt from Glasgow to Edinburgh and Dundee, with 200,000 in Aberdeen, the European centre of the North Sea Oil industry. Scottish cities such as Edinburgh and Glasgow were concentrated and had a greater affinity with European cities than to the more dispersed cities of England. The picture has changed with the considerable suburban expansion of this century.

The uplands and mountain areas of Scotland in contrast have some of the lowest population densities in Europe with people living mainly in the more fertile river valleys and along the coast. In the far north west where only one per cent of the land can be classified as arable, there is an average population density of 1.25 persons/sq. km.

The rights to land had, and still have, a major impact on rural Scotland. Basically all land is privately owned, although some land is held by the Forestry Commission, some by the water authorities, some now by Scottish Natural Heritage and some by non-governmental organizations, such as the National Trust for Scotland and the Scottish Wildlife Trust. The Crown Estates own the coast between high and low water mark on the mainland of Scotland as well as some land holdings (Livingstone and Lloyd 1990).

In the lowlands, or more arable areas of Scotland, land ownership was firmly based on the feudal system. The king granted out land to his faithful followers in exchange for their support in times of war. In turn these lords leased out the land to tenants in exchange for military support and food. The pattern of estates with their defensive castle the symbol of feudal power, their good mains or home farm and tenanted farms is still there. The present agricultural landscape dates from the late-eighteenth and early-nineteenth century, later than much of England. The farms were laid out on patterns set down by the landowners, not however on a strict grid pattern, but rather superimposed on the existing agricultural landscape. There was a movement of people from the land in the lowlands from the late-eighteenth century right to after the Second World War as happened all over Western Europe.

In many of the lowlands areas, although the estate structure can still be seen in the landscape, it has largely gone. After the First World War and during the agricultural depression of the 1920s and 1930s, many of the agricultural estates were broken up and sold to the tenants. The land ownership pattern is now mostly one of owner-occupied farms.

In the Highlands, the story is somewhat different. The union of the two nations in 1707 brought improved conditions for trade and an increasingly money-based economy. (Earlier on, Scotland had much closer trading links with France than with England as often the border was closed). The population of the Highlands rose with the introduction of small pox vaccination and the increased cultivation of potatoes for winter food. The traditional, communal, pastoral system based around clan or tribal territories began to change and was finally destroyed after the aborted attempts of Catholic "Bonnie Prince Charlie" to gain the Crown in 1745. The lands of his followers were forfeited and many went into exile. There was considerable investment by the government in development with the construction of roads and military forts to ensure the keeping of the peace, new rural industries and agricultural improvements were introduced and fishing towns and harbours built along the coast.

A significant number of the jacobite followers of Bonnie Prince Charlie ended up in Canada forming the loyalist regiments that fought the Americans. Highlanders also were involved with founding the North West Company in Montreal and the opening up of the west. Many people, both from the Highlands and Islands of Scotland and the lowland agricultural areas, left Scotland either voluntarily or were "cleared off the land" going either to the industrial towns, to new settlements first in the Maritimes, Quebec and Ontario and later to the Prairies. In the Highlands, those who remained were moved to crofting townships or "reservations" along the coast to make a living by fishing and subsistence agriculture. (James Hunter's *Making of the Crofting Community (1975)* gives a very readable if somewhat one-sided picture. *The Scottish Tradition in Canada* (1975) edited by W. Standford Reid takes up the story in Canada).

In the Highlands, much of what had been used as grazing land in the summer was taken over by the clan chief, now seen as the legal land owner and it was advertised for sheep farming. The communities traditional rights to fish, hunt, graze animals, plant and fell trees and cut peat for fuel were lost largely by default. It is interesting to note that there has been a successful bid, recently, by local people in Deeside to regain their historic communal rights and use them to prevent commercial afforestation. For the most part, the people were moved off the land at much the same time as the native people of southern Ontario were being displaced during the late-eighteenth and early-nineteenth centuries.

Land ownership in Scotland is one of the most concentrated in Europe with a few people owning large areas of land. A useful, if somewhat inaccurate figure is 7:84, seven per cent of the people own 84 per cent of the land. 7:84 was the name of a very lively theatre company started in the 1970s, one of the first to take political plays to the Highlands and Islands. "The Cheviot, the Stag and the Black Black Oil" is their best remembered. It made local communities aware of the history of exploitation of the Highlands using the gaelic language and music.

The "Cheviot" refers to sheep. Large flocks of cheviot sheep were brought in from the south to graze on the hills. Wool production was highly profitable for a short time in the early- to mid-nineteenth century, before Australian wool flooded the market. Although numbers have declined, sheep farming still has an important place in the Highland economy and sheep still have a major impact on the vegetation.

The "Stag" refers to red deer, the native deer of Scotland which has been long hunted for sport. In the mid-nineteenth century, much of the Highlands were taken over by rich industrialists, following the fashion set by Queen Victoria and Prince Albert.

They built huge, stone, baronial castles or shooting lodges as their own glorified "holiday cottages." These were used for a few months of the summer as the private recreation retreats of these very rich men. Considerable amounts of money were put into these estates with investment into forestry, path or trail building and other construction work. Local men were employed to act as hunting guides or "stalkers and ghillies" and the women cooked and cleaned in the "big house." In some areas walkers were tolerated, along with the stalking or deer shooting season, in others, they were and still are strictly forbidden. This form of land use has continued over much of the Highlands. People own their private "acadias" and enjoy them in August and September. Large numbers of red deer stag increased the capital value of the estate and little regard was taken to the problems of over grazing and resource degradation.

The "Black, Black Oil" is the North Sea Oil industry that was developing at that time in the early seventies on the east coast and in the northern islands with wide spread repercussions. The deep sea water of the West Coast lochs was needed for the construction of drilling rigs, major industrial oil terminals had to be developed in the remote Shetland Islands and still more people left the land to work in the new industry. Was it to be the next exploitation of the Highlands?

Returning to the Scottish Park System

In the mid-1970s, the Countryside Commission for Scotland came out with its proposal for *A Park System for Scotland* (1974). The idea was that recreational areas should range from town parks through country parks to regional parks and special or national parks. Thirty country parks have been developed close to towns and cities, mainly in the central belt between Glasgow and Edinburgh. These range from a few hectares to many hundreds and are managed primarily for outdoor recreation. They are usually owned by local or municipal authorities although there are some privately owned country parks. Each park has to achieve a certain standard before being granted the title of country park. There are a number of larger regional parks, such as the Lomond Hills in Fife and the Pentland Hills, near Edinburgh. The land remains in private ownership but there may be agreements with the land owners to formalize access or to safeguard landscape features or special habitats.

Long distance walking routes, such as the West Highland Way running from Glasgow to Fort William have developed despite considerable controversy. Many people, especially the mountaineers, felt that it could be the thin edge of the wedge which would destroy people's commonly accepted rights of "Freedom to Roam" by restricting access. There was also concern about the safety of encouraging inexperienced people into the hills.

Long distance routes are now an established part of the Scottish scene beginning to create a network around Scotland. This concept is not new as the Scottish Youth Hostel Association developed a series of walking and cycling routes, from hostel to hostel, linking the popular climbing areas in the 1930s. The association is still closely involved with the setting up of new routes and links to Europe (Lawson, P. and Fladmark, M. 1993).

In addition to the parks and long distance routes there are a number of very successful "greening" initiatives in the urban fringe such as the Central Scotland Forest. Many of these have strong community involvement and some link the inner city areas with the countryside using river corridors such as the Clyde Calder Project south from Glasgow.

The CCS proposal for special parks has not yet been implemented. The situation in the Highlands is complicated and as yet no special or national park has been designated. Loch Lomond, despite much political lobbying for national park status, has been designated a regional park because of its proximity to Glasgow.

Why Are There No Scottish National Parks?

There seems to be a number of factors appearing to contribute to the elusive nature of the Scottish park system and the lack of national parks.

1. *Land ownership.*

Scotland has the most concentrated land ownership in Europe. In the past, land ownership was equated with power. This is still the case to some extent. Land owners have considerable influence and there are many long-held vested interests. In the past, there was little support of national parks from the land owning fraternity as they saw increased restrictions on how they use their land and also the introduction of hoards of visitors to, as yet, little visited areas. Many land owners now recognize that they have to maintain a careful balance between self interest and the public good. There is a lot of discussion about the estate owner as "steward of the land" and it is perhaps the veiled threat of increased regulation, of possible land nationalization that raises awareness in the most intransigent.

2. *Sectoral approach of government.*

Until very recently rural Scotland has suffered from the British "divide and rule" approach to government. Since the last war, UK agriculture policy aimed to maximize food production and increase self-sufficiency in temperate products. Forestry policy to reduce dependency on timber imports, which stood at 90 per cent, led to monoculture afforestation with quick growing Sitka spruce from the Queen Charlotte Islands. The local planning authorities controlled development and tried to safeguard amenity through the town and country planning system, but had no jurisdiction over agriculture or forestry. This again dated from post-war planning when it was felt that foresters and farmers were the natural stewards of the countryside and what was good for forestry and agriculture was good for the countryside. The Countryside Commissions promoted recreation and landscape beauty and the Nature Conservancy, later the Nature Conservancy Council, set up a sophisticated, but somewhat static, system for designating "sites" of special scientific interest and nature reserves based on existing interest and management. These cover the whole range of semi-natural habits in the UK as well as geological and geomorphological sites. Less progress has been made with marine sites because of conflicting interests. Ancient monuments and historic buildings are designated and looked after by yet another government body, now Historic Scotland.

Any integration was done at the Scottish Office level by the secretary of state with advice from each of the sectoral experts. The whole system was hierarchical and with decision making and power coming from the top. Conflicting policies of various government departments and agencies could not bring consensus about the best way forward. The management of special mountain areas involves integration, no one expert or profession has all the answers. Also, land use decision making is complex and land managers do not make decisions simply in response to government policy.

3. *Dichotomy between "wild nature" and a sense of wilderness and ideas of the "English pastoral," the well-managed countryside producing benefits for man.*
This is obviously a more nebulous issue, but it does have a profound effect on people thinking about the future. Scotland has been inhabited for 7,000 years since the last Ice Age and has a very diverse cultural and natural heritage; however, different people have different perceptions of Scotland and different views of this cultural landscape. The ideal of the well-husbanded English countryside with its hedges and small islands of nature amid verdant fields does not, quite, fit with Scotland. Dr. Johnson, who toured Scotland in the eighteenth century, saw it as desolate and godforsaken, "A tree might show in Scotland as a horse in Venice." Scotland was largely deforested by the fourteenth century.

Others of the romantic movement, for example, William Wordsworth and his sister Dorothy, Walter Scott and the author of the heroic saga of "Ossian," created the view still held by many that the bare open hillsides are "romantic and sublime." Others see the same hills as "a man created, wet desert." The ranks of Sitka spruce are seen as productive forestry by some and regenerating native pine woods as worthless scrub. Others are offended by the green pile carpet blanketing the bare, purple, heather-covered hills. The deer forest owner has looked upon increasing numbers of red deer as a valuable asset adding capital value to their estates, whilst others see the final destruction of natural vegetation. Deer numbers are very high at present because of a series of mild winters.

There has been little agreement either about what is the best future for the Highlands or the best way forward. In the past, there has been much misunderstanding coming from the very different perceptions of the Scottish countryside that people hold.

Changing Circumstances and Hopes for the Future
A number of conflicts came to a head in the 1980s which have brought changes both in Scotland and in the UK as a whole. Public concern about the environ-

mental impact of agribusiness grew, as did anger about conifer afforestation. The European Community found agricultural surplus too expensive and did a u-turn. Rural communities are now seen as valuable to the urban population as stewards of the countryside and need to be supported. Farmers are paid to set land aside and there are schemes to promote environmentally sensitive farming to conserve the landscape and the agricultural community. Social aspects are on the agricultural agenda along with the environment.

Tax relief on afforestation was withdrawn in 1987 and the plug pulled on wide-scale conifer planting. Forestry policy now aims to manage existing native woodlands and to promote planting of native species. Ideas of community forests and recreational forests are coming in and the Forestry Commission is working closely with the local authorities. This is a complete turnaround from 1980.

There were a number of very controversial battles over the management of sssis, largely about the levels of compensation paid to owners for profit that they would forego if they agreed to change existing management practice (Livingstone, Rowan-Robinson and Cunningham 1990). It has been said that this controversy led to the breaking of the power of the Nature Conservancy Council.

In Scotland, Scottish Natural Heritage was formed from the Nature Conservancy Council for Scotland and the Countryside Commission for Scotland in 1992. The Natural Heritage (Scotland) Act, 1991, introduces the concept of natural heritage and sustainable development into Scottish law. The new body has the task of designating and coordinating the management of "Natural Heritage Areas," the latest title for Scotland's special areas, and has been considering Loch Lomond and the Trossachs and the Cairngorms.

Another issue that has to be borne in mind is that the "voluntary approach" has long been part of Tory government philosophy and especially with their rural policy. The "voluntary approach" is promoted and there is an unwillingness to introduce further systems of regulation and enforcement; however, this approach is linked to policies to cut budgets, to undermine the power of local government and for centralization, rather than to education and incentives. Natural heritage areas however, will be designated from the centre by a decision from the Secretary of State on advice from snh and only then be managed locally by voluntary agreement.

In the meantime, the European Union moves towards subsidiarity and regionalization, funding rural communities to seek local solutions to sustainable development through programmes such as LEADER that provides direct support for local initiatives in rural development (Baxter 1994). Some communities, like those in the Western Isles now see that their future is closely linked to their environment and are exploring ideas of "green tourism" and appropriate agriculture and questioning unsustainable development such as super quarries.

In the mountain areas particularly, there are indications that things are changing and that people are coming together. Landowners, long antagonistic to mountaineers, are finding that conflicts can be reduced by discussion and that they can live with the hikers who also enjoy and value these areas. The mountaineers are gaining understanding of the factors involved in making a living from the hills. This new approach is by no means universal but there are hopeful signs of change. (SNH has produced *Enjoying the Outdoors: A Consultation Paper on Access to the Countryside for Enjoyment and Understanding, 1992.*)

Some estate owners have formed groups to manage what is now recognized to be a common resource and there is a new Association of Scottish Deer Management Groups. Deer forest owners are beginning to recognize that the conservationists have valuable things to say about habitat management and carrying capacity. On the other hand, the scientists are coming to realize that managing populations of wild animals is not easy and that they do not have all the answers. More attention is being given to the views and knowledge of the deer stalker.

There is much to be optimistic about as there are positive things happening in Scotland and perhaps a move towards more sustainable land management and community development. The Scottish Office has come out with *A Rural Framework* (1992) calling for partnership and cooperation, maintenance of diversity, networks and communication between agencies and communities and links with Europe.

The question of whether or not the universally accepted status of national park should be given to certain special areas continues to be debated. How can these special areas be safeguarded without formal national park status and firm financial commitment? How can the government seek World Heritage status for the Cairngorms but without ensuring a robust management structure. A public survey in 1990 asking should there be National Parks in Scotland got a 84 per cent positive response. The Scottish Office survey in 1991 found 90 per cent in favour. Will Natural Heritage Area satisfy people? It does not quite have the ring of National Park? Does Natural Heritage encompass the complexity of the Scottish cultural landscape? Will designations from the secretary of state be acceptable to local communities? Boundaries do not instill a sense of belonging or responsibility. Local communities have their own sense of commitment to an area.

Maybe special status should be allowed to develop gradually. In the west of Ireland, the local people seeing the potential economic benefits of having a national park in their area are now calling for its designation where in the past they fought against it. There is no easy answer or one right answer. The important thing is that people with previously conflicting interests are beginning to talk to each other and find that they have much common ground, not least a love of the land. The elusive Scottish park causes tremendous controversy and strong feelings but it continues to bring people together to think about the future. Maybe if it was a long-established reality, there would be misplaced feelings of complacency. Perhaps the lesson that Scotland can bring to Ontario is that moving towards a sustainable future, which protects and values special places, is an ongoing process. There is not a right way forward. What is important is that people get together with a common purpose and develop shared values and visions.

References

Baxter, S.H. *Digest of Participatory Processes in Integrated Development Programmes.* The Centre for Environmental Studies, The Robert Gordon University, Aberdeen/Scottish Natural Heritage, 1994.

Countryside Commission for Scotland. *A Park System for Scotland.* CCS, 1974.

Countryside Commission for Scotland. *The Mountain Areas of Scotland: Conservation and Management.* CCS, 1990.

Department of Health for Scotland. *National Parks: A Scottish Survey* (The Ramsay Report). Cm 6631, HMSO 1945.

Hunter, J. *The Making of the Crofting Community.* Edinburgh, 1975.

Lawson, P. and Fladmark, M. *Access through Hostelling: The Role and Policies of SYHA,* in Fladmark, J.M. (ed) *Heritage: Conservation, Interpretation and Enterprise,* London, Donhead, 1993.

Livingstone, L.H. and M.G. Lloyd. "Marine Fish Farming in Scotland, Proprietorial Behaviour and the Public Interest." *Journal of Rural Studies,* Spring 1992.

Nature Conservancy Council. *Nature Conservation in Great Britain.* ISN 0 86139 285, NCC, 1984.

Scottish Natural Heritage. *Enjoying the Outdoors: A Consultation Paper on Access to the Countryside for Enjoyment and Understanding.* SNH, 1992.

Secretary of State's Cairngorm Working Party. *Public Consultation Paper: May 1992.* Scottish Office, 1992.

Smout T.C. *A History of the Scottish People, 1560–1830* and *A Century of the Scottish People 1830–1950.* William Collins Sons & Co., 1986.

Standford Reid W. ed. *The Scottish Tradition in Canada.* Toronto, 1976.

CANADIAN PARKS LEGISLATION:

PAST, PRESENT AND PROSPECTS

Ian Attridge

With 1993 marking the centennial of Ontario's parks system, our minds naturally turn to a review of history and an examination of the future of the places we love so well. Accordingly, I will present my own personal views on the past, present and prospects of parks by looking at the law.

Now the law, and lawyers, can be pretty dry fodder at any time. But it has been legislation that has crystallized peoples' expressions of, and commitments to their concept of parks. Legislation tells us what is important, who has control and who has a role in managing our park lands. A park statute also sets out the confines within which public activities can take place, and the standards against which park managers' successes and shortcomings can be assessed.

I will focus on two themes:

- the evolution of legislation from governing a single park to presiding over a system; and

- a shift from recreation and resource use to more of an emphasis on protection.

I will track these themes as they have played out in the past, exist in the present and potentially could unfold in the future. My focus will be on legislation at the senior levels in Canada (national, provincial and territorial parks), but some references will be made to the municipal and regional levels as well, especially since both tiers have played significant roles in the history of Canada's parks movement.

The Beginnings of Parks Legislation

Legislation to provide public funds for creating public parks was passed during the decade following 1833 in Great Britain. This led to the creation of London's Victoria Park and Birkenhead Park near Liverpool in 1842 and 1843 respectively, becoming the first "outdoor recreational space on land acquired and owned by the people themselves, developed with public funds and open indiscriminately to all."[1] The commons is an ancient concept, however, that has evolved into a contemporary park context, such as the Boston Common first established in 1640.

In Canada, the earliest public park, "The Garden," was used by 1583 in St. John's, Newfoundland as little more than a vacant lot left wild.[2] The first Provincial Act to dedicate a park in Canada supposedly was for the 1763 establishment of Halifax Common.[3]

Ontario's first public parks were established in the mid-1800s. These included the leasing of the Garrison Reserve to Toronto in 1848, the transfer to Kingston of the City Park in 1851, and the park operated in Niagara-on-the-Lake since 1855.[4] However, some commentators consider early cemeteries to be the first public parks, since they were used for picnics, recreation and green space until the 1860s.[5]

Ontario's first park enactment dedicated Gore Square to the City of Hamilton in 1852 by provincial Act[6]. This individual park statute was followed some 30 years later by the Public Parks Act of 1883, the first of its kind in Canada.[7] This latter act set out the authority for municipalities to establish and manage a "system of parks, avenues, boulevards and drives" for public use, and has remained essentially the same over the last 120 years.

Moving now from the local scale, the first regional level park legislation in Ontario was passed in 1880 to enable the federal government to establish a park at Niagara Falls.[8] After tiring of federal government delays, the province went ahead and created the Niagara Falls Park in 1885, renaming it the Queen Victoria Niagara Falls Park two years later.[9]

From this individual park sprang the Niagara Parks Commission, which now operates a system of lands under the Niagara Parks Act.[10] This act contains the unusual provision that allows the commission to retain revenues from electric power generation at the Falls and thus achieve rare financial independence (having lucky 13 as the chapter number in three of the statutes setting up the park probably doesn't hurt, either!). The legislature must approve power generation agreements, and any bridges proposed to pass through the original Queen Victoria Park. These sections thus preserve substantial revenues and the scenic wonder of the Falls left unimpeded by unsightly spans.

Along with the Niagara Parks Commission, regional park legislation followed for lands remaining after the hydroelectric development at the International Rapids section of the St. Lawrence River,[11] and along the St. Clair River.[12] To integrate the growing provincial parks system with these regional and conservation authority park systems, the province established the Parks Integration Board under its own Act in 1956,[13] which was later abolished when the Department of Lands and Forests became the Ministry of Natural Resources in 1972.

A list of some of the other historical highlights of Ontario's park statutes, and of developments in the Provincial Parks Act itself, can be found at the end of this paper.

Park System Development in Legislation

We can identify six key periods in the development of the concept of a park system in legislation, beginning with individual park establishment and ranging through to potential future directions for a comprehensive protected areas system. A table of the first parks, individual and system statutes, and current act references for all of Canada's 13 senior jurisdictions is provided at the end of this paper.

1. *Individual Park Acts*

The earliest park statutes were passed to establish individual parks. These included:

- Banff National Park by Order in Council in 1885 and under the *Rocky Mountains Park Act* in 1887;[14]

- Queen Victoria Niagara Falls Park in 1885, and Algonquin and Rondeau Provincial Parks in 1893 and 1894, respectively;[15] and,

- Quebec's Laurentides and Trembling Mountain parks, established under separate but consecutive Acts in 1895.[16]

This early trend was followed by the establishment of British Columbia's Strathcona Park in 1911.[17]

2. *First System Statutes*

As new parks were developed, it became apparent that a simpler method of establishing parks was needed. More importantly, the administration of parks needed to be coordinated. Thus, the first park system statutes were passed in the early 1900s.

The first of these, the Dominion Forest Reserves and Parks Act, was passed by the federal Parliament in 1911, and included Banff National Park.[18] Two years later, Ontario passed its first Provincial Parks Act to consolidate administration of Algonquin and Rondeau Parks.[19]

3. New Authority for Park Systems

The third stage in system development occurred when constitutional authority over natural resources was transferred from the federal government. When these powers were assumed by the western provinces in 1930, Alberta and Saskatchewan quickly took advantage of this opportunity to pass their first provincial park acts, but Manitoba waited 30 years to pass such legislation.[20] Quebec added its first system statute in 1941, although this was not a new power.[21] Due to the development of a system of parks by this time, these first park acts benefitted from the Canadian and Ontario experiences some 20 and 30 years earlier.

A second wave of system-oriented acts were passed in the eastern provinces in the 1950s and early 1960s.[22] Except for Newfoundland, these were not based upon new authority, but rather a growing recognition of the need for protected areas and the desire to administer more effectively the many roadside and other sites under provincial management.

The most recent phase in this assumption of new authority came when limited jurisdiction over natural resources was transferred from the federal government to the Territories. The Northwest Territories assumed a number of federal roadside parks in 1967 with this transfer, and the larger recreational Fred Henne Territorial Park in 1970 from the City of Yellowknife.[23]

New authority was also granted to regional park systems during this period, including:

- Ontario's St. Lawrence and St. Clair park commissions and conservation authorities;
- Regional park systems in BC and Saskatchewan;[24]
- more local assemblages of lands at Niagara Falls, and in Saskatchewan and New Brunswick, for example.

4. Park System Classification

A recognition that all parks could not be all things to all people began to develop in the 1950s. This need to classify parks first gained legal expression in 1954 with Ontario's reconstituted Provincial Parks Act.[25] This act set out three classes: parks administered by the minister of Lands and Forests, by park commissions, or by another minister.

A few years later, British Columbia followed this lead with a three-part classification scheme in the Department of Recreation and Conservation Act,[26] a unique beginning of a park system within a departmental act. BC has essentially stuck to this three-part legal classification under its current Parks Act, although the Class C local parks are rarely created now.

In 1968, Ontario came forward with an innovative scheme setting out five different classes: natural environment, nature reserve, primitive, recreational and wild river.[27] While the names of these Ontario categories remain the same in the act as in 1968, several of the terms used today have changed. Primitive has become wilderness, wild river is now waterway, and an historical class has been added as an "other" class of provincial park. Based on Ontario's lead, many other provinces have adopted a similar classification system in their legislation.

5. The System Concept in Current Legislation

Today, most senior park statutes set out a classification scheme, often accompanied by specific purposes and permitted uses, especially in the western provinces. Further development of the contemporary park system concept can be observed in several legislative trends.

First, park system plans may be required. For example, Manitoba's new parks act requires that a system plan be put in place before many of the new sections take effect.[28] Similar requirements for the development of park system plans can be found in the legislation governing the National Capital Commission and the regional parks systems in British Columbia and Saskatchewan, among others.[29]

Second, the administration of a parks system has become more sophisticated, often leading to specific responsibilities being set out in the statutes for the legislature, cabinet, the minister, park superintendents and enforcement officers.

Third, reporting on the state of the parks system is also becoming more common. The federal National Parks Act requires such reporting, and Ontario may soon develop a similar approach under the new Environmental Bill of Rights that allows the environmental commissioner to report on ministries' compliance with their Statements of Environmental Values.[30]

6. Future Directions for Park Systems

In the future, certain trends are likely to expand and various legal techniques become more developed. This will respond to a contemporary recognition of what a complete protected areas system should be, its relationship to the surrounding landscape, new administrative structures, and an enhanced role for First Nations and the general public, among other dynamics.

To understand whether a particular park system configuration is in fact achieving its objectives, including representation of acknowledged features and processes, reporting on the health of park systems will become more sophisticated and spread to other provinces. System plans will become more important and thereby provide a focus on accomplishing these objectives. This is evident in the recent release of a new system plan, in Nova Scotia, while the Endangered Spaces campaign and The Wildlands Project are spurring similar developments in BC, the Territories, Alberta and elsewhere. Procedural provisions directing the development of these system plans may become more common in order to recognize their important role, as has already occurred in British Columbia, Saskatchewan, Manitoba and at the federal level.[31]

Enabling legislation for ecological and other surveys of various lands and waters will also be necessary to ensure that all potential components of a park system are assessed and then represented. The United States has already established its own Biological Survey, and we may soon be headed in a similar direction in this country.[32]

The needs of First Nations will be increasingly incorporated into park legislation. This is especially so as park management models develop in British Columbia, Ontario, and through land claim settlements in the north. As the implications become clear from the 1982 constitutional protection of Aboriginal and treaty rights and their 1990 interpretation by the Supreme Court of Canada in the *Sparrow* and *Sioui* cases, park statutes and regulations will be affected. Legislation will thus begin to provide new mechanisms to establish protected areas by First Nations for various natural and cultural heritage purposes, as the Six Nations and Nisga'a people have pursued. Further, legislation also may provide authority to enter agreements for the exercise of, or otherwise recognize, Aboriginal and treaty rights. This is essentially a further evolution of Phase C, above, where Aboriginal peoples will assume authority over some protected areas.

New park classes will be developed to make the systems more flexible or comprehensive, including:

- greenways as important recreational centres and ecological links (BC's parks authorities have long had the ability under their act to assume responsibility for trails and other greenways, and new statutes may build on this idea);[33]

- recognition of private lands and those protected by conservation groups as part of the protected areas system, such as already exist in the

Saskatchewan and Manitoba parks statutes, in some provinces' ecological reserves legislation, and under numerous natural areas statutes in various US states;[34]

- conservation reserves now under discussion for some three of 17 candidate areas in Ontario, that would permit hunting, trapping and motorized access to these areas;

- aquatic areas and their special legislative needs, which are now only minimally recognized in some provinces' waterway park classes, but do receive a higher profile as National Marine Parks under the federal National Parks Act (and apparently may soon have their own specific statute).

Finally, new classes of parks may include corridors between parks, or restoration areas within, around and between parks. I will address these again under the next theme for this paper.

Ecological Protection, Management and Integrity

Besides the development of the system concept for protected areas, the historical development of parks legislation in Canada also reveals an increasing emphasis over time on ecological protection, management and integrity. Rather than discuss this trend by identifying certain stages in this development, as above, this evolution will be presented under several sub-topics: purpose, administration, management, enforcement and ecological integrity within and outside of parks.

1. *Purpose*

The original purpose of establishing parks was primarily recreation and preserving scenery, such as in Banff and at Niagara Falls. These purposes are often set out in the implementing act's dedication clause. This clause in the National Parks Act, requiring National Parks to be "maintained and made use of so as to leave them unimpaired for the enjoyment of future generations," can be contrasted with the slightly looser Ontario act that dedicates provincial parks to those "who may use them for their healthful enjoyment and education, and ... shall be maintained for the benefit of future generations." As Kevin McNamee has noted, the provincial act provides no direction to keep parks "unimpaired," protected, or not overdeveloped, but rather the emphasis is on resource use and human benefit.[35] Other provinces have since adopted similar clauses in their legislation.

Some balance between recreation and environmental protection occurred later, but it has never been fully resolved. Managers' expertise and their budgets have tended to focus on activities that support park visitation, rather than the less quantifiable benefits of research, feature protection and management. This was also reflected in the legislation.

In 1988, this balancing act was then tipped towards protection in the amendments to the National Parks Act (Canada), where in section 5(1.2): "Maintenance of ecological integrity through the protection of natural resources shall be the first priority when considering park zoning and visitor use in a management plan." This clearly puts resource protection ahead of recreation and visitor activities where there is a conflict between these objectives. While this protection priority is suggested in some provincial policy and administrative practice, it has yet to receive legal expression within other park statutes.

2. Administration

Which department and which level of authority is responsible for managing parks can affect the protection afforded these areas. Administration of parks began under a variety of governmental departments, particularly those responsible for public lands. These included: the Department of the Interior for Banff, Department of Crown Lands for Algonquin and a Board of Commissioners reporting to the Legislature for Niagara Falls.

In a reverse of a trend in some jurisdictions towards a more specific mandate, national parks were recently moved from the Department of Environment to a new, more broadly based Department of Canadian Heritage. While Ontario's provincial parks are now run by the Ministry of Natural Resources, this ministry has evolved from and remains the administrative unit responsible for Crown lands and a wide variety of other activities. Niagara parks are still run by a Board of Commissioners with very little provincial involvement.

Like the federal and Ontario examples, British Columbia's first provincial park, Strathcona, was placed under the Department of Lands. As noted earlier, this was later followed by the province's first parks system legislation as established under the Department of Recreation and Conservation Act, thus originally tying parks to a particular administrative division. BC also retains an interesting provision that explicitly establishes the parks branch under the Parks Act, with an assistant deputy minister in charge. Today, the Ministry of Environment, Lands and Parks is responsible for these areas, representing a more specific, higher profile for parks administration than in earlier periods.

In other provinces, many amendments have been made over the years to Newfoundland's Provincial Parks Act solely due to a reorganized government administration, while some jurisdictions have decided to leave administrative responsibility to the ministry assigned by the lieutenant governor in council. Resource and tourism departments have more focused expertise than the earlier public works or lands departments, but some commentators suggest that these departments may have less commitment to the protection mandate than a Ministry responsible specifically for environmental or parks matters.[36]

3. Management

Two key management tools can be set out in legislation to support ecological protection and integrity. These are, first, specified prohibited or restricted uses, and second, management plans.

Early legislation specified certain prohibitions on uses within parks, or necessary procedures and authorizations before certain activities could occur. While this approach has been retained to a large extent, the regulation of various uses within different parks is now made easier due to the classification and zoning provisions put into legislation in the 1960s. Earlier management flexibility may have become more limited, but there is clearer guidance on what happens within certain types of parks, and this makes it easier for managers to resist pressures to overexploit park resources.

Many prohibitions and restrictions remain only in policy or regulations, rather than in the acts themselves, and this has been a departure from some earlier park statutes. One contentious issue in Manitoba's new act occurred when resource extraction within parks was to be explicitly recognized. At third reading, this provision was removed so that the act was silent on extraction; however, a close advisor to Premier Filmon informed me recently that Manitoba will always allow mining within parks since this is a key component in that province's economic development strategy.[37]

Management plans are the second key tool for protection within parks. Plans were not mentioned in the early park acts, and today they still receive limited reference. The legislation for national, Yukon and now Manitoba parks require preparation and (except for the Yukon) inclusion of certain components of management plans, while the Ontario and Nova Scotia acts leave such plans optional. Other jurisdictions may have management plans, but they are not founded upon a legal mandate.

Despite this limited recognition of management plans in senior park legislation, as noted earlier there is a strong system and individual park planning component in the regional- and local-level statutes governing the National Capital Commission, regional parks and the Creston Valley Wildlife Area in BC, Saskatchewan's regional parks and Meewasin Valley Authority and the Pippy Park in St. John's, Newfoundland.[38] It thus appears easier to specify process and components for an arm's length agency, than for governments to set out standards for themselves!

Finally, the requirement in the 1988 National Parks Act amendments placing ecological integrity as the first priority in National Park management plans gives Parks Canada more direction in how it should carry out its functions. This legislative direction has resulted in a number of internal and broader-scope conferences and thereby helped ensure a stronger emphasis on the protection mandate.

4. Enforcement

Over time, environmental protection has been enhanced by giving park officers more enforcement powers and increasing penalties for breaches of park rules. Stricter controls over hunting and fishing, increased patrols and tighter enforcement of leases in the National Parks in the first third of the 1900s had a substantial positive impact on environmental protection.[39] In Ontario, the 1961 grant to park wardens of all the powers of the Ontario Provincial Police gave them stronger enforcement authority.[40]

While I haven't compared fines with the average wage, penalties have nonetheless increased substantially in order to recognize the value placed on the features protected within parks. For example, fines under the National Parks Act (Canada) increased from an original $50 in 1885 to $5,000. This latter fine level remained for many years until the 1988 amendments created a maximum fine of $150,000. In Ontario, fines have increased from $50 to $500, and in 1989 to $5,000. Some provinces also provide for jail sentences, while at the federal level, there is now a differentiated fine structure that reflects variations in the seriousness of violations.

Today, poaching and other serious offences appear to be increasing, and we will need to build upon the techniques developed under wildlife, pollution and other laws to address such problems. These threats to Canadian parks will require new and innovative enforcement techniques and sophisticated penalties, including:

- better reporting and documenting of offences and offenders;

- penalties which strip profits and hunting licences from commercial poachers and repeat offenders, and cause their transgressions to be published;

- more officer powers such as: having peace officer protection while doing intelligence gathering and investigations outside of the park, and in some cases search warrants and the ability to stop and search vehicles.

In general, enforcement will become more proactive rather than reactive, necessitating more intelligence gathering, the monitoring of commercial and resource use sectors and ethnic markets, and high-tech surveillance and forensic methods.[41]

5. *Ecological Integrity Within Parks*

The Ontario Parks and Natural Heritage Section and Parks Canada, among others, have held a number of scientific seminars on ecological integrity, and the principles are becoming clearer for park management. While these principles have yet to see much translation into legislation, how could such principles be so applied?

First, as mentioned, system and management plans can be subject to ecological integrity as a priority, like the National Parks Act. This was a significant legal advance in 1988, and credit should be given to Parks Canada officials and other individuals such as Kevin McNamee for this accomplishment.

Second, the principles and objectives for the size and functional integrity of parks in the system could be set out in legislation. This may include a total minimum size for the parks system, as under British Columbia's Parks Act and in the original preamble to its Ecological Reserves Act,[42] or directions on area and boundary determinations for individual sites.

Third, higher standards for wildlife harvesting, pollution or construction activities could be set, to complement other acts. As noted earlier, this occurred in the early 1900s under the National Parks Act, and now section 33(t) of the new Manitoba Act provides a contemporary example to enable these enhanced standards.

Fourth, private and Aboriginal lands, lands managed by land trusts or other conservation groups, and other agencies' properties could be recognized as types of protected areas. Stewardship of these lands could also be assumed or supported under park act programs; this is occurring now under some Canadian and many US ecological reserve and natural area statutes.

6. *Ecological Integrity Outside of Parks*

Ensuring ecological integrity outside of parks is more conceptually and politically challenging. Little legal recognition of this principle has occurred for senior Canadian park systems to date, but increasing scientific interest may soon
spur new developments. None the less, under the 1992 international Convention on Biological Diversity, Article 8(e), Canada and its provinces do have a
responsibility to: "Promote environmentally sound and sustainable development in areas adjacent to protected areas with a view to furthering protection
of these areas." Promoting this idea in legislation could be accomplished in a
number of ways, such as:

- giving staff authorization outside of park boundaries to conduct
  education, landowner contact, enforcement, and acquisition programs
  and to make agreements;

- setting out financial disincentives for poor management on nearby
  lands, such as occurs under Alberta's Wilderness Areas, Ecological
  Reserves and Natural Areas Act;[43]

- requiring environmental impact assessments on lands surrounding
  parks.[44]

Connectivity could be encouraged by specific provisions for corridor and
restoration park classes and zones, inclusive of private lands, as in the proposed
American Northern Rockies Ecosystem Protection Act.[45]

Several statutes describe parks as being "set aside" or "set apart." While this
is true for municipal administration purposes, it fosters a non-integrative,
unecological perspective. This view is buttressed by enforcement and other
powers that are only valid within a park's boundaries. Such an approach and its
associated legal language will need to be altered if protected areas are to maintain their ecological significance and integrity.

Based upon these developments in purpose statements, administration,
management, enforcement and ecological integrity, one can conclude that there
has been an increased focus on environmental protection in parks legislation
over the years. It is also apparent, however, that innovations made in various jurisdictions across Canada also point to numerous opportunities where this direction could be legally and more widely enhanced.

Conclusions

There have been several generations of park statutes over the years. These have included the movement from single park and agency legislation to legal recognition of more comprehensive park systems. In addition, we have seen a shift from a recreation- and scenery-based orientation in park acts to one which increasingly puts priority on environmental protection.

The most recent expressions of these trends have been the 1988 amendments to the National Parks Act, and to a fair extent Manitoba's 1992 overhaul of its parks statute. There have been new parks and new administrative structures, such as two Ontario Ministry of Natural Resources reorganizations over the last three years, and upheavals in several other provinces; however, most reforms have been in policy, and legislation has been slower to evolve.

Now, in response to the World Wildlife Fund and Canadian Parks and Wilderness Society's Endangered Spaces campaign, many jurisdictions are developing systems plans, candidate areas, and new policies. While Endangered Spaces has generated much activity in these areas across Canada, we must also seek to rework legislation as we learn new scientific lessons, as priorities are redirected, and as comparative research reveals useful legal techniques. For it is legislation that crystallizes our commitment, demonstrates our direction, and regulates our roles in running these special areas.

I hope that this review of the past, present and prospects of Canada's parks system laws contributes to developing this new generation of protected areas legislation. I look forward to hearing about other new directions as Ontario embarks on its second century of provincial parks.

Historical Highlights of Ontario's Park Statutes

1852   Gore Square granted to Hamilton – first municipal park established by Ontario act

1883   Public Parks Act – first municipal park system act in Canada

1885   Niagara Falls Park Act – first regional park under provincial control

1893   Algonquin National Park Act – first "provincial" park act in Canada

1913   Provincial Parks Act – first provincial park system act in Canada

1946   Conservation Authorities Act – first act to create various conservation authorities

1954   Provincial Parks Act – reconstituted this act, and formed the framework and philosophy of the current act

1955   Ontario – St. Lawrence Development Commission Act – created the current St. Lawrence Parks Commission to administer regional parks

1956 Ontario Parks Integration Board Act – brought park agencies together to coordinate activities

1959 Wilderness Areas Act – early protection for ecological reserves and "wilderness," passed before the 1964 US Wilderness Act and 1971 BC Ecological Reserves Act

1966 St. Clair Parkway Commission Act – created this commission to administer regional parks

1974 Algonquin Forestry Authority Act – created an authority to coordinate logging in Algonquin Provincial Park

Key Amendments to Ontario's Provincial Parks Act

1954 The Provincial Parks Act is reconstituted, forming the framework and philosophy of the current act

1961 The Game and Fish Act prohibition on hunting in provincial parks can be overridden in specified parks
Provincial park officials are given "all the power and authority of a member of the OPP"

1968 Provincial parks can be classified into natural environment, nature reserve, primitive, recreational, wild river or other classes of park
Areas within provincial parks can be classified into historic, multiple use, natural, primitive, recreational or other zones

1970 Subject to cabinet approval, the minister is given authority to establish advisory committees

1976 The minister is given authority to prepare and review "master plans"

1989 The fine is increased for offences under the Provincial Parks Act from $500 to $5,000 (increasing from $50 in 1893)
Minor amendments were also passed in 1956, 1958, 1959, 1962, 1966, 1971, 1972 and 1984
Consolidations were made in 1960, 1970, 1980 and 1990

Historical Table of Canadian Parks Legislation

Jurisdiction	First Park	First Park Act	First System Act	Current Park Act
Canada	1885	1887 c.32	1911 c.10	1985 c.N-14
British Columbia	1911	1911 c.49	1957 c.53 [1] 1965 c.3	11979 c.309
Alberta	1932	1930 c.60	1930 c.60	1980 c.P-22
Saskatchewan	1931	1931 c.20	1931 c.20	1986 c.P-1.1
Manitoba	1961 [2]	1960 c.53	1960 c.53	1987 c.P20
Ontario	1893 [3]	1893 c.8	1913 c.15	1990 c.P.34
Québec	1895	1895 c.22 [4]	1941 c.156	1977 c.P-9
New Brunswick	1935	1961 c.14	1961 c.14	1982 c.P-2.1
Prince Edward Island	1959	1956 c.25	1956 c.25	1988 c.R-8
Nova Scotia	1958	1959 c.7	1959 c.7	1989 c.367
Newfoundland	1959	1952 c.49	1952 c.49	1990 c.P-32
Northwest Territories	1967	1973 (3d) c.5	1973 (3d) c.5	1988 c.T-4
Yukon	1987	1979 (2d) c.13	1979 (2d) c.13	1986 c.126

1. A park system was first set out in the Department of Recreation and Conservation Act (1957), and subsequently developed into the Parks Act in 1965.
2. From a chart provided by the Manitoba Parks and Natural Areas Branch, with six parks established in 1961.
3. This date is debatable, for the Queen Victoria Niagara Falls Park was established in 1885 by the province after the federal government did not establish the park under authority granted by the province in 1880.
4. See also S.Q. 1895, c.23 dealing with the creation of Trembling Mountain Park.

Endnotes

1. Norman T. Newton. 1971. *Design on the Land.* Cambridge, Mass.: Belknap Press. 267. Cited in: J.R. Wright. 1983. *Urban Parks in Ontario. Part 1: Origins to 1860.* Toronto: Ontario Ministry of Tourism and Recreation. 22.
2. Wright, op. cit., 55.
3. *Ibid.* A review of the early Nova Scotia statutes, however, did not reveal this particular Act, but Chapter XII of 1760 is a similarly early Nova Scotian enactment, being "An Act for regulating the Common belonging to the Township of Lunenburg."
4. Wright, op. cit., 55-66.
5. Owen Scott, Landplan Collaborative Consultants, Guelph, Ontario, speaking on CBC's Radio Noon program in Toronto, 26 February 1993, at 12:30 pm.
6. An Act to vest in the Corporation of the City of Hamilton, the "Gore" of King Street, for public purposes, Statutes of the Province of Canada 16 Vict. (1852), chapter 33.

7. Statutes of Ontario 1882-83, chapter 20. See Wright, op. cit., 84.

8. Niagara Falls and Adjacent Territory Act, Statutes of Ontario 43 Vic. (1880), chapter 13.

9. Statutes of Ontario 48 Vic. (1885), chapter 21; and Statutes of Ontario 50 Vic. (1887), chapter 13.

10. Revised Statutes of Ontario 1990, chapter 3.

11. Ontario-St. Lawrence Development Commission Act, Statutes of Ontario 1955, chapter 59, now the St. Lawrence Parks Commission Act, Revised Statutes of Ontario, chapter S.24. Also see: Gerald Killan. 1993. *Protected Places: A History of Ontario's Provincial Parks System.* Toronto: Dundurn Press and Ontario Ministry of Natural Resources. 88.

12. St. Clair Parkway Commission Act, Statutes of Ontario 1966, chapter 146, now Revised Statutes of Ontario 1990, chapter S.23.

13. Ontario Parks Integration Board Act, Statutes of Ontario 1956, chapter 61.

14. Statutes of Canada 50-51 Vic. (1887), chapter 32.

15. Statutes of Ontario 48 Vic. (1885), chapter 21; 56 Vic. (1893), chapter 8; 56 Vic. (1894), chapter 15.

16. Statutes of Québec 58 Vic. (1895), chapters 22 and 23.

17. Statutes of British Columbia 1 Geo.V (1911), chapter 49.

18. Statutes of Canada 1-2 Geo.V (1911), chapter 10.

19. Statutes of Ontario 3-4 Geo.V (1913), chapter 15.

20. Statutes of Alberta 1930, chapter 60; Statutes of Saskatchewan 1931, chapter 20; Statutes of Manitoba 1960, chapter 53.

21. Statutes of Québec 1941, chapter 156.

22. Statutes of Newfoundland 1952, chapter 49, passed shortly after becoming a province in 1949; Statutes of Prince Edward Island 1956, chapter 25; Statutes of Nova Scotia 1959, chapter 7; and Statutes of New Brunswick 1961, chapter 14.

23. Jim Simon, Ministry of Economic Development and Tourism, personal communication, 19 April 1994.

24. Statutes of British Columbia 1965, chapter 43; Statutes of Saskatchewan 1979, chapter R-9.1.

25. Statutes of Ontario 1954, chapter 75.

26. Statutes of British Columbia 1965, chapter 31.

27. Statutes of Ontario 1968, chapter 104.

28. Statutes of Manitoba 1993, chapter 39, section 6.

29. Revised Statutes of Canada 1985, chapter N-4, sections 11 and 13; Revised Statutes of British Columbia 1979, chapter 310, section 17; Statutes of Saskatchewan 1979, chapter R-9.1, sections 5 and 23.

30. Revised Statutes of Canada 1985, chapter N-14; Statutes of Ontario 1993, chapter 28.

31. See footnote 29, and the Provincial Parks and Consequential Amendments Act, Statutes of Manitoba 1993, chapter 39, section 6.

32. Marla Cone and Melissa Healy. 1993. U.S. is Planning Census of All Its Biological Species. *Toronto Star*, 16 October 1993. C6.

33. Revised Statutes of British Columbia 1979, chapter 309, section 6.

34. Statutes of Saskatchewan 1986, chapter P-1.1, section 8; Statutes of Manitoba 1993, chapter 39, sections 17, 18 and 40; Revised Statutes of Québec 1977, chapter R-26, section 4; Statutes of New Brunswick 1975, chapter E-1.1, sections 4 and 7.1; Revised Statutes of Nova Scotia 1989, chapter 438, sections 4, 7 and 14.1; and Revised Statutes of Prince Edward Island 1988, chapter N-2, sections 3-5.

35. Kevin McNamee. 1993. "Preserving Ontario's Natural Legacy." *Environment on Trial.* Toronto: Emond Montgomery Publications and Canadian Institute for Environmental Law and Policy. 284.

36. Paul F. J. Eagles. 1982. Commentary on Does Ontario Need a New Provincial Parks Act. *Environments 14(1)* 60-61. Paul F. J. Eagles. 1984. *A Study of the Ontario Provincial Parks Act.* Recreation Publication Series No. 1. Waterloo: University of Waterloo, Dept. of Recreation. Tom Miyata. 1982. Commentary on "Does Ontario Need a New Provincial Parks Act." *Environments* 14(1) 62-63. Kevin McNamee, op. cit.

37. Bob Sopuck, Government of Manitoba, personal communication, 11 March 1994.

38. See footnote 29, and the Revised Statutes of British Columbia 1979, chapter 82; Statutes of Saskatchewan 1979, chapter M-11.1; and Revised Statutes of Newfoundland 1990, chapter P-15.

39. H. Ian Rounthwaite. 1981. "The National Parks of Canada: An Endangered Species?" *Saskatchewan Law Review* 43, 51.

40. Statutes of Ontario 1961-62, chapter 112.

41. L.J. Gregorich. 1992. *Poaching and the Illegal Trade in Wildlife and Wildlife Parts in Canada.* Ottawa: Canadian Wildlife Federation. 24-26, 66-73.

42. Statutes of British Columbia 1971, chapter 16.

43. Revised Statutes of Alberta 1980, chapter W-8.

44. This type of provision could have been provided under the comprehensive planning policy concerning lands adjacent to significant natural heritage features, as proposed by Ontario's Sewell Commission on Planning and Development Reform, but this concept has not been adopted.

45. House of Representatives Bill 2363, introduced by Rep. Peter Kostmayer and others on 9 September 1992.

Parks –

A BRITISH COLUMBIA

PERSPECTIVE

Bruce K. Downie

Unlike the common premise of uniqueness used to identify the special characteristics of various regions of this country and what is happening there, this paper is based on what I consider to be the fundamental similarities among all parts of the country.

I feel our common experience regardless of what part of the country we're in is remarkable. It is true our geography in Canada is varied – British Columbia has a few more bumps on the landscape than many other parts of the country and I've been told that some places are a little colder than Victoria, where I now live, but from a parks and protected areas perspective we all face:

1. increasing demands on land and resources for a variety of uses increasing the complexity of protected areas establishment and management;

2. changes within government structures and the levels of influence and responsibility for protected areas;

3. difficult economic conditions that put stress on our ability as a society to protect and effectively manage resources of the common good such as parks; and,

4. the assertion of, and necessary response to, aboriginal rights for land, resources and self-determination.

It may appear that there is a tendency for us in different parts of the country to address these concerns differently, but I believe it is more common for us to do many of the same things but under different labels.

In this paper I will attempt to:

1. describe a few of the highlights of recent current events, products and processes relating to protected area establishment and management in BC; and,

2. relate a few of the highlights of a recent conference sponsored by the Canadian Parks and Wilderness Society (CPAWS), the purpose of which was to take stock of progress and give thought to the future.

To follow the media or even to listen to the high profile environmentalists (the lunatic fringe), you would think BC is going to hell in a handbasket at a furious pace and that this government is worse than the last one. It is my view that nothing could be further from the truth and I really hope that people in BC will wake up to that before the next election. The NDP is currently at the halfway point in its mandate. I am not a big fan of governments generally, politically or the bureaucracy, but I am a fan of good planning and rational decision-making, so I am certainly more generous with the current provincial administration.

Progress for the protected areas agenda is relative – there are definitely problems:

1. the slow pace;

2. many would argue that BC's diversity on a broader national and global scale deserves greater attention than the standard 12 per cent solution – many extremely significant areas are going to be utilized for other purposes, if adherence to this guideline is maintained;

3. reversing the dark history, and many would argue the present practice, of forestry in BC is a monumental task;

4. there is continuing resource extraction in "protected" areas – mining exploration and development and hunting;

5. tension over visitor use facilities impacting on the continued integrity of park values is exceptionally high and will only intensify in the future; and,

6. the continued lack of sufficient funding.

Highlights of the Protected Areas Agenda:
Changes in direction are significantly influenced by the ability of key leaders and groups to build on circumstantial opportunities for change.

One of the lessons we have learned from the historical context described in other papers in this book, is that there is no such thing as a clean slate. The historical context in BC is like a family situation I have experienced. I am sure many of you will recognize it. As a parent (government) I hear angry screaming from another room. I go to investigate and my five-year-old (forest industry) is clutching a family possession and the two-year-old (evironmentalists) wants it badly. What are my options as a parent:

1. tell them to work it out between them and leave;

2. offer a consequence for a lack of a solution and leave;

3. reason with the older child to enable her to share;

4. explain to the younger child that the older one had it first and should be allowed to keep it;

5. take it away from both of them; or,

6. discuss the solution with both to reach a solution.

In BC we're not dealing with five-year-olds. There has been a long history of the forest industry and the Ministry of Forests (MOF) controlling the entire land base of the province and the protected areas system must develop from that reality.

The protected areas system has its roots in the system planning done within the Parks Branch as far back as the early 1950s when park sites were picked from the passenger seat of a Beaver aircraft. More seriously system planning developed in earnest in the late 1970s and is evidenced by a whole series of plans and policies with respect to park system development including the development of the natural landscapes framework that was to underlie much of the subsequent system planning process. In the framework 10 eco-provinces are divided into 43 eco-regions which are subsequently divided into 110 eco-sections. The extent of representation of these landscapes throughout the province has been the subject of considerable study, gap analysis, discussion and even debate.

The protected areas system became a joint venture between the Parks Branch and the Ministry of Forests with the advent of Parks and Wilderness for the 1990s. The combined initiative resulted from the historical context of MOF control of the land base and its new legislative mandate for wilderness. This joint venture was eclipsed in 1992 with the establishment of the Commission on Resources and the

Environment (CORE). This body, independent of government, has the responsibility for facilitating land use planning throughout the province and presenting recommendations from a table of all stakeholders to government.

The Commission on Resources and Environment (CORE)

Stephen Owen is the Commissioner of CORE and as outlined in a recent presentation to a conference in Sante Fe, he identified the reason for the establishment of CORE as the dysfunction of domestic governance:

> The dysfunction expresses itself in widespread public cynicism abuout government effectiveness and fairness and a resulting dissatisfaction with the actions and decision of government. Procedurally, the public feels alienated from the decision-making process.... On the spectrum between representative and participatory democracy, our form of government has swung far to the representative side ... the public is demanding a correction towards greater participation.
>
> In the land use context, the current procedural dysfunction is demonstrated by the rejection of the results of the existing planning processes. Parties from across the spectrum of interests in land-use regularly attempt to do "end runs" around decisions reached by processes in which they have taken no meaningful part. The chief forester reduces the annual allowable cut for a corporate timber licensee and the company seeks judicial review; a permit is issued for a logging road into a pristine watershed and an environmental group resorts to civil disobedience and sets up a blockade; cabinet ministers are lobbied by various interest groups against administrative land-use decisions; and media campaigns, often spiced with exaggerated claims, are launched at home and abroad. A common tendency is for government to react to these pressures with ad hoc decisions outside formal planning processes. This response creates inconsistency and enhances public distrust and alienation.

CORE is currently working on a provincial overview for land use on the basis of principles of economic, environmental and social sustainability.

Also, processes in four regions of the province, Vancouver Island, the Cariboo/Chilcotin, the East Kootenay and the Kootenay Boundary, have begun and in only one, Vancouver Island, has a report been completed (Feb. 1994) and submitted to government for decisions and action. The intent is consensus-based negotiations involving representatives from a full range of interests. Achieving consensus and maintaining commitment from all interests to the process and the outcomes has proven difficult. Reports are required from CORE to government regardless of the level of success at the regional tables.

Vancouver Island Report Highlight

- 23 new protected areas

- protected areas increased from 10.3-13 per cent of the island

- eight per cent of the island in 16 areas of regionally significant lands were identified (lands where logging and mining are permitted but cannot jeopardize the priority ecological values)

- other land uses are identified as: settlement (three per cent); cultivation (three per cent); and multi-resource use (73 per cent)

- a foundation of the plan is an Economic Transition Strategy for the retraining of displaced workers, the diversification of local economies, and the establishment of pension-bridging programs for older workers.

Reaction to the report was swift and dominantly negative. A community-based campaign, stimulated by local logging industry interests, resulted in 15,000 demonstrators on the lawn of the legislature one month after the report's release.

The government stood behind the report and recently announced action on the transition strategy. A major job creation and retraining program was announced to be coordinated by a new agency called Forest Renewal BC. Jobs are anticipated in silviculture and environmental clean-up as well as value-added forestry related initiatives. The job program is to be financed by new taxes on the forest companies through an increase of over 80 per cent in stumpage rates which will net the government $300 million per year in new money.

Protected Area Establishment Beyond the Regional CORE Initiatives
Part of the reality of no "clean slate" is the inevitability of certain actions taking place beyond the newly established processes. This is certainly the case in the BC context. CORE has not had the time nor been given the resources immediately to take on all the pressing protected areas issues that are current. Some examples of recent protective actions beyond the CORE process include:

1. *The Tatshenshini River area*
- highly publicized

- highly political
- a cabinet decision that was based on a study of the technical implications of the proposed mining development in the area

2. *Clayoquot Sound*
- a cabinet decision based on the results of the Clayoquot Sound Sustainable Development Committee
- the Clayoquot Sound land use decision was incorporated into the Vancouver Island CORE report as concluded by cabinet in 1993
- the working forest is to be reduced from 81 per cent to 45 per cent of the land base
- special management areas cover 17 per cent of the land base
- protected area designations have increased from 14.9 per cent to 33 per cent of the land base with 14 new areas being established
- the rate of cut is set at 1,000 ha/yr resulting in a regeneration period of 80–120 years
- improved environmental standards have been imposed
- a scientific panel has been established for the area

3. *Chilko Lake*
- Ts'ilos Provincial Park announced 13 January 1994
- 233,240 ha (almost half the size of PEI)
- 160 km sw of Williams Lake
- a study team of 37 interested parties including First Nations, Energy, Mines and Resources, Tourism, MOF, Parks, Share Groups, the BC Outdoor Recreation Council and local residents collaborated over an almost two-year period to come up with the proposal
- process coordinated by an independent facilitator

4. *Gowlland Range, Mount Finlayson, Tod Inlet*
- green space acquisition of private land
- cooperative venture (BC Government; Nature Conservancy of Canada; Capital Regional District; local governments; and private land donation)
- >1,000 ha on Saanich Peninsula near Victoria

- total purchase value $8.5 million from the BC Lands acquisition fund. This one-time program called the Commonwealth Nature Legacy will result in a series of purchases of park land around the province, especially in areas where critical requirements for the protected areas system are difficult to establish due to the preponderance of privately held land

Important Related Initiatives to Land Use Planning

Also of critical importance to the implementation of a protected areas system are other initiatives aimed at improving the quality of our environment beyond protected areas and at the same time maintaining a healthy economy for the benefit of British Columbians. Without sustainable industry the achievement of a protected areas system will have little meaning and even less support.

Forest Practices Code
- tougher standards for forest practices
- significant increase in penalties and promise of tougher enforcement

BC 21
- major employment initiative involving cooperative employment and re-training programs
- significant emphasis on environmental clean-up and restoration

Another major shift in BC government policy that deeply affects the evolution of the protected areas system is the recognition of Aboriginal peoples and their efforts to gain control of their own future through a negotiated treaty process.

Aboriginal Claims
- BC Treaty Commission established
- applications for treaty negotiations being received
- first determination is identification of legitimately constituted groups for negotiation purposes
- identification of need and establishment of interim agreements

CPAWS Conference

CPAWS, along with many other parks and conservation oriented public interest groups in BC and across the country, have applied continuing pressure on government to advance conservation interests towards a vision of an ecologically representative system under protected area status by the year 2000. As part of this public pressure, support and participation in the process, CPAWS organized "The Wilderness Vision – Colloquium on Completing British Columbia's Protected Area System" that was held in Vancouver on 11–13 March 1994.

The stated purpose of the event was "to provide a forum for open discussion and review of the critical issues affecting implementation of a protected area system in BC, and to stimulate progress toward completing a protected areas system in BC by the year 2000."

A series of plenary session speakers provided varying perspectives on the experience, issues and potential futures for the planning and implementation of the protected area system. Jim Pojar, a BC Forest Service Officer in Prince Rupert, provided an assessment of the success and shortcomings of the present protected areas system for effective conservation. The Chairman of the Outdoor Recreation Council, Mark Angelo, outlined the recreation and tourism needs from the system and enunciated a clear future vision reflecting the importance of recreation as part of the lifestyle of British Columbians. Gerald Amos brought a First Nations' perspective to the discussion drawing attention to the necessary and imminent fundamental change that must characterize future evolution of the system in relation to the rights of aboriginal people. Bill Dumont, of Western Forest Products, presented a perspective from the forest industry that recognized conservation needs and the willingness of industry to contribute within the context of a sustainable and economic industry. Sierra Club's Chairperson, Vicky Husband, drew attention to the inadequacies of continuing forest practices in the province that continue to threaten the environmental agenda with respect to protected areas. Denis O'Gorman, Deputy Commissioner of CORE, reported on the foundations, progress and directions of the CORE land use planning process and the implications for protected areas. Ken Georgetti, President of the BC Federation of Labour, provided an insightful view of the process and dimensions of change in the labour force not brought about by, but inextricably linked to the forces of change in society which includes a new outlook on the environment. Mayor Anne Fiddick brought a very real and local perspective from the community of Gold River of some of the challenges that we all face in striking a new and more sensitive land management course and offered some concerns and suggestions for action.

In addition, both Premier Harcourt and the Honourable Moe Sihota addressed the conference. Two specific messages came through clearly in their presentation of the government perspective and agenda. The first was the fundamental nature of change in the relationship with First Nations that must characterize all planning and development in British Columbia. The second was government's complete commitment to the CORE land use planning process as a means of providing an appropriate forum for all interests at appropriate local and regional levels to determine land use decisions.

The second day of the conference was devoted to workshops where conference participants could become more involved in discussion of some of their most pressing concerns. At individual workshops on legislative reform, conservation, social and economic issues, land use planning and marine systems resource people provided some food for thought and offered their expertise to the ensuing discussion. Workshops were also convened to reflect on the case studies of Haida Gwaii (Queen Charlotte Islands), Clayoquot Sound, the Cariboo-Chilcotin, Crown of the Continent and the Northern Rockies. In addition other workshops specifically explored cooperative approaches among governments, the public and with industry that might provide useful ideas for the future. Concerns over the marine components of the protected areas system as a major gap were consistently voiced and Minister Sihota responded with a commitment to work with his federal counterparts to advance this aspect of the system. Finally, a special workshop was convened to explore the area of aboriginal interests including their perspectives on conservation and roles in establishing and managing protected areas.

CPAWS President Harvey Locke also addressed the conference. He eloquently articulated the tremendous threats to ecosystem values in the Rockies and the inadequacy of our protected areas, national parks in particular, to maintain their protection mandate. He encouraged vigilance in combating the erosion of park values in existing parks and outlined new cooperative efforts by the environmental community to establish a international corridor of sensitive ecological management throughout the heart of the mountain systems from "Yellowstone to Yukon."

Overall at the colloquium, discussions were characterized by a strong sense of caring, concern, respect and openness – characteristics that have not been typically associated with many of the environmental controversies of recent years. Perhaps this conference marked the beginning of a new cooperative approach to a common vision. The following outline attempts to highlight critical points in the discussion.

What has been our experience?
- We have learned that it is important to create an atmosphere where people feel accepted, heard and valued. Perhaps nowhere is this more strongly felt

than among First Nations peoples. But this has also arisen from experience in planning processes by environmentalists, recreation interests and people in our rural resource communities. We must learn to take the time to hear and truly understand and accept each others ideas, fears, and concerns.

- We have experienced a remarkable magnitude of change. Changes in technology. Changes in industry and society. Changes in the economy. And changes in the jobs and job prospects facing workers.

- We have felt appreciation for a new land use planning context within the province.

What are the issues we face?

- There is tremendous uncertainty over the land base for protected areas. How do we interpret the 12 per cent figure? There are many perspectives and this issue although energetically discussed will continue to challenge us throughout the planning process.

- The issues are complex and difficult to resolve. The solutions must also be multi-faceted. We cannot expect to establish a protected areas system without first addressing the social dimensions of the impacts of that system and the related employment transitions.

- Economic development aspects of protected areas agreements must be developed as part of the process and documented before concluding the agreement. Small communities must develop their own economic transition strategy but they need the resources and skills to make these strategies work.

- A major, aggressive effort will be needed in the area of education and communication to the public concerning the nature, importance, process and outcomes of major land use and protected areas planning and decision-making.

- Stewardship of private lands is an important goal that can contribute significantly to achieving conservation objectives on lands beyond the protected areas.

- There is a need for serious and comprehensive reform of the Parks Act including legislating boundaries and ensuring intergovernmental coordination. Such reform would include a significant process of public involvement. Legislative reform must also address First Nations interests. A provision for interim status of protected areas similar to the "park reserve" status in the

National Parks Act would ensure that treaty settlements are not prejudiced by area establishment.

What are some directions for the future?
- This government has a strong commitment to change. The status quo was seen as simply not viable. New processes have been put into place, and there is a commitment to see these processes continue, and to hold the participants accountable.
- There will be a fundamentally new context within which the entire agenda of land use planning and protected areas will be addressed. That context is the new jurisdictional map of the province following the treaty process that has just begun. Premier Harcourt clearly stated his government's commitment to this process and its implications will be far reaching.

What is our vision?
Our vision for a protected areas system and effective environmental conservation in the province includes:
- the maintenance of ecological integrity throughout the province
- long term stability of the Protected Areas System
- recognizing humans as part of the earth's ecological system
- adoption and application of environmental stewardship or land ethic
- looking for strategies to assist in the transition the resource-based communities face in the course of change
- the recognition of outdoor recreation as a cultural trademark of our society in BC.
- the adoption of a code of ethics for recreationists and tourism operators
- open communication and cooperation among all interests in the establishment and management of protected areas

What can we actively do to further the vision?
- develop and implement legislative mechanisms appropriate to the implementation requirements of the protected areas system
- develop creative partnerships and increased volunteerism

- commit adequate resources to the effective completion of the process
- implement community-based consultation and participation
- engage in the planning and management of lands beyond the protected areas for conservation purposes

These reflections on the conference proceedings were provided by the author in the closing session followed by responses from the Honourable John Cashore, Derek Thompson and Gerald Amos. Both John Cashore and Gerald Amos stressed the emerging new relationship with First Nations in BC and highlighted both the opportunities presented by this new relationship and the need for change in our typical way of doing business. Derek Thompson outlined the functions and direction of the newly formed Land Use Coordination Office and its role in the protected areas agenda of government.

"The Wilderness Vision" provided a very timely and important forum for the discussion of the protected areas system in British Columbia – its evolution, its obstacles and its opportunities. But it was not an end in itself. It marks a milestone in the on-going process of working to establish a parks and protected areas system that reflects the needs and aspirations of British Columbians and contributes to the integrity of natural systems here and in the global context.

References

British Columbia. 1993. *A protected areas strategy for British Columbia*. Government of British Columbia, Victoria, B.C.

—. 1993. *Clayoquot Sound – A balanced decision; a sustainable future*. Government of British Columbia, Victoria, B.C.

—. 1994. Chilko Lake area designated B.C.'s newest protected area. News release, 13 January 1994.

—. 1994. Province secures Gowlland, Mt. Finlayson, Tod Inlet lands: Commonwealth Nature Legacy unveiled. News release, 30 March 1994.

Commission on Resources and Environment. 1994. *Vancouver Island Land Use Plan*. CORE, Victoria, B.C.

CPAWS, In press. "The wilderness vision." Colloquium proceedings.

Owen, S. In press. "Participation and sustainability: the imperatives of resource and environmental management." Conference proceedings, Sante Fe, New Mexico.

PARKS PAST, PRESENT, FUTURE:

A NORTHERN PERSPECTIVE

Ronald G. Seale

The Northwest Territories: A Unique Jurisdiction

The Northwest Territories differs markedly from all other jurisdictions in Canada in virtually every respect. This unique character has a major influence on the parks issue, just as it does on any other contemporary issue. The NWT is distinctly different culturally, socially, economically, politically and demographically. These differences must be appreciated before the parks issue can be meaningfully discussed.

1. Cultural Considerations

The NWT is the only jurisdiction in Canada that has an aboriginal majority. There are major cultural differences between lifestyles of these communities and those typical of southern Canada. With respect specifically to the parks issue, we might note just three points:

- In the small and remote communities of the North, there is very little outdoor recreation as southerners know it. People certainly spend a great deal of time on the land, but not for recreational purposes. They spend more time on the land because it is their *life*. They have snowmobiles and motorboats, but these are not used as toys as they are in the South. Rather they are used as tools, to improve the efficiency with which Northerners pursue their traditional harvesting pursuits. On the other hand, the non-motorized recreational activities that park managers are accustomed to accommodating in the South, have virtually no following amongst aboriginal Northerners.

- Amongst "Euro-Canadians" who are the minority in the North, there *are* many keen outdoor recreationists – particularly canoeists, boaters, fishermen and hikers. For these people, however, the opportunities available to them to pursue such activities appear almost limitless. Virtually any NWT resident can leave his home and be in a wilderness environment in less than half an hour.

- The result of the two above factors is that there is almost no public constituency for parks and protected areas in the NWT. To the extent that there is a public lobby on behalf of parks, it is almost entirely southern-based. It therefore tends to be viewed by Northerners as naive and ill-informed. As a result, it also tends to be relatively ineffective.

2. Social Considerations:

The usual indicators of a dysfunctional society, such as alcoholism, suicide, family violence, school drop-out rates and so on, are all at extremely high levels in the North. As a result, the need for parks and protected areas often seems to be a relatively low priority for governments faced with such pressing social problems.

3. Economic Considerations:

In the South, the economic fabric is more or less set. Transportation networks, settlements, urban systems – all are long established and well-developed. In the North, the situation is very different. As in no other part of the country, these basic parameters remain to be determined. Only two of 62 communities are accessible by rail, and only 14 of the 62 are accessible by all-weather road. There is virtually no agriculture and almost no forestry. Even mining, which is the biggest private sector employer, is a relatively small activity, compared to the mining sectors in Ontario or British Columbia, for example. There are only six operating mines in the entire vast expanse of this jurisdiction, and three of those are within 10 kilometres of the centre of Yellowknife.

Thus, although the environmental implications of development in the North should in no way be minimized, the existing level of development is such that, relative to the rest of Canada, we have virtually a clean slate. This situation has interesting implications for park advocates. In the rest of Canada, park advocates are often approaching the resource table long after the fare has been well picked over by sundry extractive interests. Park advocates in the South often characterize their efforts as valiant fights for the last remnants of particular kinds of habitats, be they wetlands, grasslands, or virgin forests. In the North, on the other hand, park advocates are often in the position of being able to identify for protection the most outstanding examples of a particular type of habitat, rather than merely the bits that happen to be left over.

This unusual situation leads in some ways to role reversals for park advocates and other land use interests in the North. Whereas in the South it is usually the park advocates who feel threatened, in the North it is the mining industry that frequently feels threatened. It is the mining industry that often feels that it only has access to the bits that are left over, after major land use decisions have been made. It is not a position that the mining industry is either familiar with or comfortable with.

For park advocates in the North, their position of relative strength behooves them to act in a less confrontational manner than that which some of their Southern counterparts appear to favour. Given the limited state of economic development in the North, both park advocates and industry interests should find it possible to commit themselves to rational decision-making processes with respect to land use processes that have as their starting point the recognition by all parties of the legitimacy of the other competing interests.

4. Political Considerations

Another major difference between the NWT and other jurisdictions in Canada, is that the territorial legislation, at least for now, does not function on the basis of partisan party politics. Instead the legislature operates on the basis of consensus. The consensus style of government has implications for park issues as for all other types of issues. This is particularly the case for park matters, given that the very idea of a park is a concept that is alien to traditional aboriginal cultures.

5. Demographic Considerations:

One consideration that is often ignored in discussions about the North is the demographic one. The rate of natural increase within the population of the Eastern Arctic or Nunavut, may well be the highest in the world. Granted the base population is very small, but the rapid growth in population has major implications for parks and any other type of resource use further down the road.

Heritage Values: Northern Perspectives

In southern Canada, natural heritage and cultural heritage are generally considered to be distinctly different. Heritage professionals normally have experience and expertise in one or the other, but rarely in both; however, for the Aboriginal peoples who make up the majority of the population in the NWT, those distinctions between natural heritage and cultural heritage do not exist. The landscapes and wildlife populations that for Southerners constitute natural heritage values, are instead perceived to be cultural values – values that define the cultural identity of the individual and of the community.

The enormous polar bear and the magnificent canyon that are for the Southerner, outstanding natural values that are the highlights of a superb vacation, are for the Northerner, cultural values that define him as a person. Both Southerner and Northerner, however, are equally awed by the same phenomena. Perhaps we would benefit if we learned to value and appreciate our world from various perspectives. If we do, then the importance of areas that protect those features, those values, will be enhanced even further, and we shall all be the richer for it.

Evolution of Parks in the Northwest Territories:
Northern attitudes towards parks have evolved in response to various factors. Amongst them are the following:

1. Reaction to the Dominating Federal Presence
The federal government continues to be a dominant player in the NWT. In the early days of the territorial jurisdiction, the federal presence was even more overwhelming. The predictable result was that federal initiatives were widely perceived by Northerners to be actions imposed by a far-away master with little or no appreciation of circumstances or concerns in the North.

Thus in the 1960s and 1970s, national parks were perceived by many Northerners to be unnecessary initiatives imposed by Ottawa in response to Southern perceptions, and with no consideration of Northern priorities. When territorial parks were first established, the government of the NWT was determined that its parks would serve distinctly different purposes, rather than merely being imitation national parks. Rather than protecting natural values, territorial parks would have clear economic objectives. They would be established and operated to support the tourism industry. Since its inception, therefore, the territorial parks function has been lodged within an economic development portfolio, rather than within a resource management or environmental portfolio, as is more often the case in other jurisdictions.

2. Devolution of authority

Responsibility for an increasing range of authorities is gradually being devolved to the territorial government. The Department of Indian Affairs and Northern Development remains, however, the major player in the NWT with respect to land management. When responsibility for management of lands, waters and other natural resources is fully devolved, the context within which territorial parks are managed will be considerably different. Even if the parks function remains within an economic development portfolio, the other players with whom it interacts will be different. The dynamics amongst competing land interests will be significantly altered.

3. Division of the Northwest Territories

Before the year 2000, the new territory of Nunavut will be in place in the Eastern Arctic. Even before its establishment, however, Nunavut is having a substantial impact throughout the NWT. Land use decisions, including park decisions, are being made in anticipation of Nunavut, with a view to making today's decisions and actions compatible with the expected direction that Nunavut will take. Primarily this means making land use decisions compatible with the final land claims agreement under which Nunavut is to be established. The decisions in question impact not only upon Nunavut, but upon the whole of the NWT. With respect specifically to protected areas and other heritage issues, the Nunavut agreement is quite supportive.

4. Aboriginal self-government

Nunavut is the most obvious expression of the rise of aboriginal self-government in the NWT. Given the overwhelming Inuit majority in the new territory, the government of Nunavut will be de facto self-government for the Inuit. The character that aboriginal self-government will have in the Western Arctic is less clear, but it will obviously become an increasingly important factor. Throughout the NWT, therefore, we can look more and more, for heritage initiatives to reflect the aboriginal perspectives discussed above in Section II.

A Policy for Territorial Parks

The government of the NWT is currently developing its first comprehensive general parks policy. This policy will set out the bases upon which territorial parks are to be established, developed, and operated. The various kinds of benefits that parks are to provide will be explored at some length. Particular attention will be paid to economic benefits, but also to less tangible kinds of social and cultural benefits. The latter are especially important to the varied people of the NWT at a time when their traditional cultures are under severe stress. In these circumstances, parks and protected areas that reflect aboriginal perspectives of heritage referred to above, can be critically important in providing a heightened sense of self-esteem, both for individuals and for entire communities.

A System Plan for Territorial Parks

As well as developing a parks policy, the territorial government is also developing a park system plan. This system will reflect the need for parks to provide socio-economic benefits, particularly for small and remote communities. Cultural values and access will also be major considerations. Given that parks will be expected to support the sustainable development policy adopted by the territorial government in 1990, biophysical criteria will be taken into account. Such criteria will not comprise the major driving force in the parks system plan as they do in Parks Canada's system plan and in those of most provincial jurisdictions.

Conclusion

The Northwest Territories continues to be a markedly distinct jurisdiction within Canada. The establishment, development and operation of parks within this unique jurisdiction reflect that distinct cultural, social, economic and political character. Perspectives on heritage are different in the Northwest Territories, and parks reflect those differing perspectives. As governments in the North come increasingly to reflect the unique character of this part of Canada, parks will continue to be distinctly different here. The planning and management of parks is becoming more sophisticated, but parks in the Northwest Territories will continue to reflect different concerns and to serve different needs than those in southern Canada.

GREENWAYS:

THE SECOND PARK MOVEMENT

George B. Priddle

In 1978 a significant event took place in the history of the province of Ontario. Ontario's new provincial park policy was released in what has come to be known as the "Blue Book." The official title is: *Ontario's Provincial Parks: Planning and Management Policies* (Ontario Ministry of Natural Resources, 1978). This document stated the types of parks and the type of zoning within parks that was to make up the provincial park system. It also stated what kind of activities could take place in each type of park within each type of zone. The document also went on to state the basic rationale for determining where and how many of each type of park there should be in the overall system based on the goals of protecting the natural and cultural landscape, providing outdoor recreation opportunities, allowing for heritage appreciation and providing for tourism.

In spite of the sophistication of this systems thinking about parks, only one form of linear park was identified and that was waterway parks. In many cases the proposed waterway provincial parks are a downstream extension of an existing park or they pass through other provincial parks. Americans were at the same time identifying and dedicating scenic and wild rivers in the United States. Federally, in Canada the heritage rivers program was evolving.

We were not however seeing these linear corridors as important and vital links in an overall "linked open space system." The idea of linked green space has really been around for a very long time and indeed goes back to the thinking of island biogeography that had begun to emerge in the 1930s (Smith and

Hellmund, 1993). Indeed Frederick Law Olmsted and his followers had been designing open space systems for the urban milieu since before the advent of the motorcar (Little, 1990). Prospect Park in Brooklyn with its parkway to the coast, the Emerald Necklace in Boston and the interconnected system of Greenways around Minneapolis-St. Paul are outstanding examples that come to mind (*National Geographic*, June 1990).

In England, Ebenezer Howard and Patrick Abercrombie had begun to realize the dream of garden cities and greenbelts to define and keep the urban and rural components of the landscape separate. In Southern Ontario the evolution of the conservation authorities and the resulting restriction of development on floodable and hazardous lands has given us the basic building block for the development of a greenway system.

The Ontario Trails Council did emerge in Ontario at the instigation and with the support of the Ministry of Natural Resources shortly after the emergence of the "Blue Book." In spite of the strong cabinet support it received from Bert Lawrence, a minster of the Crown in the Davis government, it never really received the political support it needed to survive. Before the demise of the initial Trails Council it did play an instrumental role it getting a well-developed system of snowmobile trails established in both northern and southern Ontario. The truly valuable lesson that can be learned from all of this is how effective the snowmobile fraternity has been in not only developing their system of trails, but in taking on the responsibility for the ongoing management and regulation of them. Within the last five years the Ontario Trails Council has re-emerged, this time as a non-government organization thanks in large part to the dedication of one Mavis McCallum, a member of the original Trails Council. This re-emergence is in no small part, attributable to the rapid abandonment of railway rights of way by the CNR and the CPR. The Ontario Trails Council and the Heritage Resources Centre at the University of Waterloo have hosted three workshops over the last four years on the topic of converting rails to trails. The Ontario Government has also responded by establishing the Interministerial Committee on the Abandonment of Railroad Rights of Way. This committee has sponsored an excellent background study on the topic and has assisted in the acquisition of abandoned lines that were deemed to be of provincial interest.

In the United States there is now a very active Rails-to-Trails Conservancy and in Canada we now have the Rails to Greenways network actively promoting the development of a national greenway system.

In the US the greenway movement has been heralded as the Second National Park Movement. With a little imagination one can easily envisage a linked open space system consisting of national parks, provincial parks, conservation areas, ANSIS, environmentally sensitive areas, wetlands, existing trails and rail trails making up an effective greenway system that extends from the local neighbourhood to our provincial and national parks .

The Royal Commission on the Future of the Toronto Waterfront, more commonly know as the Crombie Commission, began its mandate in 1988 (*Regeneration*, 1992). The commission soon realized that to be concerned with the waterfront it was necessary to take an ecosystem approach to planning and look at the entire Greater Toronto Bioregion bound by Lake Ontario, the Niagara Escarpment and the Oak Ridges Moraine. It soon became obvious that the headwaters and reaches of all of the rivers and streams in the entire watershed of the GTA had to be of concern if one was to plan for the future of the Toronto waterfront. The concept of greenways fits in perfectly to this type of thinking and indeed chapter five of the final report of the Commission entitled *Regeneration* deals with and is titled "Greenways" (*Regeneration*, 1992). It states: "The essence of greenways is connections – not simply connecting recreational areas through trails, but connecting wildlife habitats to each other, human communities to other human communities, city to country, people to nature." It goes on to discuss the benefits of greenways under the following headings:

- Greenways as ecological connectors
- Greenways as enhancers of water quality
- Greenways provide recreational opportunities close to home
- Greenways bring economic benefits to communities
- Greenways make more liveable communities
- Greenways help to strengthen communities
- Greenways provide links among existing programs

So far this paper has been all good news. Unfortunately the recent commission dealing with the future of land use planning in the province of Ontario, the Sewell Commission, tends not to deal with the concept of greenways and the need for taking a bioregional approach to planning (Commission on Planning and Development Reform in Ontario, 1993).

They do, however, call for watershed-based planning as does the government response to the Sewell Commission (*A New Approach to Land Use Planning*,

1993). Many presentations were made to the Sewell Commission calling for the concept of greenways and bioregional planning to be incorporated into their thinking, but alas to no avail.

Meanwhile on the ground and in specific locations a great deal is happening in terms of rail trail conversions and in the identification of greenways through ecosystem-based planning.

The Howard Watson Trail in Clearwater Sarnia, the Uthoff Trail in Orillia, and the Lynn Valley Trail linking Simcoe with Port Dover are cases in point. In all of these cases the trails have come about and are being maintained because of strong non-government local community initiative. The conversion of the abandoned rail lines from Cambridge to Paris, from Hamilton to Jerseyville, and from Elora to Cataract, are excellent examples of the rail trail greenways coming about because of conservation authority initiatives, with the help of local interest groups and the support of the Interministerial Committee

Professor David Brown from Brock University has been instrumental in instigating the development of a Niagara Greenway system by bringing together a great number of provincial and regional government agencies and local interest groups.

In my home region of Waterloo we are currently reviewing the Regional Official Policies Plan (Regional Official Policies Plan, 1994). In the draft document that has just been released for review a number of interesting maps have emerged, showing not only the existing protected spaces be they ESPAS, ANSI, provincially significant wetlands, floodplains and hazard lands, but a second map indicates how a total greenway system could be realized by protecting key woodlots, and stream valleys. What is really needed now is a series of greenway maps, showing:

1. the green areas that can serve both an ecological and trail function,

2. links and areas that have strictly a natural function, and

3. links that serve purely a recreational and nonmechanized transit function.

In the region of Waterloo, watershed and subwatershed planning have received a good deal of attention of late and seem to be gaining local acceptance as the way to go in future land use planning .

Greenways have certainly become a movement, in the USA, and I think in Canada. Certainly in Ontario, greenways and ecosystem-based planning have the potential of becoming a movement. This is understandable for a number of reasons:

1. it allows for community-based planning;

2. it allows for bottom up as well as top down planning;

3. it requires government agencies to work as facilitators and not just regulators;

4. it takes an environmentally sound approach through ecologically based planning.

Greenway and ecosystem based planning will "stick" hopefully and we will have the ecological support system and the nonmechanized corridors we need to support sustainable development.

References

1. Ontario, Ministry of Natural Resources. *Ontario's Provincial Parks: Planning and Management Policies.* Toronto: 1978.
2. Smith, D.S. & Hellmund, P.C. *Ecology of Greenways.* Minneapolis: University of Minnesota Press, 1993.
3. Little, C.E. *Greenways for America.* Baltimore: Johns Hopkins Press, 1990.
4. Royal Commission on the Future of the Toronto Waterfront. *Regeneration.* Toronto: Queen's Printer of Ontario, 1992.
5. Commission on Planning and Development Reform in Ontario. Toronto: Queen's Printer of Ontario, 1993.
6. Ontario Ministry of Municipal Affairs. *A New Approach to Land Use Planning.* Toronto: 1993.
7. Region of Waterloo. *Regional Official Policies Plan.* March 1994.

Ecotourism and Parks:

DO OR DIE

Paul F. J. Eagles

Parks in provincial and federal levels in Canada are widespread, highly valued and endangered. Over the last decade a fundamental shift in societal attitude has occurred towards these institutions. Even as more and more parks were created, the expenditure allocation, at all levels, was reduced. This apparent contraction sees society creating parks at a frequent rate, but reducing the money available for their maintenance. This attitude shift sees society expressing higher importance for parks, but stating, simultaneously, that the parks must earn more for themselves. Therefore, the environmental protection and the outdoor recreation costs inherent in these institutions are being shifted from the existing and future, in the case of deficit financing, taxpayer, to the existing user.

The salvation of Canadian parks, and those in most other places in the world, lies with the users. The users must pay more. The parks' administration must operate in a businesslike fashion so that sufficient funds are raised. Recreation costs cannot exceed income.

If the park user and the park administration are unable to develop a financial structure that sees the costs of operation covered by the users, many Canadian parks will fall to the state found in third world countries. The parks will look great on paper, but in actuality will have insufficient infrastructure to ensure proper facility maintenance, to enforce carrying capacity decisions and to halt deprecative activities.

Ecotourism is an essential component of this future. Since ecotourism depends upon high quality environments, the finance and administration of parks must be structured so that these high quality environments are preserved. If environmental quality is reduced, ecotourism will suffer and so will income. Therefore, in ecotourism there is a self-serving link between protective management and financial sufficiency. With a carefully constructed park administration, ecotourism has the potential to protect sensitive environments while providing outdoor recreation opportunities.

Background

During the last 20 years the number of parks and the area of parkland have been increasing in Ontario, in Canada and worldwide. Accordingly the number of visitors to these parks has been increasing; however, the budgets of Canadian park systems have been shrinking over the same period. In many locales the spread between the area and visitors to be managed and the resources available to do the management has been widening. In this paper, the Canadian national parks system and the Ontario provincial parks system are presented as examples of these trends.

Park Establishment

Worldwide the creation rate of parks and protected areas has been high during the last two decades. Since 1970 the number of protected areas has increased by over 150 per cent, to around 8,100. Correspondingly the area of parks has increased from 1,800,000 million square kilometres to over 7,500,000 million square kilometres (WRI, IUCN, UNEP, 1992), an increase of 316 per cent. Canada and Ontario show similar trends with increasing number of parks and parkland area.

Since 1980 many national parks or national parks reserves have been established in Canada. This includes Grasslands (1981), Mingan Archipelago (1984), Ivvavik (1984), Ellesmere Island (1986), Bruce (1987), Gwaii Haanas (1988), Aulavik (1992) and Vuntut (1993) (Table 1). In addition, in 1992, 22,252 square kilometres of area were withdrawn for the future establishment of the North Baffin National Park, assuming land claim negotiations are concluded. These nine parks and reserves have added 89,446 square kilometres of area to the national parks system (Colombo 1994). In 1980 the national parks system contained 129,457 square kilometres of area. The nine new parks added 89,446 square kilometres or 69 per cent to this 1980 total. By 1993 the total area of national parks had become 218,902.9 square kilometres (Nilsen, pers. comm.),

if North Baffin is included. These figures do not include 4514.9 square kilometres in four national marine park areas, all established since 1980.

Table 1: Canadian National Park Trends

Year	1980	1981	1982	1983	1984	1985	1986	1987	1988	1989	1990	1991	1992	1993
Parks	28	29	29	29	31	31	32	33	34	34	34	34	36	37
Area	129.5	130.4	130.4	130.4	140.7	140.7	178.5	178.6	180.1	180.1	180.1	180.1	214.6	218.9

Figure 1 shows that since 1980 the number of national parks has increased 32
per cent, while the area of national parks has gone up 69 per cent. If national
marine park areas are included, the number of national parks and reserves has
increased to 41 (46 per cent increase) and the area to 223,418 square kilometres
(73 per cent increase) since 1980. Therefore, since 1980 the Canadian national
parks system has increased dramatically. The Green Plan for Canada suggests
that the national parks system is only 50 per cent complete and only two out of
29 marine regions have marine national parks. Clearly, many new national
parks and marine national parks are likely to be created in the future
(Environment Canada 1991).

In 1980, the Ontario provincial parks system contained 131 parks with a total
area of 4,256,729 hectares (MNR, 1981). Since 1980 many provincial parks have
been established in Ontario, with the 1983 parks establishment initiative quite
prominent. By 1993 the system had risen in size to 259 parks, with a total area of
6,328,590 hectares. Over the 1980 to 1993 period the number of parks increased
by 127 or 96 per cent. In the same period the area of parkland increased by
slightly over 2,000,000 hectares or 49 per cent (Table 2 and Figure 2).

Figure 1: National Park Trends

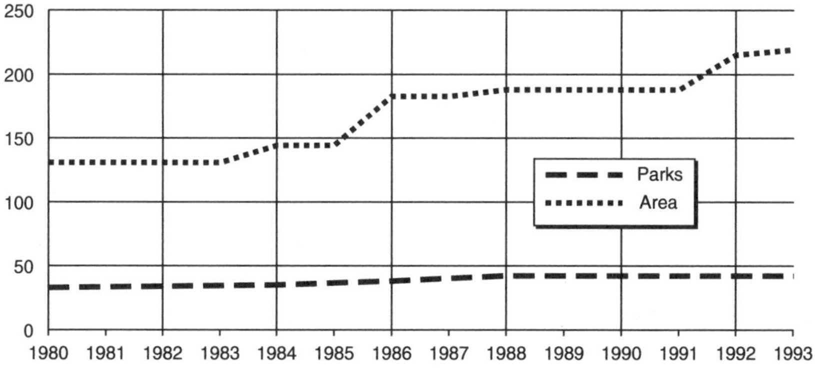

In 1994 Howard Hampton, the minister, announced the potential creation of 14 new parks, with a total area of 64,379 hectares plus a 1,521 hectare addition to an existing park (Hampton 1994). Therefore, further increases in park numbers and area are likely.

Table 2: Ontario Provincial Park Trends

Year	1982	1983	1984	1985	1986	1987	1988	1989	1990	1991	1992	1993
Parks	132	138	138	220	219	219	217	261	261	261	260	260
Area: ha millions	4.25	5.48	5.48	5.66	5.66	5.66	5.62	6.33	6.33	6.33	6.33	6.33
Visitors: millions	6.25	7.65	7.34	7.52	7.49	8.01	7.77	7.79	7.72	8.45	6.98	8.43

Visitor Numbers and Visitor Satisfaction

Data on the visitor numbers and visitor satisfaction levels in parks worldwide are not available; however, both Canada and Ontario have developed good data bases in this regard.

In 1988 the Canadian parks system served 20,240,000 visitors. By 1993 it catered to 21,160,000 visitors, an increase of 4.4 per cent, due to a modest increase each year. The visitation numbers before 1988 cannot be compared to those after that date due to a change in the data collection procedures. Therefore, long-term trend comparisons are not possible. In 1980 the Ontario parks system served 5,210,712 visitors (MNR 1981). By 1993 the system visitation had risen to 8,430,318 (MNR 1994), an increase of 62 per cent.

The Ontario Ministry of Natural Resources undertakes surveys of the campers and the day users of the provincial parks. All parks are surveyed, on a rotating basis, over a period of years so that each park has visitor data, none of which is over six years old. The surveys collect information for park planning and management purposes. The 1990 survey was conducted in 48 parks, providing a data base from 14,094 campers (MNR 1990a). One of the questions asked the campers to provide an overall rating of the park they were visiting. The responses provided a high rating of approximately 1.6, on a scale of one to five. This shows that even with the budget restraint, the average camper in Ontario provincial parks is expressing a high park satisfaction level. When asked if they were receiving value for their fees the ranking was similarly high, with a figure around 1.75 on a scale of one to five. Interestingly, the visitors to wilderness class parks gave the highest level of park ranking and expressed getting the highest value for their fees, while the recreation class visitors had significantly lower rankings in both categories (Murray 1994). The day use only visitors also reported

Figure 2: Provincial Park Trends

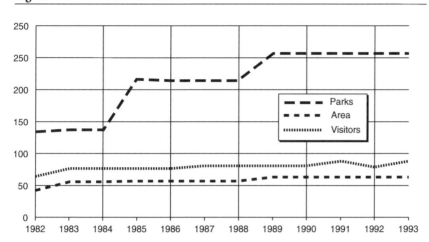

high levels of satisfaction with their visit and would give good recommendations to their friends (MNR 1990b), but at slightly lower levels than the campers.

When asked what programs or facilities the park could provide to encourage more visitation, only one activity in one park class, interpretation programs in wilderness class parks, was agreed to by the majority of campers. All other choices, such as lower fees or improved hospitality, received only lukewarm interest. This shows that provincial parks will have trouble getting the existing campers to lengthen their stays or to visit more often (Murray 1994).

Between 33 per cent and 50 per cent of the outdoor recreation market has camping as its primary accommodation form, while the rest prefers roofed accommodation such as lodges, cabins or cottages (Laventhol and Horvath 1988). Therefore, most of the parks in Canada, which have a lack of roofed accommodation, cannot serve at least 50 per cent of the outdoor recreation overnight market.

There are trends which suggest, that in the medium term, park visitation may decline. Park visitation that relies on camping is primarily concentrated in the younger sector of the population. In 1982, 34 per cent of the 18-to-24-year-old population cohort participated in camping, compared to only 15 per cent of the 45 to 64-year cohort (Robinson 1987). Foot (1990) suggests that the median age of the Canadian and American population will continue to rise as the baby boom generation moves into its senior years. Therefore with an aging population structure and a lack of roofed accommodation, it can reasonably be predicted that the park visitation market will shrink in Canada. Therefore, park visitation may be at a peak. Demographic trends particularly, point to a long, slow visitation decline.

Laventhol and Horvath (1988) conclude that the Ontario provincial parks are poorly positioned to take advantage of the market possibilities and changes over the next 20 years. Of the key problems shown in Table 3, all can be addressed by park management except for park location.

Table 3: Key Market Issues

---

1. Provincial parks are generally too remote from the large Ontario, Canadian and American population centres.
2. The parks lack all-season and roofed accommodation.
3. There is a severe lack of tour packages and the associated connections with the travel industry.
4. There are financial limitations due to the inability to raise funds from the clients.
5. There are inherent conflicts with the existing market if more intensive infrastructure is developed.

To sustain or increase visitation to provincial parks the managers must look seriously at broadening the options available for accommodation. Appropriate connections to the local tourist industry should be forged. The worldwide tourist industry uses a standardized booking and information system based on travel agents. The Ontario and Canadian parks are almost totally isolated from this system, to their disadvantage. The issues of revenue retention and revenue enhancement must be addressed. All of these changes can be made without unduly impacting existing uses or users.

Finance

The 1992 world parks congress concluded that the economic difficulties facing many countries restrict the investment required for adequate management of protected areas (McNeely 1993). This problem is particularly severe in the poorest countries, but the financial situation in Canadian parks is also a problem.

In the 1994-1995 fiscal year Parks Canada had a budget of $364,000,000. This money manages national parks, national historic parks, national marine parks, national historic sites, Canadian heritage rivers and world heritage sites (Government of Canada 1994). An analysis of the budget estimates tabled in parliament

Figure 3: Provincial Park Budgets

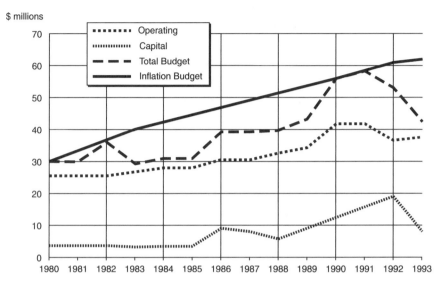

shows that from 1983 to 1993 Parks Canada lost a total of $70,240,000 through budget cuts. In addition, for the 1980 to 1991 period inflation cut an additional $17,000,000. Therefore, the 1994-1995 budget would be $451,240,000 if the 1983 budget had been maintained without cuts or inflation. This means that the latest expenditure levels are 19 per cent lower in spending power than 11 years earlier.

Riley (1989) showed, for the 1975 to 1986 period, a select sample of Ontario provincial parks lost 50 per cent of their purchasing power. A detailed analysis of the 1980 to 1993 period shows that the parks' system lost slightly over 30 per cent of its purchasing power. Figure 3 also shows that the capital expenditures increased considerably in the late 1980s as special funding was made available for projects associated with the 1993 centennial; however, in 1993 the capital funds fell back to a more normal level. Reid (1994) suggested that over the longer period, since 1974, the Ontario parks have lost approximately 60 per cent of their budgetary purchasing dollar. Clearly, the latest expenditure levels of Ontario provincial parks are severely reduced over those in place 20 years ago.

Obviously the Canadian and Ontario governments have cut parks' budgets to a considerable degree. The Canadian parks operation has been strongly hit with a one fifth reduction but the Ontario parks operation has been decimated with over a 50 per cent reduction.

Managing More with Less

How have the parks systems managed to survive in this period of rapid growth in responsibility and rapid decline in available financial resources?

Parks Canada has had a substantial budget reduction which has largely been absorbed through program reduction and staff loss. In the 1983 to 1993 period, a total of 155 person years of employment was permanently lost in that system. The management of the many new parks has been made possible by the transfer of staff positions from operations elsewhere, such as existing parks and regional offices. Overall, the field management has seen a general watering down of activities as fewer people do more activities across a much larger area.

The agency started a major thrust towards the use of volunteers and cooperation with voluntary organizations (D'Anjou 1989; Environment Canada, 1991). Starting cautiously in 1978, by 1986 there were over 5,500 active volunteers in all aspects of the Parks Canada operation (D'Anjou 1989). This has helped replace some functions of the lost staff, but more significantly has increased the ability of the operation to move into service functions that are not traditional undertaken by federal administrations, such as local fund raising, fee for service operations and mercantile operations. It can be argued that the volunteer sector involvement in Parks Canada has enabled the agency to both strengthen local support and to tap new sources of finance.

The Ontario provincial parks system has had nothing less than a devastating loss of resources over the last 15 years. The losses have been many and only a few will be discussed.

The level of visitor safety protection, such as through the use of life guards, has been considerably reduced. Many beaches now have no guarding or rescue services. The park management planning exercise has ground to a crawl. The desire to have each park with its own management statement is still only a dream. Very few parks have professionally trained natural resource managers. Natural resources and visitor management research have been reduced to a very low level. Most provincial parks have no resident staff for most of the year. Only 108 have any form of fee collection or gate control. More of the park functions are being operated on a District or Regional level as staff within the Ministry of Natural Resources add parks' management as one responsibility within a broader job responsibility. It has been said that Ontario provincial park operations have been reduced to campground management, probably an overstatement but unfortunately too close to the truth to be ignored. Fortunately, the campers and day users were still reporting a high level of satisfaction with their view of this part of the park operation in 1990 surveys (MNR, 1990; Murray, 1994). In May 1994 the Minister of Natural Resources announced that eight small provincial parks would remain closed throughout the year due to a lack of operating funds (*Kitchener-Waterloo Record*, 1994).

The Consolidated Revenue Fund

Canada and Ontario have an old tradition of having all government income deposited into one large pot, the consolidated revenue fund. This money is then doled out, along with borrowed money in recent years, to expenditure units throughout the administration. This approach is designed to avoid having rich agencies, those who have access to much income, and poor agencies, those that have no such access. It also avoids having many little pots of funds scattered around the government administration.

This approach turns parks agencies into expenditure units only. Earned income is relatively unimportant because it is not relevant to the next budget allocation from the central government. As a result, budgeting in parks agencies is the perverse exercise of deciding how much money is to be spent, with little or no emphasis placed on the collection of income. Parks managers during budget cutting exercises sometimes have cut fee collection staff because it was deemed to be of minor importance! Many parks have reduced the length of period that fees are collected, usually called reducing the operating season, giving those who visit during the rest of the year free access. Table 4 shows that the expenditures per visitor are much higher in those agencies that operate under the expenditure influence of the consolidated revenue fund. It is important to recognize that Parks Canada manages a widely spread set of parks, many of which are located in remote areas. The Niagara Parks have the advantage of having a large number of clients in a small area, a situation conducive to higher service efficiency.

Table 4: Park Expenditure Analysis

Park System	Expenditures	Visitors	Cost Per Visitor
National Parks	$364,000,000	21,160,000	$17.20
Provincial Parks	$43,281,200	8,430,318	$5.13
Niagara Parks	$39,000,000	12,000,000	$3.25

I would argue that this financial approach also has deep and profound impacts on the psychology of the organization. The lack of emphasis on fee for service means that issues such as service quality, return visitation and client satisfaction are given short shrift because they do not really matter in the decision structure. Since government runs on a long line of administrators whose job it is to decide who gets the money, the key emphasis for a park manager is to please the upper administrators who control the money. Therefore, the agencies spend much too much time with internal resource allocation machinations, and too little time on the management of the natural resources or the park visitation.

Table 5 shows that the Niagara Parks Commission, which has internal revenue retention, has arranged its operations to gain considerably more income per visitor, than the other agencies. The Niagara example is particularly noteworthy as virtually none of this income comes for the typical gate fees that are charged as visitors enter an area. The viewing of Niagara Falls and the use of the 40-kilometre-long parkway are both free to visitors. Table 5 suggests that a park agency which has the ability to operate like a business, with revenue retention, is able to develop successful strategies for increasing the return from their clientele.

Table 5: Park Income Analysis

Park System	Expenditures	Visitors	Cost Per Visitor
National Parks	$37,000,000	21,160,000	$1.75
Provincial Parks	$16,277,081	8,430,318	$1.93
Niagara Parks	$44,000,000	12,000,000	$3.67

Riley (1994) reports that the City of Etobicoke parks and recreation operation has revenue retention. As budget pressures have mounted in recent years, the earned income has increased to 34 per cent of expenditures, up from 8 per cent a few years ago. He reports that with careful management and aggressive income collection systems, income can be increased.

In the late 1980s the US Congress gave partial revenue retention powers to the National Parks Service. A modest fee increase occurred and each park was able to retain the income due to the increase. Starting in 1994 the Canadian government expects Parks Canada to earn $37,000,000 from operations, the traditional income in recent years. Over this amount, 25 per cent of the total can be retained by the agency (Whitfield 1994). These two major park management agencies are now moving towards higher levels of revenue generation, tied to the reward of increased internal resources if the income increases. The Ontario provincial parks have increased the income effectiveness as the income per visitor has increased from $1.34 in 1980 to the present figure of $1.93.

Clearly those agencies that operate on standard business principles relating to revenue generation and expenditure provide recreation services to the visitors at a more economically efficient rate. This phenomenon is becoming more recognized and administrative alterations are underway to increase financial efficiency in many parks agencies around the world.

The Building Competition

There is often a perception amongst national and provincial park managers that they sit on priceless resources that are unique. Since there is no substitute for that park, there is no perceived need to worry about visitor needs or satisfaction. Add this to the structural deficiencies in the systems and one can see the reasons for low emphasis on a client focus.

Competition is rearing its head across the world. The increase in world-wide travel by the outdoor recreation market gives any one park or one park system competition from many sources. Within Ontario the camping market has four major players, with the resultant highest level of competition anywhere in Canada. The national parks, provincial parks, conservation areas and private campgrounds provide thousands of potential camping sites across the province. Outside Ontario, the provincial park systems in many provinces are increasing in size and offering more product. Across the world the number of new parks has almost doubled in the last 30 years, providing even more competition.

The private sector is faster moving than government and is rapidly developing services and products that are value added to the existing park programs. A typical example might be Algonquin Park. Algonquin is a world-class park that is heavily used by people from Ontario and nearby provinces and states; however, it is very difficult to use by international travellers from outside North America. Key limitations include a poor marketing effort, the complete isolation from the travel industry allocation system of agents and carriers, the need for sophisticated equipment (tents, canoes, sleeping bags, etc.), and many difficulties with language and information. The private sector has stepped into this market in a sophisticated way and is now developing a steady and growing business in serving the European market. These outfitters provide all the information, all of the equipment, multilingual guides and sell their product through the standard tourism provision infrastructure. The private sector is developing a service-oriented market that the public sector is uninterested in or incapable of developing.

Costa Rica is now well known as providing one of the best ecotourism experiences in tropical environments in the world. The country has developed a diverse national park and wildlife refuge system to protect representative examples of every major ecosystem in the county. The world media have exploded their coverage of the parks and their visitation providing a rich market exposure. The resultant visitation has created a rapidly increasing ecotourism market. Fennell (1990) studied the Canadians who had visited Costa Rica on an ecotourism travel experience. He found that many parks and reserves were visited, presumably to experience the diversity of ecosystems that occur in the country. He asked the travellers to rank the parks that they visited. Surprisingly, the highest ranked destination in the country is not one of the world famous parks or reserves; it is a privately operated park, the Monteverde Cloud Forest Reserve.

The Monteverde Reserve is owned and operated by local conservation organizations, the Tropical Science Centre and the Monteverde Conservation League. The reserve protects 10,500 hectares of land, has 28 employees and serves slightly under 40,000 visitors a year (Rojas 1992). Monteverde protects an ecosystem of cloud forest and the associated attitudinal variations on the Caribbean mountain slope, very similar to the ecosystems in Brauillo Carillo National Park. But the visitors ranked Monteverde far ahead of the similar national park. Fennell's study showed that it was more than the natural environment alone that determined ecotourist visitor satisfaction. He found that the ecotourists were very interested in learning and experiencing nature. Monteverde provides basic services to the tourists that are not available in the national park. There is a visitor centre with displays, books and up-to-date information. There are many, well-marked and managed trails through various ecosystems. There are knowledgeable guides available for hire. There are hotels in the local village that can be booked in advance through travel agents. These simple, but effective, visitor services provide the necessary information, accommodation and travel services to the ecotourists that result in high levels of satisfaction. The Monteverde Reserve has placed a visitor limitation of 100 people a day and charges $7.00 US per visit. This income of $700.00 a day is sufficient to operate the most highly valued ecotour experience in the country.

The national parks in Costa Rica are at a considerable disadvantage. All of their income must return to a consolidated revenue fund. Even if they charge money for services, they cannot keep it. They are not allowed to charge the international tourists more than the poorer local people. Their major emphasis is on resource protection, with very few services for the visitors. There is only one functioning visitor centre in all of the parks and reserves. There are a few camping sites but visitors must bring all of their own equipment and food which eliminates most of the international visitation. There are no lodges in the parks; however, the parks see their visitation increasing dramatically as tropical ecotourism becomes very popular. Over the last decade the Costa Rican parks have had to make do with a static or declining budget allocation from the central government. Some parks can now not afford basic equipment, such as a boat in a marine park. As a result, the national parks are also experiencing a resource quality decline as the visitation increase impacts negatively on the environment.

The contrast of the private and public ecotour operations in Costa Rica reveals some fundamental principles. The private sector can and will provide high quality visitor services. The public sector could provide those services but the central budget does not provide sufficient money and the agency cannot charge the tourists for the services. Therefore, needed services are not operated! The private sector must provide high quality natural environments to maintain high nature tourist interest. The public sector has the mandate to provide high quality natural environments, but sees the environmental quality being reduced by rapid increases in visitation and the associated impacts. The structural defects in the public system almost direct long-term degradation of the environment and of the associated visitor satisfaction.

The Critical Link Between Finance and Protection

The Ontario, Canadian and Costa Rica examples show that these governments are following similar trends of making more parks and encouraging higher visitation levels, all the while choking the financial health out of the management agencies. If this continues increased resource degradation, decreased ecotourist satisfaction levels and the virtual destruction of management structures are predicted. This cannot be allowed to occur.

There is a silver lining to this cloud and the Monteverde, Canadian and Ontario experiences cast considerable light. Parks management requires two fundamental concepts, the protection of nature and the management of visitors. The former is a right and proper role for all of society, because everyone benefits. Therefore, governments are behooved to provide continuous tax-based, funding for the maintenance of the important ecosystems that occur in and near the parks; however, the recreation services provided should be bought and paid for by those who do the consumption. There is no good reason why the outdoor recreation of the middle and upper classes of society should be subsidized by tax dollars. Monteverde shows that a large and significant natural area can be managed in an environmentally sensitive fashion with funds entirely derived from tourism.

In Canada and elsewhere, the parks agencies must be released from the bondage of the consolidated revenue fund and its stifling influences. The agencies must be encouraged to develop administrative and financial structures that charge the tourists for the recreation services that they use. There is no alternative. Either the tourists pay their way, or the visitor services and the associated environments will sink into disarray.

Revenue Generation and Willingness to Pay

Revenue generation occurs in parks, typically from entrance and camping fees. The US Parks Service takes in approximately 10 per cent of its expenditures (Ridenour 1993). Parks Canada takes in $37 million, which is 10 per cent of a $364 million budget (Whitfield pers. comm.). The Ontario provincial parks earn 38 per cent of their very modest expenditures (Reid 1994). The conservation authorities come closest to earning self-sufficiency in income in their parks and outdoor recreation expenditures, many authorities earning from 75 per cent to 100 per cent of their expenditures through income.

Conservation authorities have the advantage in being able to operate in a businesslike fashion. The recreation operations have internal revenue retention and therefore the operations are encouraged to live off their income. Some authorities earn high incomes on intensive recreational operations, such as ski tows and swimming beaches, and use this money to subsidize more extensive recreation activities such as hiking or nature observation.

There are a variety of revenue retention ratios in parks operations. Those systems that have revenue retention and operate in a standard business fashion, earn much higher proportions of their expenditures.

Murray (1994) reports that Ontario provincial park campers report a high level of satisfaction with the value they obtain for their park fees. They also report that lower fees will not lead to longer or more visitation, suggesting that existing fees levels are not a critical decision component of the trip experience.

Riley (1989) analyzed the Ontario provincial park visitors' willingness to pay for higher service levels. She found that 41 per cent of visitors were willing to pay for a higher level of specific services in provincial parks. The willingness to pay was most concentrated in the three variables: food, restaurants and convenience stores, lodging and rental of equipment. A breakdown of visitor categories showed that 56 per cent of day users and 32 per cent of campers were willing to pay more. She found that collection of increased fees is best done through conditional fees attached to specific services being offered, rather than an all encompassing usage fee increase. She also found an impressive 54 per cent of visitors willing to donate money on a one-time basis. The average suggested was $64.13 a person. An impressive 30 per cent of visitors were willing to donate some time to the park they were visiting. Riley's work showed that there is upward flexibility in the users' willingness to pay; however, they wanted certain products and services, that apparently were not sufficient at present. There is also a huge potential to raise donated money and time from the visitors.

The Niagara Parks Commission as a Model

The Niagara Parks Commission is a scheduled provincial agency. It has the responsibility to manage the tourism facilities along the Niagara River and Niagara Falls area in Ontario. The agency is a Crown corporation with specific legislation that provides for its operation. It is governed by a board of directors, the members of which are appointed by the province and by designated local municipalities. The agency operates like a private corporation. Its financial and managerial operations encourage entrepreneurial and financially efficient behaviour.

The Niagara Parks Commission has 240 full-time staff and 1,100 seasonal staff. It serves 12 million visitors on 1,400 hectares of land. In 1993, the commission earned a profit of $5,000,000 on gross revenue of $44,000,000 (Schaefer 1993). Remarkably this profit was earned without charging fees for the primary attraction, the viewing of Niagara Falls and the visitation of the parkland along the Niagara River and gorge.

The primary sources of funds for the commission, in order of importance are: gift shops, food services, attractions and hydroelectric generation. The latter income comes from Ontario Hydro, a major industry along the gorge and falls. If this industrial income did not occur, the commission would still be close to breaking even. The attractions' income comes from parking fees, and from special attractions such as boat rides, tramway rides and gorge viewing sites. The gift shops are specially located at prime sites along the Niagara Parkway and sell a typical variety of souvenirs. Speciality shops are now being developed, for example a Christmas store and a nature store.

The two primary sources of income for this agency, merchandising and food, are not now tapped by most parks agencies. Neither the national parks nor the provincial parks earn significant funds from merchandise sales or from food sales. Where these operations occur, the parks have turned over these profit centres to the private sector for operation. Dennis Schaefer, the general manager of the Niagara Parks Commission, states that he does not use concessionaires for any potential profit making enterprises. If there is a profit to be made, he wants his agency to earn that profit.

The operating surplus of the Niagara Parks Commission is used to upgrade facilities and services. For example, a recreation trail from Fort Erie to Niagara-on-the-Lake costing four million dollars was constructed and made available for free use. This basic idea of dispersed recreation services being paid for by specific profit generation centres is innovative.

The commission has a tourism management mandate. The agency does not have a key environmental protection mandate, beyond the protection of scenic landscapes and views. This relieves the agency from the management of large expanses of sensitive lands that do not generate high levels of funds. The commission also has the significant advantage of large numbers of visitors in a concentrated area. This provides for efficiencies of scale that are not available to parks that provide outdoor recreation in a dispersed fashion in a sensitive environment; however, the Niagara example shows that the most lucrative sources of income for parks, merchandising and food, are not being tapped by most parks agencies. The emerging Friends of Parks cooperating associations are starting to tap such markets in some national and provincial parks. Where present, these Friends' operations are now providing key funds to the visitor information and visitor services components of some parks.

The Niagara Parks Commission operations show that with proper business practices a much higher level of economic efficiency can occur in park agencies. Dispersed wilderness recreation can never earn the level of income that Niagara Falls can, but a park system with a mixture of park types and facilities can earn a substantial part of its expenditures. A reasonable goal would be to earn at least one half of its expenditures through recreation-based income. The other half is the responsibility of society for the environmental protection element inherent in parks.

Summary
In the last 15 years the Canadian national parks system has had the national park area under management double in size and has had the visitation increase 4 per cent. All of this has occurred while the money available for the system has decreased by 19 per cent. In the same period the Ontario Provincial Parks System has had even more dramatic changes. It has seen a 50 per cent increase in the area

to be managed and has served an increase in visitation of 60 per cent; however, the budget needed to manage this area and these recreationists has declined a crippling 62 per cent.

The Ontario provincial park campers and day users report high levels of satisfaction with the parks they visit and say that they are getting good value for their fees. The lack of roofed accommodation and the aging population will serve to limit, and possibly reduce, overnight stay levels in Canadian parks over the next 20 years unless administrative and marketing changes are undertaken.

A restructuring of parks operations in Canada, and elsewhere, is needed. In the long term, either the tourist use must pay for itself or else the tourist use will prove to be destructive to itself and to the park on which it depends. This reality must cause the parks to operate with business like principles of service quality and financial return. This will require a total restructuring of the administrative, financial and personal structure of the parks' operations.

Most parks systems have a critically important environmental protection mandate. This environmental protection is a public good and in wealthy countries, such as Canada, should be paid for by general tax revenues. In poorer countries the public good is still present but the governments are not able to provide environmental protection funds. In these cases there is little choice but the tourists for gaining suitable income. Either the tourists pay the costs of operation, or the parks are insufficiently protected and managed.

Canada, nationally and provincially, must move to a more businesslike park management structure. The key concepts must be resource protection, high levels of visitor satisfaction, fee for service and financial self sufficiency in tourism. Such a mix of ideas is emerging in many operations across the world, with large private ecotourism reserves leading the way.

References Cited

Colombo, J. R. 1994. *The Canadian Global Almanac.* Macmillan, Toronto.

D'Anjou, Alice. 1989. *A Comparative Study of Volunteers in Selected Canadian National Parks.* Unpublished thesis, Department of Recreation and Leisure Studies, University of Waterloo, Waterloo, Ontario.

Environment Canada. 1991. *State of the Parks.* Parks Service, Minister of Supply and Services, Ottawa.

Fennell, David. 1990. *A Profile of Ecotourists and the Benefits Derived from their Experience: A Costa Rican Case Study.* MA thesis, Department of Recreation and Leisure Studies, University of Waterloo, Waterloo.

Foot, D. 1990. The Age of Outdoor Recreation in Canada. *Recreation Canada*, December.

Government of Canada. 1994. *Main Budget Estimates – Part III.*

Hampton, Howard. 1994. *Keep It Wild: Our Natural Heritage Areas.* Ministry of Natural Resources, Toronto.

Kitchener-Waterloo Record. 1994. *8 Ontario Parks to stay shut as money-saving measure.* May 4.

Laventhol and Horvath. 1988. *Ontario Provincial Parks Market Analysis.*

McNeely, J. A. 1993. *Parks for Life.* Report of the IVth World Congress on National Parks and Protected Areas, International Union for the Conservation of Nature, Gland, Switzerland.

Ministry of Natural Resources. 1981. *Ontario Provincial Parks Statistics 1980.* Parks and Recreational Areas Branch, Outdoor Recreation Group, Toronto.

Ministry of Natural Resources. 1990a. *Provincial Park Camper Survey: Statistical Summary.* Provincial Parks and Natural Heritage Policy Branch, Toronto.

Ministry of Natural Resources. 1990b. *Provincial Park Day Visitor Survey: Statistical Summary.* Provincial Parks and Natural Heritage Policy Branch, Toronto.

Ministry of Natural Resources. 1992. *Ontario Provincial Parks Statistics 1991.* Provinical Parks and Natural Heritage Policy Branch, North York.

Ministry of Natural Resources. 1994. *MNR Parks and Recreational Areas Expenditures 1981-1992.* Data Sheet provided by Dan Mulrooney.

Murray, Christine. 1994. *Ontario Provincial Parks Visitor Analysis.* Paper prepared for Dan Mulrooney based on the 1990 provincial park camper survey data. Department of Recreation and Leisure Studies, University of Waterloo.

Nilsen, Per. 1993. *Data Sheet of Canada's National Parks and National Park Reserves.* Parks Canada, Hull.

Reid, Ronald. 1994. *Delivering Ontario's Provincial Parks: A Review of Management Alternatives.* Consultant report for the Federation of Ontario Naturalists.

Ridenour, James. 1993. Speech given to the Joint U.S. and Canadian Federal/Provincial/ State Parks Directors Meeting, Niagara Falls, September.

Riley, Jill. 1989. *An Analysis of Visitor's Willingness to Pay for an Expanded Service Level at Ontario Provincial Parks.* MA Thesis, Department of Recreation and Leisure Studies, University of Waterloo, Ontario.

Riley, Tom. 1994. Personal Communication.

Robinson, J. P. 1987. Where's the Boom? *American Demographics* 8(3):34-37.

Rojas, Carmen. 1992. *Ecotourism in Monteverde.* Paper presented at the World Parks Congress, Caracas, Venezuela, February.

Schaefer, Dennis. 1993. Speech given to the Joint U.S. and Canadian Federal/Provincial/ State Parks Directors Meeting, Niagara Falls, September.

Whitfield, Carol. 1994. Telephone Conversation. Parks Canada, Hull.

World Resources Institute, World Conservation Union and United Nations Environment Programme. 1992. *Global Biodiversity Strategy.*

Parks and Protected Areas and Sustainable Development[1]

J. G. Nelson

The Challenge

The vitally important links between parks and protected areas and sustainable development are not sufficiently appreciated by many public officials and citizens – to the detriment of natural and human well-being now and in future. Most people still see parks and protected areas as essentially scenic, natural and historic heritage areas, whose principal use is recreation. The many environmental, economic and social services which parks and protected areas offer to society are generally not well understood. The contribution that they can make in providing equitable access to socio-economic and environmental opportunities – or sustainable development – now and in future, is insufficiently recognized and supported in Canada.

Background

Parks and protected areas can be understood as part of our evolving natural and cultural heritage. For as long as we have knowledge of human history, a struggle has existed between using and conserving the resources and environments that sustain us (Nelson, Needham and Mann 1978). Since "Stone Age" times people have husbanded plant, animal and other resources by setting areas aside in various types of reserves or sacred ground. Taboos or social or legal regulations have been invoked by many folk to provide for conservation and use of wildlife, water and other resources more generally. In early Eastern societies, parks were set aside to protect the wildlife and habitat valued by the ruling classes for hunting and for recreation (Shepard 1967). In the eleventh century, the Norman invaders established Royal Forests in England to protect deer and other animals for the subsistence and pleasure of the King's roving court. These forests protected not only deer and other wildlife but oak, beech and other ancient woodlands that have succeeded to the present day. The management of these Forests involved making arrangements for local people to continue some collecting, grazing and other economic and social activities while not killing the game. Agricultural activities and settlements were also maintained in and around Royal Forests in different parts of England. These arrangements still continue in the New Forest of southern England and can be seen as a form of sustainable development (Nelson 1995).

In Europe the idea of the park appears to have merged with the garden and landscaping in seventeenth, eighteenth and nineteenth-century country estates. These estate parks were created in the image of the savannah, the wooded and grassy landscape which reputedly is preferred above most others by humans. The estates consisted of intermingled woods, lawns, deer and other animals as well as land for agriculture and ponds for fish. Such country parks conserved resources for aesthetic purposes and also supported owners and workers through production of food and other commodities for subsistence and for sale outside the estates. The country parks were therefore a key part of the environmental, social and economic system of historic England and essential to its sustainable development – which was shattered by the first Great War and the technical, economic and political changes that ensued.

Parks and protected areas also were inextricably intertwined with the development of the United States of America and have played an important role in Canada and other countries. According to historians such as Huth (1957), Nash (1968) and Runte (1979), the idea of wilderness and the social invention of the national park were part of the American effort to establish itself as a distinctive country among the nations of the world in the nineteenth and twentieth centuries. Europe had its culture, its old ruins, its growing urban areas. The US had its great wild areas which were perceived as essentially untouched by human activity, in spite of considerable evidence of centuries of use by native or indigenous people for agriculture, collecting, hunting, and other purposes. Many of the early American and Canadian national parks were created for conservation and enjoyment in relatively isolated areas where agricultural or other activities were not economically feasible. Many of the national parks were also established primarily for geologic rather than biological reasons. An example is Yellowstone with its mountain and canyon scenery, its hot springs and geysers.

Over the decades, the roles of national parks in the US and Canada have multiplied, although their wide-ranging functions and contributions are still not sufficiently well understood and valued. The contributions to recreation and tourism are relatively widely recognized. Many citizens also see national parks as playing an important role in protection of biological features and processes and rare and endangered species of plants and animals. Contributions to air and water quality and to regional development are less well understood as is the evolving role of parks and protected areas in conserving a wide range of plant and animal species, natural communities, landscapes and biodiversity more generally (Mosquin et al 1995, Hummel 1995).

The development of national parks and protected areas in Canada has more or less paralleled that in the US (Nelson and Scace 1969; Nelson et al. 1979; Scace and Nelson 1986). Many of the early Canadian national parks were created in remote places for geologic, scenic, tourism and later for biological and ecological reasons. Since the 1960s the national parks have been established in accord with a systems plan designed to have at least one representative national park in each of the natural regions of Canada. At various times in the last decade in particular, various proposals have been made for a more co-operative approach among the federal government and the provinces for conservation of areas representative of the national or Canadian landscape, for example, National Heritage Areas.

In Canada, the US and internationally, many other types of parks and protected areas have developed in association with national parks (McNeely and Miller, 1984). In Canada as well as in provinces such as Ontario, provincial parks, national wildlife areas, conservation authority conservation areas, national heritage rivers, local and regional parks, agreement forests, areas of natural and scientific interest (ANSI), municipal environmentally significant areas (ESA), federal and provincial historic parks and sites, biosphere reserves and World Heritage Sites are among those that come to mind. Some of these different types of protected areas are publicly owned. Some are privately owned. Others are a combination. The different types have developed historically, more or less in accordance with the needs of the day and *not* as part of any predetermined plan.

Parks and Sustainable Development

Figure 1. Functions of National Parks and Protected Areas in National Conservation Strategies

---

1. Conservation and use of forests, water, soil, wildlife

2. Conservation of genetic resources

3. Science and environmental monitoring

4. Protection and appropriate use of lakes, rivers, wetlands

5. Protection and appropriate use of coastal and marine areas

6. Protection and appropriate use of historical, cultural and archaeological resources

7. Protection and appropriate use of "green space" or "natural framework" in and near cities

8. Protection and appropriate use of resources for recreation and tourism

9. Protection of resources for appropriate use by indigenous people

10. Protection and appropriate use of resources, environment and heritage areas as part of regional planning and management

11. Protection and appropriate use of resources, environment and heritage as part of comprehensive land use planning/management

Modified from Nelson, J.G. 1987, National Parks and Protected Areas, NCS and Sustainable Development. Geoforum, 18, 3, 291 - 319.

Figures 1 and 2 are intended to summarize or highlight the many uses, functions, and services offered to Canadians – and other people of the world – by parks and protected areas. It is difficult to list all of the uses in a distinct way, because many of them are interrelated, overlapping and mutually reinforcing.

Figure 1 is an attempt to list the uses or services in a reasonably systematic fashion. Not everyone will agree with the classes and divisions but the list does show that the uses and services are numerous, varied, comprehensive and essential to society and sustainable development.

In its 1980 World Conservation Strategy the International Union for the Conservation of Nature and other international agencies put forward three basic elements of sustainable development:

1. to preserve essential ecological processes;

2. to protect diversity; and

3. to maintain resource productivity.

Figure 1 shows that parks and protected areas play an essential role in regard to all three of these basic elements of sustainability.

Figure 2 shows that parks and protected areas have important roles to play in many specific types of land uses as well as in general classes of land management ranging from preservation and protection of wildlands and species, to multiple and intensive use. Various kinds of protected areas offer various services at different points or places along the land use spectrum. At one end of the

Fgure 2. Land Use Spectrum

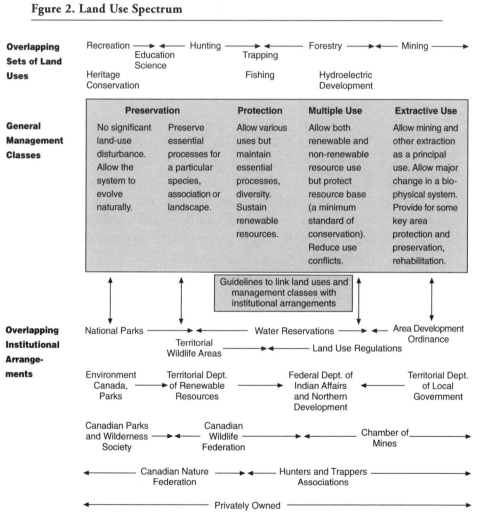

Modified from Bastedo et al., (1984).

spectrum large national and provincial parks conserve and provide for the appropriate use of substantial areas representative of ecosystems or natural areas of Canadian significance. At the other end of the spectrum, in more intensely settled areas, parks and protected areas play an important role in conserving smaller natural and human heritage areas that offer key services to society. These services range from protection of water quality, aquifers, wetlands and other important plant and animal habitats, to providing the woodlands, marshes or other areas upon which ecological restoration programs can be based after mining and other development activities are completed.

Figure 2 also underlines the fact that the organizational or institutional arrangements for parks and protected areas extend beyond public ownership and government responsibilities to include private ownership and stewardship and the programs of agencies such as The Canadian Nature Federation or the Canadian Parks and Wilderness Society, whose forerunner was the National and Provincial Parks Association.

In thinking about parks and protected areas in the foregoing context, it is important to recognize that they offer many opportunities for employment and economic returns through business and investment as well as maintaining the environmental and resource capital that is essential to the sustaining of nature, society, and quality of life. We have not done enough in recognizing the significant direct and indirect employment and socio-economic benefits of protected areas. In many cases, these are more longlasting than those of mining, forestry, or other often more highly valued alternative forms of land use.

One of the main challenges – if not the main challenge for sustainable development in future – is to extend many of the foregoing ideas, principles and approaches developed over the years for public or government protected areas, into the private domain – and vice versa. The UNESCO Man and Biosphere program and the National Park Greater Park Ecosystem approaches are two relatively recent attempts to effect such links among public and private ownership and activities in the lands surrounding parks and protected areas.

Current Concerns
The big problem is that in spite of having many different kinds of parks and protected areas, and a growing number of private efforts, we are still losing ground in terms of sustainable development, i.e. in conserving parks and protected areas and enhancing the environmental and socio-economic opportunities needed to provide effectively and equitably for people today and tomorrow

(Hummel 1995; Mosquin et al 1995). Many important wild or "natural areas" remain unprotected or inadequately conserved. Numerous existing national parks and protected areas are unevenly managed. Wood Buffalo National Park is a good example, with the direct and indirect effects of hunting, water power development, agriculture and other activities in and outside the park, presenting challenges to the integrity and maintenance of the system. Other protected areas are a bone of contention among agencies and groups that have been competing when they could be co-operating more closely with one another. One example has been the Grasslands National Park in southern Saskatchewan that has varying wildlife, vegetation, historic and other characteristics that require a strong co-operative public and private stewardship approach. Another example is Riding Mountain National Park in Manitoba that is stressed inside by recreation pressures and outside by agriculture.

Increasingly parks and protected area officials are dealing with these stresses through buffer zone or biosphere approaches that attempt to link the park with surrounding land uses in more sensitive and effective ways. These arrangements involve co-operation in activities such as research, education and monitoring of land use and environmental changes around and within parks and protected areas. Yet the challenges are formidable for many protected areas lie amid areas of accelerating development, such as Fundy National Park, New Brunswick; Rondeau Provincial Park, Ontario; Banff National Park, Alberta; and Pacific Rim National Park, British Columbia.

Central and southern Ontario is a classic example of the foregoing situation with its maze of different types of federal national and historic parks, provincial parks, waterfowl and wildlife management areas, conservation areas, provincially designated wetlands, flood plain zones, ANSIs and ESAs. All these different types of protected areas tend to be managed with a generally low level of co-ordination among responsible parties and without much thought for connections among the different protected areas in the sense that this is promoted by recent advances in landscape ecology and conservation biology (Woodley et al 1992). These advances suggest that in general, biological diversity is better maintained by a system of connected and interrelated natural areas than by isolated ones. These advances – and general experience – also suggest that natural and human heritage areas and approaches should be brought more closely together in protecting and using the various kinds of significant habitats and human communities that make up areas such as central and southern Ontario. In this respect, the idea of landscape – involving as it does understanding of and sensitivity to the interaction of natural and human influences – is a powerful unifying or integrating force.

Recent government initiatives such as the proposal for 17 new Wild Places in Ontario are very welcome; however, they are insufficient to meet the growing need for protected areas offering wildland, biodiversity, rare species, water quality and quantity, natural history, monitoring, science, educational and other interrelated functions often requiring large areas to be effective. New wild places should be planned as part of networks or "green frameworks" for sustainable development in Ontario – as well as other areas. Examples of such systems have been developed in a general way for some of the states in the US (Nelson, 1991; Noss, 1987).

In my home area of Waterloo and the Grand River Valley, many people welcomed the recent work of the Sewell Commission with its support for improved planning and management of environmentally significant areas at the regional and municipal government level in Ontario. The Sewell recommendations laid the basis for bringing small dispersed Environmentally Significant Policy Areas (ESPAs and locally ESAs) into a linked protected area network that could provide many functions or services required for balanced land use and sustainable development locally and regionally.

One result of the commission's work has been concern among planners for improved definitions of "ecological significance" in order to provide a better scientific or technical basis for protecting as much as possible of the woodland, prairie and other natural areas remaining in the Waterloo and Grand River region. Yet only about 16 per cent of the Grand River basin is still wooded and it could be argued that all of it is needed or significant in terms of the many services that parks and protected areas offer to society and quality of life. It has been highly encouraging nevertheless, that the last Ontario government passed new planning legislation based on the recommendations of the Sewell Commission. Of further importance were the recent revisions of regional and municipal plans to reflect many of the ideas in the Sewell Commission report, for example, those of the regional governments of Waterloo and Haldimand-Norfolk. What is worrying is the move by the Harris government in Ontario to revise and amend the new act in ways that will make it more difficult to strengthen the role of protected areas in sustainable development at the local and regional level.

Similar situations could be described in other parts of Ontario and Canada; and these apply to other needs as well, for example historic and cultural heritage. In this case the focus has been and still is, on individual buildings and structures. Relatively few historic heritage areas, districts or landscapes have been set aside to date in Ontario, even though provincial and other legislation makes this possible. Little has been done to promote historical or cultural corridors or to link nature and culture through landscape planning. The highly sectoral approach that is still dominant in Ontario is illustrated by the fact that recent major provincial reviews of the Heritage Act and the Planning Act were undertaken separately at about the same time by the last provincial government. These reviews, and possible changes ensuing from them, continue to be treated distinctly from one another, even though much could be gained by making them mutually reinforcing. Insufficient cross-departmental or cross-sectoral activity is taking place, in spite of the rising interest in government and the citizenry in linking environment, economy and society in sustainable development.

Needs

Some major changes need to be made in the near future if we are not to suffer major losses in regard to parks and protected areas and sustainable development for present and future generations.

1. A fundamental need exists in Ontario – and other provinces – for broad federal and provincial strategies for parks and protected areas in the context of sustainable development. We need to review the whole range of institutional arrangements that make up the current historically evolved system. A framework is needed that will allow us to move beyond the sectoral approaches and conflicts that typify the situation today. Broad strategies involving intergovernmental, interagency, and public and private sector co-operation, are urgently needed in Ontario and other parts of Canada if parks and protected areas and related forms of public and private stewardship, are to make their essential contributions to maintenance and enhancement of natural and human well being.

The strategic approaches need to be formulated and undertaken at national, provincial, regional and local levels. Government people, businessmen and citizens must be better informed about the important functions or services that parks and protected areas offer to land use, conservation and sustainable development at all scales of endeavour. Some examples of useful strategic approaches have been developed in the last decade or so. These include the federal Green Plan that provided funding for relevant activities ranging from pollution control to research and planning for protected areas throughout Canada. The Green Plan is, however, reportedly to be terminated in 1997. An example of an appropriate strategy at the provincial level is the work of the Sewell Commission on "the greening" of official planning in Ontario. This initiative is however, apparently destined to be weakened by the Harris government. An ongoing example at the local level is the Crombie Commission and the Toronto waterfront restoration program. An excellent ongoing example in the private domain is the Endangered Spaces Program of World Wildlife Fund Canada (Hummell 1995). This program has placed pressure on both government and private agencies and groups to co-operate more fully in protecting wild areas throughout Canada. The emphasis in this program is however, on the creation of enough large national parks and comparable reserves to complete the protection of representative samples of all the natural regions of Canada. It is not concerned so much with improved management of existing national parks, nor with the creation and development of smaller parks and protected areas in more settled regions.

2. A major need also exists for a broader political voice for the conservation and appropriate use of natural and cultural heritage in Canada and for their place in sustainable development. Such conservation and use fundamentally depends on the growth and effective management of a system of parks and protected areas. It also depends upon ecologically and historically based land use planning, where this includes not only zoning and other regulations and policies, but also economic instruments such as tax and other financial incentives. These help recompense land owners and managers for the contributions or services that their protected lands make to society.

Major decisions are now being made about key elements of the management or institutional mosaic responsible for the future state of our natural and human heritage. These decisions are generally being made separately in different administrative units such as national parks, provincial parks, regional parks, and conservation authorities. Currently these decisions are threatening because they involve major budget cuts, downsizing and re-organization. Such changes could negatively affect not only the nature of individual programs but the relations among them and the capacity of the whole to serve society. We lack a citizens group or voice – an advocate – for the promotion of a broader view of natural and cultural heritage in Ontario and the country as a whole.

3. A much more vigorous educational program is needed to help people understand the essential role that parks and protected areas, and related public and private stewardship programs, play in maintaining and enhancing the natural and cultural well-being of ourselves and our children. More vigorous environmental education work is especially important in urban areas where most of the people live and where an increasing proportion of land use and environmental problems arise and spread to the countryside and rural areas.

A century ago Caucasian settlement had seriously damaged bison, other wildlife, waters, forests, soils and other resources in Canadian hinterlands, to the point of crisis in terms of environmental sustainability. In consequence, at the end of the nineteenth and in the early-twentieth century, national parks and other protected areas, as well as related conservation laws and institutions, were developed to deal with these challenges. Many of these conservation efforts arose from the work of the federal Conservation Commission, which provided relevant information and guidance from about 1911 to 1922.

Today, at the end of the twentieth century, we face an array of comparable challenges; however, these arise as much if not more in the city than the countryside. In this respect, we need centres and programs across the country to make urban and rural dwellers more understanding of and better prepared to deal with the challenges. One little used and promising means at the federal level is the National Landmarks Program set up in the late 1970s to conserve valued geologic, archaeological, biological and other resources at many relatively small sites in Canada, in co-operation with other governments and interested parties. The role of government in supporting development and operation of such sites, centres and institutions, should be a strong one. The same could be said for universities, colleges and schools. But ongoing budget cuts limit these roles and leave much to private initiatives.

4. Universities and colleges can play a strong role by attempting to provide needed information and support through educational and research activities undertaken in co-operation with government agencies and citizen's groups. An example is the Long Point Environmental Folio project undertaken at the Heritage Resources Centre, University of Waterloo. For several years faculty and graduate students at the University of Waterloo and other nearby universities have conducted various geological, biological, land use, flood hazard, protected area and other studies in the Long Point region. The Point consists of marshes, wetlands, beaches and dunes stretching about 40 km into Lake Erie. It is one of the longest freshwater peninsulas in the world and of high scientific, ecological and heritage interest because of its significance as a waterfowl and passerine bird staging area, a home for rare plant and animal species and its importance as a nursery area for fish. Such qualities earned Long Point area recognition as an international Biosphere reserve in 1986. The Long Point Biosphere program is administered by a management committee that consists of people employed or associated with the many agencies and groups involved in the area including the Canadian Wildlife Service, Ontario provincial parks, and the Ontario Ministry of Natural Resources, as well as naturalist and citizen groups.

The Long Point Biosphere Reserve Committee has been the principal point of contact between the Heritage Resources Centre folio research group, local people and concerned government personnel. This contact has made it possible to discuss and jointly decide upon the water quality, waterfowl, flood and erosion, forest history and other themes considered significant enough to be included in the first folio of maps and text. In other words the Long Point Folio is one example of a co-operative university, government and citizen approach to the identification of issues and the analysis, assessment and presentation of relevant information in maps and ways that are useful to researchers, government and citizens more generally (Nelson et al., 1995).

5. Finally, interactive and wider ranging civic approaches to decision-making have to be built into a commitment to broad social learning. Individuals, groups and agencies with different backgrounds and interests need to exchange information and ideas on values as well as on issues, planning, management and decision-making. The mainly top-down approach of governments in the past has resulted in some major achievements such as the current system of protected areas, and associated economic, social and environmental benefits. But this system has also led us to many of the important challenges that we face today.

A key challenge therefore is to find more effective, efficient and equitable ways of co-operating in planning, management, and decision-making, basically through active social learning. Some ways of doing so have been referred to previously, for example civic learning centres and multi-interest groups such as Biosphere Committees. Other examples include the Round Tables on Sustainable Development that have been active across the country in the last five to 10 years, although some of these have recently been cancelled by provinces.

A key requirement is for *fundamental ideas or concepts* that can provide the basis for bringing agencies, groups and individuals of different backgrounds together. These ideas or concepts need to draw attention to fundamental values and to common concerns although they may well be ambiguous in their more specific operational meaning. An example is the concept of "sustainable development" that many professionals and citizens see as contradictory in meaning and impossible to achieve. Yet the term has brought many people of different interests to the table because they all are concerned with their own survival and sustainability and ultimately in reconciling, and resolving conflicts about economy, society and environment.

Another fundamental concept which can be used as a focus for a civics approach, especially for parks and protected areas, is the idea of ecological integrity or ecological health. The idea of ecological integrity was included in the 1988 amendments to the Canadian National Parks Act as a result of citizen presentations to parliamentarians at House of Commons Committee meetings on this act. The main citizen group involved in this action wished to introduce a new basic idea to add to wilderness which has been a fundamental guiding concept for national and provincial parks for many years.

The wilderness idea – in the sense of a pristine environment largely undisturbed by human actions – has been challenged in recent decades by research that shows that many national park and protected area landscapes or ecosystems, were considerably changed by historic hunting and other activities of native peoples as well as by agriculture and other activities of early European settlers. Yet many people still feel strongly about wilderness as a way of thinking about, enjoying, planning and deciding upon parks and protected areas.

On the other hand, the concept of ecological integrity has greater power in the scientific or professional sense. The term ecological integrity rests on the improved scientific and scholarly understanding of environment or ecosystems which has developed in the last two decades in conservation biology, stress biology and landscape ecology (Woodley 1991; Woodley 1996). Ecological integrity has more explicit links to plant succession, animal migration, lake and river fluctuations, fire dynamics, predators, disease and other natural and human processes than does the more general concept of wilderness. In this sense, the term, ecological integrity, provides a better basis for understanding why controlled burns or other human interventions are now considered a necessary part of management in many protected areas. Fires occurred frequently prior to creation of parks and protected areas with their control policies and programs. These fire control policies led over the decades, to the growth of species and communities quite unlike those of pre-European days. These control policies were in large part based on the idea of wilderness and the associated practice of allowing systems to evolve "naturally" without human interference.

The fundamental point however, about ecological integrity, wilderness and other basic concepts is that people should be encouraged to think about the underlying ideas upon which we build planning, management, decision-making, learning and enjoyment. In a time of increasing uncertainty about the nature and future of parks and protected areas, it is as important to attempt to comprehend the roots of our understanding as it is to think about actions on the ground.

Summary

Parks and protected areas have been viewed historically as a field of interest separate from development. Yet in practice they have also been part of evolving efforts made by various communities and societies to use or gain services sustainably from the land, water, air, wildlife, habitat and other resources needed for natural and human well-being. This should be even more the case today, given the growing array of population, land use, water, air, biodiversity and other challenges facing us now and in future. It is therefore very important that much effort be devoted by all concerned parties to *understand, communicate and jointly use information* about the vital roles and functions of parks and protected areas in sustainable development.

This approach will require much more interaction and co-operation among government, agencies, public and private groups and individuals as well as much stronger overall environmental stewardship than has been the case in recent decades. It will also require the development of a broader and stronger research, educational and social learning approach, as well as a more active political voice for the role of parks and protected areas in land use and sustainable development than has been the case to date. Universities and colleges can help at many levels, including locally through projects such as the Long Point Environmental Folio that uses a civics approach to provide information in a form that helps people make better decisions. Ultimately there is a need for a major review of parks and protected areas and sustainable development nationally, possible in the form of a commission like the Conservation Commission of the early 20th century or the Commission on the Heritage Estate which dealt with similar challenges in Australia in the 1980s.

References

Hummel, Monte (ed.). 1995. *Protecting Canada's Endangered Spaces: An Owner's Manual.* Key Porter Books, Toronto.

Huth, H. 1957. *Nature and the American.* University of California Press, Berkeley and Los Angeles.

McNeely, Jeffrey, A. and Kenton R. Miller (eds.) 1984. *National Parks, Conservation, and Development. The Role of Protected Areas in Sustaining Society.* Proceedings of the World Congress on National Parks, Bali, Indonesia, 11-22 October 1982.

Mosquin, Ted, Peter G. Whiting, and Don E. McAllister. 1995. *Canada's Biodiversity.* Canadian Parks and Wilderness Society, Henderson Book Series, No. 23, Canadian Museum of Nature, Ottawa.

Nash, R. 1967. *Wilderness and the American Mind.* Yale University Press, New Haven and London.

Nelson, J.G. 1995. "The New Forest, England: A Threatened Landscape of Global Significance," *Natural Areas Journal.* 15.2: 168-74.

Nelson, J.G., Patrick Lawrence, Karen Beazley, Ron Stenson, Andy Skibicki, Chi-Ling Yeung, and Kerrie Pauls. 1993. Preparing an Environmental Folio for the Long Point Biosphere Reserve and Region. Working Note 1. Heritage Resources Centre, University of Waterloo, Waterloo, Ontario.

Nelson, J.G. and R. Serafin. 1992. "Assessing Biodiversity: A Human Ecological Approach," *Ambio.* 21.3 212-18.

Nelson, J.G. 1991. "Beyond National Parks and Protected Areas: From Public Ownership and Private Stewardship to Landscape Planning and Management," *Environments.* 21.1 23-34. Reprinted in Parks and Protected Areas in Canada: Planning and Management (eds. Philip Dearden and Rick Rollins), Toronto, Oxford University Press, 1993, pp. 45-57.

Nelson, J.G. and R.D. Needham, S.H. Nelson and R.C. Scace (eds.). 1978. *The Canadian National Parks: Today and Tomorrow Ten Years Later.* University of Waterloo, Waterloo, Ontario, 2 Volumes.

Nelson, J.G., R. Needham and D. Mann (eds.). 1978. *International Experience with National Parks and Related Reserves.* University of Waterloo, Department of Geography Publication Series, No. 12, Waterloo, Ontario.

Nelson, J. G. 1976. *Man's Impact on the Western Canadian Landscape.* McClelland and Stewart Ltd., Toronto.

Nelson, J. G. and R. C. Scace (eds.). 1968. *The Canadian National Parks: Today and Tomorrow.* University of Calgary, Calgary, Alberta, 2 Volumes.

Noss, Reed F. 1987. Protecting Natural Areas in Fragmented Landscapes, *Natural Areas Journal.* 7.1 2-13.

Runte, Alfred. 1979. *National Parks: The American Experience.* University of Nebraska Press, Lincoln and London.

Scace, R. C. and J. G. Nelson (eds.). 1986 and 1987. *Heritage for Tomorrow*. Canadian Assembly on National Parks and Protected Areas. A National Park Centennial Project. Minister of Supply and Services Canada, Ottawa, 5 Volumes.

Shepard, Paul. 1967. *Man in the Landscape*. Ballantine, New York.

Woodley, Stephen, G. Francis, J. Kay. (eds.). 1993. *Ecological Integrity and the Management of Ecosystems*. St. Lucie Press, Florida.

Woodley, Stephen. 1996. "A Scheme for Ecological Monitoring in National Parks and Protected Areas." *Environments*. 23.3: 50-73, Faculty of Environmental Studies, University of Waterloo, Waterloo, Ontario.

INDEX

ACC (see Alpine Club of Canada)

ANSI (see Areas of Natural and Scientific Interest)

Abercrombie, Patrick, 257

Aberdeen, 212

Abitibi Power and Paper Company, 118

Abitibi region, 21, 150

Aboriginal (First Nations) (Native peoples), ix, 50-57, 60-62, 64-70, 72, 73, 98, 103, 185, 225, 226, 231, 243, 244, 245, 247, 249, 253, 254

Acadienis, 21

Adams, G.F., 113, 132

Addington County, 83

Ad Hoc Committee to Save Algonquin Park, 61, 62

Adirondack Park, 58

Advisory Board on Wildlife Protection, 97, 98

"Air of Death", 44

Alaska, 181

Alberta, 16, 94, 169, 170, 183, 224, 226, 232, 235, 285

Algonquins, 56-63

Algonquin Forest Authority, 45

Algonquin Forestry Authority Act (1974), 234

Algonquin National Park, 196, 197, 198, 200-202

Algonquin National Park Act (1893), 233

Algonqiun Park Act, 36

Algonquin Provincial Park, vii, viii, ix, 2-4, 25, 34-37, 39, 40, 43, 45, 53, 57-64, 67, 69, 78, 82, 89, 189, 196, 223, 224, 226, 271
—Interim Hunting Agreement (1991-92), 63
—2nd Interim Hunting Agreement (1992), 63

Algonquin Wildlands League, 43, 45

Allin, C.W., 39, 48

Alnwick Band of Mississauga, 95

Alpine Club, The, 161

Alpine Club of Canada (ACC), viii, ix, 160-176
—Banff Clubhouse, 163, 166, 173
—Fay Hut, 163

Alsek River, 181

Alternatives, 13

American Historical Association, 2

American Rivers, 181

Amérique du Nord, 149, 153

Amos, Gerald, 245, 249

Anaquot, Lester, 70

Anansi (House of), 21

Angel, Mark, 245

Arctic, 14, 15, 83, 87, 252, 254

Arctic Waters Pollution Prevention, 11

Areas of Natural and Scientific Interest (ANSI), 90, 259, 281, 285

Aristotle, 18

Arkansas Hot Springs, 190-192, 196, 201

Armstrong, William, 3

Anthony Island Planning Task Force, 185, 186

Aotearoa/New Zealand, 195

Artillery Park (see Quebec City)

Ashworth, W., 45, 48

Association of the Scottish Deer Management Groups, 219

Atikokan (ON), 66

Atlantic Ocean, 211

Attawapiskat (ON), 67

Attawapiskat (Band) First Nation, 67, 68

Attridge, Ian, viii, 221

Atwood, Margaret, 12-14, 16, 26

Aolavik National Park (or Reserve), 262

Australia, ix, 189-195, 197-203, 292

Australian National Parks and Wildlife Service, 195

BC (see British Columbia)
BC, 21, 244
BC Federation of Labour, 245
BC Lands, 244
BC Mountaineering Club, 168
BC Outdoor Recreation Council, 243, 245
BC Studies, 21
BC Treaty Commission, 244
Back, —, 15
Backus, Edward, 38
Baden Baden (Germ),191
Baldwin, N.S., 113, 132
Ballance, John, 197
Bancroft (ON), 61
Banff (AL), 94, 163, 227
Banff Clubhouse (see Alpine Club of Canada)
Banff Hotsprings Reserve (see Banff National
    Park)
Banff National Park, viii, ix, 3, 160, 163, 170,
    171, 175, 196, 198, 223, 224, 285
Bark Lake (ON), 3
Barnes, T.J., 109, 132
Barry's Bay (ON), 61
Bas Saint-Laurent, 153
Bastedo, —, 283
Batchawana Bay, 113, 116
Batchewaung Lake, 66
Bath (U.K.), 191
Batiscan, riviére, 145
Battle of Wounded Knee, 2
Bay of Fundy, 135, 139
Baxter, S.H., 218, 219
Beausoleil Island, 98, 99
Beauty, Health and Permanence (1987), 43, 49
Benidickson, Jamie, viii, 77
Bennett, Peter H., 178, 180-183, 186
Bennett, R.B., 170
Bennett, W.A.C., 17
Bennett, W.H., 98
Bennett Dam, 18
Berger, Carl, 5, 6, 12, 26
Berger, Thomas, 13, 26
Berger Inquiry, 23
Berger Report, 13
Berkes, Fikret, 23, 26
Bering Land Bridge, 184
Bernier, Leo (Minister), 65
Bertram, John, 82
"Big Tow", 118-121
Biological Survey, 226
Biosphere Committees, 290
Birkenhead Park, 222

"Blue Book" (see *Ontario's Provincial Parks:
    Planning and Managements Policies*)
Black Robe (1985), 14, 28
Board of Commissioners, 228
Boisvert, riviére, 145
Bond Head, Sir Francis, 70
Bonnechère River, 3
Bonnie Prince Charlie, 213
Bordo, Jonathan, 3
Boston, 137, 257
Boston Commons, 222
Boston University, 135
Bouchard, Russel, 151
Boundaries Water Canoe Area, 64, 66
Bourassa, Robert, 17, 18, 26
Bramwell, Anna, 19, 26
Bravillo Carillo National Park, 272
Brazil, 16
Breakwater Press, 21
Breen, David, 22
Bremner River, 124
Brink, Jack, 183, 184, 186
Britain, 41, 160, 190, 193, 199, 200
British Columbia, x, 3, 13, 16, 17, 21, 56, 123,
    169, 177, 178, 181, 182, 185, 223-226, 228,
    230, 231, 234, 235, 238-240, 242-246, 248,
    249, 251, 285
British Ecological Society, 210
British Empire, 71
British Naval Department, 98
British North America Act (BNA) (1867), 52,
    55
Brock University, 259
Brockville (ON), 95
Brook, Rupert, 131, 132
Brooklyn (NY), 257
Brown, David, 259
Brown, R. Craig, 95, 142, 176, 205
Browne, J.C., 100
Bruce Peninsula, 47, 69, 70, 103
Bruce Peninsula National Park, 70, 94, 103,
    262
Brunelle, Rene, 67
Brunton Township, 59, 63
Buies, Arthur, 153
Burgess Shale (see Canadian Rocky Mountain
    Parks)
Butala, Sharon, 22
Byrne, Jim Dr., 183, 187

CBC (see Canadian Broadcasting Corporation)
CBC *Ideas*, 12

CCS (see Countryside Commission of Scotland)
CED (see Community Economic Development)
CORE (see Commission on Resources and the Environment)
CNR (see Canadian National Railway)
CPR (see Canadian Pacific Railway)
CRAWS (see Canadian Parks and Wilderness Society)
Cabinet Committee on Aboriginal Affairs (ON), 54
Cadwell First Nation, 72
Caithness, 210
Cairngorm Mountains, 209, 210, 218, 219
—*Public Consultation Paper* (1992), 209
Calder Case, 13
Calgary (AB), 164, 171
Calgary Power Company, 170, 171
Calgary Ski Club, 168
California, 191, 194
Callicott, J. Baird, 19, 26
Cambridge (ON), 259
Cameron, Christina, 184, 187
Camp Mercier, 148
Campbell, Kim, 186
Canadian Alpine Journal (CAJ), 161, 166, 173, 174
Canadian Arctic Resources Committee, 13
Canadian Audubon Society, 41
Canadian Broadcasting Corporation (CBC), 12, 44
Canadian Consultative Council on Multiculturalism, 21
Canadian Ethnic Studies, 21
Canadian Heritage Rivers System, 16
Canadian International Paper, 144
Canadian Institute, 36, 200
Canadian National Exhibition Stadium, 44
Canadian National Parks Branch, 135, 136
Canadian National Parks Association, 171
Canadian National Railway (CNR), 257
Canadian Nature Federation, ix, 283, 284
Canadian Newsletter of Research on Women, 21
Canadian Pacific Railway (CPR), 80, 83, 94, 160, 163, 257
Canadian Parks and Wilderness Society (CPAWS), ix, 43-45, 172, 233, 239, 244, 245, 246, 283, 284
Canadian Parks Service, x
Canadian Point, 117
Canadian Rockies, 160, 162-165

Canadian Rockies Archive, 161
Canadian Rocky Mountain Parks, 178
—Burgess Shale, 178
Canadian Shield, 3, 77, 79
Canadian Wildlife Federation, 283
Canadian Wildlife Service, 290
Canmore (AB), 170
Cannon, Kerry, A., ix, 50
Canoe Lake (ON), 3
Canot de maître, 25
Canot du nord, 25
Cantin, Gisèle, 184, 187
Capital Regional District (BC), 243
Carless, Ric, 181, 182, 187
Careless, J.M.S., 6-11, 21, 26
Cariboo/Chilcoton region, 241
Caribou Island, 116, 117
Carmichael, Frank, 3
Carolinian flora and fauna, 97
Carolinian forest, 72
Caron, Ivanhoë, 150
Carr, Emily, 3
Carson, Rachel, 44
Carter-Edwards, Dennis, viii, 94
Cartier, Jacques, 1, 11, 12, 25
Cascade River, 124
Cashore, John, 249
Cataract (ON), 259
Catlin, George, 192, 205
Centennial (1967), 21, 24
Central Boreal Uplands, The, 103, 112
Central Scotland Forest, 215
Century of the Scottish People, A., 1830-1950, 211
Chadwick, G.F., 203
Chant, Donald, 13
Champagne-Aishihik band, 186
Charlevoix, 153, 155
Charlottetown Accord, 51, 52
Chatham (ON), 198
Chemin des Jésuites, 145
"Cheviot, the Stag and the Black Black Oil, The", 214
Chicago (IL), 2
Chicoutimi (PQ), 144
Chiefs of Ontario, 54
Chilko Lake, 243
Chisasibi, 18
Chippewas (Ojibwa), 57
Chrétien, Jean, 103
Churchill Falls Hydro development, 17
Churchill River, 17, 18

City Park, 222
Clancy, James, 36
Clarendon Lectures, 12
Clark, Judson, 87
Clarke, C.H.O. 36
Clay Belts, 79
—Great Clay Belt, 7
—Little Clay Belt, 84
Clayoquot Sound, 243, 246
Clayoquot Sound Sustainable Development
Committee, 243
Clearwater Sarnia, 259
Clinton, Bill, 181, 182
"Clio in Canada" (1946), 10, 28
Clyde Calder Project, 215
Clyde Township, 59, 63
Coach House Press, 21
Cobalt (ON), 84
Cochrane, Frank, 85
Columbia River, 17
Columbia River Treaty (1964), 17
Collins Inlet, 69
Columbia University, 180
Columbo, John Robert, 12, 26, 262, 277
Commercial Empire of the St. Lawrence, The,
(1937), 5
Commission géologique du Canada, 148
Commission on Conservation, 97, 289, 292
Commission on the Heritage Estate, 292
Commission on Planning and Development
Reform in Ontario (1993), 258, 260
Commission on Resources and the
Environment (CORE), 241, 245
Committee for an Independent Canada, 14
Commonwealth Nature Legacy, 244
Community Economic Development (CED),
24
Confederation, 51-53, 79
congrès de l'Association forestière americaine,
141
Congress of the American Forestry Association,
80-82
Conservation Authorities Act (1946), 233
Conservative (Party), 81, 84, 85, 87, 88
Constitution Act (1867), 54
Constitution Act (1982), 56
Convention for the Protection of the World
Cultural and Natural Heritage (Canada
1979), 177-180
Convention on Biological Diversity, 232
Conway, Abbot, 43
Cook, Ramsay, 21, 24, 26

Coppermine River, 15
Cormier, Mrs., 130
Côte-du-Sud, 153
Costa Rica, 271-273
Cosgrove, D., 109, 132
Countryside Commission (England and Wales),
211
Countryside Commssion for Scotland (CCS),
209, 211, 215, 216, 218, 220
Countryside (Scotland) Act (1967), 211
Cramahe, Hector, 57
Cree(s), 13, 18, 52, 67
Creighton, Donald, 5-7, 10, 11, 26
Creston Valley Wildlife Area, 230
Crombie, David, 22, 23, 26
Crombie Commission (see Royal Commission
on the Future of the Toronto Waterfront)
Cronon, William, 2
Crosby, Alfred W., 2
Crown, 57, 77, 79, 83, 88, 95, 96, 98, 102,
213
Crown Estates, 212
Crown Land(s), 58, 200, 228
Crown Management Units, 45
Crown of the Continent, 246
Crown Timber Act (1952), 88
Cunningham, —, 218

DLF (Ontario Department of Lands and
Forests), 36, 37, 40, 59, 67, 223
—Parks Branch, 42
D'Anjou, Alice, 268, 277
Dalibard, Jacques, 180, 181, 183
Daniels, S., 109, 132
Davis, E.J., 83
Davis, William (Premier), 45-47
Deeside, 213
Dene, 12, 13
Dene Declaration, 13
Department of Canadian Heritage, 228
Department of Crown Land, 228
Department of Environment, 228
Department of Fisheries, 8
Department of Indian Affairs and Northern
Development, 98, 283
Department of Lands, 228
Department of Mines and Resources, 65
—Indian Affairs Branch, 65
Department of Indian Affairs and Northern
Development, 254
Department of the Interior, 81, 95, 228
—Indian Affairs Branch, 54, 95

Department of Labour, 99
Department of Municipal Affairs, 37
Department of Recreation and Conservation
  Act (1957), 225, 228, 235
Depression (Years), 79, 88, 89, 171
Deschênes, F.G.M., 144
Deseronto (ON), 82
DeWolf, Harold, 136-138
DeWolf, Madeline, 137
Diefenbaker, John, 12
Dinosaur Provincial Park, 179, 183
Discovery of Strangers, A, (1994), 14, 28
Dogrib, 15
Dominion Forests Reserve and Parks Act
  (1927), 162
Dominion Forests Reserves and Parks Act
  (1911), 162, 223
Dominion of the North (1944), 6, 26
Dominion Parks, 161, 165
Douglas, Howard, 165
Douglas & McIntyre, 21
Dower Commission, 210
Downie, Bruce, x, 238
Dream Like Mine, A (1987), 14, 27
"drive camps", 119
—Angel Falls
—Dam Camp
—Swamp Creek
Drew, Wayland, 14, 27
Dunbar (Scotland), 209
Dundee, 212
Duncan, J., 109, 132
Dunphy, Miles, 194
Dumont, Bill, 245

ESAC (see environmentally significant areas),
  281, 285
ESPAC (see Environmentally Significant Policy
  Areas)
E.B. Eddy, 144
Eagles, Paul, x, 261
East Kootenay region, 241
Eastern Forest Reserve, 82
Eastern Provincial Forest, 88
Ecological Reserves Act (1971), 231, 234
Economic Transition Strategy (BC), 242
Edinburgh, 212, 215
Edmonton (AB), 162, 166
Edwards, R. Yorke, 45, 48
Eganville Leader, 62
Eisvik, Harold, 182
Elk Lake, 85, 91

Ellesmere National Park (or Reserve), 262
Elliot, Nancy, viii, 177
Emerald Necklace, 257
Empire and Communications (1950), 4, 27
Endangered Spaces Campaign, 226, 233, 288
Enduring Dreams: An Exploration of Arctic
  Landscape (1994), 12, 28
England, 16, 97, 131, 210-213, 257
Enjoying the Outdoors: A Consultation Paper on
  Access to the Countryside for Enjoyment and
  Understanding (1992), 219, 220
Environment Canada, 13, 263, 268, 277, 283
Environmental Bill of Rights, 225
Environmentally significant areas, (ESAS), 281,
  285, 286
Environmentally Significant Policy Areas, 259,
  286
Essex County and Wild Life Association, 97
États-Unis, 145, 150
Etobicoke (ON), 270
Europe, 160, 163, 190, 209, 210, 212, 214,
  216, 219, 280
European Community, 218
European Union, 218

FON (see Federation of Ontario Naturalists)
Fathom Five Marine Park, 103
Faulkner, J. Hugh, 178, 187
Fay Hut (see Alpine Club of Canada)
Federal Fisheries Act, 56
Federation of Ontario Naturalists (FON), ix,
  35, 38, 39, 41, 42, 45, 59, 62, 66, 68
Fennell, David, 272, 277
Fentress, James, 111, 132
Ferguson, Howard, 87, 88
Fernow, Bernhard E., 77, 87
Fiddick, Anne, 245
Fife, 215
Fillion, A.B., 143
Filmoni Gary (Premier), 229
Finlayson, E.H., 89
Finlayson, William, 88
Finlayson Point Park, 70
First Nations (see Aboriginal First Nations)
First Nations of Ontario, 54, 55
First World War (Great War), 17, 163, 212, 280
Fish River (Jenolan) Caves, 193
fjord du Saguenay, 153
Fladmark, M., 215
Fleming, Sanford (Sir), 162
Flow Country, 210
Flower Pot Island, 98

Flynn, Edmund James, 143, 145
"Focus on the Future" (Ontario), 104
Foot, D., 265, 277
Forest Conservation Act (1883), 196
Forest Renewal BC, 242
Forest Reserve Act (1898), 82, 89
Forestry Act (1927), 79, 88
Forestry Board (Ontario), 88
Forestry Commission (Scotland), 212, 218
Fort Chipewyan, 18
Fort Erie (ON), 276
Fort Severn First Nation, 68
Fort William, 215
Fortin, Thomas, 147
Fortress Lake, 164
Fournier, Marcel, 144, 145
Fox (Premier), 196
France, 213
Francis, Douglas, 22
Franklin, John, 12, 14
Fred Henne Territorial Park, 224
"Freedom to Roam", 215
Freisen, Gerald, 22
French Lake, 66
French River, 69
Frey, Patrick, 185, 187
Friars, Robert, 136-138
Friends of the Boundary Waters Canoe Area
    (BWCA), 66
Friends of Quetico Park, 66
Friends of the Rideau, 182
Frontenac County, 82
*Frontier and Metropolis: Regions, Cities and
    Identities in Canada before 1914* (1989), 6,
    26
"Frontierism, Metropolitanism, and Canadian
    History" (1954), 6, 26
Frontier Thesis (Frederick Jackson Turner), 1, 2,
    6, 7, 25
Frost, Leslie, 40-42
Frye, Northrop, 11, 25
Fundy National Park, 135-138, 285
Fundy Park Chalets, 136, 137
Fur Trade In Canada, The (1930), 4, 27
Fur Trade Routes of Canada/Then and Now
    (1969), 25, 28

GTA-Greater Toronto Area
Gaffield, Chad, 21, 27
Gaian Expedient, The (1985), 14, 27
Game and Fish Act (1961), 60. 234
Gananoque Reporter, 96

"Garden, The", 222
Gargantua, 113, 116
Garrison Reserve, 222
Gaspésie region, 21, 153, 155
Gayton, Don, 22
Geddes Resources Ltd., 181
General Grant National Park, 194
Generelle Morphologie (1866), 18
Georgetti, Ken, 245
Geographic Board of Canada, 169
Georges River, 194
Georgian Bay, 51 98
Georgian Bay Islands National Park, 94, 98-
    100, 102
Georgian Bay Provincial Forest, 88
Geraldton (ON), 91
Gertler, Leonard, 42
Gibson, Roy A., 165
Gibson, Thomas W., 36, 48
Gillis, Peter, viii, 77, 141
Gilpin, William, 152
Girard, François, 12, 27
Glacier National Park, 163
Glasgow, 212, 215
Glen Affric, 210
Glen Coe, 210
Gold River (BC), 245
Golden Lake (ON), 56, 57, 59, 60-62
Golden Lake Algonquin First Nation, 57-63, 67
Gore, Al, 181
Gore Square, 222, 233
Gone Indian (1973), 14, 27
Govin, Lomer, 142
Gould, Glenn, 12, 27
Gouveneur Général du Canade et Lady
    Wellington, 148
Gowganda (ON), 85
Gowwlland Range, 243
Government of Canada, 51, 52
Government of Ontario, 51
Grand River, 286
Grand River Valley, 286
Grande Baleine, 17
Grant, Shelagh, 12
Gras, Norman, S.B., 8, 10, 27
Grasslands National Park, 262, 285
Gravel River, 116
Gray, Walter, 43
Great Britain, 210, 222
Great Britain's Woodyard (1973), 8, 27
Great Lakes, 44, 103, 113
Great Lakes Ornithological Club, 97

Greater Toronto Bioregion, 258
Green Plan for Canada (1990), 104, 263, 287, 288
Greenpeace, 14
"Greenways" (see *Regeneration*)
Greenways, system of, 257
Grey Cup (1962), 44
Grip (commercial advertising firm), 3
Gros Morne National Park, 179, 184
Group of Seven, 3, 6, 53
Gwai Haanas National Park (or Reserve), 262

Haeckel, Ernst, 18
Haida, 25, 185
Haida Gwaii, 246
Hakluyt, Richard, 1
Haldiman-Norfolk Region, 286
Halfway Man (1989), 4
Halifax Common, 222
Hall, W.J.C., 147, 148
Hamelin, Louis-Edmond, 12
Hamilton (ON), 222, 233, 259
Hampton, Howard, 264, 278
Harcourt, Mike (Premier), 181, 245, 248
Hardie, Duncan, 178, 187
Hardy, Patrick, 41, 43, 58
Harkin, James Bernard, 97, 98, 165-167, 170
Harris, Lauren, 3
Harris, Mike (Premier), 286, 288
Harvest House, 21
Harvey, Fernand, 21
Harvard University, 8
Hayden, Scott, 61
Hays, Samuel, P., 43, 44, 49
Haywood Lake, 118
Head-Smashed-In Buffalo Jump, 179, 183
Hearne, Samuel, 14
Hébert, Yves, ix, 140
Hellmund, P.C., 257
Henderson, Gavin, 43, 45
Hepburn, Mitch, 102
Heritage Act, 287
Heritage Canada, 180
Heritage Resources Centre (see University of Waterloo)
Heritage Rivers (see Canadian Heritage Rivers System)
Herrick Lake, 118
Hewitt, Gordon, 97
Highlands of Scotland, 209, 213-215, 217
Highway 60 (ON), 39
Historic District of Quebec (see Quebec City)

Historic Scotland, 216
—Scottish Office, 217
History of the Scottish People, The, 1560-1830, 211, 220
Hodgins, Bruce, viii, ix, 50, 77
Hôpital Notre-Dames de Montréal, 143
Hopkins, Gerard Manley, 109
Horvath, —, 265, 266
Horwood, Harold, 14, 27
Houston, Stuart, 12
Howard, Ebenezer, 254
Howard Watson Trail, 259
Hudson Bay, 68, 209
Hudson Bay Lowland, 64
Hull (P.Q.), 144
Hummel, Monte, 281, 285, 288, 293
Hunter, James, 213, 220
Hunter's Island, 64
Hunters and Trappers Association(s), 283
Huntsville (ON), 61
Huron(s), 56
Huronia, 56
Hurtig Inc., 21
Husband, Vicky, 245
Huth, H., 203, 204, 280, 293

ICOMOS (see International Council of Monuments and Sites)
ICUN (see World Conservation Union)
Ice Age, 217
Idea of the North, The, 12, 27
In Defense of the Land Ethic (1989), 19, 26
Indian Act (1876), 52, 54
Industrial Revolution, 190
Inuit, 12, 13, 15, 18
Inuit Tapirisat, 13
Inner and Outer Hebrides, 212
Innis, Harold Adams, 4-7, 10, 11, 27
Interim Enforcement Policy, 61
Interministerial Committee, 259
Interministerial Committee on the Abandonment of Railroad Rights of Way, 257
International Council of Monuments and Sites (ICOMOS), 178, 181
International Rapids (see St. Lawrence River)
International Union for the Conservation of Nature, 282
Introduction to Economic History (1922), 8, 27
Institut québécois de recherche sur la culture, 21
Ipperwash Provincial Park, 35
Ivvavik National Park or Reserve, 262

Jackfish (ON), 113, 116
Jackson, A.Y., 3
Jackson, J.B., 108, 133
Jacques-Cartier Park, 56
Jacques Cartier, riviére, 145
James Bay, 8, 18, 52, 68
James Bay and Northern Quebec Agreement, 13, 18
James Bay Power Project, 17
James Bay Treaty, 9, 52
James Lorimer Co., 21
Jasper National Park, 163, 164, 169
Jerseyville (ON), 259
Joanisse, Carole, 182, 187
Johnson (Samuel) Dr., 217
Johnson, Lydon B., 44
Johnston, Franz, 3
Johnston, Margaret, 168, 174
Jones, D., 95
Jones, David, 22
Jourdain, Leon, 67
Jourdain, Steve, 65

Kamouraska, 153
Kananaskis Provincial Park, 170
Kane, Paul, 3
Kavanagh, Kevin, 35
Kawartha Provincial Forest, 88, 90
Keenan, James, 42
"Keep It Wild", Natural Heritage Areas, 90
Kelly, M.T., 14, 27
Kennedy, John F., 44, 137
Kenora, 51
Kent County, 72, 198
Killan, Gerald, viii, 34, 37-40, 42, 45, 47, 49, 207, 208, 236
Killarney Provincial Park, 43, 45, 68, 69
Kinesis, 21
King, —, 15
King, Mackenzie, 102
King, Martin Luther Jr. (Dr.), 135-137
King, Mrs. Martin Luther Jr., 136
Kingston (ON), 77, 95, 222
Kirkwood, Alexander, 3, 27, 34, 35, 37, 49, 58
Kitchener Waterloo Record, 269, 278
Kluane National Park Reserve, 179
Kolinosky, D.P., 113, 132
Kolodny, Annette, 2
Kootenay Boundary, 241
Kootenay National Park, 163
Kroetsch, Robert, 14, 27
Kurszewski, George, 185, 187

LEADER, 218
l'Abatis, 151
l'Abitibi, region, 151
l'Ile-aux-Coudres, 154
l'Ile-d'Orléans, 154
L'Anse Aux Meadows National Historic Site, 179, 182, 183
Lac LaCroix First Nation, 63-67
Lacoursière, Jacques, 149, 152
La Grande River, 17, 18
Labrador, 17
Labour/Le Travail, 21
Lachine Canal, 5
Lady Evelyn-Smoothwater Wilderness Park, 70, 71, 90
Langford, N.P., 200
Lady Evelyn Wild River Park, 90
Laing, Arthur, 101
Lake District, 210
Lake Erie, 45, 97, 289
Lake Louise, 165
Lake Nipissing, 57
Lake-of-the-Woods, 51
Lake O'Hara, 170
Lake Ontario, 22, 258
Lake Superior, 25, 45, 51, 83, 112-116, 118, 127
Lake Superior Provincial Park, 35, 36, 43
Lake Temagami, 71, 83-85, 89
Lake Timiskaming, 57
Lake Traverse, 41
Land and Water Conservation Fund (1965), 44
Land Use Coordination Office, 249
Laurentian thesis, 5, 7, 9
Laurentides Provincial Park, ix, 198, 223
Laurentides region, 21
Laurier, Wilfred (Sir), 97
Laventhol, —, 265, 266, 278
Laviolette, Camille, le docteur, 143
"lay-over" harbours, 115
    —Playter Harbour
    —Morrison Harbour
    —Oiseau Bay
    —Simon's Harbour
    —Triangle Harbour
    —Old Dave's Cove
    —Otter Cove
    —Richardson Harbour
    —Ganley Harbour
    —Pilot Harbour
    —Dog Harbour
Lawrence, Bert, 257

Lawson, P., 215, 220
Leather, Jay, 67
Lemoine, James MacPherson, 147
Leopold, Aldo, 41
"Letters from America" (1916), 131
Liberal (Party), 47, 54, 60, 83, 84
Lion's Club of Toronto, 100
Lique Anti-tuberculeuse de Montréal, 144
Lismer, Arthur, 3
Little, C.E., 257, 260
Liverpool, 222
Livingstone, Louise H., ix, 209, 212, 218, 220
Lloyd, G. Mr., 212, 220
Loch Lomond, 210, 215, 218
Locke, Harvey, 246
Lomond Hills Park, 215
London (ON), 95
London (UK), 44, 162, 222
Long Point (ON), 289, 290
Long Point Environmental Folio, 289, 290, 292
Long Point Biosphere Reserve, 290
Long Point Biosphere Reserve Committee, 290
Long Point Provincial Park, 35, 37, 38
Long Sault Rapids, 57
Lopez, Barry, 109
Los Angeles (US), 44
Louis Lake, 124
Lowenthal, D., 108, 133
Love Canal, 180
Lower, Arthur, 8, 9, 27
Lunenburg (NS), 178, 180, 182-184
Lurch River, 124
Lynch, William, 141
Lynn Valley Trail, 259
Lyons, —, 194

MOF (see Ministry of Forests [BC])
Mt. Robson, 164
MacDonald, Alan, R.K., 40
MacDonald, G.A., 123, 133
MacDonald, John A. (Sir), 6, 12, 81, 94
MacDonald, J.E.H., 3
MacDougall, Frank, 35, 39-41
MacEachern, Alan, ix, 135
MacFarlane, J.D.B., 137
Mackenzie, —, 14 (Arctic explorer)
Mackenzie Valley Pipeline Inquiry, 13
MacLaren, Ian, 12
MacLeod, Lynn, 71
Macobe River, 86
Madawaska River, 3
Makobe-Greys Waterway Park, 90

Making of the Crofting Community (1975), 213, 220
Maligne Lake, 169
Man and Biosphere program (UNESCO), 284
Manitoba, 17, 224-227, 229, 233, 235, 285
Manitoba Free Press, 161
Manitoba (Parks) Act, 231
Manitoba Parks and Natural Areas Branch, 235
Manitoulin Island, 56, 69
Manitoulin Island Treaty (1862), 51
Manhattan (ship), 11
Mann, —, 279
Manyfingers, Kirby, 183, 187
Maori, 195, 197
Maple Mountain, 85
Marathon (ON), 62
Maritimes, 21, 137, 213
Marsh, John, 168, 174, 175
Maslin, Ronald William, 174
Master of Norriya, The (1986), 14, 27
Mathieu, Jacques, 149, 152
Mattawa, 61, 80
Mattawa River, 42, 52, 57
Maurice region, 21
Mawhinney, D. Laurence, 182, 184, 187
McCallum, Mavis, 257
McCullough, Graham A., 113, 133
McLuhan, Marshall, 4
McMillan, Tom, 185-187
McNamee, Kevin, 181, 188, 227, 231
McNeely, Jeffery A., 266, 278, 281
McTaggart, W. Donald, 22, 28
Meewasin Valley Authority, 230
Media and Communications (1951), 4
Meinig, D.W., 108, 133
Memories of Alcheringia, The (1984), 14, 27
Memphremagoa, le lac, 153
Meness, Clifford, 60
Mercier, Honoré, 142
Merck, Frederick, 8
Mesopotamia, 17
Metabetchuvan, riviére, 145
Métis, 11, 13, 18, 50
Mica Dam, 17
Michipicoten Bay, 116
Michipicoten Harbour, 113
Michipicoten Island, 113-116
Micmac, 25
Mid-Canada Corridor project, 11
Midland (ON), 98
Miller, Kenton R., 281
Miller, Perry, 191, 205, 208

Miquasha Provincial Park, 177, 178
Miner, Horace, 153
Mingan Archipelago National Park or Reserve, 262
Ministry of Environment, Lands and Parks, 228
Ministry of Forests (MOF), 240, 243
Ministry of Natural Resouces (MNR), viii, 46, 51, 54, 55, 60, 62, 65, 66-69, 72, 73, 202, 208, 223, 228, 233, 256, 257, 260, 263-265, 268, 269, 278, 290
—Parks Division, 46
Minneapolis-St. Paul, 257
Minnesota, 38, 64
Mississagi Forest Reserve, 83, 86
Mississagi Park, 90
Mississagi Provincial Forest, 88
Mississagi (Wild River) Waterway Park, 90
Mississippi Basin, 7
Mobert (ON), 124
Moffat, Thomas, 163
Mont Tremblant Provincial Park, ix
Montana, 170
Monteverde Cloud Forest Reserve, 272, 273
Monteverde Conservation League, 272
Montreal (PQ), 5, 80, 141
Montreal Congress (see Congress of the American Forestry Association)
Montreal River, 85, 86, 113
Moore, Brian, 14, 28
Moraine Lake Road, 165
Morgan, J.H., 81
Morgan, Rick, 61
Morissonneau, Christian, 150
Morrison Harbour, 115
Morse, Eric, 25, 28
Morton, W.L., 9-15, 22, 23, 28
Mosely, Geoff, 194, 205, 206, 208
Mosquin, Ted, 281, 285, 293
Moss, John, 2
Montmorency, riviére, 145
Mount Finlayson, 243
Mountain Areas of Scotland: Conservation and Management, The (1990), 209
Mowat, Oliver, 197
Muir, John, 2, 169, 193, 209
Mulroney, Brian, 182
Munday, Don, 170, 172
Murphy, J.J., 3, 27
Murray, Christine, 264, 265, 269, 274, 278
Murray, riviére, 145
Murtha, Mike, 181, 182, 188
Museums of Canada, 97

Mushkegowuk Tribal Council, 68
Muskoka River, 3
Musqueam First Nation, 56

NAC (see National Archives of Canada)
NC (see Nature Conservancy)
NDP (see New Democratic Party)
NGO (non-government organization), 173, 181, 183
NPAC (see National Parks Association of Canada)
NWT (see Northwest Territories)
N'Daki Menan, 71
Nahanni National Park, 179
Narrative, 12
Nash, R., 204, 205, 280, 298
National Action Committee, 21
National Archives of Canada (NAC), 174, 175, 176
National Park, The (Australia) (see Royal National Park)
National Archives of Canada, 161
National Geographic, 257
National Heritage Areas, 281
National Landmarks Program, 289
National and Provincial Parks Association of Canada (NPPAC) (see Canadian Parks and Wilderness Society)
National and Scenic Rivers Act (1968), 44
National Capital Commission, 225, 230
National Marine Parks, 227
National Nature Reserves (UK), 211
National Park Greater Park Ecosystem, 284
National Parks Act (1930), 99, 100, 102, 162, 171, 186, 202, 225, 227, 228, 231, 248, 291
—amendment (1988), 202, 230, 231, 233, 291
National Parks and Access the Countryside Act (1949), 210
National Parks Association of Canada (NPAC) (formerly Canadian National Parks Association), viii, 171, 172
National Parks Service (US), 101, 137, 138, 270, 274
National Policy, 6, 95
National Research Council of Canada, 41
National Scenic Areas, 211
National Trails Act (1968), 44
National Trust, 210
National Trust for Scotland, 212
National Wildlife Federation, 44
Native Affairs (provincial), 54

Native Studies, 13
Natural Heritge Areas, 218
Natural Heritage (Scotland) Act (1991), 218
Nature Conservancy (NC), 210, 211, 216, 220
Nature Conservancy of Canada, 90, 243
Nature Conservancy Council for Scotland, 211, 216, 218
Nature Conservation in Great Britain, 210, 220
Needham, R.D., 279, 293
Nelson, J. Gordon, x, 279-282, 286, 290, 293, 294
Nelson River, 17, 18
New Approach to Land Use Planning, A, 258, 260
New Brunswick, 135, 136, 224, 235
New Democratic Party (NDP), 55, 56, 61, 239
"New Ontario", 80, 85
New Plymouth (New Zealand), 195
New South Wales, 193, 194, 200
New Zealand, ix, 189, 194-203
—North Island, 196
New Zealand Forests Bill (1874), 196
New Zealand State Forests Act (1885), 196
"New Regional History, The", 21, 27
New York (NY), 162, 180
Newfoundland, 9, 178, 222, 224, 228, 230, 235
Newman, Billy, 129, 130
Newton, Norman T., 235
Niagara Escarpment, 43, 258
Niagara Escarpment Commission, 90
Niagara Falls, 269, 275, 276
Niagara Falls (NY), 191, 192, 199
Niagara Falls (ON), 179, 191, 199, 222, 224, 227, 228, 270, 275
Niagara Greenway System, 259
Niagara Falls Park Act (1885), 222, 233
Niagara-on-the-Lake, 222, 276
Niagara Parks Commission, 222, 223, 270, 275, 276
Niagara Parkway, 275
Niagara River, 180, 275
Nilsen, Per, 262
Ninstints, South Morresby Island, 179, 185
Nipigon Bay, 116, 117
Nipigon Forest Reserve, 83
Nipissing highlands, 35, 36
Nisqa'a, 56, 226
Nishga, 13
North America, 41, 46, 81, 189, 209, 271
North American Assault on the Canadian Forest (1938), 8, 27

"North" in Canadian Historiography, The" (1970), 10, 28
North Baffin National Park, 262, 263
North Bay (ON), 84
North Channel, 51
North Island (see New Zealand)
North of Summer: Poems from Baffin Island (1967), 14, 28
North Sea Oil industry, 212, 214
North West Company, 5, 213
Northern Frontier, Northern Homeland (1977), 13, 26
Northern Nishnawbe-Aski Nation, 56
Northern Perspectives, 13
Northern Rockies, 246
Northern Rockies Ecosystem Protection Act, 232
Northwest Territories (NWT), x, 224, 226, 235, 250-255
Noss, Reed F., 286, 293
Nottaway-Broadback-Rupert river systems, 17
Nova Scotia, 178, 226, 229, 235
Nunavut, 23, 252, 254

OFAH (see Ontario Federation of Anglers and Hunters)
ONAD (see Ontario Native Affairs Directorate)
ONAS, 69
OPP (see Ontario Provincial Police)
Oak Ridges Moraine, 28, 258
Oates, Stephen, 136
Obabika Waterway Park, 90
Office of Indian Resource Policy, 54
Office of Land Claims, 54
O'Gorman, Denis, 245
Oelschlaeger, Max, 2
Oiseau Bay, 115, 118
Oiseau Harbour, 116, 130
Ojibway, 51, 64
OjiCree, 51
Oka Algonquin, 57
Old Crow band, 184, 185, 188
Old Dave's Cove, 115
Old Woman Bay, 116
Oldman Project, 16
Oldman River, 18
Olmsted, Frederick Law, 257
Ommer, Rosemary, 9
Ontario, vii, viii, ix, 3, 21, 34-38, 40-43, 45-48, 50-55, 57-66, 69, 71-73, 77-90, 94, 95, 99, 102-104, 146, 178, 189, 195-203, 212, 213, 219, 222, 224, 225, 227-230, 233-235,

251, 256, 257, 259, 262-264, 266-274, 277, 285-288
—Bureau of Forestry, 82, 87
—Department of Agriculture, 81, 87, 97
—Department of Crown Lands, 81
—Department of Lands, Forests and Mines, 85, 87
Ontario Federation of Anglers and Hunters (OFAH), 60-62
Ontaro Hydro, 17,. 275
Ontario Ministry of Natural Resources (OMNR) (see Ministry of Natural Resources)
Ontario Native Affairs Directorate (ONAD), 55, 59
Ontario Parks Integration Board Act (1956), 234
Ontario Provincial Parks, x, 231, 266, 276, 290
Ontario Provincial Park Council, 66
Ontario Provincial Parks Planning and Management Policies (1978), 46-48, 256, 257, 260
Ontario Provincial Police (OPP), 230, 234
Ontario Trails Council, 257, 257
Opeongo Road, 3
Orillia (ON), 259
Orkney Islands, 212
Orr, Rowland B. (Dr.), 98
Osborne, Brian S., ix, 107, 109, 113, 133
Ottawa (ON), 17, 61, 65, 84, 137, 160, 164, 166, 167, 170, 181, 183, 253
"Ossian", 218
Ottawa - Huron Tract, 79
Ottawa River, 5, 11, 16, 52, 80
Ottawa (River) Valley, 57, 60, 84
Otter Cove, 115, 116, 127-130
Otter Head, 116
Outaovais, riviére, 142
Outaovais region, 21
Outaouais, la riviére, 142
Out of the Whirlwind (1995), 14, 27
"Outline of a Basis for a Parks Policy for Ontario" (1958), 41, 42
Owen, Stephen, 241
Owram, Doug, 22
Oxford University, 12

PEI (see Prince Edward Island)
Paradise Valley, 164
Parc Algonquin, 145, 146
Parc de la Gaspésie, 142
Parc des Grands Jardins, 143

Parc de la Jacques Cartier, 143
Parc des Laurentides, 140, 142-144, 146-148
Parc de la Montagne Tremblante, 140, 142-146, 149
Parc du Mont Orford, 142
Parc National des Laurentides, 148, 154
Parc nationaux canadiens, 142
Parc Yellowstone, 145
Paris (ON), 259
Parker, Elizabeth, 161, 169, 172, 174-176
Park Integration Board, 223
Park System for Scotland, A (1974), 215
Parks Act (1965), 225, 228, 231, 235, 247
Parks Branch (BC), 240
Parks Canada, 174, 178, 180-185, 230, 231, 255, 266-270, 274, 275
Parks and Wilderness (BC), 240
Pacific Ocean, 2
Pacific Rim National Park, 285
Parent, Simon-Napoléon, 142
Parkland Forest Reservation Act, 58
Parti National, 142
Peace-Athabasca Delta, 18
Peace River, 17, 18
Peace River country, 7
Peawanuck First Nation, 68
Peltier, Henry, 69
Pembroke (ON), 61, 62
Penetanguishene (ON), 98
Pent Land Hills Park, 215
Perrault, Joseph-Edovard, 148
Petawawa River, 3
Peterborough (ON), vii, 71
Peterson, David, 47, 48, 54, 55, 57, 59
Petroglyphs Provincial Park, 42, 71, 72, 90
Pettigrew, —, 194
Phipps, Robert W., 81
Pic River, 112, 116, 126
Pickerel Lake, 66
Pink and White Terraces, 199
Pimlott, Douglas, 43
"Pioneers", 107
Pippe Park, 230
Places Far From Ellesmere (1990), 14, 28
Playing Dead: A Contemplation Concerning the Arctic (1988), 14, 28
Pleistocene ice sheets, 16
Point Grandine Reserve, 69
Point Pelee, 97, 98
Point Pelee National Park, 97-102
Point Pelee National Park Development Plan, 101

Pointe aux Pins, 36
Pojar, Jim, 245
Polar Bear Primitive Park, 42, 43
Polar Bear Provincial Park, 67, 68
Polar Bear Provincial Park Management Plan, 68
Pollution Probe, 13
Pope, Alan, 47
Porcupine-Timmins gold rush, 85
Portages (1993), 14, 28
Port Coldwell (ON), 113-116
Port Dover (ON), 259
Port Maitland (ON), 44
Porteous, D., 109, 133
Potts, Gary (Chief), 71
Power from the North (1985), 18, 26
Prairie Forum, 21
Prairies, 21, 213
Precambrian Shield, 7
Presqui'ile Provincial Park, 35, 37
Price, Uvedale, 152
Priddle, George B., viii, 256
Prince Albert, 214
Prince Albert (SA), 12
Prince Edward Island, 235, 243
Prince Rupert (BC), 245
Principal Navigations, Voyages, Traffiques and Discoveries of the English Nation, The, 1
Proescholdt, Kevin, 66
Proceedings Against the Crown Act, 60
Protected Areas System (see "Wilderness Vision")
Prospect Park, 257
Province of Canada, 51
Provincial Parks Act (NFLD), 228
Provincial Forest Act (1929), 79, 89
Provincial Parks Act (1913), 63, 233
Provincial Parks Act (1954), 233, 234
Provincial Museum (Toronto), 98
Provincial Parks Act (1913), 223, 224
Provincial Parks Advisory Council, 45
Prudhoe Bay, 11
Public Lands Act, 89
Public Parks Act (1883), 222, 233
Purvis Company, 113-116
Purvis, Mr. —, 115
Pukaswkwa fishing groundings, 116-118
Pukaskwa National Park, ix, 45, 94, 103, 108, 112, 113, 119, 123, 124, 127-131
Puckaskwa Pits, 112
Pukaskwa River, 112, 116, 118, 124, 126, 127, 130
Purdy, Al, 14, 28

Quebec, ix, 14, 17, 18, 21, 56, 57, 78-81, 103, 140, 141, 142, 146, 148-152, 154, 155, 177, 178, 180, 198, 213, 223, 204
Quebec City, 180, 181
—Artillery Park, 180
Québec, la ville de, 144, 145
Old Historic Quebec, 180, 183, 184
Quebec Harbour, 113, 116
Québécoises deboutlee!, 21
Queen Charlotte Islands, 216, 246
Queen Victoria, 195, 214
Queen Victoria Niagara Falls Park, 197, 198, 201, 222, 223, 235
Queensland, 194, 201
Queen's University, 77
Quetico Boundary Reserve, 83
Quetico Forest Reserve, 64
Quetico Guides Association, 66
Quetico Foundation, 38
Quetico Provincial (Wilderness) Park, 35, 37-39, 43, 45, 53, 64, 65, 90
Quetico Wilderness Park, 63, 65-67
Quetico-Superior Council (QSC), 38

Rae, Bob, 51, 57
Rafferty-Alameda Project, 16
Raffin, James, 12
Ragweed Press, 21
Rails to Greenways network, 257
Rails-to-Trails Conservancy, 257
Rainy River (ON), 51
Ramsay Commission (1945), 210, 211
Rathburn, E.W., 82
Red Bay basque whaling site, 178
Rees, Ronald, 22
Regan (ON), 118
Regeneration (1992), 22, 26, 258, 260
Regional Official Policies Plan (1994), 259
Reid, Ronald, 267, 274
Reichwein, PearlAnn, ix, 160
Reserve #24C (see Sturgeon Lake Indian Reserve #24C)
Réserve faunique des Laurentide, 144
Resources for Feminist Research, 21
Rideau Canal, 178, 180, 182, 183
Riding Mountain National Park, 285
Richardson Harbour, 115, 116
Riddell-Latchford Timber Commission, 87
Ridenour, James, 274
Riley, Jill, 267, 274, 275, 278
Riley, Tom, 270, 278
Riverrun (1973), 14, 28

Riviére-du-Loup, 153
Riviére Ouelle, 153
Rocky Mountains, 192
Rocky Mountain National and Provincial Parks, 179
Rocky Mountains Park (see Banff National Park)
Rocky Mountains Park Act (1887), 94, 162, 223
Robarts, John, 42
Roberts Treaty, 32
Robertson, —, 194
Robinson, J.P., 265, 278
Rocky Mountains (see Canadian Rockies)
Robinson, Homer, 166
Robinson, W.B., 51
Robinson Treaties (1850), 51, 69, 70
Rogers, Maynard, 166
Rohmer, Richard, 11
Rojas, Carmen, 272, 278
Rondeau Bay, 36
Rondeau Park Act, 36
Rondeau Provincial Park, 35, 37, 72, 198, 223, 224, 285
Ross, George 84
Rossport (ON), 113, 116
Rouge, Riviére, 144
Routhier, Adolphe Basile, 153
Round Tables on Sustainable Development, 290
Rowan-Robinson, —, 218
Rowe, J. Stan, 19, 28
Royal Canadian Mounted Policeman, 24
Royal Commission on Aboriginal Peoples, 70
Royal Commission on Forest Protection (1897), 82
Royal Commission on Forestry (1947), 88
Royal Commission on Forest Reservation and National Park (1893), 58
Royal Commission on the Future of the Toronto Waterfront (1988), 22, 258, 260, 288
Royal Commission on Game and Fish (1892), 198
Royal Commission on the Status of Women, 21
Royal Forests, 280
Royal National Park (The National Park), 193, 194, 200
Royal Proclamation of 1763, 50, 57
Rozell, Jane, 182, 188
Runte, Alfred, 280, 293
Rural Framework, A (1993), 219
Russia, 15, 17

SLUP (see Strategic Land Use Planning)
SNH (see Scottish National Heritage)
SSSIS (see Sites of Special Scientific Interest)
St. Catherine's Milling and Lumbering Company, 53
St. Catherine's Milling Case of 1884, 53
St. Clair Park Commission, 224
St. Clair Parkway Commission Act (1966), 234
St. Clair River, 223
St. John's (NFLD), 222, 230
St. Lawrence Development Commission Act (1955), 233
St. Lawrence Islands National Park, 94, 96, 98-100, 102
St. Lawrence Lowlands, 103
St. Lawrence Parks Commission, 224, 234
St. Lawrence River, 5, 11, 95, 96
—International Rapids, 223
Saalfield, R.W. 113, 132
Saanich Peninsula, 243
Sage, Walter, 21
Saint-Laurent, fleuve, 141
Sainte-Anne, riviére, 145
Sainte-Anne-de-la-Pérade, riviére, 145
Sainte-Irénée les Bains, 153
Sale, Kirkpatrick, 20, 28
Sallenaue, John, 23, 28
Sanctuaries and Preservation of Wild Life in Ontario (1934),
Sand County Almanac, A (1949), 41
Sante Fe, 241
Saquenay-Lac St. Jean region, 21, 151
Sarazin, Greg, 62
Saskatchewan, 12, 16, 224-227, 230, 235
Saskatoon (SA), 162
Satellite fishing stations, 115
—Otter Cove
—Old Dave's Cove
—Simon's Harbour
—Morrison Harbour
Sauer, —, 108
Saugeen (Ojibway), First Nations, 56, 69, 70
Sault Ste Marie, 51, 80, 118, 121, 123
Savard, F.A., 151
Sayyea, Bill, 130
Scace, R.C., 281, 293, 294
Schaefer, Dennis, 276, 278
Schäffer, Mary, 169
Scotland, ix, 209-219
Scott, Ian, 54, 60
Scott, Owen, 235
Scott, Walter, 217

Scottish Natural Heritage (SNH), 211, 212, 218-220
Scottish Tradition in Canada (1975), 213, 220
Scottish Wildlife Trust, 212
Scottish Youth Hostel Association, 215
Seaforth (touring yacht), 130
Seale, Ronald (Ron) G., x, 250
Second National Park Movement, 258
Second World War, 35, 39, 43, 53, 79, 164, 212
Selkirk Mountains, 163
Sequoia National Park, 194
Serpent Mounds Provincial Park, 72
Seton, Ernest Thompson, 4
Settlement and the Forest Frontier in Eastern Canada (1936), 8, 27
Seventeen (touring yacht), 130
Sewell Commission, 258, 260, 286, 288
Shepard, Paul, 280, 293
Shetland Islands, 212, 214
Shields, R., 109, 133
Shields, Carole, 107, 108, 133
Short, J.R., 109, 133
Shultis, John, ix, 189
Sibley Forest Reserve, 102
Sibley Provincial Park, 35, 36
Sibley Township, 83
Sierra Club, 2, 44, 169, 245
Shihota, Moe, 245, 246
Silent Spring (1962), 44
Simcoe (ON), 259
Simon's (Spruce) Harbour, 115, 116, 130
Siou case (see Supreme Court of Canada)
Sites of Special Scientific Interest (SSSIS), 211, 218
Sitka spruce, 216, 217
Six Nations, 226
Skidegate Indian Band, 185
Sleeping Giant Provincial Park, 90
Smart, James, 168
Smith, D.S., 256, 260
Smout, T.C., 211, 220
Social Memory: New Perspectives on the Past, 111
Solace Waterway Park, 90
South Australia, 194
South Leeds, 95
Southworth, Thomas, 81, 82, 85
Spanish River Lumber Company, 86
Sparrow, Reginald, 56, 61, 69
Sparrow case (see Supreme Court of Canada),
Special Joint Committee of the Senate and the House of Commons (1948), 53

Spray Lakes, 170, 171
Stanford Reid, W., 213, 220
Statement of Political Relationship (1991), 55
Stilgoe, —, 108
Storemann, W.F., 203
Stoney Lake, 42
Strategic Land Use Planning (SLUP), 46, 47
Strathcona Park, 223
Strong, B.I.M., 137, 138
Sturgeon Lake, 64, 65, 67
Sturgeon Lake Indian Reserve #24C, 64, 65, 67
Sturgeon River, 83, 86
Sturgeon Waterway Park, 90
Such, Peter, 14, 28
Sudbury (ON), 69, 80, 85
Sulphur Mountain, 163
Surfacing (1972), 14, 26
Superior National Forest, 38, 64
Superior Shoal, 116, 117
Supreme Court of Canada, 50, 56, 62, 71, 226
—Siou case, 226
—Sparrow case, 226
Sutherland, 210
Swallow River, 127
Sydney (AUS), 193, 194
Sylvia (touring yacht), 130

T-AA (see Teme-Augama Anishnabi)
TEK (traditional ecological knowledge), 23, 24
Talonbooks, 21
Tasmania, 194, 201
Tatshenshini International, 181
Tatshenshini River, 181, 242
Tatshenshini-Alsek Watershed, 181
Tatshenshini-Alsek Wilderness Park, 177, 178, 180-183, 186
Taverner, Percy, 97
Temagami, viii, 57, 70, 78, 79, 83
Temagami First Nation, 71
Temagami Provincial Forest, 71, 88-90
Temagami Forest Reserve, 83-86
Teme-Augama Anishnabi, 55, 70, 71
—Memorandum of Understanding (190), 71
—Wendaban Stewardship Authority, 71
—Agreement-in-Principle (AIP), 71
Témiscaminque, région, 151
Temiskaming and Northern Ontario Railway, 84, 86
Territorial Department of Local Government, 283
Territorial Department of Renewable Resources, 283

terres de la Couronne, 141, 143, 145
terres de la division de Greenville, 143
Thensen, Cliff, 183, 188
Thermal Districts, 201
Thermal Districts Act (1881), 196
Thomas, K., 203
Thompson, Derek, 249
Thompson, John Herd, 22
Thomson, Tom, 3, 4, 12, 53
Thirty-Two Short Films About Glenn Gould, (1993), 12, 27
Thousand Islands (ON), 95, 96
Thunder Bay (ON), 66, 102
Tod Inlet, 243
Tongariro National Park, 196, 197
Toronto (ON), 3, 22, 36, 44, 58, 82, 162, 222, 258, 288
Trail Riders of the Canadian Rockies, 168
Trans-Canada Highway, 36
Treaty No. 3 (Ojibwa and Ojicree), 63, 64, 67
Treaty No. 72, 70
Treaty of Co-existence, 71
Treaty of Waitangi, 195
Tremblante, la montagne, 143
Trembling Mountain Park, 223, 235
Trent Severn Waterway, ix
Trent University, vii, 13
Triangle Harbour, 115, 116
Tropical Science Centre, 272
Trossachs, 218
Trudeau, Pierre, 13, 25
Ts'ilos Provincial Park, 243
Tuan, Yi-Fu, 108, 134
Tukino, Te Heuheu, 197
Turner, Frederick Jackson, 2, 3, 8
—Tunerian agrian landscape, 9
—Turner thesis (see Frontier Thesis)
Turner, Larry, 182, 188
Turtle Bay, 100
Twin Lakes, 129
"Two Rivers Policy", 17

UK - United Kingdom, 210, 216, 217
UNEP (see United Nations Environment Programme)
UNESCO (see United Nations Educational, Scientific and Cultural Organization)
Undeveloped Lands in Northern and Western Ontario, The, 3, 27
United Chiefs and Councils of Manitoulin, 69
United Farmer administration, 87
United Nations Educational, Scientific and Cultural Organization (UNESCO), 177, 179, 185, 284
United Nations Environment Programme (UNEP), 262, 278
United States (US), ix, 7, 11, 17, 20, 21, 24, 44, 64, 77, 79, 103, 138, 160, 179-203, 226, 227, 231, 234, 256-259, 270, 272, 280, 281, 286
—U.S. Forest Service, 39
University of Calgary, 21
University of Saskatchewan, 19
University of Toronto, 87, 89
—Faculty of Forestry, 87, 89
University of Waterloo, 257, 289
—Heritage Resources Centre, 257, 289, 290
Upika, riviére, 145
Upikkauba, riviére, 145
Uthoff Trail, 259

Vallée du Sainte-Laurent, 150, 151, 155
Van Herk, Aritha, 14, 28
Vancouver (BC), 56, 162, 181, 245
Vancouver Island, 241-243
Varley, Frederick, 3
Victoria, 194
Victoria (BC), 162, 238, 243
Victoria Park (U.K.), 222
Vigneault, Gilles, 14, 28
Vogel, Julius, 195
Volunteers, The, 110
Vuntut National Park (or Reserve), 262

WRI (see World Resources Institute)
Wabeno Feast, The, (1973), 14, 27
Wadland, John, viii, 1
Waiser, Bill, 22
Wales, 16, 210, 211
Walker, James, 138
Walker, W.J. Selby, 171
Wanapitei Provincial Forest, 88
Ward, Peter, 61
Warecki, G., 38, 45
Warkentin, John, 22
Waterloo Region, 259, 260, 286
Waterman, F.W., 167
Watershed (1990), 22
Waterton Lakes, 166, 169, 170
Waterton Lakes-Glacier National Parks, 177, 178
Weenusk First Nation, 68
Weidman, Gus, 129, 130
Wendaban Stewardship Authority, 79, 90

Werlen, Benno, 109, 134
West Coast (Scotland), 210, 214
West Highland Way, 215
Western Forest Products, 245
Western Isles, 219
Wester Ross, 210
Western Australia, 194
Western Prairie Producer Press, 21
Wheatley, A.B., 40
Wheeler, Arthur, 161, 163, 164, 166, 167, 169, 170, 172, 174
Wheeler, Edward Oliver (Sir), 164, 167, 172, 174
White, Aubrey, 64
White Eskimo, (1972), 14, 27
White Lake, 119
White River, 112, 118-123, 131
White River Rafting Camp,
White Paper (1969), 13
Whitfield, Carol, 270, 274
Whitney (ON), 58
Whitney, James, 84
Whyte Museum, 161
Wickham, Chris, 111, 132
Widgeon Lake, 124
Wiebe, Rudy, 14, 15, 18, 28
Wikwemikong (ON), 69
Wild Places, 286
Wilderness Act of 1964, 2, 44, 234
Wilderness Areas Act (1959), 42, 234
Wilderness Areas, Ecological Reserves and Natural Areas Act, 232
"Wilderness Vision—Colloquium on Completing British Columbia's Protected Area System", 245, 248, 249
Wildlands League, ix, 34, 66
Wildlands Project, The, 226
Wildlife Research Area, 39
Wildman, Bud, 60, 65, 71, 73
Williams, Raymond, 110, 134
Williams Lake (BC), 243
Williams Treaty (1922-23), 57
Wilson, Alexander, 17, 28
Williston Lake, 18
Windy-Craggy copper mine, 181

Winks, Robin, 138
Winisk River, 42
Winisk (Wild River) Waterway Park, 68
Winnipeg (MN), 161, 162
Winter Lake (NWT), 15
Wood Buffalo National Park, 179, 185, 186, 285
Woodcock, George, 22
Woodley, Stephen, 285, 291, 294
Wordsworth, William, 217
World Conversvation Strategy, 282
World Conservation Union (ICUN), 178, 262
World Conservation Strategy, 282
World Heritage Convention (see Convention for the Protection of the World Cultural and Natural Heritage)
World Heritage List, 178, 180, 181, 183-185
World Heritage Site(s), 177, 178, 181-183, 185, 186, 219, 281
World Resources Institute (WRI), 262, 278
World Wildlife Fund, ix, 233, 288
World War II (see Second World War)
World's Columbian Exposition (1893), 2
Worster, Donald, 2, 20, 28
Wrangell-St. Elias-Glacier Bay Parks, 181
Wright, J.R., 235, 236
Wyatt, Paul, 69

YMCA (Young Men's Christian Association), 100
Yellowknife (natives), 15
Yellowknife (NWT), 15, 224, 251
Yellowstone Lake, 200
Yellowstone National Park, 96, 191-194, 196-198, 200, 246, 281
Yeltsin, Boris, 181
Yoho National Park, 163
Yosemite National Park, 191, 192, 194, 196, 197
Yukon, 181, 184, 229, 235, 246

Zaslow, Morris, 11
Zauitz, E.J., 87
Zelinsky, Wilbur, 109, 134